# Relational Database Systems

## Analysis and Comparison

Edited by
Joachim W. Schmidt and Michael L. Brodie

Springer-Verlag
Berlin Heidelberg New York 1983

Joachim W. Schmidt
Fachbereich Informatik, Universität Hamburg
Schlüterstraße 70, D-2000 Hamburg 13
FRG

Michael L. Brodie
Computer Corporation of America
575 Technology Square, Cambridge MA 02139
U.S.A.

ISBN 3-540-12032-7 Springer-Verlag Berlin Heidelberg New York
ISBN 0-387-12032-7 Springer-Verlag New York Heidelberg Berlin

Library of Congress Cataloging in Publication Data
Main entry under title:
Relational database systems.
1. Data base management. 2. Information storage and retrieval systems.
I. Schmidt, Joachim W., 1941- . II. Brodie, Michael L., 1948- .
QA76.9.D3R44   1983   001.64'42   82-19175
ISBN 0-387-12032-7 (U.S.)

Printing: Beltz Offsetdruck, Hemsbach. Bookbinding: Schäffer, Grünstadt.
2145/3140-54321

# Foreword

After a long period of research, development, test and trial, relational database management systems are at last being marketed in force. The feedback from early installations of these systems is overwhelmingly positive. The most frequent comment by users is that productivity has been increased by a significant factor (from 5 to 20 times what it was using previous approaches). Another comment is that, in many cases, end users can now handle their own problems by direct use of the system instead of using application programmers as mediators between them and the system.

As the reputation of relational systems for ease of use and enhanced productivity has grown, there has been a strong temptation for vendors of other approaches to exploit the label "relational" somewhat indiscriminately. In some cases the label is being misapplied to a whole data system; in others it is being misapplied to an interface.

It is therefore worth developing criteria which database management systems (DBMSs) should have in order to be called "relational". The Relational Task Group (RTG) of the American National Standards Institute (ANSI) undertook such an effort by developing a characterization of RDBMSs and analyzing fourteen DBMSs per this characterization. The result of this work is presented in this book.

The conclusions of the RTG are in agreement with my view that a DBMS should not be called "relational" unless it satisfies at least the following conditions:

1. All information in the database is represented as values in tables.

2. There are no user-visible navigation links between these tables.

3. The system supports at least the select, project, and equi-join or natural join operators of the relational algebra - in whatever syntax is found convenient, but without resorting to commands for iteration or recursion, and with the provision that none of these operators is restricted by whatever access paths have been predefined.

Of course, a system that meets only these requirements should be called minimally relational. Furthermore, a system that meets the first two (structural) requirements, but fails to meet the third (relational processing), should not be called relational at all, but instead tabular.

Note that it would clearly be misleading to call an interface "relational" if there existed queries that a user could not get the system to execute without first going to the database administrator and requesting that some new access paths be defined. Such a state of affairs would be a violation of requirement 3 above.

For a database management system to be called _fully relational_ it must satisfy the following additional _conditions:_

1.  It must support all of the operators of the relational algebra in whatever syntax is convenient, but without resorting to commands for iteration and recursion, and without restrictions due to predefined access paths.

2.  It must support the two general integrity rules of the basic relational model (entity integrity and referential integrity).

Most existing relational products fall somewhere between being minimally relational and fully relational. They all need to be strengthened in integrity support, and no doubt they soon will be.

Some relational systems support a data sublanguage that is usable in two modes: 1) interactively at a terminal and 2) embedded in an application program written in a host language. There are strong arguments for such a _double-mode_ data sublanguage:

1.  Using such a language, application programmers can separately debug, at a terminal, the database statements they wish to incorporate into their application programs.

2.  Such a language significantly enhances communication among programmers, analysts, end users, database administration staff, etc.

3.  Frivolous distinctions between the languages used in these two modes place an unnecessary learning and memory burden on those users who have to work in both modes.

The importance of this feature in productivity suggests that relational DBMSs be classified according to whether they possess this feature or not. Accordingly, we call relational DBMSs that support a double-mode data sublanguage _uniform relational_. Thus, a uniform relational DBMS supports _relational_ processing at both an end-user interface and at an application programming interface _using a data sublanguage_ common to both interfaces.  The natural term for all other relational DBMSs is non-uniform relational.

Most database management systems today (whether relational or non-relational) provide weak support or no support for distributed databases - and that applies to the relational systems discussed in this book.  Soon, however, we shall see extremely powerful distributed database management systems emerge - systems that not only permit data to be distributed to geographically dispersed sites in a very flexible way, but also permit transactions that require data from multiple nodes to be specified as if all the data were stored in a single centralized database.  The engineering prototypes of these systems are all based on the relational model, and the majority of them are, in fact, extensions of existing relational systems.  Why is this so?

There are four main reasons why the relational approach lends itself to distributed data:

1.  Relational databases offer great decomposition flexibility when planning how a database is to be distributed over a network of computer systems.  Tables may be sliced vertically or horizontally, and they may be glued together by joins and unions (by contrast, databases based on the network or hierarchical models are constrained in their decomposition by the entanglement of their navigation links).

2.  The relational operators provide great recomposition power for dynamic combination of decentralized information (by contrast, the network and hierarchical models do not possess operators of comparable power).

3.  The concise high-level languages of relational systems offer considerable economy of transmission when compared with the record-at-a-time languages of non-relational systems;

4.  The concise high-level languages of relational systems make it feasible for a node to analyze the intent of a transaction and speedily decompose it into parts that can be handled locally and into parts that will have to be shipped off to other nodes.

The systems described here are therefore likely forerunners of tomorrow's distributed database management systems.

Today, much is being made of the theme of integration of database products.  By this is meant the degree to which the various members of a database family work together.

Typically, a database family would include a database management system, a query facility, a logical database design aid, a physical database design aid, an application generator, and a data dictionary. These components are well integrated if:

1.  Users of the family of products need to familiarize themselves with only one data model.

2.  The data dictionary is the principal repository of all data description for the entire family, including (but not limited to) that needed dynamically by the database management system and the application generator (in other words, data descriptors can be declared once for the entire family of products and stored with the minimal redundancy required by performance considerations).

At the present time, there are few (if any) database management systems that are members of such a tightly integrated family. However, relational systems offer the immediate possibility of attaining integration of this kind. In fact, we may expect that relational families soon will be developed that have a greater degree of integration than any family based on either the hierarchical or network approach. One reason is that the same tabular structure and high-level languages supported by relational database management systems are precisely what is needed for managing and interrogating the dictionary by a staff not trained in the details of regular programming and for supporting high-level generation of application programs.

The fourteen systems discussed in this book are a representative sample of systems now being marketed. They differ from one another in three important ways: first, in the degree and kind of support for the semantic features of the relational model (especially domains, keys, nulls, and the integrity rules); second, in the syntax adopted for expressing the relational processing capability; third, in the degree to which they provide the many services expected of a database management system today.

We are entering an exciting period for relational database management systems - a period in which there will be rapid growth in both the numbers of these systems installed and in the size of databases managed by them. There will also be rapid development in their performance and in their capabilities, especially extensions of the following kind: semantic support, well integrated data dictionaries, application generators, and database design aids.

In conclusion, I wish to congratulate the members of the Relational Task Group of ANSI and the task group leaders, Dr.

Michael L. Brodie and Dr. Joachim W. Schmidt, for their work on the relational data model and on characterizing the features of RDBMSs.

The findings of the RTG with regard to possible standardization were published in the ACM SIGMOD Record of July 1982. I fully support the RTG's view that the relational data model can be defined by means of a set of functions, and these in turn provide a sound basis for the definition of a wide variety of database retrieval and update languages. In the database standards context, this means that RDBMSs can be standardized by means of this set of functions together with one or more of the relational languages already in widespread use.

E. F. Codd

San Jose, California

June 24, 1982

# Preface

In May 1979, the ANSI/X3/SPARC DBS-SG Relational Database Task Group (RTG) was chartered to investigate the justifiability of proposing to the American National Standards Institute (ANSI) that a project be initiated to develop a relational standard.

The RTG concluded that such a proposal is justified based on the result of the two tasks, namely:

(1) Identification of the fundamental concepts of the Relational Data Model (RDM)

(2) Characterization of existing and proposed Relational Database Management Systems (RDBMSs).

To perform these tasks the RTG developed a "Feature Catalogue of Relational Concepts, Languages and Systems". The catalogue was intended as an abstract (i.e., implementation independent) characterization of RDM and RDBMS concepts.

The feature catalogue served several groups of authors as a common basis for a detailed feature analysis of a number of DBMSs that were claimed to support aspects of the RDM. The RTG used these feature analyses to "identify or establish aspects of the RDM and RDBMSs that might be appropriate for standards development" (*).

The feature catalogue is given in its entirety in Chapter 2. Chapter 3 presents 14 individual feature analyses that resulted from applying the catalogue to 14 DBMSs which were claimed to support aspects of the RDM. Chapter 4 concludes the book with a detailed summary and comparison of the 14 feature analyses.

This book consists entirely of working documents prepared to assist the RTG in completing the tasks described above. Now that the analyses have been completed, it is clear that improvements could be made. Some feature analyses would benefit from revision by the system's designers familiar with the system's most recent version and by users with practical experience. The book as a whole could be improved by small conceptual changes and some restructuring of the feature catalogue itself. However, the working documents are completely adequate for the reader to develop a detailed understanding of the RDM, RDBMSs, and the state-of-the-art in RDBMS technology. In addition, the documents constitute the most comprehensive collection on the increasingly important relational technology.

---

(*) part of the RTG's charter

For these reasons and to respond to a growing demand for the documents, the documents have been collected and published as a book.

The results of the RTG's work are presented in this book and in the RTG's final report. The final report includes an introduction to the RDM, an RDM definition and a survey of over 80 DBMSs which are claimed to support aspects of the RDM. "The Final Report of the ANSI/X3/SPARC DBS-SG Relational Database Task Group" was published in July 1982 as a special issue of SIGMOD RECORD. SIGMOD RECORD is a publication of the Special Interest Group on the Management of Data of the Association of Computing Machinery. The report is available from the Association of Computing Machinery, 11 West 42nd Street, New York, NY10036, USA.

The Relational Database Task Group had the following members at the time that its final report was completed:

Michael L. Brodie, co-chairman              University of Maryland
                        and Computer Corporation of America
Joachim W. Schmidt, co-chairman             University of Hamburg
                        and Computer Corporation of America
Alex J. Arthur              International Business Machines Corp.
Margret Ball                            Intel Systems Corporation
                                     and Burroughs Corporation
Charlie Bontempo (Alternate for Arthur)            IBM Systems
                                          Research Institute
Harrison R. Burris                                    TRW Inc.
Beth Driver                       PRC Information Sciences Co.
                        and Technology Service Corporation
Roy Hammond                                 Statistics Canada
Peter Hitchcock                       University of Victoria
                and British Columbia Systems Corporation
Kate Kinsley                  University of Central Florida
Nancy McDonald                  University of South Florida
Alain Pirotte         PHILIPS Research Laboratory, Brussels
                        and Computer Corporation of America
Daniel R. Ries                  Lawrence Livermore Laboratory
                        and Computer Corporation of America
Edgar H. Sibley                        Alpha Omega Group, Inc.

Others who contributed to this document are:

| | |
|---|---|
| A. Blaser | International Business Machines Corp. |
| R. E. Brinegar | Honeywell Information Systems |
| K. Bratbergsengen | Sperry Rand and University of Trondheim |
| E. F. Codd | International Business Machines Corp. |
| N. S. Davids | Honeywell Information Systems |
| W. Dotzek | University of Hamburg |
| J. Driscoll | University of Central Florida |
| H. Eberle | International Business Machines Corp. |
| R. Erbe | International Business Machines Corp. |
| O. Friesen | Honeywell Information Systems |
| K. Grammel | University of Central Florida |
| J. Z. Kornatowski | University of Toronto |
| W. Kent | International Business Machines Corp. |
| M. Lacroix | Philips Research Laboratories |
| H. Lehmann | International Business Machines Corp. |
| G. Mueller | International Business Machines Corp. |
| M. Mall | University of Hamburg |
| J. McNally | University of South Florida |
| C. M. Robertson | University of Toronto |
| M. Schauer | International Business Machines Corp. |
| H. Schmutz | International Business Machines Corp. |
| T. Stahlhane | University of Trondheim |

# Table of Contents

# 1. Introduction

For more than one decade the relational database model (RDM) has received considerable attention in the research community and is now receiving attention by database practitioners. The RDM's simplicity and formality continue to inspire a large amount of research and development. Many practical and theoretical advantages have been demonstrated or claimed, for example, high level relational languages have strongly influenced the development of database query languages and theoretical results have provided database design aids.

Over the last ten years the relational approach to databases has become a dominant factor in database education. It is used for database design, analysis, and query formulation. Close to one hundred DBMSs have been reported that are said to support relational concepts and languages. Extensive interest in these systems indicates that they soon will come into widespread use.

From their initial formulation to their precise definition and their final realization in a Relational Database Management System (RDBMS), the concepts that constitute the RDM are defined in different ways. There are three distinct steps in this progression:

The Relational Data Model is the collection of basic concepts that underlies the relational approach to data definition, manipulation, query, and integrity.

A Relational Data Model Definition provides a notation (syntax) to identify the concepts of the RDM and an unambiguous specification of the meaning (semantics) associated with this notation.

Relational Database Management Systems are software systems that provide interfaces with the functionality specified by an RDM definition. Languages (syntax and semantics) at these interfaces are tailored to meet users needs.

The purpose and relative importance of the steps are clear. RDM concepts are fundamental. A RDM definition is one of many possible expressions of the RDM concepts. A RDM definition should provide guidelines for the specification and implementation of an RDBMS.

The three step progression outlined above is idealistic

for the development of an RDBMS. For pragmatic reasons, steps may be left out or be reordered. The Relational Task Group (RTG) began its work with the third step, the characterization of RDBMSs. Results of this step were used in developing several candidate RDM definitions from which the basic RDM concepts were (substantially) extracted as the common core.

This book presents the results of the third step, the RDBMS characterization and analysis. The main objective of this step was to develop a RDBMS characterization which was consistent with existing relational technology. In practice, database management systems seldom provide a definition of the data model on which they are based, nor is there precise or concise characterization of the system itself. RDBMSs, like other complex systems, are informally described by their user's guides and operator's manuals. Even for one RDBMS, these documents [BREAK]use different concepts and terminology.

The RTG developed the characterization as follows. First, a feature catalogue was prepared as a common framework for the subsequent RDBMS analyses. The catalogue gives a functionally organized list of the potential features of an RDBMS. Each feature was characterized independently of implementation details and individual systems. Second, the feature catalogue was used with 14 RDBMSs to develop a complete feature analysis of each system. Finally, the resulting feature analyses were summarized in detail, and compared.

The empirical material presented in this document is intended to provide a deeper insight into the RDM definitions implemented by various RDBMSs, and a better understanding of the relational approach in general.

# 2. Features of Relational Database Systems

In his 1981 Turing Award Lecture E.F.Codd stated that

"A data model is, of course, not just a data structure, as many people seem to think. It is natural that the principal data models are named after their principal structures, but that is not the whole story.

A data model [...] is a combination of at least three components:

(1) A collection of data structure types (the database building blocks);

(2) A collection of operators or rules of inference, which can be applied to any valid instance of the data types listed in (1), to retrieve, derive, or modify data from any parts of those structures in any combinations desired;

(3) A collection of general integrity rules, which implicitly or explicitly define the set of consistent database states or changes of state or both - these rules are general in the sense that they apply to any database using this model" [CODD82].

The feature catalogue presented in subsection 2.2 follows that notion of a data model and clearly distinguishes the structure of the various database constituents, the operations to be applied, and the integrity constraints to be maintained. The catalogue also distinguishes several possible perceptions of a relation (e.g. as sets, tables, predicates). RDBMSs are further characterized in terms of their interfaces, their architecture, and various operational aspects (i.e., security, integrity, and recovery).

## 2.1  Development Of The Feature Catalogue

The feature catalogue was developed by the RTG to guide the analyses of selected relational database management systems. The purpose of using a feature catalogue was to ensure that all systems were described in the same format and that all features of interest to the RTG were considered in the analyses.

The purpose of the analyses was to gain insight into:

1. RDM
   a. essential or core concepts, and
   b. additional concepts or extensions.

2. Systems issues concerning the support and use of the RDM:
   a. aspects closely tied to the model, such as the design of interfaces, and
   b. general system features (e.g., locking, concurrency, security, access control).

Non-relational features were included in the feature catalogue for two reasons:

1. The analyses were required to decide whether a particularly common DBMS feature was related to the RDM. One objective of performing the analyses was to determine what DBMS features were dependent on the RDM.

2. One reason for supporting the development of a relational standard was the task group's finding that there is a significant number of complete, useable DBMSs supporting aspects of the RDM. If the only implementations of the RDMs were research vehicles, a standard might be premature. Therefore it was important to determine the full capabilities of the systems being analyzed.

The intent of the task group was to categorize the features on the basis of the analyses according to the following taxonomy.

1. Features that appear in every system that are claimed to be relational.

2. Features that do not appear in every system but are rapidly being added to many systems.

3. Features that are felt to be important but do not yet appear except in the literature or in research systems.

4. Features that have been in some systems for some time but do not appear to be spreading to other systems.

5. Features that distinguish the relational approach from other approaches.

Features in categories 1 and 2 would form the basis for a standard, while features from categories 3 and 4 could be used as a basis for future developments. Features in category 5 would be used to exclude non-relational systems.

Besides supporting a standard, the analyses based on the feature catalogue were expected to be useful in the following ways:

1. To relate specific knowledge of the state-of-the-art to research and development results.

2. To demonstrate the amount and nature of work in implementations, applications, and literature.

3. To determine to what extent RDM concepts are constrained by implementation concerns.

The feature catalogue on which the analyses are based is the third version developed by the RTG. The initial version was based on the Generalized DBMS Survey completed by the CODASYL System Committee in 1969. This version was tested by asking members to analyze selected systems. The catalogue was found to be incomplete since some hierarchical DBMSs could be described as "relational" following the catalogue. A second version of the catalogue placed more weight on purely relational features, but it appeared to be too detailed for the RTG's purpose. In the third version of the feature catalogue this problem is not completely solved. However, the overall organization of information is clear and easy to follow.


The relative importance of relational concepts, languages, and systems is reflected in the structure of the catalogue. First, RDM concepts are considered, followed by associated functional capabilities and ending with DBMS features. Within the categories of functional capabilities, query and manipulation are considered before definition, generation, and administration. This ordering indicates the distinction between RDM concepts and RDBMS features in response to the RTG charter.

2.2   THE FEATURE CATALOGUE


FEATURE CATALOGUE OF

RELATIONAL

CONCEPTS, LANGUAGES and SYSTEMS

May 1980

Working Paper RTG-80-81

of the

Relational Database Task Group

of

ANSI/X3/SPARC - Database System Study Group

reply to: Michael L. Brodie
          Dept. of Computer Science
          University of Maryland
          College Park, MD 20742
          (301) 454-2002

          Joachim W. Schmidt
          Fachbereich Informatik
          Universitaet Hamburg
          Schlueterstr. 70
          D-2000 Hamburg 13
          W. Germany
          011-49-40-4123-4154/4164

Please refer to RTG-80-90 for comments on completing a
feature analysis based on this feature catalogue.

by


Michael L. Brodie,* University of Maryland


and


Joachim W. Schmidt,** Universitaet Hamburg



with contributions from RTG members and others:


Margret Ball, MRI-Intel
Kjell Bratbergsengen, University of Trondheim
Wolfgang Dotzek, Universitaet Hamburg
Beth Driver, PRC Information Sciences Co.
Kate Kinsley, University of Central Florida
Manuel Mall, Universitaet Hamburg
Daniel Ries, Lawrence Livermore Laboratory



and suggestions from the Relational Database Task Group members:


Alex Arthur, IBM Santa Teresa Lab
Charlie Bontempo, IBM Systems Research Institute
Harrison R. Burris, TRW, Inc.
Jim Driscoll, University of Central Florida
H. Randall Johnson, Boeing Computer Services Co.
Michel Lacroix, Philips Research, Brussels
Jim Larson, Sperry Univac
Nancy McDonald, University of South Florida
Ken Paris, Peat, Marwick, Mitchell and Co.
Alain Pirotte, Philips Research, Brussels
E.H. Sibley, University of Maryland

*Dr. Brodie's work was supported, in part, by the Army Research Office Grant DAAG 29-78-B-0162, for AIRMICS.

**Dr. Schmidt's work was supported, in part, by the Federal Ministry of Research and Technology of W. Germany.

# Table of Contents

# 1. Introduction

## 1.1 Identification

Give the name of the system (and version where applicable) together with some information about its origin.

## 1.2 Status

### 1.2.1 System

Give the development status of the system together
with the appropriate release dates. Planned extensions
and their proposed dates can be identified. More details
can be given later in the appropriate sections; however,
the features should be clearly marked as proposals.

### 1.2.2 Applications

Describe briefly the class of applications for which
the system is intended and those applications for which it
may be less well suited. Characterize the limits placed by
the system applications, e.g., total size. List the know
applications; these may be described in more detail, in
section 8.0.

## 1.3  System Background

Describe briefly how the system came into being, what (if any) family of similar systems it belongs to and on which systems (if any) it is based.

## 1.4  Overall Philosophy

If possible, give a statement of overall philosophy including motivation for designing and developing the system, objectives for the system, major contributions and features unique to or emphasized by the system, and the design rationale for meeting these goals.

## 1.5  Essentially Relational Characteristics

Recently (TODS Vol. 4, No. 4, Dec. 1979), Codd wrote that for a system to be considered _fully_ _relational_ it would have to support:

(i) structural aspects of the relational model;

(ii) the insert, update, and delete rules; and

(iii) a data sublanguage at least as powerful as the relational algebra, even if all facilities the language may have for iterative loops and recursion were deleted from that language.

(For further details see the referenced paper.)

He also stated that if the data sublanguage was not supported, then the system might be considered _semirelational_.

There may be varying degrees of semirelational systems, depending on the level of the data structures and languages and on the restrictions placed on relational operations.

The level of the data sublanguage is significant. The relational algebra operators, i.e., extended cartesian product, union, intersection, difference, projection, selection, restriction, join, and possibly division, must be atomic. These operations could be implemented in assembler which is not relational in nature.

A DBMS which places restrictions on the use of the relational algebra operations such as join (i.e., more restrictions on join than union compatibility of join attributes) may be considered as semirelational or even not relational in nature. The following are examples of restrictions which reduce the power of the join operation:

(i) cycles are not permitted. In the relational approach, any series of joins including those that result in a cycle can be expressed. Some database models do not permit cyclic relationships.

(ii) a relation cannot be joined with itself. Some database models do not permit an entity (e.g., a record type) to be related to itself.

(iii) only one join is permitted between two relations. In the relational model, a join is permitted between two relations as long as the join attributes are union compatible. There is no other restriction, such as the number of such pairs or join attributes between relations.

(iv) relations must be connected by joins. The relational model permits relations to exist independently of any other relations. DBMSs which are based on explicit links make few provisions for this case.

The following advantages have been claimed for the relational database model and used to distinguish relational systems from those that are not relational in nature:

1. no access path dependencies such as information bearing links, e.g., a relation can exist independently of any other relations;
2. no order dependencies among tuples;
3. no index dependencies for database access;
4. no insert, update or delete dependencies such as storage and removal classes, e.g., unconditional delete of dependent tuples when the parent tuple is deleted;
5. high-level, non-procedural, set-oriented qualification primitives (see Section 3.1);

6. the ability to derive and maintain dynamically a user
   view (i.e., derived relation) from one or more existing relations;
7. the ability to add and delete semantic integrity constraints during the lifetime of the application.

[Please make suggestions for extending this list. See
also Section 7.0 for advantages of relation approach.]

   If the system or language under consideration does
not possess one or more of the advantages then it may not
be relational in nature.

   This section is intended to distinguish between systems that are fully relational, semirelational, and those
that are not relational in nature. This distinction
raises the question whether there is an essential difference between, for instance, the relational, hierarchic,
and network database models. If there is no essential
difference it would seem unlikely that a relational standard be justifiable.

   Based on the above information (and on additional
proposals by you) classify the system or language being
considered as fully relational, semirelational, or not
relational in nature.

## 1.6  Interfaces

   A database management system presents, through one or
more interfaces or languages, some of the following capabilities (after each capability is a list of sections in
the feature catalogue in which the capability is
described):

(1) Database Schema Definition                     4.1
(2) Query Language                                 3.1,3.2,3.4
(3) Database Altering                              3.1,3.3,3.4
(4) Constraint Definition                          2,4
(5) Database Generation and Regeneration           4.2,4.4
(6) Database Schema Redefinition and Renaming      4.3
(7) Report Generation                              3.1,3.2,3.4
(8) Data Entry
(9) Security Definition, Monitoring and Control    6.1
(10) Database Control (utilities): load, dump       6.2,3.2,3,
     backup, restore, recovery, monitoring, etc.    3.4.7
(11) Definition of Storage Structure, Indexes,

and Access Paths
(12) Database Dictionary (database design,
     dictionary query, etc).          3.2.2,4.5
(13) Special Purpose Language

For the system under consideration, identify its
interfaces or languages. Briefly characterize each
language in terms of its capabilities. A more detailed
description of the interfaces is given in Section 5.

## 1.7 Documentation

Give a bibliographic list of documentation available
on the system (especially those documents used for the
feature analysis). Also, give a list of technical papers
that discuss the system.

## 1.8 General System Description

Briefly describe any important characteristics of an
introductory nature, perhaps unique to the system, that
have not yet been described in the introduction.

## 2. Database Constituents

A database may be perceived as consisting of a number of constituents. Each constituent may be viewed as a structure, together with a fixed set of operators, with both the structure and operations restricted by some constraints.

There are a number of distinct perceptions of relational databases. A relation may be perceived, e.g., as: a _set_ of tuples, _array_ (table) of tuples (rows), an n-ary _predicate_, a n-ary _function_, and as a file. A system may present only one such perception at all interfaces, different but distinct perceptions in different interfaces (e.g., set-oriented queries, predicate-oriented queries, functional queries, arrays for programming language interfaces, and files for the DBS interface) or a mixture of perceptions (e.g., both set and array oriented operations).

The perceptions presented should be characterized. If more than one perception is presented and each has different characteristics (i.e., operational semantics), they should be treated distinctly (i.e., apply section 2 to each perception).

## 2.1 General Description

List the constituents of a database and their relationship; e.g., the feature catalogue assumes the following constituents. A particular system may have more constituents, or less.

The constituents of a System N database are: DB(=database), R(=relation), V(=view), T(=tuple), A(=attribute), D(=domain).

These constituents are related as follows: A relational DB consists of R's of possibly different type. An R consists of T's of identical type. A V is an R derived from one or more R's by means of qualification operations.

A T consists of A values of possibly different type.   A's are defined in terms of a D.  Finally, a D is a user defined data type.

Note that DB, R, V, T, A, D are the system's terms which should be used but equated to the feature catalogue terms using "(=F.C. term)" where the terms differ. For quick reference a term translation table should be given in this section.

[2.X Constituent

For each constituent in Section 2, describe the structure and constraints in detail. Operations should be listed with a brief description of their effect (semantics).  A more detailed description of operations is given in Sections 3 and 4.]

## 2.2   Database

### 2.2.1   Database Structure

Describe a database structure at the schema level (type level) at the instance level (value level). Describe the mechanism for naming (identifying) a database. What is the role of relations and views in database structuring?

### 2.2.2   Database Operations

List the operations for defining, generating, and manipulating a database structure.

### 2.2.3   Database Constraints

Characterize the constraints (e.g., global assertions) that can be defined on a database structure and its operations. How are these constraints maintained over a database and how are violations handled?

## 2.2.4  Additional Database Properties

Describe properties about a database not given in the above sections.

## 2.3  Relation

### 2.3.1  Relation Structure

Give the system's definition of a relation. Keep in mind that the schema level notion of a relation may differ from the instance level notion. What is the predominant perception of a relation (i.e., table of rows and columns, set of tuples, entities over which functions or predicates can be evaluated). Describe the naming (identification) mechanism for relations. What is the role of tuples and attributes in relation structuring? Are duplicate tuples allowed? Is attribute order significant? Can alias names be defined?

### 2.3.2  Relation Operations

List the operations for defining and manipulating a relation structure. Is the design of the operations oriented more toward formal rigor (relation or set algebra, applied predicate calculus, mappings, etc.), procedurality and control (variables, operators, expressions, control variables, control statements, etc.), end-user convenience, or semantic richness? What is the role of tuples and attributes in these operations, e.g., what are the compatibility requirements for operands in these operations?

### 2.3.3  Relation Constraints

Characterize the constraints (e.g., functional dependencies, keys, predicates, joining restrictions) that can
be defined on a relation structure and its operations.
Give the system's definition of key and its roll as a
relation constraints. Are constraints on relations perceived as query modifiers, as definitions of exception or
trigger-raising conditions? Or are they considered to be
like datatype definitions leading to type violations? How
do constraints interact with the database manipulation
facilities? Are there any query facilities based on the
definition of constraints (e.g., on relation keys)? What
are the constraints imposed on relations through attributes? How are constraint violations handled?

### 2.3.4  Additional Properties of Relations

Are there any additional properties of relations? Can
a short statement be made about the use of relations in
"real world" modeling?

### 2.4  Views

### 2.4.1  View Structure

Give the systems definition of a view. The schema
level and instance level notions of view may differ. How
does a view structure differ from a relation structure?
Can views be dynamic and static? How are views derived?
What is the role of (base) relations and views in view
structuring? Describe the naming mechanism for views. Are
keys definable for views or are they inherited from the
(base) relations?

### 2.4.2 View Operations

List the operations for defining and manipulating views. Are view definition operations a subset of the qualification (3.1) operations? Are view manipulation operations a subset of the relation operations? Are there operations and views that are not available on relations? Under what conditions can relation operations be applied to views?

### 2.4.3 View Constraints

Characterize the constraints (e.g., access control, subsetting, logical restrictions, general assertions) that can be defined using views. Compare view constraints with relation constraints emphasizing those unique to and specialized for views. How are view constraint violations handled?

### 2.4.4 Additional Properties of Views

Are there any additional properties of views? Are views intended to be treated or seen as different from relations? Characterize if applicable dynamic and static views (snapshots). What is the intended role of views for modeling, querying, assessing parts of the database? Can a brief statement be made on the use of view in conceptual modeling.

### 2.5 Tuple

### 2.5.1 Tuple Structure

Give the system's definition of a tuple. Describe a tuple structure (i.e., record type) and a tuple value (i.e., record instance). In some systems a tuple may be defined implicitly when a relation is defined. What is the role of attributes and domains in tuple structuring? Are keys definable at the tuple or relation level? Describe the mechanisms for unique tuple qualification, e.g., based on unique key values.

## 2.5.2  Tuple Operations

List the operations for defining and manipulating tuples. Are there explicit or implicit tuple-oriented operations (e.g., existence test, equality test, read, write, replace) or control structures (e.g., FOR EACH e in EMPL)?

## 2.5.3  Tuple Constraints

Characterize the constraints (e.g., uniqueness, order, assertions, inter-attribute restrictions) that can be defined on tuples. How are tuple constraint violations handled?

## 2.5.4  Additional Properties of Tuples

Are there any additional properties of tuples? Is there an exclusive tuple-oriented interface? Are tuples addressed explicitly or implicitly? Are tuples treated as elements of a set? Are tuples treated as entries in an array? Are tuples treated as values in the domain of an n-ary function or predicate? Can a brief statement be made on the use of tuples in conceptual modeling?

## 2.6  Attribute

### 2.6.1  Attribute Structure

Give the system's definition of an attribute. The schema and instance level notions of attribute may differ. Is the concept of an attribute supported independently of domains or primary data types? What is the role of domains and primary date types in attribute structuring? How do attributes differ from domains? Describe the naming mechanism for attributes. Can alias names be defined? Are there any distinguished attribute values (e.g., null, unknown, undefined, etc.)?

List the operations for defining and manipulating attributes (e.g., the relational comparison operators <, <, =, >, > / ; arithmetic operations +, -, -, *; aggregation functions SUM, COUNT, MAX, MIN, etc.). Give the compatibility and coercion rules for these operators. Do attributes have different compatibility rules than the underlying domains or primary data types? Can attribute operations be defined or are they inherited for the underlying domains?

### 2.6.2  Attribute Operations

### 2.6.3  Attribute Constraints

Characterize the constraints (e.g., assertions, value restrictions, operation restrictions) that can be defined on attributes. How are attribute constraint violations handled? Distinguish attribute and domain constraints and emphasize constraints unique to attributes.

### 2.6.4  Additional Properties of Attributes

Are there any additional properties of attributes? Are attributes supported implicitly or explicitly? Can a brief statement be made on the use of attributes in conceptual modeling?

## 2.7 Domain

### 2.7.1 Domain Structure

Give the system's definition of domain. Is a domain a set of fundamental objects or entities, a set of values, part of a type definition, etc. Which kinds of domain exist (predefined) or can be defined (integer-based, string-based, etc.)? Is an order defined on domains? Are there any distinguished domain values (e.g., null, unknown, undefined, etc.)? What is the role of predefined data types in defining domains?

### 2.7.2 Domain Operations

List the operations that are defined or can be defined together with domains (e.g., tests, comparisons, arithmetic, Boolean). What are the compatibility and coercion rules for this operation? Compare domain and attribute operations and describe those operations associated with domains. Can domain operations be defined or redefined?

### 2.7.3 Domain Constraints

Characterize the constraints (e.g., value set restrictions, operation restrictions, compatibility of domains, upper and lower limits on value sets, etc.) that exist or that can be defined on domains. How are domain constraint violations handled?

### 2.7.4 Additional Properties of Domains

Are there any additional properties of domains? Can a brief statement be made on the use of domains in conceptual modeling?

## 2.8  Additional Database Constituents


Are there any additional constituents in  a  database in  the  system  being  described  (e.g.,  transaction, triggers, data  dictionary,  procedures,  etc.).  Describe additional  constituents  in  the same manner as the above constituents. Does  the  system  support  assertions?  Can assertions be defined and dropped dynamically?

# 3. Functional Capabilities

The functional or operational capabilities of the system or language(s) under consideration are those facilities used to select and manipulate database constituents. A distinction is made between qualification and operations over selected constituents. Qualification is the selection of a subset of the database for subsequent operations. The selected constituents may be presented to the user, as in the case of queries, or they may be used as arguments in database altering operations.

Functional capabilities are presented to users differently in different systems. All functional capabilities may be provided in one language or in several languages. Please maintain the distinctions given in the feature catalogue and name the interfaces (languages) providing each capability. Some capabilities may be provided through more than one interface, in which case deal with semantic differences here and with syntactic differences in Section 5.0 (do not repeat information).

Different perceptions of relations (see 2.0) may be presented for various functional capabilities. In particular, querying may be done through a set-oriented or n-any predicate (or function-oriented) interface, while updates may be done through an array-oriented interface. Make these distinctions where they are appropriate. See comment j in RTG-80-90 concerning an example.

## 3.1 Qualification

This section deals with the approach or philosophy taken in the system for selection. Qualification facilities (i.e., selection mechanisms) are used to select database constituents, usually tuples of a relation, for retrieval or altering.

Give a general description of qualification: the nature of the selection mechanism (algebra- or calculus-oriented); the perceptions of relations; the interfaces.

How are the results of qualification perceived by the user? How are exceptional conditions handled?

In the following subsections list and define each qualification mechanism. The operators of the relational algebra and the selection predicates of the calculus should be described in these subsections. An operator is defined by: its arguments, its effects (if any) on its arguments, failure and success conditions, and how it is perceived by the user. What is the role of domains and attributes for each operator? You may have to define or refer to such concepts as tuple variables.

### 3.1.1 Restriction

List and define the simple conditionals (e.g., $<$, $\leq$, $=$, $\geq$, $\neq$) that can be used to select tuples from a relation. For example, can tuple attributes be compared only to constants or also to the value of other attributes? Specify which types of comparisons are supported for which types of attributes or domains. Are there any restrictions, such as not being able to compare a packed decimal type value to an integer type value. (Give the coercion rules.)

In addition, specify if and how the simple selection conditions can be combined into a more general Boolean expression. The relational algebra operators selection, restriction, and projection should be defined here. Give a small example.

### 3.1.2 Quantification

If the selection mechanism is calculus-oriented, universal and existential quantification must be supported. What kinds of predicates can be defined? Are predicates explicitly defined as Boolean expressions? e.g., "SOME e IN EMPL (...)", "ALL e IN EMPL (...)". Are they implicit in other operators such as count, group by, divide, subset? Is absolute quantification supported, e.g., "there is at least 3..." "there is at most 10..."? Give small examples.

### 3.1.3   Set Operations

List and define the supported set operators, i.e., union, intersection, difference, and extended cartesian product. What conditions do the arguments have to fulfill? Describe any other set-oriented operators, e.g., set inclusion. Give small examples.

### 3.1.4   Joining

List and define each join operation supported, e.g., equi-join, natural join. Describe constraints on the relations to be joined. How many relations can be joined? What conditions on the joining attributes must be met in order to join relations? Must joining attributes have indices or other access paths? Can a relation be joined with itself? Are there any other constraints on joining? (See restrictions on joins in Section 1.5.) Give small examples.

### 3.1.5   Nesting and Closure

Describe the way in which the qualification facilities interact. Are qualification operations closed, i.e., can the result of a qualification be further qualified? Can simple qualifications be combined (nested) to make more complex qualifications? Are there different (levels of) constructs or languages with which to express more complex queries? How do the qualification facilities interact with other facilities in subsections 3.2, 3.3, and 3.4? Are the qualification facilities "relationally complete"? Give small examples.

### 3.1.6   Additional Aspects of Qualification

Describe other important qualification facilities not described earlier. For example if relational division is supported, describe it as join was described.

## 3.2  Retrieval and Presentation

The results of qualification operations can be used to retrieve database constituents and present them in some form of output or report. For each subsection, describe its relationship to qualification described in 3.1 and, if needed, define its own selection mechanism. Give a small example of each facility.

### 3.2.1  Database Queries

Characterize the facilities for defining queries only in as much as they differ from those for qualification. How are queries expressed? Are there specific facilities for queries that result in a variable number of tuples? Are there specific facilities for 1-element queries (defined by a maximum/minimum condition, or by identity or order of the key values, etc.)? Are there specific facilities for Boolean-valued queries (equivalence to propositional or predicate calculus expressions, membership tests, inclusion tests)? What is the perception of the effect of a query evaluation (a relation, a file, a sequence of actions returning partial results, a Boolean value)? What is the role of domains in queries? Do you consider the query facility as being "relational complete" (i.e., with respect to DSL ALPHA)?

What operations beyond the qualification operations are used in querying, e.g., projection, permute, absolute qualification, user defined functions? How does the query facility relate to the other facilities described in Section 3.

### 3.2.2  Retrieval of Information About Database Constituents

Describe the facilities that support the query and retrieval of schema information (e.g., database definitions -- what constituents exist, how they are defined, current constraints or assertions over the database). If these facilities depend on authorization over the standard query facilities, do not repeat information in Sections 3.1, 3.2, or 6.1. Describe how these facilities interact with other facilities, e.g., can the result of a schema query be used in a database qualification?

### 3.2.3  Retrieval of System Performance Data

Describe the facilities for retrieving performance data for an application, e.g., statistical information, performance monitoring information, information about indices, directories, and access paths. If this interface is essentially relational in nature, also refer to it in Section 7. Describe the relationship of this retrieval with respect to qualification described in 3.1.

### 3.2.4  Report Generation

Describe report generation facilities based on the qualification described in Section 3.1. Pay particular attention to those features that have a relational flavor. Stand-alone report generators not based on Section 3.1 should be listed here and described in detail in Section 5.0.

### 3.2.5  Constraints and Limitations

Describe any constraints and limitations on the use of retrieval and presentation facilities. These may be related to security, the nature of the interface, the development status of the system, etc. Future developments could be listed here together with proposed release dates.

### 3.2.6  Additional Aspects of Retrieval and Presentation

Describe any important aspects that were not described in the subsections of 3.2. For example, can a brief statement be made about the philosophy or approach taken to retrieval and presentation.

Can data be retrieved for purposes other than presentation and altering?

## 3.3  Alteration

The result of a database altering operation is a database state transition; the new state generally depends on the old state of the database and on user-supplied input data.

Depending on the altering facility, the perception of database constituents may vary. The role of relations may be that of a left-hand-side variable in an assignment statement, or a value/result parameter in a function. A relation may also be perceived as a function redefined by the relation altering facility.

The following subsections deal with the basic altering facilities and their relationship. The presentation of the basic concepts should be illustrated by means of examples. The operations described here should refer to but not repeat the information in Section 2.

### 3.3.1  Insert Facilities

Which of the database constituents can be altered by insertion (relations, views, tuples, attributes, domains)? For each constituent that can be inserted, describe the insert by its effect on the constituents into which insertion is made. Characterize the facility for the definition of insert operations. What is the perception of the user-supplied parameters in the insert operation (are they perceived as relations, as tuples, as input data used by a general facility for the redefinition of relations, etc.)?

What are the roles of tuples, attributes and domains in the insert operation? What is the role of general constraints (e.g., keys, type constraints) and how are constraint violations handled?

Can results of queries be used as parameters in insert operations? Give a small example.

### 3.3.2  Delete Facilities

Which of the database constituents can be altered  by
deletion?  For  each  constituent  that  can  be deleted,
define the operation by its effect on the constituent from
which  the  first constituent is being deleted.  Characterize the facility for the definition of delete  operations.
What  is the perception of the user-supplied parameters in
the delete operation (are they perceived as relations,  as
tuples,  as information used by a general facility for the
redefinition of relations, etc.)?  What  is  the  role  of
tuples,  attributes,  and domains in the delete operation?
What is the role of general constraints and how  are  constraint  violations  handled?   Can  results  of queries be
used as parameters in delete  operations?   Give  a  small
example.

### 3.3.3  Modify Facilities

Which of the database constituents can  be  modified?
For  each  such constituent, describe the operation by its
effect on the constituent being modified and on any  other
constituents.

Characterize  the  facility  for  the  definition  of
modify  operations.   What  is the perception of the user-
supplied parameters in the modify operation (are they perceived  as  relations,  as tuples, as input data used by a
general facility for the redefinition of relations, etc.)?
What is the role of tuples, attributes, and domains in the
modify operations?  What  is  the  role  of  general  constraints and how are constraint violations handled?

Give a small example.

### 3.3.4  Commit and Undo Facilities

Does the  system  provide  facilities  for  making  a
sequence  of tentative alterations which can, e.g., at the
user's discretion, be committed (made permanent) or undone
(called  back  to  the  state  of  the database before the
alteration sequence).

### 3.3.5 Additional Alteration Facilities

Describe any facilities for altering database constituents other than by single insert, delete, and modify
operations. Do not duplicate information in Section 3.4.

## 3.4 Additional Functional Capabilities

The following subsections describe features used to
support the combined use of qualification, retrieval, and
alteration.

### 3.4.1 Arithmetic and String Operations

What simple arithmetic expressions are supported?
What substring and embedded string operations are supported? Do not repeat information in Section 2.

### 3.4.2 Sorting

Describe the facility for ordering the tuples in a
relation; give the time period during which the ordering
is supported.

### 3.4.3 Library Functions

Describe the library functions that are supported,
e.g., aggregate functions such as MAY, MIN, SUM, COUNT,
AVERAGE.

### 3.4.4  User Defined Functions

Describe the mechanisms that can be used to define functions over some database constituents. Can these functions be defined, added, deleted, and redefined through time?

### 3.4.5  Transactions

Does the system permit altering users to define "units of operations", i.e., transactions that perform meaningful database state transitions or state evaluations? How are these transactions defined? Is the user aware of concurrency of transactions?

### 3.4.6  Multi-tuple Alterations

Can more than one tuple of one relation be altered (i.e., inserted, modified, or deleted) using some tuples of another relation as arguments to the operation.

### 3.4.7  Grouping

Describe the facilities for grouping tuples (i.e., partitioning sets of tuples into distinct subrelations) for processing. What functions (library, user defined, sorting) can be applied to the resulting groups or partitions (average salary of employees grouped by department, count people grouped by age, etc.)?

### 3.4.8  Exception Handling Mechanism

Describe the mechanisms provided by the system for handling exceptional and error conditions. Can a user-specified sequence of operations be triggered automatically by some change in the database state or by the execution of some specified operations?

## 3.4.9  Additional Functional Capabilities

Describe any functional capabilities not described in subsections of 3.4.

## 4. Definition, Generation, and Administration Facilities

The development and maintenance of a database application involves at least the following four stages: database design, defining the database constituents to form a schema, generating an actual database by creating instances of the constituents (population is done by the facilities described in Section 3), and administering the maintenance and evolution of both logical and performance properties of the application. The facilities to support these states are described in the following subsections.

The description of these facilities should relate as closely as possible to the database constituents described in Section 2.0. However, the facilities may address different "levels" of the constituents, e.g., derived relations, base relations, domains, access paths, storage structures, etc. Difference in the levels of perception between Sections 2 and 4 should be distinguished. The "level" of each facility should be characterized. The various levels and their relationship should be characterized briefly here. The ANSI/SPARC architecture should be used _if_ it is appropriate.

Describe how the definition, generation, and administration facilities interact.

## 4.1 Definition Facilities

The following subsections deal with the definition of database constituents to form a database schema. Describe how the definition facilities interact (e.g., parts of one uniform language). Each subsection should describe definitional aspects only (e.g., notation, defining properties of constituents, naming limitations, expression of application rules) so as not to repeat information in Section 2. Give an example of a small database definition and refer to it in each of the following subsections. See comment j in RTG-80-90.

### 4.1.1  Constituents of a Database Definition

List the constituents of a  database  schema  definition,  e.g.,  the constituents described in Section 2 plus
constraints, operations, and access paths. Place each constituent  in a level given in Section 4.0 and characterize
the relationships among constituents.

### 4.1.2  Database Definition

How are the properties of a database  (2.2)  defined?
Are  there  limitations such as the number of constituents
(e.g., relations)? Refer to the example.

### 4.1.3  Relation Definition

How are the properties of a relation  (2.3)  defined?
Are  there  limitations  such as the number of attributes,
the order of definition, restrictions  on  defining  keys?
Are there extensions such as the ability to define foreign
keys? Refer to the example.

### 4.1.4  View Definition

How are the properties of view (2.4) defined?  Are
there restrictions on defining these properties? If applicable, describe how dynamic and static  derived  relations
(views)  are  defined. Describe  how  the view definition
determines the operator  set  available  for  manipulating
views.

Refer to the example.

### 4.1.5  Tuple Definition

How  are  the  properties  of  tuples (2.5)  defined
(either  explicitly  or implicitly). Are there limitations
on defining these properties?

Refer to the example.


### 4.1.6 Attribute Definition

How are the properties of attributes (2.6) defined (either explicitly or implicitly)? Are there restrictions on defining these properties, e.g., unique attribute name, aliases? What is the role of domains in the definition of attributes?

Refer to the example.


### 4.1.7 Domain Definition

How are the properties of domains (2.7) defined? List the built-in types on which domain definition is based. What are the restrictions on defining properties of domains? Can built-in data types be constrained to form new domains (restricted value set or operations)? Can a value set for a domain be defined by enumeration or other means? Can operations be defined over domains?

Refer to the example.


### 4.1.8 Definition of Additional Database Constituents

Describe the definition of any additional database constituents, e.g., snapshots, transaction, triggers, procedures. Database dictionary is to be described in subsection 4.5.


## 4.2 Generation Facilities

The generation of a database involved the processing of a database schema, the creation of (possibly empty) instances of database constituents, and possibly the population of the database. Some aspects of database generation are defined as part of the system generation while others are defined as part of the application generation. This section describes the facilities for database generation.

Give a brief description of how a database is generated. Auxiliary mechanisms such as search aiding structures and details of how the database is generated need not be discussed.

Describe how these generation facilities relate to the other facilities of this section, i.e., 4.1, 4.3, 4.4, 4.5, as well as to the functional capabilities 3.0, if appropriate.

## 4.2.1 Constituents of a Database Generation

List the database constituents that are created during database application generation. Relate this list to Section 4.1.1. Only some of the constituents defined in 4.1, e.g., attributes, tuples, and relations, may be used to populate a database.

## 4.2.2 Generation of Database Constituents

Describe the facilities available for processing and populating database constituents. Briefly characterize any database load facilities and facilities for copying relations, particularly if they are relational in nature.

## 4.3 Database Redefinition

During the lifetime of the database it may become necessary to change the database definition. This may be as simple as renaming database constituents or it may require a redefinition of one or more database constituents.

### 4.3.1  Renaming Database Constituents

Describe the facilities for renaming each of the database constituents. Distinguish renaming from aliasing, which is the addition of synonyms to an existing name for a constituent. What are the restrictions on renaming? What is the effect on other database constituents that reference the constituent to be renamed? When does a schema change require changes to the database? To programs accessing the database?

### 4.3.2  Redefining Database Constituents

Describe the facilities for redefining database constituents.  What changes to database constituents are permitted? What is the effect and required change to the schema and to the database?  Can you redefine domains, attributes, tuples (by adding or deleting attributes), relations?  Are there any restrictions on defining new views other than those given in 4.1.4? What is the effect on views based on relations that are redefined? Under what conditions can constraints be added to or deleted from the schema. What restrictions are there on redefinition?

### 4.4  Database Regeneration and Reorganization

During the lifetime of a database, logical changes to the application and the need to improve performance may require the database to be regenerated or reorganized. This section describes the facilities provided for these changes.  Emphasize features that are relational in nature.

### 4.4.1  System-Controlled

Describe the changes to the database organization that are supported automatically by the system. Under what condition(s) does the system regenerate or reorganize the database?  What is the extent of the changes that are system controlled (e.g., partial or full).

### 4.4.2 DBA-Controlled

Describe the facilities that the DBA can use to regenerate and reorganize the database. Under what conditions are such changes permitted, necessary, or desirable? Can a database be used to load a second database? What is the effect of each change?

### 4.5 Database Dictionary

Define the concept of database dictionary as supported by the system. What are its constituents? What information is stored in the data dictionary? What operations does it support (e.g., schema queries, system performance, data queries). How is authority granted to the facilities of the data dictionary? Does the data dictionary support database design, schema generation, etc.? Do the data dictionary languages differ from the database languages? Give a small example of their use.

# 5. Interfaces and DBMS Architecture

The purpose of this Section is to describe the various interfaces named in Section 1.6 and to describe their relationship within the DMBS architecture.

## 5.1 System Architecture

The various languages or interfaces of a DBMS are related in a DBMS architecture (e.g., the ANSI/X3/SPARC architecture). In this feature catalogue we are interested only in those interfaces or languages used by humans. We are not concerned with interfaces between system modules nor with any other implementation details. Describe the DBMS architecture as the relationship among the interfaces named in Section 1.6. Make this description as simple as possible by drawing a diagram of the architecture based on those used by C.J. Date in his book Introduction to Database Systems published by Addison-Wesley, second edition, 1976. Use two or three level schemas only if they are applicable.

## 5.2 Interface Descriptions

For each language named in Section 1.6, this Section should contain a subsection (e.g., 5.2.1, 5.2.2, etc.) which describes the language. The descriptions should be brief, not repeating information given elsewhere in the feature analysis. The following is an incomplete list of characteristics (and the subsection of the feature catalogue where they are described) to be considered in the description.

⊕ name and purpose (1.6)

- ⊕ problem class for which the language is intended (8.0)
- ⊕ for what type of user is the language intended (ad hoc query, dba,...)?
- ⊕ semantics: what database constituents (2) are accessible? what functional capabilities (3,4) are available?
- ⊕ language form: linear (e.g., such as PL/1, PASCAL); graphic (e.g., tabular, menu); single or mixed (e.g., light pen and keyboard)
- ⊕ language type: search/qualification complexity (3.1); relational algebra; relational calculus; block structured mapping; "natural" language.
- ⊕ perception of relations (2.0): sets, tables, predicates, functions, etc.
- ⊕ interactive features: are choices for responses fixed? is the dialogue user- or system-driven?
- ⊕ self-contained features: Can parts of the language be used on a stand-alone basis? What is the computational power of the self-contained portion of the language (e.g., relational algebra, relational calculus, see Sections 3 and 4)?
- ⊕ host language features: is access to a relational database provided by features that are extensions to (e.g., procedure calls that put results into workspaces) or embedded in the related database management system (e.g., relation-like structures built into the language)? Describe the interface between the host language and the relational database facilities. How is database status information passed to the host language? How is data from the database passed to the host language? Does the user access the database through procedure calls or directly through the data structures and operations in the language? Characterize the level of procedurality (e.g., record or set oriented, power of qualification).
- ⊕ What the the security features provided by the language? (6.1)
- ⊕ Describe the recovery features of the language. (6.2)
- ⊕ Describe any special features of the language.
- ⊕ Give a brief example to illustrate the use of each main feature of the language. Refer to examples given in Sections 3 and 4 for features already illustrated.

# 6. Operational Aspects

## 6.1 Security

This section discusses the security features provided by the system.

### 6.1.1 Access Control

Describe the facilities provided by the system to protect against unauthorized access. Describe the logging and audit trail facilities. How are users identified or authorized in access control based on operations, access paths, data values, etc.? How are security violations handled? Does the system support the definition and maintenance of private relations?

### 6.1.2 Capability

Describe the possible security domains and their potential capabilities. How are these domains and capabilities defined?

## 6.2 Physical Integrity

This section describes the mechanisms for ensuring integrity of the database under sequential and concurrent access.

### 6.2.1  Concurrency Control

Discuss how the system handles the concurrent alteration problem.  Are these aspects transparent to altering
users or can they control the level and effects of concurrency.  How are concurrency related problems (lost
updates, phantoms, deadlock) resolved?  Can database
queries be executed concurrently?

### 6.2.2  Crash Recovery

Describe the capabilities provided to ensure  against
failure, e.g., backup, restart, checkpoint, logging,
restore, undo.

### 6.3  Operating Environment

This section discusses the hardware and software
environment of the DBMS.

### 6.3.1  Software Environment (Operating System)

The reliance of data management systems on executive,
control, or operating systems varies widely.  Some rely
heavily on manufacturer's supplied operating systems, others rely only on programming language compilers, while
some include, within the data management system, those
functions normally performed by the operating system. This
section attempts to characterize the system being discussed according to the above spectrum.

### 6.3.2  Hardware Environment
#### (CPU, Memory, Peripherals)

All systems are implemented or are being  implemented
on at least one hardware configuration and may be implemented on many. The description of the  hardware  environment  covers  the  CPU, memory,  and peripherals that are

minimum, and which is recommended.

What is the size in bytes of the relational  database
system?  Differentiate, if possible, by giving the size of
the major components.

# 7. Essentially Relational Solutions for Generalized DBMS Problems

Research and development based on the relational approach to databases has provided solutions applicable to generalized DBMS problems, i.e., applicable to more than just the relational approach. This Section describes these solutions and other advantages of the relational approach to databases.

Consider each of the following <u>claimed</u> advantages of the relational approach and, where applicable, describe briefly how the advantages are realized in the system or language under consideration. (Feel free to add to the list of claimed advantages.)

- Simplicity. Based on the simple and well understood nature of set-theory and predicate calculus there is an economy of concepts. There is one major data structure, the relation, and a small set of operations forming the relational algebra.
- Uniformity. Relational algebra and relational calculus exhibit closure and can be used as a basis for all forms of interaction with the database.
- Data Independence. Relational schemes and languages are free of many representational details such as access paths, ordering, and indexes. The relational algebra and calculus are high-level (non-procedural) and set-oriented.
- Permits optimization. The lack of representational detail in relational languages allows for the possibly automatic optimization of database interactions. (You may wish to describe any optimization the system does for interactions.)
- Basis for high level interfaces. Non-procedural, set-oriented relational languages permit the user to deal with the information in an application-oriented manner by being able to ignore many representational details. Relational languages can be extended easily to other high level interfaces. Considerable research on query languages is based on the relational approach.
- Natural. The set, table-like or predicate perceptions of data may be particularly appropriate for certain classes of applications.
- Efficient storage and retrieval potential. The high level, set-oriented nature of the relational model can be used to take advantage of database machines.

⊕ Multiple views of data. The relational algebra permits dynamic definition of new user views which can be derived from existing relations.

⊕ Advantages for distributed databases? Relational languages are independent of access paths and location of the data. This may provide benefits for distributed databases where distribution is intended to be transparent to the user.

⊕ Security? Access paths are defined by the use of the relational algebra or calculus rather than being explicit.

⊕ Basis for database semantics. The relational approach permits a distinction between data structure and data semantics. Data structure concerns relations, the representational tools. Relations are simple and "uninterpreted". Data semantics concerns the properties of the database application that are to be represented using relations plus additional constraint mechanisms. In this approach the relational database model is a basis for database design and semantic database models, e.g., constraints can be expressed using first order predicate calculus.

Some other advantages for database semantics are:
- Relationships are explicit in relations. Relationships exist either in relations or can be derived dynamically from existing relations using the relational algebra.
- Relativism. A relation can be viewed as representing an entity or an n-ary relationship.
- Symmetry. A relationship A O B can be accessed and expressed with equal facility in both orders A to B and B to A.

⊕ Strong theoretical foundation based on the mathematical concept of relation, on set theory, and on first-order predicate calculus. This theory has provided a basis for the study of the following aspects of databases:

- normalization theory
- consistency
- redundancy
- derivability
- analysis of relational schemes, altering operations and queries
- schema mappings
- completeness of database languages with respect to relational calculus (or DSL ALPHA) as a means for evaluating database languages
- query processing, i.e., logical deduction, optimization of query evaluation
- database design

## 8. Database Applications Using the System

This Section is intended to characterize the practical uses of the system: How widely used is the system (number of running applications)? What is the nature of the class of actual uses of the system? Give statistics concerning known applications, i.e., numbers and sizes of database constituents. Give the actual use of functional capabilities, transaction types (e.g., insert, update, delete) and loads, query activity, types of interfaces and their actual usage. How often has the schema been altered since the database was first loaded? What types of views (e.g., dynamic, static, snapshot) are used? How important is security? How complex is semantic integrity? What is the size of the schema and its associated procedure library (i.e., number of schema constituents and number of procedures)? How long have these applications been in existence? Describe unique or novel features common to applications using the system. What characteristic of these EBMSs is unique to the relational approach? What type of system (if any) was it running on in the past?

# 3. Analysis of Relational Database Management Systems

The following 14 systems were analysed using the feature catalogue of chapter 2:

3.1   ASTRAL   ( University of Trondheim )

3.2   IDAMS   ( IBM Heidelberg )

3.3   IDM   ( Britton-Lee )

3.4   INGRES   ( University of California )

3.5   MRDS   ( Honeywell )

3.6   MRS   ( University of Toronto )

3.7   NOMAD   ( National CSS, Inc. )

3.8   ORACLE   ( Relational Software Incorporated )

3.9   PASCAL/R   ( University of Hamburg )

3.10   PRTV   ( IBM, United Kingdom )

3.11   QBE   ( IBM, Thomas J. Watson )

3.12   RAPID   ( Statistics Canada )

3.13   RAPPORT   ( LOGICA Ltd., London )

3.14   SYSTEM R   ( IBM, San Jose )

3.1  Feature Analysis Of ASTRAL

by

Kjell Bratbergsengen

Tor Stalhane

Division of Computer Science
The University of Trondheim
Trondheim, Norway

January 1982

# 1.0 INTRODUCTION

## 1.1 Identification

ASTRAL, A Structured Relational Application Language, is a complete, general programming language. It developed as a joint effort between the Department of Computer Science and the Computer Center at the University of Trondheim, Norway, and A/S Norsk Data, a Norwegian computer systems company.

## 1.2 Status

### 1.2.1 System -

At present, a pilot compiler, featuring the major parts of ASTRAL and producing P-code, is running on a NORD-10 computer. Along with the developement of the programming language and the data base system, the developement of a special purpose data base computer is also going on. ASTRAL will finally run on this computer. No release dates have yet been set.

### 1.2.2 Applications -

ASTRAL is still an experimental system and not yet ready for applications.

## 1.3 System Background

The work on extending SIMULA with relational data types and relational calculus like statements, started in 1975 at the Department of Computer Science, University of Trondheim. A compiler for this language, which gave a sequence of SIMULA-statements and traditional DML-like subroutine calls as object code, was built. A Norwegian computer systems company took interest in the project and proposed new hardware for more efficient execution of relational operations. This then became the ASTRA project.

ASTRAL has been redesigned a number of times, and PASCAL was chosen later to form the basis for the programming language. The main reason was PASCAL's stronger type concepts. But still ASTRAL is very much influenced by SIMULA.

The development of ASTRAL is only one of several activities in the ASTRA project. There are other activities such as implementing a data dictionary system, an interactive update and query language, a subroutine interface to be used from FORTRAN and COBOL, a data base management system and new hardware.

The work has been sponsored by the Norwegian Government Research Agency since 1977.

## 1.4   Overall Philosophy

ASTRAL is a general purpose programming language. No distinction is made between database and non-database (temporary) data. ASTRAL is block structured. Transaction programs are inner to blocks or modules defining the database. Data are accessible within their scope of definition. Data allocation, indices, etc., are not controlled by the programmer, but these functions are taken care of by the runtime (database) system.

The overall motivation is to improve productivity in developing information systems and also open up for exploiting new hardware through parallel processing.

Contributions: The database description and transaction programs form an open ended, but integrated hierarchy. Common data and common code might be declared at the lowest common level, providing shelter against unnecessary interference, and better security. Processing of data, not only traditional database processing like searching and sorting but also complex arithmetic operations, might be performed in parallel. It is the task of the ASTRAL compiler and the database system to exploit the parallelism imbedded in the ASTRAL program and the database computer.

## 1.5   Essentially Relational Characteristics

The relations are perceived as flat tables. There is no ordering of the rows of the table and identical rows are not allowed. A row has one or more (multiattribute) unique keys. No index or storage structure is used or assumed by the user.

The following set and table operators are found explicitly in the language: selection, projection, union, difference, intersection, and join. The relational algebra operations are all imbedded in a general predicate and table constructor.

In addition, there are statements for operations on a row by row basis. No sorting sequence is assumed unless the relation is subject to a sort operator.

There are no restrictions on any operation imposed by the underlying storage structure. Dynamic views are maintained. Constraints have to be explicitly specified, and might be changed over the lifetime of the database. ASTRAL is a fully relational system.

## 1.6 Interfaces

There are activities implementing an interactive update and query interface and a subroutine interface to be used from FORTRAN and COBOL.

## 1.7 Documentation

Amble, T., K. Bratbergsengen and O. Risnes: "ASTRAL – A Structured and Unified Approach to Data Base Design and Manipulation". Proc. of the IFIP TC-2 Working Conference on Data Base Architecture, Venice 1979, North Holland 1979.

2.0   DATABASE CONSTITUENTS

2.1   General Description

Constituents of the database are the modules.   A  module
is  either   a   transaction  program  or a data declaration and
description module.  Declarations of datatypes and  variables,
views and assertions are part of a declaration module.

2.2   Database

2.2.1   Database Structure -

An ASTRAL database consists of a model and possibly a set
of submodels.  The model and its submodels define a collection
of tables and restrictions on their relations and data.

2.2.2   Database Operations -

Databases can be defined, created and deleted.  Data  can
be  inserted,   retrieved,   updated,   and   deleted using ASTRAL
assignment statements.

2.2.3   Database Constraints -

Constraints exist on three levels:

- on components of a   tuple,  mostly  imposed  by  the  value
  domains.   In  addition  it is possible to specify one or a
  certain combination of component values to be unique.

- on  relations  between  components  in  a   tuple.   These
  constraints are imposed by on access statements.

- on relations between components in different tables.  These
  are also imposed by on access statements.

## 2.3  Relation

### 2.3.1  Relation Structure -

A relation (called a table in ASTRAL) consists of identically structured, unordered tuples (PASCAL records). Tuples are uniquely defined by a specific combination of attributes contained in a tuple (see 2.2.3). Primary and secondary keys are specified when the relation (ASTRAL table) is declared.

### 2.3.2  Relation Operations -

The following operations may be performed: union, intersection, difference, simple selection, join selection, simple delete, join delete, projection, and assignment (insert or update).

In addition, the following standard procedures are available:

SUM, AVG (average), MAX, MIN, COUNT, SORT, SOME, and NO.

### 2.3.3  Relation Constraints -

See 2.2.3 (Database Constraints)

## 2.4  View

### 2.4.1  View Structure -

A view in ASTRAL is a table obtained by a projection or join of tables, possibly restricted by a predicate.

Example:  <P.name, P.price>(.P in parts.)
Example:  <E.name, B.name>(.E in emp, B in emp:
          E.mgr = B.name and E.sal > B.sal.)

## 2.4.2  View Operations –

A view may be used wherever a table may appear, except in the case stated in 2.4.3 (view constraints).

## 2.4.3  View Constraints –

- a view cannot have an <u>on access</u> statement attached to it.

- a view may only be exported in read-only-mode (see 4.1.8).

- elements of a view may not be updated or deleted and no new elements may be inserted.

## 2.5  Tuple

### 2.5.1  Tuple Structure –

A tuple in ASTRAL is a PASCAL record without variants.

### 2.5.2  Tuple Operations –

An ASTRAL tuple may be assigned to a PASCAL record provided the tuple is unique.  By using a standard table function it is possible to check whether a particular tuple is a member of a table or not.  Tuples may be changed, inserted or deleted in a coherent manner.

Insertion:  Tabl := Tabl + tuplel;

Deletion :  Tabl := Tabl - tuplel;

Tuples may be selected by predicates, for example

: tuple := Tabl(.a > 7 <u>and</u> b < a.);

where a and b are components in Tabl.

: tuple := Tabl(.x <u>in</u> Tab2 : x.a > a.);

Tuples may also be selected by means of a <u>for</u>-statement:

```
Example:    for x in Tabl(.a = 4.) do
            begin
              ...
              x.h := 7;
              x.s := 'new';
              ...
            end;
```

or, in a shorter form

```
Example:    in Tabl(.a = 4.) do
            begin
              ...
              h := 7;
              s := 'new';
              ...
            end;
```

Tuples may be deleted by predicates, for example:

```
Example:    T(.i < 7 .) := empty;
```

or in a for-statement:

```
Example:    for x in Tl do
            begin
              ...
              if x.i < 7 then  delete(x);
              ...
            end;
```

## 2.5.3  Tuple Constraints -

A tuple may be any PASCAL record which does not contain a variant part.  See also 2.6.3, attribute constraints.

## 2.5.4  Additional Properties Of Tuples -

Tuple components may be initialized like any usual ASTRAL record.

```
Example:    type dl = rec    s: string(6) := '      ';
                             age: integer := 21;
                    end;
            var Tl  : table of dl;
                    end;
```

## 2.6  Attributes

### 2.6.1  Attribute Structure -

An attribute in a tuple is identified  by  its  name  and qualified by a tuple name (compare example in 2.5.2).

### 2.6.2  Attribute Operations -

The rules for attribute operations are the same as  those defined for record components in PASCAL.

### 2.6.3  Attribute Constraints -

Attribute constraints are the same as those  defined  for PASCAL  variables of the same type.  In addition, an attribute may not be of type file, pointer or table.

## 2.7  Domain

### 2.7.1  Domain Structure -

In addition to the standard PASCAL types,  ASTRAL  offers the following extensions:

- fixed (<positive integer constant>)

  which is a two-word number with a  fixed  number  (<positiv integer constant>) of decimal digits:

  Example: <u>var</u>  fl :  fixed(2);
  ```
            ...
            fl := 1.03;      (* ok            *)
            fl := 1.035;     (* round to 1.04 *)
  ```

- <u>string</u> (<positive integer constant>)

  which is a packed  array  of  <positive  integer  constant> characters.

  Example: <u>var</u>  s :  <u>string</u>(6);
  ```
            ...
            s := 'AB';       (* 4 trailing blanks *)
  ```

2.7.2   Domain Operations -

They are the   same   as   in   PASCAL,   with   the   following
extensions:


- all kinds of fixed numbers may be mixed in expressions

- fixed(0) is equivalent to integer

- it is possible to select a character or a substring from   a
  string

    Example:   S1 := S2(3);
               S2 := S2(2:5);

- character   and   (sub)strings   of   size   1   may   be   used
  interchangeably.



2.7.3   Domain Constraints -

The actual implementation of ASTRAL constrains the:

- size of real and integer constants, and the

- number of members in a set.

## 3.0 FUNCTIONAL CAPABILITIES

### 3.1 Qualification

A table in ASTRAL may be qualified by a predicate. The result itself is a table which may appear wherever an unqualified table is allowed.

#### 3.1.1 Restriction –

#### 3.1.2 Quantification –

The quantifiers SOME, NO are available.

Example: if NO(.x in Tabl : x.i > k.) then ...

#### 3.1.3 Set Operations –

An ASTRAL table may be treated as a SET and the typical set-operations may be performed:

```
T1+T2  :  table union
T1*T2  :    "   intersection
T1-T2  :    "   difference
```

Set and element-inclusion may be performed by predicates.

#### 3.1.4 Joining –

A join predicate is defined as

<rec> in <tab>, <rec> in <tab> : <simple pred>

Example: Emp(.B in Emp : B.name =mgr and B.salary > salary.)

#### 3.1.5 Nesting And Closure –

Boolean expressions using tables may not be staticaly nested.

## 3.2   Retrieval And Presentation

### 3.2.1   Database Queries -

An ASTRAL database may be used in the following ways:

- to obtain a single record:

  R := Tab(.predicate.)

  The exception of 'NOTUNIQUE' will be raised  if  more  than
  one table element satisfies the predicate;

- to obtain a subtable:

  Tabl := Tab2(.predicate.);

- to obtain a Boolean result:

  SOME(.x in Emp :  x.salary > 10000.);

- to search through a table or subtable:

  for x in Tab(.predicate.) do ... ;

  This statement will provide all  table  elements  which
  satisfy  the predicate, one at a time.  The components of a
  table element are available through quantification with the
  controlled  variable,  x.   It  is  also possible to search
  through the table in the following way:

  in Tab(.predicate.) do ... ;

  where the table element components  are  available  without
  qualifications.

  When no updating is performed, a table may be replaced by a
  table constructor.

  Example:  R  := <A.x, B.a, A.z>(.A in Tl, B in T2.)

  Example:  Ta := <A.x, A.y, B.c>
                      (.A in Tl, B in T2 : A.y > B.a.)

### 3.2.2   Retrieval Of Information About Batabase Constituents. -

All  ASTRAL  databases  are  defined  by  models   and/or
submodels.   These are ASTRAL programs which may be inspected,
changed and recompiled by the person who  has  access  to  the
appropriate program files.

### 3.2.3  Retrieval Of System Performance Data -

No such data are currently available.

### 3.2.4  Report Generation -

ASTRAL offers currently no report generation facilities.

### 3.2.5  Constraints And Limitations -

- Table constructs may not be used in (for...) in statements.

- A maximum of two tables may be used in a range part
  (i.e., <auxillary variable> in <table>).

- A maximum of two tables may be used in a predicate.

- A predicate may use only comparison operators and the
  logical operators AND, OR, and NOT.

## 3.3  Altering

### 3.3.1  Insert Facilities -

A new element may be inserted into a table in the
following ways:

- by set addition
  Tl := Tl + r;

- by direct insertion (subtable replacement)
  Tl(.none.) := r;
  (none denotes the empty subtable of Tl)

Similarly, a new table may be added to an already existing
table.

- by addition
  Tl := Tl + T2;

- by direct insertion
  Tl(.none.) := T2;

In all four examples, the tables on the right hand side
of the assignment may be replaced by a table qualified by a

predicate, or a projection.

Example:  T1(.none.) := <X.a, X.b>(.X in Emp.);
          T1 := T2(.A in Emp : A.b = V.);


## 3.3.2  Delete Facilities -

An ASTRAL table, or some elements of a table, may be deleted.

Deletion of a table:

Tab := empty;  (* empty record *)

Deletion of some element in a table:

Tab (.predicate.) := empty;

(only those elements for which the predicate yields true are deleted)

```
  for x in Tab do
  begin
    ...
    if C then  delete(x);
    ...
  end;
```

The current element x in the table is deleted if C is true. The table, Tab, may be qualified by a predicate.


## 3.3.3  Modify Facilities -

Components of a table element may be changed directly in a for...in - or an in - statement.

Example:  for x in T1 do  x.b := m;

Example:  in T1 (.b > n .) do
            begin
              a := m;
              b := b + 1;
            end;

See also 2.5.2 (tuple operations) and 3.3.1 (insert facilities).

### 3.3.4  Commit And Undo Facilities -

Since ASTRAL is a multiuser system, a user may reserve a table or a subtable by a region statement. All changes to the tables inside the region are immediately performed on the database. By definition, the changes made to the database are confirmed (committed) when the region-statement is completed. However, the changes may be undone by the statement restart region.

```
Example:   region reserve T = Tabl(.predicate.) do
           begin
              ...      (* Tabl(.predicate.) is reserved *)
              ...      (* inside this region           *)
              if bool expr then
                 restart region;
              ...
           end;
```

## 3.4  Additional Functional Capabilities

### 3.4.1  Arithmetic And String Operations -

In addition to the operations given in 2.7.1 to 2.7.3 all standard PASCAL operations are available.

### 3.4.2  Sorting -

Sorting is achieved by the following construction:

```
Tab(.predicate.).SORT(sortlist)
```

Sortlist is a list of elements given by {ASC/DESC} (attribute-id).
In order to save a sorted table, it must be assigned to a file.

```
Example:   sortfile := Tl.SORT(ASC(name));
           sortfile := Tl(.age > 20.).SORT(DESC(wage));
```

### 3.4.3  Library Functions -

In addition to the standard PASCAL library functions, ASTRAL provides the following functions:

```
High(A)     : upper bound of a one-dimensional array
Low(A)      : lower bound of a one-dimensional array
```

```
Tab.avg(id)   :  gives the average of all occurrences of id in
                 Tab
Tab.sum(id)   :  gives sum of all occurrences of id in Tab
Tab.max(id)   :  gives the maximum value of all occurrences of
                 id in Tab
Tab.min(id)   :  as for max, but the minimum value is returned
Tab.count     :  gives the number of elements in Tab
```

### 3.4.4  User Defined Functions -

In addition to the facilities inherited from PASCAL, ASTRAL supports external functions and procedures.

### 3.4.5  Transactions -

Database transactions may be defined by the region statement (see 3.3.4).

### 3.4.6  Multi-Tuple Alterations -

Multi-tuple alterations are achieved by controlled loops

Example:  <u>for</u> x <u>in</u> tab <u>do</u> ...;
   or
Example:  <u>in</u> tab <u>do</u> ...;

For additional information see 2.5.2 (tuple operations) and 3.3.1 to 3.3.3.

### 3.4.7  Grouping -

3.4.8  Exception Handling Mechanisms -

A function, procedure, region (see 3.3.4), or program may have an exception part.  This is defined in the following way:

{ head of func/proc/reg/prog }

{ body }

exception

{ except-tag : statement; }

end;

An exception may be raised in two ways:

- by an error occurring in the program, or

- by a signal, explicitly programmed by the application programmer.

When an exception is raised, the following actions take place:

- the internal variable STATUS is given the appropriate value, depending on the exception raised;

- the ASTRAL runtime system finds the innermost surrounding block (in a dynamic sense) where the exception is handled;

- the STATUS variable is set back to normal and the statement connected to the except-tag is entered.

If no appropriate except-tag can be found, the runtime system will display an error message and terminate the program.

The following exceptions are defined:

leave, overflow, truncation, subscript, endoffile, notuple, error, catastrophe, caseindex, duplicate, emptytable, emptypointer, storeoverflow, stringerror, unimplemented, illegal, astrerror, outofrange, notunique.

A signal is raised by the statement:

signal <except-tag>;

Example:  if a > b then  signal catastrophe;

# 4.0   DEFINITION GENERATION AND ADMINISTRATION FACILITIES

## 4.1   Definition Facilities

### 4.1.1   Constituents Of A Database Definition –

An ASTRAL database definition consists of:

- a set of table types (PASCAL record types plus the enhancements mentioned in 2.7.1 (domain structure));

- a set of table definitions, containing the table type and the <u>unique</u> and key-specification.

In addition, the database definition may contain definitions of views, integrity constraints (<u>on</u> access-definitions), and definitions of external routines.

The database information is passed on to the application programs by export statements.

### 4.1.2   Database Definition –

A database is defined in the following way:

```
model <model name>;
{ constant definitions }
{ type definitions }
{ variable definitions }
{ view definitions }
{ proc/func definitions }
{ integrity constraints (on access) }
{ export <exportlist> to <address>; } *
end;
```

It is possible to augment or restrict the database by one or more submodels.  A submodel is defined as

```
<model name> (address) submodel <submodel.name>;
import <importlist>;
   ...
(* see model definition *)
   ...
end.
```

Example:   <u>model</u> A;

        <u>type</u> person = <u>record</u> name    : <u>string</u> (12);
                           address : <u>string</u> (24);
                           age     : 0..120;
              <u>end</u>;

        data   = <u>record</u> name    : <u>string</u> (12);
                           dep     : <u>string</u> (24);
                           mgr     : <u>string</u> (12);
                           roomno  : 1000..9999;
                           wage    : fixed(2);
              <u>end</u>;

      <u>var</u>   emp   : <u>table</u> of person;
                 <u>unique</u> name, address;
                 <u>end</u>;

        jobb  : <u>table</u> of data;
                 <u>unique</u> name, dep;
                 <u>end</u>;

     <u>virtual</u> Pl : &lt;A.name, A.age, B.dep&gt;
                (.A <u>in</u> emp, B <u>in</u> jobb.);
     <u>export</u>  jobb, <u>protected</u> emp to B;
     <u>export</u>  <u>protected</u> Pl to C;
     <u>end</u>.

    A(B) <u>submodel</u> AB;
    <u>import</u>  jobb, <u>protected</u> emp;
    <u>virtual</u> P2 : &lt;A.name, A.address&gt;
                (.A <u>in</u> emp : age &gt; 50.);
    <u>export</u>  jobb, <u>protected</u> P2 to progl;
    <u>end</u>.

This will create the following structure:

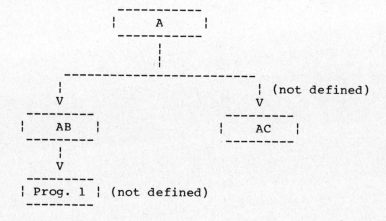

## 4.1.3  Relation Definition -

A relation (ASTRAL-table) is defined as:

```
<name>   :   table of <table type>;
             {unique <uniquelist>;}
             {primary <prim-list>;}
             {secondary <sec-list>;}
             end;
```

A <uniquelist> specifies a component or a set of components which will be unique in the table.

The keywords primary and secondary specify a primary key and a secondary key respectively. Each consists of one or more attributes.

## 4.1.4  View Definition -

Views may be defined in the following way:

```
<name>  :   '<'<complist>'>'(.<rangelist>{':'<predicate>}.)
```

Example:  P : <A.x, B.y, A.z>
                    (.A in T1, B in T2 :  A.x > 12 and B.y < m.);

## 4.1.5  Tuple Definition -

A tuple (table element) is defined as a PASCAL record.  A tuple may not have a variant part.

## 4.1.6  Attribute Definition -

The types ^<name> (pointer), file, and table are not allowed.  See 4.1.5 and 2.7, otherwise

## 4.1.7  Domain Definition -

The domain definitions are the same as for PASCAL, that is:

integer, real, char, boolean, set, and subranges plus the

ASTRAL types <u>string</u> and <u>fixed</u>:

   <string def> ::= <u>string</u> (<positive integer constant>)

where <positive integer constant> is the string length in characters, and

   <fixed def> ::= <u>fixed</u> (<pos const>)

where <pos const> is the number of digits after the decimal point.

   In addition to the standard PASCAL subrange definitions, it is also possible to define subranges of fixed numbers:

Example:  measure : 0.96..1.04;


4.1.8  Definitions Of Additional Database Constituents –

   A relation (table) may be made available to the user in two ways:

   <u>export</u> <name>...

in which case it may be retrieved and updated, and

   <u>export</u> <u>protected</u> <name>...

where it may be retrieved only.


4.2  Generation Facilities

   The ASTRAL compiler generates a stand alone program when a model or submodel is compiled.  This program, when executed, will catalog all tables which are defined in this model or submodel.

## 4.3   Database Redefinition

### 4.3.1   Rename Database Constituent -

No renaming is allowed in ASTRAL.

### 4.3.2   Redefine Database Constituents -

An existing database may not be redefined.

## 4.4   Database Regeneration And Reorganisation

### 4.4.1   System Controlled -

This facility is not yet available.

### 4.4.2   DBA-controlled -

It is currently not possible for the DBA to reorganize an ASTRAL database.

## 4.5   Data Dictionary

Currently, there is no integrated data dictionary available to ASTRAL and the ASTRA DBMS.

The ASTRAL compiler uses its own dictionary based on the compilation of models and submodels. The dictionary entries are stored on special system defined files. There is one such file (ASTRAL dictionary module) for each compiled model or submodel.

The database computer maintains another dictionary - the ASTRA dictionary system. The ASTRA dictionary is a relational database containing tables describing the databses stored on the database computer. The information is entered into the dictionary by the ASTRAL runtime system, and is based on the commands from executing ASATRAL programs.

The user is not able to access any of the dictionaries. This will be a feature of the integrated dictionary system when implemented.

# 5.0  INTERFACES AND DBMS ARCHITECTURE

## 5.1  System Architecture

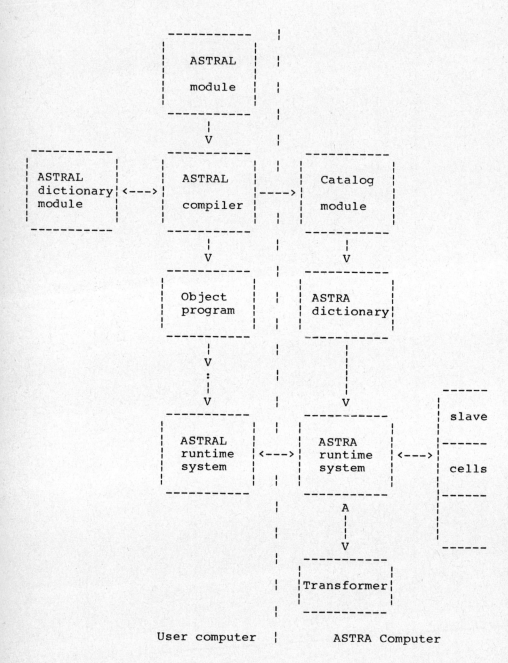

The ASTRAL compiler takes as input a model, a submodel, a routine (function or procedure) or an application program.

When the input is a model, the input ASTRAL dictionary is empty. For all other inputs, the compiler will get the appropriate ASTRAL dictionary module as specified in the submodel/routine/program heading (see 4.1.2 and 4.1.3).

The compiler generates a new ASTRAL dictionary module and an object code file.

The absolute program communicates with the ASTRAL Database Computer where the workload is distributed to the slave cells via the ASTRAL runtime system.

## 5.2 Interface Description

The user interfaces with the database through an ASTRAL program. Each relation in the database is available to the user as an ASTRAL table. It is possible to:

- select one or more elements from a table, possibly depending on a predicate;

- construct new tables, consisting of all or some of the elements in one or two other tables (by a projection);

- search through a table (or part of a table) and change or delete elements;

- build table unions, intersections and differences;

- sort a table with respect to one or more of the element components and assign the table to a file;

- obtain largest/smallest value of a component in a table, compute a component average etc. by means of standard table functions and procedures.

# 6.0 OPERATIONAL ASPECTS

## 6.1 Security

### 6.1.1 Access Control -

An application program may only obtain access to a database when the model name is known (see 4.1.2) and the model information has been exported to that application program (see example included in 4.1.2). By preceding an exported variable with the reserved word <u>protected</u>, the variable will be a read-only variable.

## 6.2 Physical Security

### 6.2.1 Concurrency Control -

The ASTRAL database computer guarantees that the relevant part of the table is updated by only one application program at a time.

It is possible for an application program to reserve one or more tables or parts thereof for a critical region of the program (i.e., transaction) by a region statement.

Example:  <u>region reserve</u> T1 = emp(.salary > 50000.) <u>do</u>
                <u>begin</u>
                  ...
                <u>end</u>;

All tuples in the table emp which satisfy the predicate 'salary > 50000' are reserved for this application program until the corresponding <u>end</u>.

### 6.2.2 Crash Recovery -

The crash recovery is provided by the ASTRA relational database management system.

## 6.3 Operational Environment

### 6.3.1 Software Environment (Operating System) -

The ASTRAL system consists of an ASTRAL compiler, written in PASCAL, a runtime system, also written in PASCAL and a set of utility routines written in PLANC, the NORD implementation language. The whole system runs under the NORD operating system SINTRAN III.

The compiler and runtime system are both easily portable, while the utility routines are very machine-dependent and would need a complete rewrite in case of a new computer.

### 6.3.2 Hardware Environment (CPU Memory Peripherals Etc.) -

The compiler and runtime system runs on a two-bank NORD-10 computer (64 k, 16 bit words per bank). The number of slave cells is optional. The performance of the system increases with the number of cells.

The current version uses discs as the peripheral storage medium.

3.2   Feature Analysis Of IDAMS

Integrated Data Analysis and Management System
(IDAMS)
Feature Description

by

A. Blaser, H. Eberle, R. Erbe, H. Lehmann,
G. Mueller, U. Schauer, H. Schmutz

IBM Scientific Center Heidelberg

March 1982

# CONTENTS

# 1. INTRODUCTION

## 1.1 Identification

The Integrated Data Analysis and Management System (IDAMS used as abbreviation) is an enduser oriented system providing a customizable interactive problem solving environment. IDAMS /1,2,3/ offers access to a relational data base and to a program library via a common, uniform, high level query language.

IDAMS has been developed at the IBM Heidelberg Scientific Center as an experimental system.

## 1.2 Status

### 1.2.1 System

The final version of IDAMS as described in the following sections, was accomplished in June 1981.

### 1.2.2 Applications

IDAMS has been developed to support interactive data analysis (and management) by application specialists, i. e., technical or business professionals. To test IDAMS in a real world environment studies and master theses with the following applications have been performed from 1978 to 1981 (for details see section 8):
- Monetary Investment Decision and Analysis Support
- Operating System Tuning
- Analysis of Traffic Accidents Data
- Analysis and Administration of Data on Human Stress
- Research on Human Hereditary Diseases
- Development of a System for Thermo-Regulation-Diagnosis
- Engineering Design Optimization
- Analysis of Data Collected in a Display
  Terminal Study

## 1.3 System Background

IDAMS has been largely implemented in the interactive APL language. It runs under VSAPL of the IBM VM/370 Conversational Monitor System (VM/CMS) /4/.

The IDAMS high level query language Extended Query by Example (EQBE in abbreviated form) is an extension of the syntactic idea of the Query by Example language proposed by M. Zloof /5/. The two major extensions are the use of the table skeleton mechanism also for application programs and the use of logical APL expressions for the specification of query predicates and constraints.

Extended Relational Memory (XRM /6/) and - alternatively - the Research Storage System (RSS) of System R /7/ serve as underlying data management components.

The following systems could be regarded as similar to IDAMS or to individual IDAMS components: QBE /5/, SQL /8/, INGRES /9/, MAGNUM /10/, NOMAD /11/.

## 1.4 Overall Philosophy

IDAMS aims at a comprehensive problem solving/decision support environment embedded in APL and providing for high level querying of a relational data base and data analysis combined with graphical data presentation and report writing facilities, with access to application program libraries, and with on-line user guidance and training facilities.

IDAMS has been developed for detailed analysis and non-routine usage of large quantities of data. Application specialists with little DP training may apply IDAMS to support and improve their planning, data analysis, and reporting activities in industry and science. To support the envisaged endusers (e.g., planners, scientists, engineers) various components are integrated in one system environment, with a simple and uniform language interface suitable for non-programmers but also attractive to people with programming skills. The system and its user language have sufficient flexibility to be adaptive to particular applications and to evolving DP experience of users.

## 1.5 Essential Relational Characteristics

IDAMS supports
- the structural aspects of the relational model, excluding the domain concept
- insert, update, and delete operations
- a table oriented high level language for querying and altering.

## 1.6 Interfaces

IDAMS offers the following user interfaces:

- for table-, function-, view-definition
- for generation and interrogation of information for interactive user guidance
- high level skeleton and linear language for query and altering
- the high level programming language APL
- for integrating application programs
- for data presentation (Graphics, Report Writing)
- for data base utilities: Dump, Restore, etc.

## 1.7  Documentation

/1/  R. Erbe, et al.: Integrated Data Analysis and Management for the Problem Solving Environment, Information Systems, Vol. 5, pp. 273 - 285, 1980.

/2/  H. Lehmann, et al.: Integrated Data Analysis and Management System, Command Language User's Guide, Heidelberg Scientific Center TN 79.04., July 1979.

/3/  U. Schauer, et al.: Integrated Data Analysis and Management System, Publication of the GI Special Interest Group on Methods Data Bases, February 1981.

/4/  IBM Virtual Machine Facility/370, CMS User's Guide, IBM Form-No. GC20-1819.

/5/  M. M. Zloof: Query By Example, IBM Research Report RC 4917, July 1974.

/6/  R. A. Lorie: XRM An Extended (N-ary) Relational Memory, IBM Technical Report 320-2096, January 1974.

/7/  Donald D. Chamberlin: Relational Data Base Management System, Computing Surveys, Vol. 8, No. 1, March 1976.

/8/  Donald D. Chamberlin, et al.: SEQUEL 2, A Unified Approach to Data Definition, Manipulation, and Control, IBM J. RES. 20:6, pp. 560 - 575, 1976.

/9/  M. Stonebraker, E. Wong, P. Kreps, and G. Held: The Design and Implementation of INGRES, ACM TRANS. on Data Base Systems 1:3, pp. 189-222, 1976.

/10/ Tymshare Inc. MAGNUM Reference Manual, November 1975.

/11/ National CSS Inc. NOMAD Reference Manual, Form-No. 1004, April 1976.

/12/ R. Erbe, G. Walch: A General Interactive Guidance for Information Retrieval and Processing Sytems, APL76 (ed. G.T. Hunter), pp. 127-140, Ottawa September 1976.

/13/ APL-Language, IBM Form-No. GC 3847.

/14/ C. J. Date: An Introduction to Data Base Systems, 2nd Edition, page 52.

/15/ H. Eberle, H. Schmutz: Calling PL/I or FORTRAN Subroutines Dynamically from VSAPL, IBM Scientific Center Technical Report TR 77.11.007.

/16/ W. H. Niehoff and R. J. Alan: APL-GRAPHPAK, Program Description, IBM Endicott Laboratory, 1978. Form-No. GC20-1819.

/17/ IBM Virtual Machine Facility/370, System Programmers Guide, IBM Corp., Data Processing Division, White Plains, New York.

## 1.8 General System Description

IDAMS offers access to the multi-user relational data base system
System R /7/ and to a program library of APL and non APL programs via a
non procedural, simple, but powerful query language encompassing all
facilities of the APL host language. IDAMS supports all APL data structures, i. e., scalars, vectors, matrices, and arrays of higher
dimension, as well as units of measurement. Unit checking and unit
mapping is performed.

A dictionary captures the definition of data and programs, i. e.,
formatted description of table and program structures.

The semantic meaning of tables and programs are described in the interactive user guidance component IUGS /12/. This textual, application
oriented information is structured as an information network to allow a
guided tour for the identification of tables and programs. In addition
the IUGS component provides online training for newcomers to get
acquainted with the IDAMS facilities and help when needed.

IDAMS offers two language levels for the user:

- menu level for the beginner or the casual user
- command level for the advanced user, the application developer and the
  application programmer.

The menu level allows adaptation to the user's skill. The user may ask
for additional explanations, skip menus by specifying selections in
advance, or switch to the command level, such that the menu level can
also efficiently be used by the advanced user.

## 2. DATABASE CONSTITUENTS

### 2.1 General Description

Term Translation Table

```
-----------------------------------------------------------
| IDAMS term              | Feature catalogue term        |
-----------------------------------------------------------
| database                | database                      |
| table                   | relation                      |
| row                     | tuple                         |
| value                   | attribute                     |
| column name             | attribute name                |
| column type             | attribute type                |
-----------------------------------------------------------
```

An IDAMS database consists of one or more tables. A table consists of rows of identical type. A row consists of values of possibly different type. A field is the cross-section of a row and a column. A field contains a value. Columns are denoted by column names; column types define the set of legal values and operators for the fields of the columns IDAMS values may be scalars, vectors, and matrices of arbitrary dimension.

The central part of the schema definition in IDAMS is the description of a table with the association to a database, with the column names and their types, and optionally the key nomination, and with a semantic description.

In general, the qualification, querying, altering, and constraint definition are row (= tuple) oriented.

## 2.2 Database

### 2.2.1 Database Structure

A database is a variable set of tables. During a single session only the tables of one database can be accessed.

### 2.2.2 Database Operations

A database is generated and defined in two independent steps:

- A special  utility is used for generation, reorganization, space allocation, and naming of a database.
- Once  access  is granted to a named database, tables belonging to this database can be defined and deleted, interactively.

Utilities are available for dumping and restoring the database.

### 2.2.3 Database Constraints

Constraints on the database level are not supported.

## 2.3 Table

### 2.3.1 Table Structure

A  structure  of type table consists of rows of identical type.  A table may be perceived as a set-like structure with first-order predicates for subset definition.

During  table definition a set of key columns can be defined.  Rows with identical key columns are rejected.

## 2.3.2 Table Operations

Within IDAMS operations on tables are those for defining, and deleting tables. In addition, features are provided for retrieving information on table structures and table semantics.

The rows of a table are not ordered. They are clustered according to the defined single or composite key.

## 2.3.3 Table Constraints

A table is constrained by its optionally defined key. The key may be composed of several columns. The system enforces that there are not two rows in a table that coincide for all key fields.

## 2.4 Views

IDAMS does not support views in the usual sense. Rather, it provides a MACRO facility that offers similar functions.

A macro is defined as a set of query language statements. When a macro is specified in a query it is replaced by the original statements before the query is compiled. Macros are more like functions to manipulate data in 'logical tables' than like 'logical tables' themselves.

## 2.5 Rows

## 2.5.1 Row Structure

A row is a structure consisting of a fixed number of fields, possibly of different types. The column order is immaterial.

## 2.5.2 Row Operations

Rows can be retrieved, inserted, updated, and deleted by specifying predicates for the corresponding rows. There exists a test operation to check whether a row is in the table or not, based on the values of one or several fields.

2.5.3 Row Constraints

Constraints for insertion, update and deletion of rows can be defined, specifying triggers, assertions and reaction rules. Assertions are specified as predicates for rows, whereas reaction rules can be regarded as whole queries.

2.6 Values

2.6.1 Value Structure

A value is perceived as an object of fixed type, and is identified by the column name.

A type information is composed of the data type, the dimension, and optionally a unit. The following data types are available: integer, real, boolean, and character. The dimension is used for defining non-scalar data. It may be of arbitrary size. Units are user defined units of measurement.

No distinguished column values like NULL are defined.

2.6.2 Field Operations

All APL functions and operators are available. Their semantics is described in APL Language Manual /13/.

Additional functions with compatibility and coercion rules can be defined by the user, and embedded in a query. These functions can be written in APL, Assembler, PL/I, FORTRAN, and COBOL.

## 2.6.3 Field Constraints

Field constraints are implied by the column type definition (s. 2.6.1).
Additional constraints can be defined using the constraint subsystem.

## 2.7 Domains

The concept of domains is not explicitly supported.

## 3. FUNCTIONAL CAPABILITIES

The Extended Query by Example (EQBE) language of IDAMS is
non-procedural. EQBE can be used in the menu mode in skeleton form,
similar to QBE (for details see 5.2.3) and in the command mode in a
linear form. The examples of this chapter are written in the linear
form.

A query consists of one or more statements called predicates. The order
of the predicates is not essential.

EQBE is based on APL. The syntax of the predicates is rather similar to
APL syntax with only minor restrictions and some additions for data base
manipulation.

Predicates are subdivided into 'input predicates' which select data, and
'output predicates' which manipulate data or alter the data base.

The examples of this chapter use a data base described in /14/. Section
4.1 of this paper contains its IDAMS definition.

## 3.1 Qualification

IDAMS selection mechanisms are content-oriented. Rows of tables are
selected by means of selection and restriction predicates that have to
be fulfilled by the values of the fields of the selected rows.

3.1.1 Restriction

There are two different predicates to select elements from a table:

(p1) tablename [col1=x1;col2=x2;...]

   returns one tuple x1,x2,... at a time for further manipulation.

(p2) tablename[col1€y1;...coli=x1;...]

   aggregates  the selected values from column col1 into y1, etc.  and
   returns  the  aggregates  that can be further processed.  x1, etc.,
   can be used to specify restriction predicates on the tuples.

The  selection  of  values  can  be restricted by additional predicates,
i. e.,  arbitrary  boolean APL expressions.  Among others all arithmetic
and comparison operations and the logical operators AND, OR, and NOT are
available.  Each expression is valid
- that is correct according to APL syntax rules, and
- that is correct according to APL and IDAMS rules for data compatibility, and
- that is correct regarding units of measurement, and
- that  yields  a  0 or 1 or an array of zeroes and ones.  In the latter
  case, only the first element of an array is relevant.

For  a  selection predicate of type p1 a restriction predicate on one or
several  of  the  variables  x1,... restricts the selected tuples. For a
predicate of type p2 the variables x1,... must be bound by another predicate;  a  predicate  on  the  variables  y1,... is a restriction on the
aggregates, not on the single elements.

Any  number  of  predicates  can  be  specified.  By  default,  they are
connected by AND. Predicates can also be connected by OR using 'alternatives' (ref. 3.1.6).

Projection is done by omitting the column names of the irrelevant columns from the selection predicate p1.

Simple equality restrictions can be directly stated in the selection predicate.

Examples

```
PART[PNAME=NAME;COLOR='RED';WEIGHT=W]
W<100×KG
```

selects all red parts from table PART that weight less than 100 kilogram. It places the corresponding values of the column PNAME into variable NAME and of column WEIGHT into variable W, such that these values may be further processed.

```
SUPPLY[SNR;PNR∈P;QTY∈Q]
SNR=123
```

returns a one-column matrix P containing the part numbers of the parts supplied by supplier 123 and another one-column matrix Q containing the quantities in the same order.

3.1.2 Quantification

Quantification is not directly supported by operators. The selection predicate p1 is treated as an existence test if all variables x1,... are bound by other predicates.

In most cases aggregates (s. 3.1.1) together with APL array operations can be used to answer questions containing quantification, including questions containing absolute quantification like 'there are at least 3...'.

Examples:

```
PART[PNR;COLOR='BLUE']
SUPPLY[PNR]
```

returns  all  part numbers of blue parts for which there exists an entry
in SUPPLY.

```
SUPPLY[PNR=222;SNR∊S]
(ρ,S)≧2
```

is true if there are at least two suppliers for part number 222.

3.1.3 Set Operations

EQBE  provides an IN operator to test whether a value is contained in an
aggregate.

Example:

```
SUPPLY[SNR=51;PNR∊P1]
SUPPLY[SNR=52;PNR∊P2]
(222 IN P1) v (222 IN P2)
```

is true if part 222 is either supplied by supplier 51 or by supplier 52.

3.1.4 Joining

Equi-join  is  supported.   Two tables can be joined according to one or
more  columns  if  the  corresponding  columns  have  compatible  types.
Equi-join  is  expressed  by  using  the same variable for corresponding
columns.  Joining more tables can be specified accordingly.

Example:

```
SUPPLIER[SNR=S;CITY='HEIDELBERG']
SUPPLY[SNR=S;PNR=P]
PART[PNR=P;PNAME]
```

returns the names of all parts supplied by a supplier located in Heidelberg.

## 3.1.5 Nesting and Closure

EQBE queries are compiled; the compiled query is an ordinary APL function. The result of a query can be stored in APL variables, and APL data can be input to a query. Thus, simple queries can be combined in APL functions to build more complex queries.

It is also possible to execute an APL function within a query. This means, queries can be nested, and can be used recursively, too.

Example:

```
EMPL M
DEPT[NAME;MGR]
MGR=M
EX NAME
EX EMPLPP NAME
```

Assume, table DEPT contains for each employee, given by his name, the name of his manager. The EX predicate executes an arbitrary APL expression. This query with name EMPL and parameter M calls itself recursively (the name of the compiled query is EMPLPP). For a given name M it finds the names of all employees reporting directly or indirectly to that manager. The first EX predicate displays the employees' names, the second one calls the query again to find the employees directly reporting to these employees. Recursion terminates when no found employee is itself a manager. Thus, the query returns the names of all employees reporting directly or indirectly to the manager M.

### 3.1.6 Alternatives

The predicates in a query can be grouped together to build alternative groups of predicates. Predicates that belong to the same group are prefixed by the same label (an identifier followed by a colon). A predicate may have several labels indicating that it belongs to several alternatives. A predicate without labels belongs to all alternatives.

This feature can be used to process selected data differently depending on some conditions.

Example:

```
PART[PNAME=NAME;PNR]
SUPPLY[PNR;QTY∈Q]
SUM=+/Q
SOME:SUM>0
NONE:SUM=0
SOME:EX NAME,'   ',(ΦSUM),'PARTS SUPPLIED'
NONE:EX NAME,'   NO PART SUPPLIED'
```

displays for each part in table PART the name and either the total number of supplied parts or the text 'NO PART SUPPLIED'.

### 3.2 Retrieval and Presentation

### 3.2.1 Database Queries

The result of querying a IDAMS database is either a boolean value or a set of tuples.

If it is a boolean value it determines whether some action is done.

Example:

```
PART[PNAME='BOLT';COLOR='RED']
EX 'THERE ARE RED BOLTS'
```

The text 'THERE ARE RED BOLTS' is only displayed if the selection predicate is fulfilled by at least one row of table PART.

If the result of querying a database is a set of tuples, these tuples consist of database elements and aggregates of database elements. These tuples are available one at a time and can be processed successively. Each element of the tuple is stored in a separate variable.

## 3.2.2 Retrieval of Information about Database Constituents

The database schema is stored in a dictionary (s. 4.5). IDAMS provides several commands to retrieve information from the dictionary. Since the IDAMS commands are APL functions, since the information retrieved from the dictionary is the result of these functions, and since any APL function can be executed in a query, dictionary information can be directly used in queries.

## 3.2.3 Retrieval of System Performance Data

IDAMS is conceived as a system for non-DP professionals. Therefore, the user does not have access to system performance data. System performance data is kept in the dictionary and used by the IDAMS compiler to determine the optimal access path.

## 3.2.4 Report Generation

There are several facilities to assemble a report:

- The EX predicate can be used to format the elements of a resulting tuple.

Example:

```
PART[PNR;PNAME;COLOR]
EX 'PART NUMBER ',(ΦPNR),' IS A ',COLOR,' ',PNAME,'.'
```

  lists sentences of the form 'PART NUMBER 222 IS A RED BOLT'.

- The user can easily write his own report writing function and execute it in a query. For this purpose IDAMS supports SINK functions. SINK functions are called once at query start, once for each resulting tuple, and once immediately before leaving the query. This type of function can be used to write header lines followed by lists followed by summary lines.

- The result of a query can be stored in a global APL variable and transferred to some independent report generator.

- The Menu Interface of IDAMS (s. 5.2.6) contains special report writer facilities.

3.2.5 Constraints and Limitations

Conceptually there are no limitations on the number of tables accessed or on the number of variables used in a query. But IDAMS runs in an APL workspace and uses auxiliary areas. If the workspace or an auxiliary area is too small this may restrict the capabilities. There are means to enlarge the workspace and the other work areas.

3.2.6 Graphical Data Presentation

IDAMS provides functions to display the result of a query as a graph at a graphical display terminal. It supports drawing of curves, scatterplots, histograms, and surfaces with grids, contourlines etc.

### 3.3 Alteration

Database alteration is done by output predicates that insert, delete and replace tuples. These output predicates can be specified in a query together with input predicates that state additional conditions. For each tuple that fulfills the input predicates the output predicates must be satisfied (executed), too.

### 3.3.1 Insert Facilities

EQBE provides an insert predicate of the following form:

tablename [→col1=expr1;col2=expr2;...]

Only complete tuples can be inserted, i. e., the list of column names in the above predicate must be complete. Their order is not relevant. expr1,... may be any APL expression over bound variables, that yields a value whose type, rank and unit are compatible with the respective column type.

If all key columns of a tuple to be inserted have the same values as the corresponding key columns of a row already in the table, insertion is rejected.

Example:

    PART[→PNR=234;PNAME='SCREW';WEIGHT=12×G;COLOR='GREY']

inserts a new part into the table PART if part number 234 does not yet exist in table PART.

### 3.3.2 Delete Facility

EQBE provides an output predicate to delete rows from a table. It has the following form:

~tablename [→coli=expri;colj=exprj;...]

expri,... can be arbitrary APL expressions over bound variables that yield a value whose type, rank and unit is compatible with the corresponding column type.

Those rows are deleted whose specified columns contain the values resulting from the evaluation of the corresponding expressions. Only those columns are specified whose values are used to select the rows to be deleted.

Example:

    SUPPLY[PNR∈SUPPART]
    PART[PNR∈PARTNR]
    ~PART[→PNR=P]
    P IN PARTNR
    ~(P IN SUPPART)

deletes all parts from table PART for which there is no entry in table SUPPLY.

IDAMS does not provide facilities to delete individual column values because it does not support NULLs. It provides a command to empty a whole table without destroying its dictionary entry, and it provides commands to erase a table from the database schema.

3.3.3 Modify Facilities

EQBE provides a predicate to update rows of a table. Its general form is:

    tablename[coli=expri;...→colj=exprj;...]

exprj,... (right of the arrow '→') may be arbitrary APL expressions over bound variables that yield values whose type, rank and unit are compat-

ible with the corresponding column type. expri,... (left of the arrow
'→') may also use unbound variables.

The column specifications left of the arrow are used to select the rows
to be updated and to return 'old' values; the specifications right of
the arrow specify the new values.

If an update operation requests to change a key value such that the key
of the row would no longer be unique, this update operation is rejected.

Example:

    SUPPLY[PNR=222;QTY=Q→QTY=1.1×Q]

increases the quantities of each supply of part 222 by 10 percent.

3.3.4 Commit and Undo Facilities

All changes of a table affect only the 'current version' of the table.
IDAMS always keeps an unchanged 'shadow version' of a table. The user
must explicitly save a segment (s. 4.1.2) to make changes of its tables
permanent, i. e., to make the shadow version equal to the current
version. By 'loading' the shadow version before saving the changes, he
can undo the changes. Loading makes the current version equal to the
shadow version.

3.4 Additional Functional Capabilities

3.4.1 Arithmetic and String Operations

EQBE supports all APL primitive functions and operators. Additionally
it provides the IN comparison operator which tests whether some element
is contained in an aggregate, and it supports a more general reduction
facility that applies not only to APL primitive functions but also to
user written functions.

3.4.2 Sorting

APL provides an ascendingly and a descendingly ordering function that can be applied to vectors.

Additional sorting facilities are offered in Menu mode (s. 5.2.6).

3.4.3 Library Functions

Simple functions like MAX or COUNT can easily be directly expressed with APL primitives.

Example:

```
PART[WEIGHT∈W]
EX(Γ⌿W)÷KG
```

displays the maximum weight in KG contained in column WEIGHT of table PART.

IDAMS offers about 30 more complex functions, most of them for statistical analysis. The system contains a User Guidance Component to help the user to find the functions appropriate for his needs (s. 5.2.2).

3.4.4 User Defined Functions

A user may write his own functions and execute them in a query. These functions may be written in APL, PL/I, FORTRAN, COBOL, or Assembler. If a function is not written in APL a small APL driver must also be coded to invoke the non-APL function dynamically.

The user may define his functions in the IDAMS dictionary. Then, the query compiler can check whether - at usuage time - the arguments of the function are compatible with the parameter definition.

EQBE provides a special output predicate for function execution. It is similar to the table selection predicate, according to the fact that functions may be regarded as relations.

IDAMS distinguishes between three types of functions that are treated differently by the query compiler:

- Single-valued functions are invoked for each tuple of input arguments qualified by the corresponding input predicates.

- 'Sources' are executed repeatedly for one single tuple of input arguments until the return code of the function indicates a terminating condition. A typical use of this type of function is reading an external file until an end-of-file condition is reached.

- 'Sinks' are invoked once before a qualifying input tuple is available to allow to initialize variables or to open a file, once for each qualifying tuple of input arguments, and once to close processing. Sinks are typically used to write query results onto external files, or to format reports.

Functions may also be used in a query without being previously defined in the dictionary. But they must be made known to the compiler by specifying them in the header line of the query. They can then be used in expressions but not in function predicates. The compiler can only check whether they are used syntactically correctly; it cannot ensure compatibility of arguments and parameters.

3.4.5 Transactions

The user is not aware of transactions, although the system uses this concept to assure data consistency in a multi-user environment. The user cannot explicitly start or close a transaction. Transactions are controlled by the system.

### 3.4.6 Multi-tuple Alterations

Multi-tuple alterations are supported. Tuples from other tables can be used as arguments to this operation. For an example, see 3.3.2.

### 3.4.7 Grouping

Aggregates as described in 3.1.1 are a means to group the resulting tuples of a selection.

Example:

```
PART[PNR ]
SUPPLY[PNR;QTY∊Q]
EX PNR,+/Q
```

displays for each part contained in table PART the part number and the sum of the supplied quantities.

### 3.4.8 Exception Handling Mechanisms

The EQBE compiler checks the syntax of the predicates, and as far as possible the compatibility of types (data type, rank and unit). It returns an error message pointing to the erroneous syntactical unit.

At execution time mainly the exception handling mechanisms of the underlying systems (VM/370 CMS, VSAPL, RSS) are active.

# 4. DEFINITION, GENERATION AND ADMINISTRATION FACILITIES

## 4.1 Definition Facilities

The definition of an IDAMS database can be divided into two steps:

1. Definition of logical and physical address space of the data base. This step includes the naming of the data base and is technically done using a generation utility.

2. Defining the data base constituents to form a schema.

Example Database Schema Definition

The example is taken from /14/.

The example database consists of three tables named SUPPLIER, PART, SUPPLY, and the units of measurement kilogram (KG), gram (G), and ton (T). Mathematical expressions define the relationships of the units. They are defined in statements ([1], [2], [3]). The table SUPPLIER is defined in statement [4] to [8] by the description of a headerline [4], providing the table name and a logical realm where to store the data. Statements [5] to [8] supply the data manager with the attribute names and their characteristics, i. e., whether they are a key, represented by K, their representation and rank. E. g., [1] C means the individual data element is a vector consisting a character data.

```
∇DATABASE
 [1] U: KG=U[1] □
 [2] U: G=0.001×KG □
 [3] U: T=1000×KG □
 [4] T: SUPPLIER RSS [1]
 [5] SNR K I
 [6] SNAME N[1] C
 [7] STATUS N I
 [8] CITY N[1] C □
 [9] T: PART RSS [2]
[10] PNR K I
[11] PNAME N[1] C
[12] COLOR N[1] C
[13] WEIGHT N R[KG] □
[14] T: SUPPLY RSS [3]
[15] SNR K I
[16] PNR K I
[17] QTY N I □
```

## 4.1.1 Constituents of a Database Definition

An IDAMS data base definition contains the description of the

- data base name, the physical and logical address space;
- tables (= relations);
- rows (= tuples);
- columns (= attributes);
- fields (= instances of attributes).

This information is stored in the IDAMS dictionary. In addition to the possibilities of name resolution and access control, the dictionary keeps information about:

- indexes to be maintained for the tables;
- clustering information;
- statistical data for access path selection.

This information is stored in the physical database dictionary.

## 4.1.2 Database Definition

IDAMS defines a database without considering the tables to be stored. Technically, a data base is defined by naming the database, nominating the database administrators, defining the addresses and the data extents, and subdividing the physical space into logical units (= segments).

## 4.1.3 Table Definition

A table is a rectangular structure, has a name and consists of a fixed number of columns and (during its life time) a variable number of rows. The sequence of rows is irrelevant. The intersection of a row and a column determines a field. Each field contains a value. All values within one column must be of the same type.

One or more columns of the table form the key. The field values in the key column determine uniquely one row within a table.

The names of a table and of its columns are specified together with other information when the user introduces (defines) a new table.

The user defined set of tables can be regarded as the database schema.

A table definition consists of a header entry followed by a column entry for each attribute.
The header entry has the following syntax:

Table:tname RSS[[sgtno]]

tname      is the name of the table to be defined.
sgtno      is the number of the RSS segment where the table shall be
           stored.

## 4.1.4 View Definition

In IDAMS views are defined according to the database manipulation operations. As a consequence, the same view has to be defined twice when it
is intended to have a read-only and a write-only version. Therefore, an
IDAMS view can be described by pointing to the similarities between a
macro and an IDAMS view.

A view is an object representing a whole or partial query. It is
defined as a set of predicates together with the information about binding und usage rules of its variables.

It can be described as a function delivering data: it is called with
some input parameters and returns at each invocation one instance of the
set of tuples of the output p.

A view definition consists of two parts: the definition of the parameters and the definition of the body containing the predicates.

The view parameter definition consists of a header entry, optionally
followed by parameter entries:

header [parameter] ...

The header entry has the following syntax:

VIEW : vname Body=cname

vname    is the name of the view.
cname    is the name of a collection containing the basic query.

A parameter entry has the following general syntax:

pname use [dim] type [unit]

pname   is the name of the parameter. Any identifier is valid that is unique within the view definition.

use     Input | Output

Input   this variable must be bound outside the view;

Output  this variable may be used outside the view; it is bound within the view.

dim     as for fields (see 4.1.5)

type    as for fields (see 4.1.5)

unit    as for fields (see 4.1.5)

Example:

This example uses the tables PART and SUPPLIER as defined in 4.1. The view has one input and two output parameters:

∇SUPPLIED
[1] VIEW: SUPPLIED BODY=DELIVERY
[2] SNAME OUTPUT [1] CHAR
[3] PNAME OUTPUT [1] CHAR
[4] WEIGHT OUTPUT R[KG]∇

Its body has the name DELIVERY and looks like a query.

∇DELIVERY
[1] SUPPLIER[SNAME;SNR=SUPPNR]
[2] SUPPLY[PNR=PARTNR;SNR=SUPPNR]
[3] PART[PNR=PARTNR;PNAME;WEIGHT]∇

This view can be used in a query like a function that, e. g., returns for a given supplier name the names and the weights of his delivered parts. The view body may contain any number of arbitrary predicates.

- The following variables are bound:
  -- all input parameters,
  -- all variables bound by a predicate of the body.
- All variables used in the body and all output parameters must be bound.

4.1.5 Row, Column, and Field Definition

IDAMS differentiates between rows, columns, and fields, but does not define them as explicitly described objects. Each column name together with the characteristics of the column-instances, is defined in one row of the table definition.

A column definition has the following general syntax

cname use [dim] type [unit] [repr]

cname      is the name of the column. Any identifier is valid, which is
           unique within one table.

use        has the syntax

           Key|Nokey

           Key    indicates that the column participates in the key (con-
                  catenated key) or is the only key column. When updating
                  a table, IDAMS ensures that the table will not contain
                  two rows with identical values for the key.
           Nokey indicates that the column does not participate in the
                  key.

dim        has the syntax

           [n]

           where n is an integer, $0 \leq n \leq 64$. It indicates the rank of the
           values of the column. n = 0 is the default and expresses that
           the field values are scalars. In case n = 1 they are vectors,
           for n > 1 they are matrices of rank n.

type     has the syntax

        Boolean|Integer|Real|Character

        and specifies the data-type of the values in the column.

        Boolean   the only possible values are 0 and 1
        Integer   any positive or negative integer between $-2*31$ and
                   $(2*31)-1$
        Real      any real value representable in VSAPL
        Character the items are character data or arbitrary rank.

unit     has the syntax

        [uexpr]

        It is only meaningful for real values and specifies the unit
        associated with the values in the column.

repr     is the representation code. The following codes are possible

| type | default | also compatible with type |
|------|---------|---------------------------|
| BOOLEAN | BZ | BT |
| INTEGER | I4 | I2, I1 |
| REAL | R8 | R4,I4,I2,I1 |
| CHARACTER | CZ | CT |

## 4.1.7 Domain Definition

The concept of domains is not supported.

## 4.1.8 Semantic Integrity Constraints

The definition of semantic integrity constraints consists of the following parts:

- the identification containing: the constraint name, (e. g., in example below: INSSUP) the trigger, specifying the action that invokes
  constraint checking, (e. g., INSERT (SUPPLY RSS[3]))

- the global definition, that provides information which is used in the
  open-phase of the triggering query to links the variables used in the
  constraint definition to the variables used in the query, (e. g., GD::
  SUPPLY [PNR=P] to link variable P to the query variable used to identify column PNR in the INSERT predicate for table SUPPLY)

- the trigger conditions, that allow to specify the trigger in a more
  detailed way,

- the constraint conditions, that must not be violated, (e. g.,
  CC:: PART[PNR=P] requiring P to be contained in table PART)

- the reaction rule consisting of reaction options (REJECT, ACCEPT,
  STOP, CONTINUE), and violation actions, formulated as a query (see the
  last two lines of the example below).

Example:

```
CONSTRAINT:INSSUP INSERT(SUPPLY RSS[3])
GD::SUPPLY[PNR=P]
AC::
CC::PART[PNR=P]
RC:: ACCEPT CONTINUE
     PART[→PNR=P;PNAME='XX';COLOR='XX';WEIGHT=0×KG]
```

This constraint checks whether a part to be inserted into table SUPPLY
is contained in table PART. If not, the insertion is nevertheless
accepted, but a corresponding tuple for this part is also inserted into
table PART.

## 4.2 Generation Facilities

An IDAMS database is generated by a utility program providing the physical space and the logical subdivision. The other database constituents
are defined via a IDAMS commands.

Before an IDAMS object (a table, function, or unit) can be used in a
query, it must be defined and added to the Dictionary (for dictionary
see 4.5). Normally, definitions are constructed as an APL collection.
The name of the collection, enclosed in quotes, is then passed to the
commands DDEF or DPDEF in the form in the form

    DDEF 'cname'
    or
    DPDEF 'cname'

The command DDEF adds the definition only to the Active Dictionary,
while the command DPDEF adds the definition also to a Permanent Dictionary.

Instead of building the definition in a collection one can use the
command

DDEFP

that prompts the user for pieces of information.

More than one definition may be entered. In this case, the last line of
each definition must be followed by the symbol '□'.

## 4.3 Database Redefinition

In a strict sense of the word a database cannot be redefined, it can
only be destroyed by allocating the physical space to another database.
All the database constituents will be erased. On the other hand, individual constituents of the database can be emptied or deleted. This

allows  a redefinition of the schema by adding or deleting new constituents.

## 4.4 Data Base Regeneration and Reorganisation

### 4.4.1 System-Controlled

IDAMS  provides an extensive tool to measure the system performance.  It provides  a set of counters to check workloads, transaction and resource collisions,  preferred  access  paths,  and  allows to realize preferred access  patterns.  The  system  checks  the use of indices, investigates redundant  indices,  and deletes all indices being either superfluous or not used.

### 4.4.2 DBA-Controlled

The evaluation of the performance measurement facility of IDAMS provides the DBA with data about the physical status, the available access paths, the amount of calls to the data manager, the usage of tables, and information about collisions of transactions.  The DBA has the possibility to dump  the  data  base,  to  redefine  the physical and logical space, to reload the data base.  New acces paths will only be build when needed by database requests.

## 4.5 Data Dictionary

The  dictionaries  administrated by IDAMS contain formal and descriptive information about IDAMS objects.

Starting  a  session  the  Active  Dictionary  (AD)  is initialized.  It contains  the  definitions  of  some  built-in  functions, the so-called Hidden Dictionary (HD), and the definitions of the user's objects stored in  the  AD  when  the  workspace was last saved.  The AD determines the immediate environment in which a user operates.  An object which is only known  in  the  AD  is  called  temporary. It becomes inaccessible after session end or after the command START.

Entries from a <u>Permanent Dictionary</u> (PD) may be copied into the AD via the <u>D</u>LOAD, <u>D</u>COPY, and <u>D</u>PCOPY commands.

Permanent Dictionaries reside on RSS segments. Objects have unique names within one dictionary. To distinguish objects with the same name in different dictionaries, the reference to permanent objects is via an object identifier consisting of a name and the location of the dictionary; i. e., the segment number.

The descriptive information on all system objects in the database can be invoked and consulted by using the IDAMS component IUGS (Interactive User Guidance System, s. 5.2.2).

## 5. INTERFACES AND DBMS ARCHITECTURE

### 5.1 System Architecture

Figure: The IDAMS Architecture

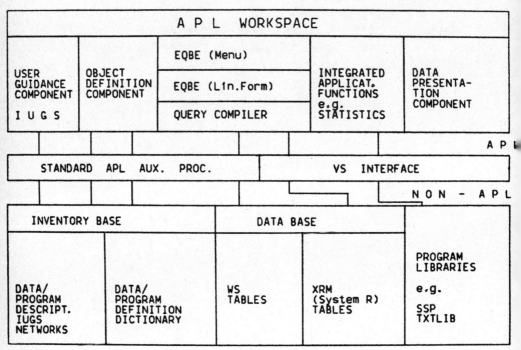

The architecture shows two main system environments linked together by a central interface (standard APL auxiliar processors and the interlanguage communication facility VS-Interface /15/):

- the APL environment (APL workspace)
- the non-APL environment (CMS host system, System R data base, ASSEMBLER-, FORTRAN- and PL/I-libraries)

The APL workspace contains all user interfaces. The object definition component and IUGS are high level interfaces to process data- and program-table definitions, and the corresponding application oriented descriptive texts. EQBE is a high level language to retrieve, insert, delete, update and process data stored in the System R data base. It can be used in the skeleton mode or in the linear form. The EQBE query created in skeleton mode is automatically translated into the linear form which is input for the query compiler generating executable APL code. In addition integrated application programs can be used inside or outside EQBE queries. The data presentation component is applied to present query output via graphical facilities or/and via report writing tools. For details see section 5.2.

## 5.2 Interface Descriptions

### 5.2.1 Table (Function) Definition Component

The table (function) definition component may be used in command mode or in menu mode. On the command level the user enters the definitions according to a given syntax and executes it via the DDEF or DPDEF command as described in section 4. The menu form prompts for the respective definitions column by column and automatically processes them.

## 5.2.2 Interactive User Guidance System (IUGS)

To facilitate the use of data and programs contained in the IDAMS system, the Interactive User Guidance System (IUGS) has been integrated as an IDAMS interface. IUGS supports the enduser in two ways:

1. IUGS allows to enter, store, administrate and retrieve application oriented descriptive information about permanent IDAMS objects.

2. IUGS supports the user via a guided search through information networks in identifying pertinent data and programs, whose documenta- tion is contained in the end nodes (leaves) of the networks. Thus, it delivers information about the data contained in the IDAMS data base, i.e., about its meaning, its origin, relationships etc., about programs in program libraries, and about the features of the system which are at his disposal.

IUGS is a menu oriented system with the following two main options:

1. The insert/update option is intended for the expert (e.g., the appli- cation programmer, the data base admininstrator) to generate the information network containing guidance information and structured documentation of data and programs.

2. The search option enables the enduser to identify data and programs, and to better understand their meaning and the prerequisites for their application by navigating him from general to more specific problem oriented description.

Since the permanent IDAMS objects (tables, functions) are formally defined in the dictionary and textually described in IUGS there is some interaction between the definition component and IUGS. The insertion (deletion) of an IDAMS object into (from) the permanent dictionary as described in section 4, implies the automatic insertion (deletion) of a corresponding IUGS node. The input of the node text is controlled by the associated dictionary information, i.e., the user is prompted to enter textual information for individual columns and for the object as a whole. Additional nodes containing application oriented information may and should be introduced to support the enduser's need to identify data and programs. The creation, update and deletion of this guidance information as well as establishing its links to the corresponding permanent object nodes is done via the IUGS insert/update option.

After the respective application or data base specialist has established an application oriented guidance network and introduced its links to the nodes of the permanent objects the enduser can apply the IUGS search option to identify pertinent data and programs. The tables and programs identified are automatically copied into the active environment. Since the IUGS-documentation of activated tables and programs is available in the active environment too it can be accessed directly in the skeleton mode of EQBE by a '?' or on the command level by the HOW-command. HOW'SUPPLY.QTY' or ?SUPPLY.QTY deliver descriptive information about the QTY-column of the table SUPPLY.

5.2.3 High Level Interface (Skeleton- and Linear Form) for Query and Data Manipulation

Defined tables and programs can be processed by a data base query formulated in the non-procedural high level query language EQBE, where the full screen skeleton version can be understood as an extension of the Query By Example (QBE) language developed by M. Zloof /5/. EQBE as an extension of QBE uses the syntactic idea of communicating with tables by 'filling-in the blanks' not only for data tables but also for functions and it allows to specify arbitrarily complex APL expressions as query predicates. EQBE is available in a full screen version where the enduser directly writes into skeletons of tables and functions, and in a linear form where the more advanced user creates a query according to a given syntax as described in section 3.

The skeleton form of EQBE is designed for users with little APL knowledge and virtually no data processing background. The language is table oriented and highly descriptive. The user inserts 'example elements', i.e., variables or literals into displayed skeletons which provide table/program names and column/parameter names (tables and programs are treated uniformly). Further, the user specifies selection- and restriction-predicates, which must hold true for his example elements, in form of APL expressions.

All features of EQBE described in its linear form in section 3 are available in the skeleton form, too. To illustrate the difference between the linear form and the skeleton form, some selected query examples in linear form given in section 3 are repeated here in the skeleton form. The definitions of the respective tables (e.g., PART, SUPPLY) and of the units used (e.g., KG, G) are listed in section 4.1. Example 1 shows a query to select the names (without display) of all red parts (stored in the table PART) that weigh less than 100 kilogram:

```
1 | APL |  EXPRESSIONS    |
--|--0--|--1-------------|
1 |  *  |  W < 100 x KG   |
```

```
2 | PART | PNR | PNAME | COLOR | WEIGHT |
--|--0---|--1--|--2----|--3----|--4-----|
1 |  *   |  *  | NAME  | 'RED' |   W    |
```

The skeleton layout is offered by the system. To formulate the selection criteria the user has to fill-in the 'RED'-restriction into the COLOR-column and the variables, e.g., W into the WEIGHT-column and NAME into the PNAME-column of the PART-table, and the weight-constraint into the APL-EXPRESSIONS-table, which is a kind of a scratch pad area to formulate additional restrictions.

Example 2 shows a query which selects and displays (see the 'quad'-symbol in the APL-column of the APL-EXPRESSIONS-table) the names of all parts supplied by a supplier located in Heidelberg (joining of tables):

```
1 | APL  | EXPRESSIONS |
--|--0---|--1-----------|
1 |  □   | PNA          |
```

```
2 | SUPPLIER | SNR | SNAME | STATUS | CITY        |
--|--0-------|--1--|--2----|--3-----|--4---------|
1 |    *     | S   |   *   |   *    |'HEIDELBERG'|
```

```
3 | SUPPLY | SNR | PNR | QTY |
--|--0-----|--1--|--2--|--3--|
1 |    *   | S   | P   |  *  |
```

```
4 | PART | PNR | PNAME | COLOR | WEIGHT |
--|--0---|--1--|--2----|--3----|--4----|
1 |   *  | P   | PNA   |   *   |   *    |
```

Example 3 shows an insert of one tuple into the PART-table. A new part is inserted with partnumber 234, partname SCREW, weight of 12 G, and GREY color. The tuple is inserted if partnumber 234 does not yet exist in table PART:

```
1 | PART | PNR | PNAME | COLOR | WEIGHT |
--|--0---|--1--|--2----|--3----|---4----|
1 |  □   | 234 |'SCREW'| 'GREY'| 12 x G |
```

The □ under the table name indicates that a tuple shall be inserted into the table. If the □ occurs in the APL-EXPRESSIONS-table it requests the display of results (see example 2).

Example 4 shows a query which requests some calculation too, expressed in APL. The total quantity of part 222 stored in the SUPPLY-table is calculated and displayed:

```
1 | APL   |     EXPRESSIONS |
--|--0---|--1--------------|
1 |  □   | M               |
2 |  *   | M = +/Q         |
```

```
2 | SUPPLY | SNR | PNR | QTY |
--|--0-----|--1--|--2--|--3--|
1 |   *    |  *  | 222 |  °Q |
```

The second row in the APL-EXPRESSIONS-table represents the calculation of the total value (by an APL expression), the first row requests the display of the result. In section 5.2.4 the example is shown with a modification, instead of the calculation of the total value by an APL expression the calculation is performed by a predefined summation-program.

5.2.4 The High Level Programming Language APL

The IDAMS beginners or/and casual users need a minimum of APL knowledge to formulate the selection- and restriction-predicates for the queries written in the IDAMS high level query language (menu- or linear-form).

Since a beginner may gradually become an advanced user, he may want to incorporate more and more complex parts of APL into his data analysis task, e.g., data extracted by the query may be further processed by user written APL functions or by APL expressions. Since IDAMS is implemented in APL a smooth transition from the menu- and command-mode to APL, and vice versa is possible.

More experienced users may use the menu level interface, the command level interface and native APL interchangeably. A variety of IDAMS commands may be used directly instead of interfacing them through the menu level interface. Extensibility by introducing user generated commands is easily achieved at the command level by just adding the pertinent (user written) APL functions.

This principle of extensibility applies also to the high level query language. Special (application specific) data manipulation requirements, beyond SUM, AVERAGE, COUNT etc. can be made available through APL functions written spontaneously. The interface to such functions is either the standard APL call mechanism or a skeleton oriented function presentation.

The following example shows the same query including total-value calculation as in section 5.2.3. However, the calculation is done via a predefined program TOTAL:

```
1 | APL   |  EXPRESSIONS |
--|--0---|--1-----------|
1 |  □    |  M           |


2 | SUPPLY | SNR | PNR | QTY |
--|--0-----|--1--|--2--|--3--|
1 |   *    |  *  |  *  |  °Q |


3 | TOTAL | INPUT | OUTPUT |
--|--0----|--1----|--2-----|
1 |   *   |   Q   |   M    |
```

This query shows the situation that an application program (e.g., TOTAL) is defined as an IDAMS object and is presented as a skeleton during the fill-in-phase. An alternative would be that an application program is spontaneously written without being defined as an IDAMS object. In this case the query would be slightly modified, i.e., the TOTAL-skeleton would be dropped and the entries in the APL-EXPRESSIONS-table would be changed as follows:

```
1 | APL  |  EXPRESSIONS |
--|--0---|--1-----------|
1 |   □  |   M          |
2 |      |   M = TOTAL Q |
```

## 5.2.5 Integrated Application Programs

Integration of application programs means:

A.) Syntactic definition of input/output parameters by the function definition component.
B.) Generation of an APL driver which serves as interface to non-APL programs.
C.) Textual description generated via IUGS

The integrated application programs can be used inside a query in skeleton mode (see example in section 5.2.4) or outside of a query via the IUGS execution option with prompting and checking of input parameters. The latter is done with respect to correct data type and rank as well as to constraints between the individual parameters. In case that the program identification step via IUGS is not needed the IUGS execution option can also be used outside IUGS through the RUN-command. The following example shows the monitored execution of the polynomial regression function named REGPOL:

```
RUN'REGPOL'
PARAMETER INPUT:
X←: ?
X : EXPECTS THE VALUES OF THE INDEPENDENT VARIABLE
    AS A VECTOR.
X←: 'ABCE'
***ERROR(S) FOR VARIABLE X:
    WRONG TYPE, CORRECT TYPE HAS TO BE REAL
X←: 1 2 3 4 5 6 7 8 10
Y←: 2,10+X*2
WEIGHTS←: 10ρ1
DEGREE→: 2
***THE FOLLOWING CONSTRAINTS ARE VIOLATED :
    NUMBER OF X-VALUES HAS TO BE EQUAL TO THE NUMBER
    OF Y-VALUES.
X→:
Y→: 10+X*2
RESULTS:
POLYNOM→: 10 0 1
        : ?
POLYNOM : COEFFICIENT OF THE POLYNOM IN ASCENDING ORDER
          POLYNOM[1] IS THE CONSTANT COEFFICIENT
          POLYNOM[2] IS THE COEFFICIENT FOR X*1
          POLYNOM[3] IS THE COEFFICIENT FOR X*2
          POLYNOM[4] IS THE COEFFICIENT FOR X*3
          ETC.
```

If the prompting of input parameters is not needed the integrated application programs can be invoked on the native APL level with or without
error checking depending on the user's choice to switch the error facility on or off.

5.2.6 Data Presentation Component (Graphics, Report Writing)

If not specified otherwise, the results of a query are displayed on the
terminal. The standard report has the format of the table(s) involved in

the query. The contents of the selected columns are assigned to APL variables whose name(s) may be the respective column name(s) or user chosen names. This allows to further process displayed values by means of APL.

The following example shows a simple query generating a standard report containing the partnumbers and the partnames of a PART table (defined in section 4.1) sorted in ascending order with respect to the part names:

```
1 |   APL |  EXPRESSIONS |
--|--0----|--1-----------|
1 |   □   |    ↑ P2,P1    |


2 | PART  | PNR | PNAME | COLOR | WEIGHT |
--|--0----|--1--|--2----|--3----|--4-----|
1 |   *   | P1  | P2    |   *   |   *    |
```

Partnumber and partname of the PART table are referenced by the freely chosen names P1 and P2, respectively. The □ in the APL-EXPRESSIONS table invokes the listing of the results and the '↑' causes sorting by partnames in ascending order. The results of the query are available in the APL workspace in the APL variables P1 and P2.

In addition to the standard query output described above IDAMS offers report writing facilities which allow the incorporation of query results into interactively designed layouts of reports. The layouts can be stored separately from the query results such that layouts created earlier can be combined with results of a query to be processed in the future.

The report writing option is complemented by graphical facilities based on the APL GRAPHPAK program package /16/. The following one- and two-dimensional plots are supported: (A1) line plots, (B1) barcharts,

(C1) histograms, (D1) scatter plots, (E1) scatter/line plots, (A2) perspective views, (B2) contour lines, (C2) three-view projections.

## 5.2.7 Database Utilities (Dump, Restore, Setupdb)

In addition to the normal VM/370-CP-commands DDR DUMP and DDR RESTORE which dumps the data cylinderwise from disk to tape and restores them from tape to disk, the IDAMS commands TDUMP and TRSTR allow to dump the data tablewise from the RSS data base to normal CMS files and to restore them from the normal CMS files to the RSS data base. The IDAMS commands TDUMP and TRSTR require as arguments table- and dictionary-name as well as CMS filetype and filemode for the file keeping the data. Its filename is identical to the table name. The CMS files created can easily be dumped on a tape by the normal CMS TAPE DUMP command and restored by the CMS TAPE LOAD command.

The SETUPDB is an IDAMS (EXEC) utility to define the physical extensions of a new RSS data base. Calling SETUPDB the user is prompted for the addresses and the respective disk space (number of cylinders) of the segments to be defined.

## 6. OPERATIONAL ASPECTS

### 6.1 Security

#### 6.1.1 Access Control

Currently, access to the IDAMS data base is controlled through the standard features of the underlying operating system. These features are extended by a password protection for logical address spaces. The view mechanism as a primitive for access protection is available, but not yet used in an authorization subsystem.

## 6.2 Physical Security

IDAMS is a multi user system and uses the System R lock manager /7/ to guarantee data base integrity under concurrent access. For crash recovery the System R log facility /7/ is used which allows to back-up an individual transaction, to recover from soft failures, and to restore the data base via archive dumps whenever a media failure occurs.

## 6.3 Operating Environment

### 6.3.1 Software Environment

IDAMS is mainly implemented in APL and runs under VM370/CMS /4/. As data base manager the Research Storage System (RSS) /7/ from System R is used which contains all access-, lock-, log-, and storage-capabilities of System R.

### 6.3.2 Hardware Environment

IDAMS can run on all IBM processors that are supported by VM/370 with the possibility to define at least 2 MB virtual storage. IBM32XX display terminals and IBM3277 GA graphics work stations may serve as user communication stations. IBM3330 or IBM3350 disk devices are used for online storage of the data base, the program libraries and the system. Tapes are only used for back-up copies.

## 7. SOLUTIONS FOR GENERALIZED DBMS PROBLEMS

DBMS is just a component of IDAMS. Its scope reaches beyond DBMS. IDAMS may be viewed as a Decision Support System and as a system supporting application development done by endusers.

Particular emphasis has been put on the following issues:

- Uniformity:
  IDAMS provides a uniform interface for data base query, for data base modification, for data analysis, for using predefined functions, and for presenting results either in report form or via graphical display.

- Model Base:
  IDAMS is not limited to the functions provided a priori by the EQBE language. Rather, the system allows to add user written functions, to define them in the dictionary, to describe them textually in IUGS, and to store them in a model base. The functions can be linked to a facility which checks type, rank, and constraints of its parameters.

- Basis for High Level Interface:
  IDAMS provides a menu and a command mode. The commands are APL functions and can therefore be used to build application specific high level interfaces. To support this process a set of utilities for screen handling, menu construction, dialogue management and data presentation is provided.

- Multiple Views of Data:
  IDAMS permits dynamic definition of new user views which can be derived from existing relations.

- User Guidance:
  For the casual user the guidance component provides the facility to learn about the system itself and about existing applications, to get help in specific problem situations, and to describe ones own application.

## 8. DATABASE APPLICATIONS USING THE SYSTEM

### 8.1 Monetary Investment Decision and Analysis Support

The Monetary Investment Decision and Analysis Support (MIDAS) application was implemented by a guest scientist from the University of Bonn and finished by an economics student early 1979. Its result is a valuable data base on daily stock quotations - values in raw form and adjusted by splits and dividends etc. - of the German stocks traded at the Frankfurt Stock Exchange over a period of 6 years (1971 - 1976), together with a set of functions for the analysis of this data. The data base consists of 4 tables, i.e., 3 auxiliar tables containing company names, industry codes and dates, and the 'main'-data table containing the stockrates (raw and adjusted) for 240 companies as time series of 1530 values each.

### 8.2 Operating System Tuning

The operating system tuning application deals with the implementation of a data base for the administration and evaluation of system measurement data collected via the VM/370 Monitor /17/, and the development of parametric queries for the display and analysis of the monitored data.

The respective data base consists of 22 tables corresponding to the 22 different record types of the VM/370 monitor. The number of columns per table varies from 3 to 13. The size of the data base is varying dependent on the time interval to be considered. Disk space for a maximum of 35 megabytes is provided for the current application.

### 8.3 Analysis of Traffic Accidents Data

This application deals with the administration and analysis of data collected from traffic accidents in the area of Berlin and Hannover. Data collection is done by members of the Institute for Vehicle Technology of the Technical University of Berlin within a research project sponsored by the Bundesanstalt fuer Strassenwesen (BAST - Federal Institute for Streets) at Koeln. The data base includes interrelated information on persons, vehicles, damage, injuries, external traffic conditions, etc., observed in a large number of traffic accidents.

Data from about 1600 accidents are stored in 18 tables. The number of columns per table is varying from 5 to 133, the number of tuples per table covers the range from 4 to 3920. The whole data base takes about 8.8 megabytes.

## 8.4 Analysis and Administration of Data on Human Stress

This study deals with the analysis of data on physical and mental human stress in the working environment, collected by members of the STRESS research team of the University of Heidelberg within a research project sponsored by the Bundesministerium fuer Forschung und Technologie (BMFT - Federal Ministery for Research and Technology) at Bonn.

The STRESS data base consists of 20 tables covering disk space of about 4.5 megabytes.

## 8.5 Research on Human Hereditary Diseases

IBM Brussels, Belgium, supports the Institute for Cellular and Molecular Pathology of the University of Louvain on the basis of a national project in its research on Human Hereditary Diseases. In a preliminary step IDAMS was used by an IBM Systems Engineer to design the data base and to efficiently and economically develop parametric queries (application programs), which satisfy most of the DP needs of the university researchers. The complete application system based on IDAMS was transferred to the university in 1980.

## 8.6 Development of a System for Thermo-Regulation-Diagnosis

With the Institute for Labour and Social Medicine of the University of Heidelberg, a masters thesis is being supervised aiming at the management and interactive analysis of Thermo-Regulation-Diagnosis (TRD) data.

In a first step data of about 400 patients will be fed into IDAMS. The record of each patient consists of 48 temperature measurements and of about 50 anamnestic data. The present size of the TRD-data base (including derived items) takes about 0.5 megabytes.

## 8.7 Engineering Design Optimization

This application is a joint study with the Institute of Space Propulsion of the University of Stuttgart. Since June 1980 IDAMS is used as a tool for engineering design optimization of space engines combining turbo, ramjet, and rocket concepts. The respective data base consists of 13 tables covering about 2.5 megabytes.

## 8.8 Display Terminal Study

The application aimed at the administration and analysis of data collected as part of an IBM internal Display Terminal Study. During a survey, data was collected by means of a questionaire of appr. 500 items from 1200 users of display terminals and from a smaller control group. These data were loaded into the IDAMS data base for their evaluation. IDAMS was particulary helpful for data screening and correction of data acquisition errors. A preliminary evaluation aiming at a first overview through count statistics, cross tabulations, and correlations was quickly performed by means of 5 parametric queries implemented via the IDAMS High Level Query Language EQBE. More complex reports were generated by nested queries. The extensibility of the EQBE through APL was found extremely important to handle very specific report writing and data selection requests.

3.3   Feature Analysis Of IDM

Feature Analysis of Relational Concepts,
Languages, and Systems for IDM

by
Daniel R. Ries

Computer Corporation of America
575 Technology Square
Cambridge, Massachusetts 02139

October 1980

Feature Analysis of Relational Concepts, Languages
and Systems for IDM[TM]


Prepared by:

Daniel R. Ries
October, 1980



FORWARD

This report was prepared for inclusion in a Feature Catalogue of
Relational Concepts, Languages and Systems being prepared by the
Relational Database Task Group of ANSI/X3/SPARC - Database Systems
Study Group.  The format and content of the report are based on the
Working Paper RTG-80-81 of the relational database task group.  This
report compared IDM to the terms and definitions of that paper and
not to other commercial products.



NOTICE

[TM]Intelligent Database Machine (IDM), Intelligent Database Language
and IDL are (applied for) trademarks of Britton-Lee, Inc.

1    INTRODUCTION

1.1   Identification

Intelligent Database Machine (IDM) 500

Developed by:   Britton-Lee, Inc.

Albright Way

Los Gatos, California

1.2   Status

1.2.1   System

The IDM will be released in the 4th quarter, 1980.

1.2.2   Applications

The IDM is designed for use by OEM companies who will provide
the direct support and/or applications for the end users.

1.3   System Background

The IDM system is a database machine and as such is not part of any
particular family of systems.  The reference manual uses the Intelligent
Data Language (IDL) to describe the functionality of the IDM and IDL
very strongly resembles the Quel language of INGRES.  However, other
relational languages could also be interfaced to the IDM.

1.4   Overall Philosophy

The IDM is a self-contained system that serves as a dedicated peripheral
providing a relational database management system.  The IDM provides a
high level 'host independent' interface to OEM supplied programs running
on the host.  The OEM supplied interface can support an interactive
set oriented language based on the relational calculus (or algebra)
and/or a tuple at a time interface.

## 1.5 Essentially Relational Characteristics

The system is fully relational. It provides all of the power of the join operation including cycles, self-joining relations, multiple joins, and independent existence of relations.

It has the advantages of a relational system including no access path dependencies, no order dependencies, no index dependencies, no altering dependencies, high-level interface, and dynamic views. It does <u>not</u> specifically support semantic integrity constraints except through the use of stored user commands. It does allow protection constraints to be dynamically added and deleted.

## 1.6 Interfaces

(1)   Database Schema Definition

(2)   Query Language

(3)   Database Altering

(4)   Constraint Definition

(5)   Database Generation and Regeneration

(6)   Database Schema Redefinition and Renaming

(9)   Security Definition, Monitoring and Control

(10)   Database Control Utilities

(11)   Definition of Storage Structure, Indexes and Access Paths

(12)   Database Dictionary

The language for all of these interfaces is basically a set of <token, values> that result from the OEM supplied parser or program interface.

IDM provides guidelines and a suggested End User Language (IDL) for implementing: a full purpose query language, a specific subroutine call interface and an imbedded programming language.

Regardless of the interface the OEM provides, it must be translated into the 'correct' sequence of tokens and values. That sequence is described as a post-order traversal of the IDL parse tree.

Results, both status and data, are returned to the host using the same <token, values> protocol.

## 1.7 Documentation

IDM Software Reference Manual Version 1.0 Copyright 1980.

"Aid in the '80s" by Robert Epstein, Paula Hawthorn in DATAMATION, February, 1980.

"Design Decisions for the Intelligent Database Machine", by Robert Epstein, Paula Hawthorn in Proceedings of the 1980 NCC, June, 1980.

## 1.8 General System Description

One unique aspect of this system is that it supplies a very high-level interface to databases for one or more host systems. The IDM is thus a Backend System that is designed to free the host resources which would otherwise be consumed by the Database Management System.

# 2. DATABASE CONSTITUENTS

## 2.1 General Description

The constituents of an IDM database are:

      Database
      Relation
      View
      Tuple
      Attribute

These constituents are related as follows: A database consists of relations of possibly different types. A relation consists of tuples of identical types. A view is a relation derived from one or more relations by relational calculus operations. A tuple consists of attribute values of possible different types. An attribute consists of values from one domain type. The domain type is one of a fixed set of system provided domain types. The user does not explicitly define domains independent of the attributes.

## 2.2 Detailed Description

### 2.2.1 Database Structure

An IDM database is named at database creation time. Relations and views are added and deleted to an 'open' database at any time. Database names are up to 12 characters long.

### 2.2.2 Database Operations

Databases can be created, opened, closed, destroyed, dumped and loaded.

### 2.2.3 Constraints

The creator of a database is declared the database administrator and only she can destroy the database. It is the responsibility of the host to determine and govern who can create a database.

## 2.3 Relation

### 2.3.1 Relation Structure

A relation is viewed as a set of n-tuples and is defined by naming the n attributes and specifying their types and lengths. Duplicate tuples are surpressed on any relation having a suitable access method. It was deemed too expensive to surpress duplicates on completely 'unstructured' relations. Attribute order is not significant. Aliases are defined through views.

### 2.3.2 Relation Operations

Relations can be created, destroyed, indexed, dumped, loaded and audited.

Predicate calculus operations are supported. The basic IDL command for manipulating relations is in the form:

Command Relation (target-list) qualification.

Commands include:

APPEND - to add tuples to a relation

RETRIEVE - to retrieve tuples into the host

RETRIEVE INTO - to create and add tuples to a new relation

DELETE - to delete tuples from a relation

REPLACE - to replace attribute values in tuples of a relation

The target-list defines, by name, the attributes (or expressions) of the relation. The qualification determines which tuples are to be effected by the command.

In the target-list or qualification, all attribute names must be preceded by a 'tuple variable' which ranges over one relation (or view). The tuple variable, say t, is bound to a relation before each command by:

Range of t is relation_name.

Note that within one command a relation can have more than one associated tuple variable. (Recall that all of these commands are sent to the IDM by a sequence of <token, value(s)> pairs. More details on the qualification and commands are found in Section 3.

## 2.3.3 Constraints

Sets of attributes can be declared to form a unique key for a relation. A relation can have several unique keys. Protection commands, PERMIT and DENY allow the owner of a relation to specify which commands other users can apply to the relation. PERMIT and DENY allow a predicate calculus qualification to specify the set of tuples of the relation that can be operated on. A target-list can also be specified to limit or allow privileges on various columns.

## 2.4 Views

### 2.4.1 View Structuring

A user can issue a:

DEFINE VIEW name (target-list) qualification

to define a view.  These views are dynamic in nature in that
the view will reflect changes made to the base relations.  Keys
cannot be defined for views.

A user can issue a:

RETRIEVE INTO name (target-list) qualification

to create a new relation called name.  Name is in effect a
static view.

### 2.4.2 View Operations

The same operations that apply to relations can be defined
for views including the permit and deny protection operations.
There are restrictions on the updating of views.

### 2.4.3 Constraints

Update operations, APPEND, DELETE, REPLACE can only be applied
to a view if the update would only affect one base relation and
the effect on the relation can be uniquely determined.

### 2.4.4 Additional Properties of Views

The IDM allows the user to make a brief statement on the use
of views in conceptual modeling.

## 2.5 Tuple

### 2.5.1 Tuple Structure

A tuple value is described as an instance of a record in the
relation.  The definition of a tuple is implicitly defined
when the relation is defined.  The values in an initial creation
of a tuple are determined by the target-list.  Values of individual
attributes of a tuple can be changed by the replace operator.

### 2.5.2 Tuple Operations

IDM does support a tuple at a time protocol for a programming language interface running on the host machine. However, for the most part, the tuple at time flow control is considered a buffering problem for the host. The IDM software reference manual does describe how an OEM user can build such an interface.

### 2.5.3 Tuple Constraints

All tuples must be requested 'associatively' by requesting specific attribute value clauses in the qualification. If an ordering is required, an 'ORDER BY' clause can be stated on a RETRIEVE command and the tuples are returned to the host in the desired order.

In order to declare a 'key' unique, the key must in fact be a physical clustering or non-clustering index. This restriction was based on the feasibility of supporting the uniqueness of a key without such an index.

## 2.6 Attribute Structure

### 2.6.1 Attribute Structure

An attribute is defined when a relation is created by specifying its name type and length. The type is restricted to the primary data types supported by IDM. Types include bit string, integer, floating point, packed (zoned) deciman, and character strings.

### 2.6.2 Attribute Operators

Attributes can be compared with each other through the normal comparison operators $<, \leq, =, \geq, >, \neq$. Arithmetic operators $+$, $-$, $\div$, $\times$ can be used on numeric attributes; string manipulation operators can be used on string attributes. Coercions are made between the different types and lengths of numeric attributes. Specific

coercion functions are also provided for numeric to character
and character to numeric conversions.  Aggregate functions
are supported and are described in detail in Section 3.4.3.
Note that these operations can be used to create new attributes
in either static or dynamic views.

### 2.6.3  Attribute Constraints

Floating point operations are not fully supported.  The difficulty
faced by IDM was in translating different hosts floating point
representations into a representation usable by the IDM hardware.

### 2.6.4  Additional Properties of Attributes

The user can associate descriptive text with each attribute of
each relation.  A brief statement can be made on the use of
attributes in conceptual modeling.

## 2.7  Domain

Domains are not explicitly defined by IDM.

## 2.8  Additional Database Constituents.

IDM supports:

Transactions - Transactions are used as a unit of concurrency
control and recovery for IDM commands.  The user surrounds
a set of IDM commands with Begin and End transaction commands
If those are omitted, a single IDM command is treated as
a transaction.

Stored Commands -  Commands can be stored in the IDM and invoked
with different parameters.  Use of this feature is suggested
for semantic integrity assertion checks and for triggers.

Data Dictionary - The user can access the system relations to
store and retrieve constituents of a data dictionary.

Relation Logging - A user can request that a log be maintained
of all atomic changes to specified relations.  This log can
be queried using the retrieval operations.

3.    FUNCTIONAL CAPABILITIES

The general format of an IDM command is:

Command Relation (target-list) qualification.

This command is described in Section 2.3.2.  Note that the same qualification
power is allowed for retrievals and alterations.

3.1  Qualification

Qualification is basically through a calculus oriented approach.  The
results of a qualification can be thought of as a relation consisting
of tuples composed of tuples from one or more relations for which the
qualification is true.

3.1.1  Restriction

The simple comparison operators ($<$, $\leq$, $=$, $\geq$, $\neq$) are supported
for comparing 'attribute expressions' to 'attribute expressions'.
An attribute expression can be a simple constant, an attribute
name, or a string or arithmetic expression involving attributes
and/or constants.  In addition, the arithmetic expression can
include the aggregate functions described in Section 3.4.2.  The
coercion rules were specified in Section 2.6.2.

The simple selection conditions can be combined into more general
boolean expressions by ands/ors and nots.

Note that, PROJECTS are implicitly defined through the use of an
attribute name either in the qualification or the target list.

As a simple example, consider the qualification

        where P.color = "red"

which could select red parts from the parts relation.

3.1.2  Quantification

Existential quantification is supported implicitly or

explicitly through an 'any' operator.

For example:

        where ANY (P.color = "red") > 0

will be considered 'TRUE' if at least one Part is

Red.

Similarly,

        where SP.P# = P.P# and P.color = "red"

will be considered 'TRUE' for one SP tuple if there exists

a red part supplied by SP.

Universal quantification is supported through the use of count,

and count-by functions.

For example,

        where Count (P where P.color = "red") = Count(P)

is true if and only if all parts are red.

3.1.3  Set Operations

Being a calculus oriented language, IDL does not explicitly

support the set operations.  However, intersection and set

differences can be done by including the appropriate joining

clause in the qualification.  Similarly, a cartesion product can be found by including attributes of different relations in the target list with no corresponding joining clause. Also note that a two relation union operation can be realized by an append operation.

### 3.1.4 Joining

Equi-joins and natural joins and combinations are all permitted. Up to 15 relations can be joined in one command. No access path restrictions are placed on the attributes to be joined. The coercion rules for attributes can be used to compare different lengths and types of numeric attributes and different lengths of character attributes. In fact, the joining clause can compare an attribute expression to an attribute expression. A relation can be joined to itself by having another 'range' variable pass over the relation.

For example:

    where SP.S# = S.S# and SP.P# = P.P#

joins the supply, supplier and parts relations.

### 3.1.5 Nesting and Closure

The restriction, quantification, most set operations, aggregate functions, and joining are all closed in that the results of those operations can be nested and used in other commands. Examples have already been provided showing the nesting of 'count' and a 'where clause'.

Note that the UNION operation cannot be nested. The system is considered relationally complete.

## 3.2 Retrieval and Presentation

### 3.2.1 Database Queries

Queries using IDL notation are expressed through the:

Retrieve (target-list) qualification command.

The results of a retrieval operation appear as a relation containing just the attributes specified in the target list. The full range of qualifications described in 3.1 can be used. The target list can consist of a list of attribute names from possibly different relations, or new attribute names set equal to an expression. The expression can contain aggregate functions, constants or attribute names.

For example,

Retrieve (SP.S#, total = Sum (SP.QOH by SP.S#))

An optional order by clause can be used to control the order in which tuples are returned to the host from the IDM. The order by clause can include attribute names, attribute expressions of attributes in or not in the target list.

### 3.2.2 Retrieval of Information about Database Constituents

The database schema is stored in 'system' relations and can be queried and retrieved just like normal user relations. Thus, the results of schema queries can be intermixed with database queries. In addition, IDM supports a 'description' relation which contains user defined descriptions of relations/attributes. Note that names of relations, attributes and views are stored in user readable form. Other system information, however, is stored in machine readable form. IDM does allow the user to

store the text of user type definition of a veiw and/or
stored commands.

### 3.2.3  Retrieval of System Performance Data

All system performance data is also stored in 'system' relations.
Thus the database qualification and retrieval facilities can
be used to monitor disk usage, find information about indices, etc.

### 3.2.4  Report Generation

Report formating is considered the responsibility of the host
system.

### 3.2.5  Constraint and Limitations

PERMIT and DENY commands can be used to control retrieval permissions to relations and views.

## 3.3  Alteration

### 3.3.1  Insert Facilities

The basic insert operation of IDM is to 'APPEND' tuples into
an existing relation.  Since the system tables are also relations,
APPENDs could be used to alter the schema.  In general, such
use of the system tables as relations is not recommanded.  Alternately, a 'block' COPY facility is supported which allows the user
to add tuples to a relation from a file outside the data base.
IDM informs the host of type violations and if some 'unique key'
constraints have been violated in inserting tuples either through
an APPEND or a COPY.

Tuples generated during the qualification section can be inserted
into a relation through the 'APPEND' operator.

Examples

1)    APPEND COMPONENTS (MAJOR = 16, MINOR = 15)

adds one tuple to the components relation.  Note that columns not mentioned in the target list get system defined

defaults (o for numeric types, blank for character types).

2.  RANGE OF N IS NEWPARTS

APPEND PARTS (P# = N.P#,...) where N.COLOR = "RED"

adds all red parts in NEWPARTS to the parts relation.

### 3.3.2  Delete Facilities

Tuples can be deleted from a relation, and relations can be
deleted from a database.  To delete tuples from a relation Part:

Range of P is Part

delete p [where qualification]

The particular tuple deleted from parts depends on the qualification.  To delete a relation from the database:

Destroy relation_name.  This destroys all indexes, and
attribute entries for the relation.

Alternately:

Range of r is relation

delete r where qualification

can be used.  This command will not delete the attribute
entries.  Note that the user must first destroy the views
which reference this relation.

### 3.3.3  Modify Facilities

Attributes of existing tuples in a relation can be modified by
means of the 'replace' operation.

Range of u is update_parts

Range p is parts

Replace p (color = U.color) where p.p# = u.p#

updates the color attribute in parts for each tuple that has a
corresponding tuple in update_parts.

Protection constraint violations are not allowed. Note that the user is not informed that he/she has made a protection violation. Instead the user is simply told that a relation or attribute does not exist. Unique key restraint violations are reported to the host and not allowed. Note that the system relations can also be modified through the REPLACE operation. Such operations can be used to change relation or attribute names.

### 3.3.4 Commit and Undo

These operations are supported. A user issues a 'Begin Transaction' command. The user (and only the user) can see the results of his or her alterations. If the user issues an 'End Transaction' command, the results are committed. If the user issues an 'Abort', the results are undone. Note that changes to the system catalogues are not undone.

## 3.4 Additional Functional Capabilities

### 3.4.1 Arithmetic and String Operations

The standard arithmetic operations (+, -, *, /, modulo) are supported for numeric types. Concatination, substring operations are supported for character string types. In addition, 'wildcard' searching for string patterns within a field are supported.

### 3.4.2 Sorting

The user can specify an 'ORDER BY' clause stating sorting requirements on attributes of tuples which are sent to the host system. The relation itself is not guaranteed to be kept ordered by any particular attributes.

### 3.4.3 Library Functions

MAX, MIN, SUM, COUNT, AVERAGE are all supported. These functions can be combined with the Group by operation and general

qualification.  To only include unique values in a SUM,

COUNT, or AVERAGE is also supported.

For example:

> Range of e is employee
>
> 1)   Retrieve (ave = avg(e.salary)
>
>       returns the average salary of all the employees.
>
> 2)   Retrieve (ave = avg(e.salary by e.dept),e.dept)
>
>       returns the average salary of employees for each
>
>       department.
>
> 3)   Retrieve (ave = avg(e.salary by e.dept where e.age
>
>       > 30),e.dept)
>
>       returns the average salary of employees over 30 for
>
>       each department.

Note that the library group by operators can be used in

qualification, retrieval, and alteration.

### 3.4.4  User Defined Functions

Not supported.

### 3.4.5  Transactions

Transactions are supported for concurrency control and recovery

purposes.  See Section 3.3.4.

### 3.4.6  Multi-tuple Alterations

This function is supported.  See Section 3.3.3.

### 3.4.7  Grouping

Grouping is supported.  See Section 3.4.3 for examples.

### 3.4.8  Exception Handling Mechanisms

IDM allows the user to specify for each command the actions to

be taken on the following exception conditions:  violation of a unique index constraint, overflow, underflow and divide by zero. For each condition, a command can be either completely rejected or allowed to continue. If the command continues, status bits indicating that the exception condition had occurred are still returned to the user.

3.4.9 Additional Functional Capabilities

The IDM will store a sequence of parameterized commands. Use of this feature is designed to be used for semantic integrity, assertion checks and for implementing triggers.

4. DEFINITION, GENERATION AND ADMINISTRATION FACILITIES.

4.1 Definition Facilities

4.1.1 Constituents of a Database Definition

Database

Relations/Attributes

Views

Indexes/Unique Keys

Relation Descriptions

Attribute Descriptions

Protection Constraints

4.1.2 Database Definition

Create database name. The creator of the database defaults to the database administrator.

4.1.3 Relation Definition

Create relation name (attribute_names = type,

.
.
.

attribute_names = type)

A maximum of 250 attributes per relation are allowed.

A maximum of 32,000 relations are allowed.

Properties such as disk locations and sizes for relations and
auditing requirements can be specified here.

### 4.1.4 View Definition

Define view name (target-list) qualification.

### 4.1.5 Tuple Definition

Tuple types are defined in the relation definition, see 4.1.3.
Tuple instances are defined during qualification, retrieval,
and alteration.  See Section 3.

### 4.1.6 Attribute Definition

See Section 4.1.3

### 4.1.7 Additional Database Constituents

INDEX's can be added or subtracted from relations.  At that time,
the index key can be declared unique.  Note that both clustering
and non-clustering indexes can be created.  Protection constraints
(PERMIT  and DENY) can be added to relations.

## 4.2 Generation Facilities

### 4.2.1 Constituents of a Database Generation

All of the constituents of a database listed in Section 4.1.1
can be generated during the course of a database application.

### 4.2.2 Generation of Database Constituents

Database and relations can be dumped to, and loaded from other
disks or the host.

## 4.3 Database Redefinition

### 4.3.1 Renaming Database Constituents

No explicit facilities are provided for renaming database constituents.
However, the relational modify operator, REPLACE can be used to
replace a relation name or attribute names.  For example, the
following replace is allowed:

Range of A is attribute

Replace A (name = "colour") where A.name = "color".

### 4.3.2  Redefining Database Constituents

No explicit facilities are provided for redefining attribute
or changing the attributes in a relation.  These redefinitions
are supported  through combinations of retrieve into's and
alterations of the database names.

## 4.4  Database Regeneration and Reorganization

### 4.4.1  System-Controlled

The system provides monitoring of disk usage and performance.
It does not automatically reorganize a database.

### 4.4.2  DBA-Controlled

The DBA can add and delete clustering and non-clustering indexes
to any relations in the database at any time during the application
development.  Thus indexes can be added before or after a relation
is populated.  One database can be used to load another database.

## 4.5  Database Dictionary

A user can store definitions of relations and attribute-relation pairs.
The system stores information on the number of attributes, number of
tuples of a relation.  In addition, the system stores some performance
statistics such as disk allocation and usage in a relation.

The database language can be used to query any of these relations.  For
example, to find all relations that have an attribute named social_sec,
the following command could be issued:

Range of A is ATTRIBUTE

Range of R is RELATION

Retrieve (R.name) where R.RELID = A.RELID and A.name = "SOCIAL_SEC"

## 5.  INTERFACE AND DBMS ARCHITECTURE

## 5.1  System Architecture

The OEM user provides the interface to the human user.  The architecture
is illustrated below:

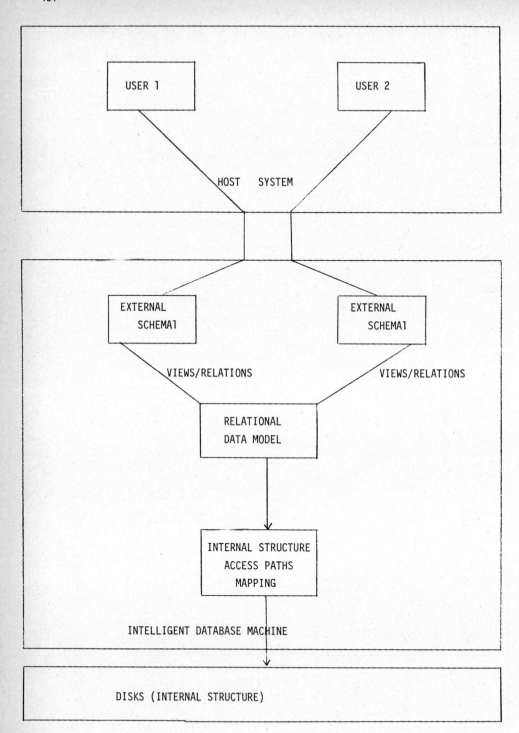

5.2  Interface Descriptions

A single interface is supported.  This interface has been described
in Sections 2, 3, and 4.

6.    OPERATIONAL ASPECTS

6.1  Security

The database administrator (DBA) creates a database and is responsible
for assigning security rights.  The user authorization is primarily the
responsibility of the host system.  The IDM does maintain two relations
that link users and hosts; and link users to names and groups of users.
The DBAs are responsible for providing the data for these relations.
The name and groups can be used by the DBA when issuing the PERMIT and
DENY commands for particular relations, attributes or parts of relations
based on a qualification. (See Section 3.0).
A user can create his/her private relations.
When a relation is created it can be declared 'with logging' and a log
of all changes (but not accesses) to that relation will be maintained.
The relational calculus commands can be used to query that log.

6.2  Physical Integrity

6.2.1  Concurrency Control

The concurrency control is for the most part transparent to the
users.  However, the concepts of transactions are supported,
allowing a user to issue several IDM commands and preventing
other users from seeing these changes until the 'End Transaction'
command is given.

Lost updates and phantoms are prevented by providing degree 3
consistency.  Since users issue several commands within one
transaction, deadlock cannot be completely prevented.  However,
the chance of deadlock is kept rather small.  If deadlock does
occur, it is detected and a transaction may be aborted.

### 6.2.2 Crash Recovery

The IDM is in complete control of the disks and makes extensive efforts to check for physical disk read and write errors; retry the I/O's in case of those errors; and keep track (in relations) of the 'flawed disk sectors'.

The IDM provides for both physical dumping/restoring of disks; and logical dumping/restoring of an entire database or selected relations.

In addition, the audit log can be used to roll forward and make the changes to a restored relation that was created 'with logging'. In the event of a crash, partially complete transactions can be rolled back to restore the database to a consistent state.

### 6.3 Operating Environment

The IDM has its own microprocessor and the basics of an operating system that it needs to support database management.  The IDM is in complete control of the disks which are attached to it.

Two types of physical interfaces are supported:  parallel and serial. Parallel I/O to the IDM is through the standard IEEE-488 bus.  The serial interface is through the standard RS232C line.

## 7. ESSENTIALLY RELATIONAL SOLUTIONS FOR GENERALIZED DBMS PROBLEMS.

### 7.1 Simplicity/Uniformity

The IDM provides the simplicity of a purely relational model and operations based on the relation calculus.  This simplicity is also utilized internally in the maintenance of the data dictionary, indexing information, protection information, stored commands, cross reference information, transaction logging, user identification, and disk allocation and usage.

7.2 Data Independence

The results of the qualification, retrieval and alteration are independent of which access paths and indices which are provided with the exception that the presence or absence of a unique index can affect the results of an IDM command.

7.3 Permits Optimization

Extensive effort is made to automatically optimize the execution of a relation calculus expression. In addition, specialized hardware is used to speed processing.

7.4 Basis for High Level Interfaces/Efficiency

One of the major contentions of the IDM developers is that a database machine must provide a high level interface to effect the communication overhead that would be unavoidable in an attribute or tuple at time database machine.

7.5 Multiple Views of Data

The IDM interface does support multiple views of data.

8. APPLICATIONS

Not yet available.

3.4   Feature Analysis Of INGRES

Feature   Analysis
of
INGRES

by
Nancy McDonald
and
John McNally

Department of Computer Science
University of South Florida
Tampa, Florida 33620

January  1981

TABLE OF CONTENTS

8.0  <u>Database applications using the system</u>

PREFACE

All examples in this feature analysis are based on the database below:


PART

| P # | PNAME | WEIGHT | CITY |
|-----|-------|--------|------|


SUPPLIER

| S # | SNAME | STATUS | CITY |
|-----|-------|--------|------|


SHIPMENT

| S # | P # | QTY |
|-----|-----|-----|


[from C. J. Date's  <u>An Introduction to Database Systems</u>, 2nd ed., p. 52]

# 1.0 INTRODUCTION

## 1.1 Identification

INGRES (Interactive Graphics and Retrieval System). This document is based on version 6.2 with relevant information included from previous versions. Developed by: University of California, Berkeley - Electronics Research Laboratory.

## 1.2 Status

### 1.2.1 System

System has been used primarily for teaching and research. Extensive improvement and elaboration to the system has been and continues to be performed.

In the later part of 1980, a company was formed to market INGRES: Relational Technology, Inc., Berkeley, CA.

### 1.2.2 Applications

INGRES is well suited to a wide variety of applications. For example, application programs written in C may access INGRES databases through the EQUEL interface. Non-programmers who are skilled database users can meet their information management needs by utilizing QUEL, an interactive non-procedural query language. Casual users can quickly and efficiently access databases through CUPID, a pictorial query language (not available for all installations). A generalized geographical data handling subsystem called GEO-QUEL is included in INGRES. It is used for research in the area of urban economics.

## 1.3 System Background

INGRES is the result of a research project at the University of California, Berkeley. Faculty and students there designed and implemented the system with graphical capabilities and mini-computer architecture in mind.

## 1.4 Overall Philosophy

The objective of INGRES is to provide a high degree of data independence and a non-procedural facility for data definition, retrieval, update, access control, and integrity verification.

## 1.5 Essentially Relational Characteristics

INGRES meets all of CODD's (TODS Vol.4, No.4) requirements for the relational database model and therefore may be classified as fully relational. One suggested criterion based upon the power of the relational algebra is not applicable to INGRES since its usage is based upon relational calculus. However, it has been shown that the relational calculus is equivalent to the relational algebra.

## 1.6 Interfaces

QUEL - General query language for INGRES based upon relational calculus with facilities for data definition, retrieval, update, access control and integrity verification.

EQUEL - Interface which allows the inclusion of QUEL statements in C programs.

CUPID - Nonprocedural pictorial query language designed for the casual user. Includes facilities for retrieval and update.

GEO-QUEL - Interface which provides users the capability of presenting geographic data in map form.

## 1.7 Documentation

Epstein; "Creating and maintaining a data base using INGRES," ERL technical memorandum M77/72, University of California.

Hawthorne, P.; and Stonebraker, M. "The Use of Technological Advances to Enhance Data Management System Performance, "ERL technical memorandum M79/3, University of California.

Held, C.D.; Stonebaker, M.R.; and Wong, E. "INGRES: A Relational Database System," Proc. ACM Pacific 75 Regional Conf., May 1975, pp. 409-416.

McDonald, N.; and Stonebraker, M. "CUPID: The Friendly Query Language, "Proc. ACM Pacific 75 Regional Conf., April 1975, ACM, New York, 1975, pp. 132-139.

Rowe, L. "INGRES Data Dictionary," memo received 23 January 1981.

Stonebraker, M. "Concurrency Control and Consistency of Multiple Copies of Data in Distributed INGRES," ERL technical memorandum reprint 1702, University of California.

Stonebraker, M.; Wong, E.; Kreps, P.; and Held, C.D. "The Design and Implementation of INGRES," ERL technical memorandum reprint 1468, University of California.

Woodfill, J.; et al. "INGRES Version 6.2 Reference Manual," ERL technical memorandum M79/43, University of California.

## 1.8 General System Description

INGRES is a relational database management system. A user may access the system interactively through the UNIX command processor. It has several interfaces for data definition and retrieval. Besides interactive use, INGRES facilities are available embedded within a procedural language for batch use.

## 2.0  DATABASE CONSTITUENTS

### 2.1  General Description

#### 2.1.1  Feature Catalog Term Translation Table

| System Term | Feature Catalog Term |
| --- | --- |
| Database | Database |
| Relation | Relation |
| View | View |
| Tuple | Tuple |
| Attribute | Attribute |
| Domain | Domain |

Note that INGRES does not maintain any functional distinction between attributes and domains. These two terms are often used interchangeably but in this document the terminology will be restricted to the word attribute. Note that this lack of explicit domains does not preclude any theoretical implications arising from the definition of relations from the cartesian product of a set of value domains.

### 2.2  Database

#### 2.2.1  Database Structure

A database is defined as a time-varying collection of relations.

#### 2.2.2  Database Operations

There are a number of operations implemented in INGRES which are relevant to the database as an RDM constituent:

CREATDB name – Establish a new, initially empty database with the given name.  The user who issues the CREATDB command is the owner of the database and is referred to as the DataBase Administrator (DBA).  Certain commands related to other RDM constituents are restricted to use by the DBA (e.g. DESTROYDB).

DESTROYDB name – Destroy a database (empty or not).  Only the DBA may issue this command.

#### 2.2.3  Database Constraints

The only global assertion which applies to the entire database is the one referred to above, i.e. the distinction between the database owner or DBA and other users.  This constraint manifests itself at other constituent levels and will be dealt with in this document when appropriate.  There is a system relation known as the USER's file which contains the information specifying which databases can be opened and by whom.

The creation and destruction of databases is tightly coupled to the UNIX operating system.  As a result, INGRES enjoys the flexibility, power and security of the UNIX file management system.

## 2.3  Relation

### 2.3.1  Relation Structure

A relation is defined as a subset of the cartesian product of N sets of attribute values.  It is generally assumed that the user's perception of a relation is an entity over which functions and/or predicates can be evaluated.  It is also possible to visualize a relation as a table in which the tuples constitute the rows and the attributes constitute the columns.  Duplicate tuples are always removed when relations are updated.

### 2.3.2  Relation Operations

There are a number of operations available in QUEL which relate to the relation as a database constituent:

| | | |
|---|---|---|
| CREATE name | – | Create a new relation with the given name.  The user issuing the CREATE command is designated as the relation's owner. |
| COPY | – | Append the data in UNIX file to an existing relation owned by the user. |
| DESTROY name | – | Delete a named relation from the database. |
| INDEX | – | Create secondary indices on existing relations |
| MODIFY | _ | Define the storage structure for a relation by specifying storage organization and keys |
| PRINT name | – | Print the entire contents of a relation. |
| SAVE | – | Change the default relation expiration date. |

### 2.3.3 Relation Constraints

Relation operations may be issued only by the owner of a relation (i.e., the user who CREATEs the relation).

### 2.3.4 Additional Properties of Relations

None found.

## 2.4  Views

### 2.4.1  View Structure

Views are defined as a set of dynamically derived relations.  A view structure is essentially a relation structure which has its operations restricted.  Statically derived relations are defined in a different manner.  The keys of a view are inherited from the base relation definition.

### 2.4.2  View Operations

Views are defined from relations in the database by the use of the QUEL DEFINE command.  View definition can be specified as a subset of the values in the base relation by means of a qualification statement identical to those used in retrieval commands.  No other form of view manipulation is possible.

All forms of retrieval on the view are fully supported

        e.g.,   range of p is part
                range of s is supplier
                define view parsup (parnan = p.pname, pnum = p.p#,
        pstat = s.status) where p.city = s.city

### 2.4.3  View Constraints

Although views are directly derived from relations, they cannot be manipulated as relations can be.

Updates are supported if and only if it can be guaranteed that the result of updating the view is identical to that of updating the corresponding real relation.

The person who defines a view must own all relations upon which the view is based.

### 2.4.4  Additional Properties of Views

None found.

## 2.5  Tuple

### 2.5.1  Tuple Structure

A tuple is an instance of a relation.  It is implicity defined when the relation is created.  Keys are defined at the relation level and only for purposes of storage structures.

### 2.5.2  Tuple Operations

There is a wide variety of operations in QUEL for manipulating tuples. Since the query languages for INGRES are based upon the relational calculus, tuples are selected from a relation which is represented by a tuple-variable. A tuple-variable is defined by use of the RANGE statement.  Once a tuple-variable is defined, the definition remains in effect until it is redefined or the user ends the QUEL session.  Operations for manipulating tuples include:

    APPEND          -   Add a tuple or tuples to an existing relation.

    DELETE          -   Remove one or more tuples from a relation.  Note
                        multi-tuple alteration capability.

    REPLACE         -   Modify one or more attribute values in one or more
                        tuples of a relation.

    RETRIEVE        -   Retrieve a subset of the tuples from a relation.

Each of these operations can include an optional qualification involving tuple-variables.  These qualifications select a subset of the tuples in a relation represented by a tuple-variable.

### 2.5.3 Tuple Constraints

Tuples may be ordered, but only if the storage structure for the relation has key ordering. When new relations are formed from the retrieval of tuples (or a subset of the attributes of the tuples) duplicates are always removed. Tuples retrieved for display do not have duplicates removed unless the UNIQUE keyword is specified in the RETRIEVE statement. The present system allows a tuple size maximum of 512 bytes with a maximum of 50 attributes.

## 2.6 Attributes

### 2.6.1 Attribute Structure

The names and characteristics of attributes are defined when the relation which contains them is defined.

### 2.6.2 Attribute Operations

Attributes (in conjunction with tuple-variables) can be used in QUEL qualification statements. These attributes are combined in qualification statements with boolean algebra and relational operators as well as implicit existential quantification. The power of the qualification statements is extended by the inclusion of a large library of computational (SIN, COS, SORT, etc.) and aggregation (SUM, COUNT, AVG, etc.) functions.

### 2.6.3 Attribute Constraints

See Section 2.5.3.

## 2.7 Domain - INGRES does not distinguish between domains and attributes

### 2.7.1 Domain Structure

Not Applicable.

### 2.7.2 Domain Operations

Not Applicable.

### 2.7.3 Domain Constraints

Not Applicable.

## 2.8 Additional Database Constraints

None found.

## 3.0  FUNCTIONAL CAPABILITIES

### 3.05  General Syntax format for QUEL

RANGE OF (tuple-variable) IS (relation-name) (repeated for each tuple-variable ranging over different relations)

Note: The tuple-variable concept has been found very useful for specifically identifying the relation being referenced.  This concept is especially useful when joining relations and in self-join operations.

RETRIEVE (target-list)  WHERE qualification

APPEND TO relation-name (attribute-name=value...)

DELETE (tuple-variable) WHERE qualification

REPLACE (tuple-variable) (target-list) WHERE qualification

### 3.1  Qualification

#### 3.1.1  Restriction

Qualification in QUEL is based upon relational calculus.  See section 2.5.2 for a discussion of the role of attributes, tuple-variables and operations involved in qualifications.  The following examples demonstrate the flexibility of the WHERE clause:

  (a) Simple
      WHERE P.COLOR = "BLUE"
  (b) Join
      WHERE S.S# = SP.S# AND SP.QTY>100

#### 3.1.2  Quantification

Existential quantification is implicit when more than one tuple-variable is present in a qualification statement.  Universal quantification is not directly supported but can be implied by the use of the COUNT function.

List the names of all suppliers who supply all parts:

RANGE OF S IS SUPPLIER

RANGE OF SP IS SHIPMENT

RANGE OF P IS PART

RETRIEVE (S.SNAME) WHERE COUNT(SP.S# = S.S# AND SP.P# $\neq$ P.P#)=0

#### 3.1.3  Set Operations

Not supported.

#### 3.1.4  Joining

QUEL supports the join operation in relational calculus.  See Section 3.1.1 (b) for an example.

### 3.1.5  Nesting & Closure

The optional ⌈into resultname⌉ clause allows the result to be created as a relation.

### 3.1.6  Additional Aspects of Qualification

None found.

## 3.2  Retrieval and Presentation

### 3.2.1  Database Queries

Queries in QUEL are almost entirely composed of qualification and so require no further discussion.  However, CUPID is so different in how qualifications are formed, it is worth mentioning here.  The relationship between attributes is implied by pictorial constructs.

### 3.2.2  Retrieval of Information about Database Constituents

The special relations known as Relation and Attribute contain the information about their respective subjects.  INGRES has no single facility known as a data dictionary.  The information considered necessary for a data dictionary is contained in the two relations already mentioned, plus four additional relations:  INDEXES, PROTECT, INTEGRITIES and TREE.  The six relations are called system relations or system catalogs and will be described in Section 4.5.

### 3.2.3  Retrieval and System Performance Data

No known.

### 3.2.4  Report Generation

No known.

### 3.2.5  Constraints and Limitations

CUPID is restricted to retrieval and update only.  Restrictions on which relations may have tuples retrieved or altered can be defined by the owners of the relation.  This feature is discussed further in section 6.1, Security.

### 3.2.6  Additional Aspects of Retrieval and Presentation

Data can be retrieved in order to construct ordinary UNIX files.

## 3.3  Alteration

## 3.3.1  Insert Facilities

Relations can be altered by appending new tuples.  If any views are based upon altered relations, they too are subsequently modified.

Add a new part to the PART relation:

    APPEND TO PART (P#=P5,PNAME="WIDGET",COLOR="GRAY",WEIGHT=50,CITY="TAMPA

### 3.3.2 Delete Facilities

Tuples may be deleted from a relation

Remove all suppliers located in Paris from the SUPPLIER relation:

    RANGE OF S IS SUPPLIER

    DELETE S WHERE S.CITY = "PARIS"

### 3.3.3 Modify Facilities

Tuples in a relation may be replaced by new tuple values.

All green bolts are now manufactured with a blue color.  Update the PART relation to reflect this change in specifications:

    RANGE OF P IS PART

    REPLACE P (P.COLOR="BLUE")

     WHERE P.NAME="BOLT"ANDP.COLOR="GREEN"

### 3.3.4 Commit and Undo Facilities

None found.

### 3.3.5 Additional Alteration Facilities

No additional features found.

## 3.4 Additional Functional Capabilities

### 3.4.1 Arithmetic and String Operations

Arithmetic operations supported by QUEL are:  addition, subtraction, multiplication, division and exponentiation.

### 3.4.2 Sorting

Ordering is specified for a relation when the keys for a storage structure are specified.

### 3.4.3 Library Functions

QUEL supports MIN, MAX, AVG, SUM, COUNT, COS, SIN, ATAN, LOG, RAND, SQRT, MOD and GAMMA library functions.  Each function has a definition which is obvious from its name.

### 3.4.4 User Defined Functions

A terminal monitor macrofacility is included to help users tailor the QUEL language.  The macro facility performs text substitution and can invoke built-in macros.

### 3.4.5  Transactions

No transaction facilities are available.

### 3.4.6  Multi-Tuple Alterations

Multi-tuple alterations are supported.

### 3.4.7  Grouping

Grouping is implicitly or explicitly performed by the use of the aggregation functions.

e.g. - implicit
    Find the sum of all quantities of supplied parts whose color is blue.

```
RANGE OF SP IS SHIPMENT
RANGE OF P IS PART

RETRIEVE (P.PNAME,QSUM=SUM(SP.QTY))
   WHERE  SP.P# =   P.P# AND P.COLOR = "BLUE"
```

e.g. - explicit
    Find the average quantity by supplier #

```
RANGE OF SP IS SHIPMENT

RETRIEVE (AVQTY = AVG(SP.QTY by SP.S#))
```

## 4.0  DEFINITION, GENERATION AND ADMINISTRATION FACILITIES

### 4.1  Definition Facilities

#### 4.1.1  Constituents of a Database Definition

A database is define by means of the CREATDB command.

> e.g. CREATDB name establishes a new, initially empty
> database with the name provided by the user.

#### 4.1.2  Database Definition

In accordance with 4.1.1, the definition of a database with the name
SUPPLIES would be accomplished by:
CREATDB SUPPLIES
The database SUPPLIES is owned by the user who initiates the CREATDB command.

#### 4.1.3  Relation Definition

To define the relations for a given database, one uses the CREATE command.

Defining the relations, their attribute names and formats for the SUPPLIES
database would be:

    CREATE PART (P#=i2,PNAME=c10,STATUS=i2,CITY=c10)
    CREATE SUPPLIER (S#=i2,SNAME=c10,STATUS=i2,CITY=c10)
    CREATE SHIPMENT (S#=i2,P#=i2,QTY=i2)

The attributes are defined wit-in the parentheses.  This subdefinition
is discussed in 4.1.6.

#### 4.1.4  View Definition

Views may be created dynamically with the DEFINE VIEW command.  To define
a view of the SUPPLIER relation such that the access is limited to tuples whose
city is London:

    RANGE OF S IS SUPPLIER
    DEFINE VIEW LONDON-SUPPLIER
        (SUPPLIER) WHERE S.CITY = "LONDON"

#### 4.1.5  Tuple Definition

Tuples are implicityly defined at the same time the relation is defined.

#### 4.1.6  Attribute Definition

Attributes are defined while relations are defined.  As noted in 4.1.3,
attribute definition takes place within parenthesis.  The form of this definition is:
attribute name = format
The _format_ represents the data type and number of bytes of storage needed.  For
example, i2 represents two bytes of integer data and c10 means ten bytes of
character data.

### 4.1.7 Domain Definition

None

### 4.1.8 Definition of Additional Database Constituents

A user may define an integrity constraint via:

DEFINE INTEGRITY on relation-name is qualification

A user may also define permission for a relation by means of:

DEFINE PERMIT retrieve, replace, delete, append or all
ON rel-name TO login-name [special times] [WHERE qualification]

## 4.2  Generation Facilities

### 4.2.1  Constituents of Database Generation

The database is populated by APPENDing or COPYing tuples into relations.

### 4.2.2  Generation of Database Constituents

Base relations are generated by the user explicitly, while derived relations are generated automatically.

## 4.3  Database Redefinition

### 4.3.1  Renaming Database Constituents

No known facilities for renaming other than redefining and copying.

### 4.3.2  Redefining Constituents

There is no known redefiniton capability for a database in general. DEFINE VIEW or the storage structures of the relation may be redefined via MODIFY.

Tuples may be redefined by APPENDing (to add, DELETEing (to delete).

Attribute values may be redefined with the REPLACE command.

## 4.4  Database Regeneration and Reorganization

### 4.4.1  System Controlled

Database reorganizations performed automatically by the system include only those techniques provided by UNIX.  If a relation has a secondary index and the primary relation changes, the secondary one is automatically updated.

### 4.4.2  DBA-controlled

There are few special DBA functions.  Typically, however, the DBA would CREATEDB and become the owner.  Owner's of databases and relations have the special operation of MODIFY which allows them to change the storage structure of a relation (dynamic storage restructuring).

Anyone has the ability to create a secondary index via  INDEX command.

## 5.0 INTERFACES AND DBMS ARCHITECTURE

### 5.1 System Architecture

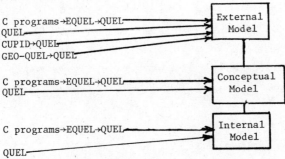

```
C programs→EQUEL→QUEL
QUEL
CUPID→QUEL
GEO-QUEL→QUEL
```
→ External Model

```
C programs→EQUEL→QUEL
QUEL
```
→ Conceptual Model

```
C programs→EQUEL→QUEL
QUEL
```
→ Internal Model

### 5.2 Interface Descriptions

#### 5.2.1 QUEL

The purpose of QUEL is to provide skilled database users who are non-programmers with a non-procedural interface to INGRES. QUEL supports a wide range of diverse functions including many especially designed for use by a DBA. QUEL is a linear relational calculus-based, stand-alone language.

The use of QUEL is clearly elucidated in sections 3.1.2, 3.3.1, 3.3.2, 3.3.3 and 4.1. Refer to the sections for examples of QUEL commands.

#### 5.2.2 EQUEL

The C programming language interface to QUEL and INGRES. EQUEL allows tuple at a time retrieval. All binding of variables to database objects is performed at run-time.

#### 5.2.3 CUPID

A pictorial query language designed for casual users. The selective powers of CUPID is equivalent to the relational calculus. The language is highly interactive (utilizes light pen) and designed strictly for interactive use.

We will present an example of retrieval using CUPID. The query answers the question "List the names of all suppliers who supply green bolts in quantities of 200 or more."

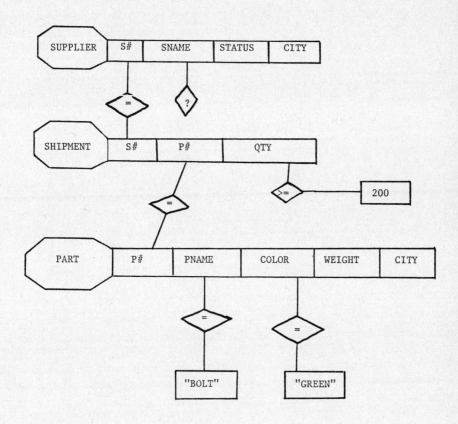

## 5.2.4 GEO-QUEL

Geographical data interface to INGRES. Contains extensive graphical capabilities including map presentation of appropriate data.

## 6.0  OPERATIONAL ASPECTS

### 6.1  Security

#### 6.1.1  Access Control

INGRES provides a high-level of access control through the QUEL DEFINE PERMIT command.  This command may be issued by the relation's owner in order to restrict access by other users to the relation and/or attributes of the relation.  This command is very flexible because it also allows restriction of the type of operation which may be performed (retrieval, update, etc.) as well as time and date of access constraints.  Data dependent access control is supported since the PERMIT command allows a qualification to be specified which restricts access to a subset of a relation's tuples.

### 6.2  Physical Integrity

#### 6.2.1  Concurrency Control

INGRES can support concurrent update at the discretion of the DBA.  It uses a preclaim algorithm to avoid deadlock.  The locking granularity is at the relation level but has the capability of working at the page level.

#### 6.2.2  Crash Recovery

A UNIX level command provides support for recovery from system failures. a QUEL command and a UNIX level command allow the creation of backup files.

The DBA may run the RESTORE command to recover from an INGRES or UNIX crash.

### 6.3  Operating Environment

#### 6.3.1  Operating System

INGRES requires UNIX to provide file management and security.  INGRES is written in C and therefore requires a C compiler.

#### 6.3.2  Hardware Environment

INGRES operates on PDP-11 architectures.  Database sizes are unlimited, but individual relations can be no larger than the maximum UNIX file size.

## 7.0 ESSENTIALLY RELATIONAL SOLUTIONS FOR GENERALIZED DBMS PROBLEMS

As a fully relational RDM INGRES clearly provides the following advantages which are generally accepted as solutions to generalized DBMS problems:

### 7.1 Simplicity

INGRES interfaces are based upon highly usable extensions to the relational calculus. As a result, a small uniform set of operations provides a wide range of selective power.

### 7.2 Uniformity

As the basis for INGRES operations, the relational calculus exhibits closure. Closure is a desirable property which simplifies user interaction with the data-base.

### 7.3 Data Independence

As a fully relational DBMS, INGRES provides a high degree of data in-dependence.

### 7.4 Permits Optimization

INGRES research has led to a technique of query processing known as decomposition. This technique facilitates query optimization. Also, data from storage structure details allows the storage structures to be optimized. This optimization can lead to faster response times for commonly used re-trieval specifications.

### 7.5 Basis for High Level Interfaces

The data independence, simplicity and uniformity of INGRES data representation and operations makes high level interfaces possible and practical.

### 7.6 Natural

There is little evidence to indicate that any one data model is particularly suited to the structural aspects of certain applications. Most of the literature in this area is based upon opinion, not experimental facts.

### 7.7 Efficient Storage and Retrieval Potential

While there is nothing in the relational model which precludes its im-plementation on a data base machine, the same may be said of other data models. The research of David Hsiao and Associates at the Ohio State University is particularly relevant to this topic.

### 7.8 Multiple views of data

The INGRES relational model does provide a flexible and highly usable method for defining view structures. (However, it would be unwise to state that this is an exclusive capability of RDMs. Note the highly developed sub-schema capability of the CODASYL (network) model.)

## 7.9  Advantages for Distributed Databases

INGRES has recently been extended to support distributed databases. However, since distributed databases are an actively on going research topic, it would seem premature to claim RDM's superiority in this area.

## 7.10 Security

Security seems to be a distinct advantage to RDMs since the access control rules can be stated using the same techniques as other operations (e.g. retrieval and update). This is further evidence of the simplicity of the relational model.

## 8.0 DATABASE APPLICATIONS USING THE SYSTEM


INGRES has been used for a variety of generalized DBMS applications in industrial, academic and governmental situations.  In particular the New York telephone company has utilized INGRES for maintaining a database relating to phone line utilization, reliability and performance.  GEO-QUEL has been used at Berkeley for urban economic analysis.  At present (8/80), perhaps the most sophisticated edition of INGRES is being used for the Department of Energy's Energy Storage database at Lawrence Livermore National laboratory.  This system uses a PDP 11/70 with 4M byte memory.  Both numerical and bibliographic databases are stored in the schema.  The laboratory has implemented a browsing data dictionary capability with self-prompting facilities on top of INGRES.  A VAX/VMS version of INGRES has been developed and is marketed by Relational Technology, Inc.

3.5  Feature Analysis Of MRDS

MRDS/LINUS
System Evaluation

by
Oris D. Friesen
N.S. Davids
Rickie E. Brinegar

Honeywell Information Systems
P.O. Box 6000
Phoenix, Arizona 85005

March 1982

# TABLE OF CONTENTS

TABLE OF CONTENTS  (CONTINUED)

1.0    <u>INTRODUCTION</u>

1.1    IDENTIFICATION

Multics Relational Data Store (MRDS) is a programming language oriented relational Data Base Management System (DBMS). The Logical Inquiry and Update System (LINUS) is an on-line query and update interface to MRDS.

1.2    STATUS

1.2.1  <u>System</u>

MRDS/LINUS is commercially available as unbundled software on the Honeywell Information Systems Series 60, Level 68 (Multics).

1.2.2  <u>Applications</u>

MRDS is designed to support application programs accessing small to large size databases.

LINUS is designed to support interactive access to MRDS databases.

1.3    SYSTEM BACKGROUND

MRDS came into being as a result of the need for a general purpose database management system for the Honeywell Multics operating system. It owes much to DSL-Alpha. It was first released as a commercial product in 1975.

LINUS drew heavily upon the SEQUEL language and was first released commercially in 1977.

MRDS and LINUS are written in PL/1.

1.4    OVERALL PHILOSOPHY

MRDS provides a relational database management system for application programs. It frees application programmers from being concerned with data storage structures and allows non-procedural access to data. It provides a high degree of program independence from the data storage structures because of its use of the data submodel. It also serves as a "tool" for the development of interactive end user facilities, such as LINUS.

LINUS provides users with an easy-to-use, mapping oriented, interactive interface to relational databases. It is built "on top of" MRDS.

1.5     ESSENTIALLY RELATIONAL CHARACTERISTICS

MRDS and LINUS are fully relational. They support the structural aspects of the relational model, including the domain concept. They support insert, update and delete operations. They both support data sublanguages which are at least as powerful as the relational algebra. The relations have no access path dependencies. There are no index dependencies for database access, nor are there any built-in insert, update or delete dependencies. The qualification principles are high-level and set-oriented. Temporary relations may be derived from one or more existing relations, and constraints can be added to domain definitions during the lifetime of an application.

1.6     INTERFACES

The interfaces to MRDS/LINUS provide the following capabilities:

o     Database schema definition including constraint definition.

o     Programming language-level querying and modification of the database.

o     Database creation and generation.

o     Interactive querying and modification of the database.

o     Definition of database views.

o     Definition of secondary indexes.

o     Securing and unsecuring the database.

1.7     DOCUMENTATION

o     Honeywell Information Systems. _Series 60 (Level 68). Logical Inquiry and Update System (LINUS) Reference Manual_. Order Number AZ49. Honeywell Information Systems, 200 Smith Street, Waltham, Massacusetts, 1980.

o     Honeywell Information Systems. _Series 60 (Level 68). Multics Relational Data Store (MRDS) Reference Manual_. Order Number AW53. Honeywell Information Systems, 200 Smith Street, Waltham, Massachusetts, 1980.

o    Weeldryer, J.A. and Friesen, O.D., "Multics Relational Data Store: an implementation of a relational database manager," in _Proc. Eleventh Hawaii International Conference on Systems Sciences_, Jan. 1978, Vol. 1, pp. 52-66.

1.8    GENERAL SYSTEM DESCRIPTION

(See 1.6)

2.0    DATABASE CONSTITUENTS

2.1    GENERAL DESCRIPTION

The constituents of an MRDS database are:

o    Database
o    Relation
o    Tuple
o    Attribute
o    Attribute name
o    Domain
o    Data Model
o    Data Submodel (=view)
o    Temporary Relation (=view)

These constituents are related as follows:    An MRDS database consists of relations of possibly different types.    A relation consists of tuples of identical type.    A temporary relation is a snapshot view derived from one or more relations by means of qualification operations (see 2.4.2).    A data model provides a global definition of the database.    A data submodel provides a view of a subset of the database and its relations allowing for synonym references to the relation names and attributes names.    A tuple consists of an ordered set of values of attributes.    Attributes are defined over a domain.    A domain is a user-defined data type.

The constituents of a LINUS database are related to the MRDS constituents as follows:

| MRDS | LINUS |
|---|---|
| database | (same) |
| relation | table |
| tuple | row |
| attribute | column |
| domain | (same) |
| data model | (same as database) |
| data submodel | (same as database) |
| temporary relation | temporary table |

2.2     DATABASE

2.2.1   Database Structure

The database structure consists of a Multics directory and a number of subordinate entries:

o     Database control file.

o     Data model file.

o     A model definition file for each relation created.

o     A keyed sequential file for each (base) relation created.

o     A secure submodels directory (secure.submodels) for the submodels that may be used if the database is secure.

The database control file contains running information related to usage of a database and concurrent access control.

The data model file contains schema-like information about the database, files, relations, attributes and domains.

The relation model files contain information about how the data is arranged in each data file.

Optionally, a number of data submodels may be created for each database. The submodels define a subset view of the data model for the user. The data submodel allows attributes to be given different names and to be reordered within their containing relations. It also allows the renaming of relations. Security restrictions may also be assigned to each relation and each attribute (see 6.1). (It does not allow relations to be joined.) (See 2.4)

2.2.2   Database Operations

Some of the operations available for database definition, generation and manipulation are:

o     Modify the database control files' contents

o     Display the contents of a data model

o     Display the contents of a database control file

2.2.3    <u>Database Constraints</u>

Database constraints are defined on the relation and domain level.

2.2.4    <u>Additional Database Properties</u>

The database may be secured (or unsecured) by a Database Administrator. In the secure state, the restrictions specified in the data submodel are enforced. In the unsecured state, the data submodel restrictions are ignored. (See 6.1)

2.3    RELATION

2.3.1    <u>Relational Structure</u>

A relation consists of tuples of identical type. An MRDS relation is perceived as a set of tuples, each containing values for the same set of attribute names. Each tuple in a relation is guaranteed to be unique from other tuples in that relation.

Relation and attribute names are fixed. They may be given aliases through use of the Data Submodel mechanism. Attributes within a relation may also be reordered through use of the Data Submodel mechanism.

In LINUS a relation is perceived as a table of rows and columns.

2.3.2    <u>Relational Operations</u>

Operations defined for relations are those for qualifying (see 3.1), querying (see 3.2), altering (see 3.3), arithmetic and string operations (see 3.4.1), standard set functions (see 3.4.3), and user-defined functions (see 3.4.4).

The primary design goal of the MRDS relation operations was to provide a high-level relationally complete programming language interface based upon the first order predicate calculus. The operations execute in piped mode allowing the application program to deal with selected relations one tuple at a time in a procedural manner.

The primary design goal of the LINUS relation operations was end-user convenience. In addition to providing the equivalent selection power provided by MRDS, LINUS allows for a more extensive use of set and scalar functions and arithmetic expressions.

The tuples of a relation are not assumed to be ordered.

### 2.3.3    Relation Constraints

Each relation is required to have at least one attribute
designated as the primary key.    A primary key may
consist of more than one attribute.    The value of the
primary key must be non-null and serves to uniquely
identify each tuple in a relation (i.e., no duplicates
allowed).    The values of attributes which are components
of primary keys cannot be modified.    Any attempt to
modify a primary key component will result in an error
message being returned to the user.

Each attribute named in a relation must be defined by
means of an attribute or a domain statement.    (The
definition of a domain implies the definition of an
attribute with a name identical to the domain name.)

### 2.3.4    Additional Properties of Relations

Although not enforced by the system, it is assumed that
the base relations are normalized.

### 2.4    VIEWS

### 2.4.1    View Structure

There are two types of views available in MRDS and
LINUS:    the data submodel and the temporary relation (or
temporary table, in LINUS).

### 2.4.2    View Operations

The data submodel operations are:

o    Create the data submodel
o    Display the contents
o    Open the submodel view
o    Close the submodel view

The data submodel allows relations and attributes to be
given new names, allows the subsetting of relations and
attributes and allows the reordering of attributes
within a relation.    Security restrictions may be
assigned to each relation and attribute (See 6.1).    The
data submodel definition is performed as a part of the
administrative function and is not a part of the
qualification operations.    Once defined, a data submodel
cannot be modified.    Since it exists as a Multics file,
it can be deleted using the Multics delete file
command.    If the data submodel relation contains less
attributes than the base relation, it is not possible to
use the store and delete operations.

The temporary relation operations are:

o    Define and load a temporary relation
o    Select data from a temporary relation

Temporary relations are defined using the selection operation at run time. Temporary relations may be created from other temporary relations as long as the selected column names are unique across the new temporary relation. The user must specify which selected attributes are to be used as primary key components of the temporary relation being defined. Temporary relations remain in existence only for the duration of the database session.

Temporary relations cannot be updated.

2.4.3    View Constraints

The constraints definable using data submodels are to provide the user with a subset of the database and to restrict access to database subsets. This is accomplished by assigning access control lists to the data submodel file, and assigning security restrictions within the data submodel. (See 6.1)

2.4.4    Additional Properties of Views

Data submodels are intended to be used for subsetting and access control purposes.

2.5      TUPLE

2.5.1    Tuple Structure

A tuple is an instance of the values of each of the attributes known to a relation corresponding to a row of a table. Tuples in a base relation are created as a result of the store operation. Each tuple is identifiable by the unique value of its primary key.

2.5.2    Tuple Operations

MRDS operates in piped mode and provides a tuple-level interface. The operations allowed are:

o    Store
o    Delete
o    Retrieve
o    Modify

The delete, retrieve and modify operations are used in conjunction with a selection expression or predicate.

2.5.3   Tuple Constraints

Tuples within base relations must be unique and are presumed to be unordered. (See 2.3.2)

Primary key values cannot be modified. Attempts to do so will generate an error status code.

2.5.4   Additional Properites of Tuples

If a view or a selection expression does not reference the entire primary key, then it is possible to retireve duplicate tuples or to eliminate duplicates, at the user's option (see 3.1).

2.6     ATTRIBUTE

2.6.1   Attribute Structure

The attribute is a named component of a relation, corresponding to the column of a table. By default, there exists one attribute name equal to each defined domain name. It is also possible to define multiple attribute names ranging over one domain. Attributes derive their data types and integrity constraints from the associated domain definition. Attribute values must be non-null.

2.6.2   Attribute Operations

The MRDS operations available for manipulating attributes are:

o    Logical operators (&,|,^)

o    Relation operators (=,<=,<,>,>=,^=)

o    Arithmetic operators (+,-,*,/)

o    Scalar functions (i.e., PL/1 built-ins: abs, after, before, ceil, concat, floor, index, mod, reverse, round, search, substr, verify, and user-defined functions)

The LINUS attribute (or column) operations include all the MRDS attribute operations in addition to the following set (i.e., aggregation) functions:

o    Average
o    Count
o    Max
o    Min
o    Sum
o    User-defined aggregate and scalar functions

2.6.3    Attribute Constraints

Attribute constraints are inherited from the underlying
domain constraints (see 2.7.3).

2.6.4    Additional Properties of Attributes

(Not Applicable)

2.7      DOMAIN

2.7.1    Domain Structure

A domain defines the set of all values an attribute
value in the database may assume.  It provides for the
definition of a domain name and the data type the
associated data values will conform to on the database.
The data types are defined using PL/1 syntax.    The
supported data types are:

o    Real fixed binary (short and long)
o    Real floating binary (short and long)
o    Complex fixed binary (short and long)
o    Complex floating binary (short and long)
o    Real fixed decimal
o    Real floating decimal
o    Packed decimal
o    Complex fixed decimal
o    Complex floating decimal
o    Bit string
o    Varying bit string
o    Character string
o    Varying character string

Data types of program data to be stored and of variables
into which data is to be retrieved in MRDS application
programs need not be the same as the data types of the
attributes, underlying domains.    Data conversion is
performed automatically by MRDS using PL/1 conversion
rules (see 3.1.1).

2.7.2    Domain Operations

Domains are not directly operated on by MRDS or LINUS
except when the database is created.

2.7.3    Domain Constraints

A check procedure may be defined for each domain to
verify data integrity prior to storage into the
database.

Encoding and decoding procedures may also be defined for each domain to convert data values upon storage into or retrieval from the database.

2.7.4   Additional Properties of Domains

(Not Applicable)

2.8   ADDITIONAL DATABASE CONSTITUENTS

(Not Applicable)

3.0   FUNCTIONAL CAPABILITIES

3.1   QUALIFICATION

In MRDS the selection expression is calculus oriented and consists of three clauses:

o   The range-clause
o   The select-clause
o   The where-clause

The range-clause allows the user to assign a tuple variable to each relation to be referenced.

The select-clause allows the user to define those tuple attributes which provide the selected attribute values.

The where-clause defines the restrictions to be applied in selecting the data values.

The values are perceived by the user as tuples, processed one tuple at a time.  A status code is returned with the results of each request.

In LINUS the selection mechanism is mapping-oriented and the range-clause is replaced by the from-clause, and the order of the clauses is select ...from...where...

The values are perceived by the user as a set of tuples (i.e., a relation).  Error status codes are translated into messages and displayed to the user.

Examples of a Data Model (=Schema) Definition
(See C.J. Date, An Introduction to Database Systems, 2nd edition, p. 52):

domain:

        integer fixed bin (17),
        character char (20),
        name char (32) -check_proc valid_name;

attributes:

| | |
|---|---|
| city-name | character, |
| supplier_name | name, |
| part_name | character, |
| quantity | integer, |
| credit_status | integer, |
| weight_units | integer, |
| color_type | character, |
| supplier_number | integer; |

relation:

company (supplier_number* supplier_name
        credit_status city)

item (part_number* part_name color_type
    weight_units city),

order (supplier_number* part_number* quantity);

The asterisk next to an attribute name indicates membership in the relation's primary key.

### 3.1.1     Restriction

Restriction is done through use of the where-clause. The allowable relational operators in MRDS and LINUS are the following:

| Symbol | Definition |
|---|---|
| = | equals |
| ^= | not equals |
| < | less than |
| > | greater than |
| <= | less than or equals |
| >= | greater than or equals |

Tuple attributes may be compared to string constants, arithmetic constants, tuple attributes within the same or different tuple variables, arithmetic expressions or scalar functions. Tuple attributes may also be compared to the values of program variables. Any domain may be compared with any other domain with conversion to a common data type performed according to Multics PL/1 conversion rules.

These relational expressions can be combined into more general expressions through the use of the logical conjunction (&), logical disjunctive (|) and logical negation (^) operators.

MRDS Example:

```
-range (i item) (o order)
-select i.part_number i.part_name
-where ((o.part_number = i.part_number) &
        (o.supplier_number = "Acme"))
```

LINUS Example:

```
select part_number part_name
from item
where part_number = {select part_number
                     from order where
                     supplier_number = "Acme"}
```

An alternative to the previous LINUS Example is:

```
select item.part_number item.part_name
from item order
where item.part_number = order.part_number
  & order.supplier_name = "ACME"
```

It is also possible to supply program variable values to the where-clause (See 3.2.1.1, example 2).

### 3.1.2 Quantification

Existential and universal quantification are implicitly supported through use of the intersection (inter), union (union) and difference (differ) set operators (see 3.1.3).

Absolute quantification is not supported.

### 3.1.3 Set Operations

The defined set operators are union (union), inter (intersection) and differ (difference).

The selected attributes must be union compatible.

MRDS Example:

```
(-range (c company)
-select c.city_name
-where c.supplier_name = "Blake")
-inter
(-range (i item)
-select i.city_name
-where i.part_name = "Bolt")
```

LINUS Example:

```
(select city_name
from company
where supplier_name = "Blake")
inter
(select city_name
from item
where part_name = "Bolt")
```

### 3.1.4 Join Operations

A relation can be joined with another relation (see 3.1.1) or with itself.

MRDS Example:

```
-range (a item) (b item)
-select a.part_name
-where ((b.part_number = 503) &
        (a.city_name = b.city_name))
```

LINUS Example:

```
select part.part_name
from part:item five_o_three:item
where five_o_three.part_number = 503 &
      five_o_three.city_name = part.city_name
```

### 3.1.5 Nesting and Closure

Qualifications can be nested. The qualifications can be used in retrieval and alteration operations. The qualification facilities are "relationally complete." The capabilities of existential and universal quantification are provided by the set operations (see 3.1.3).

### 3.1.6 Additional Aspects of Qualification

(Not Applicable)

### 3.2 RETRIEVAL AND PRESENTATION

### 3.2.1 Database Queries

### 3.2.1.1 MRDS

The manner in which the selection facility described in 3.1 is utilized in MRDS is as an argument in a CALL statement. This interface to MRDS can be used in any language containing a CALL interface that is supported by Multics (e.g., PL/1 Fortran, COBOL, etc.) provided the language supports data types that the database data types may be converted to using the PL/1 conversion rules.

Tuples are returned a tuple at a time. The first tuple is returned when the first CALL to the retrieve module is executed using a given selection expression. Subsequent tuples are retrieved by CALLing the retrieve module using the "-another" parameter in place of the original selection expression. A status code is returned when the set of tuples to be retrieved has been exhausted.

It is also possible to re-retrieve the last seen tuple by replacing the selection expression with "-current." This is useful for the modify operation (see 3.3.3).

MRDS allows for user-defined functions to be used within the where-clause. Absolute functions are not explicitly supported.

MRDS is considered to be relationally complete (see 3.1.5).

MRDS Examples using PL/1:   (Get the names of all parts weighing twelve pounds)

```
(1)   o
      o
      o
      call dsl_$retrieve (db_index,
            "-range (i item)
            -select i.part_name
            -where (i.weight_units = 12)",
            receiving_variable,
            status_code);
      o
      o
      o
      do while (status_code = 0);
      o
      o
      o
      call dsl_$retrieve (db_index,
            "-another",receiving_variable,
            status_code);
      o
      o
      o
      end;
```

```
(2)   dcl  weight_var fixed bin (35);
      o
      o
      o
      weight_var = 12;
      call dsl_$retrieve (db_index,
          "-range (i item)
          -select i.part_name
          -where (i.weight_units = .V.)",
          weight_var, receiving_variable,
          status_code);
      o
      o

      o
      do while (status_code = 0);
      call dsl_$retrieve (db_index,
          "-another", weight_var, receiving_variable,
          status_code);
      o
      o
      o
      end;
```

## 3.2.1.2   LINUS

In LINUS, the selection expression is executed
interactively as part of a LINUS Language (LILA) text
fragment. The complete set of selected rows (=tuples)
are presented to the user when the print command is
entered.

LINUS allows user-defined functiions to be used in the
where-clause and in the select-clause.

LINUS is considered to be relationally complete (see
3.1.5).

LINUS Example:   (Get the names of all parts weighing
twelve pounds).

First the user creates the desired selection expression
on a text file using LILA, as follows (underscores
indicate system generated prompt characters):

```
?  lila
=> 10 select part_name
=> 20 from item
=> 30 where weight_units = 12
=> proc
=> quit
```

The user supplied information on lines numbered 10, 20
and 30 constitutes the selection expression and is
called the LILA expression.

Satisfied that the above selection expression is correct, the user then enters:

    ? print

The prompt strings in the above examples are the default prompt strings and are changeable by the user.

The user may also create a variable to be used in subsequent selection expressions.

For example, if the LILA expression is -

    avg {select weight_units from item}

If the user then uses the assign__values command as follows:

    assign_values !avg_wu

Then the variable named !avg__wu contains the value denoting the average weight unit for all parts in the item relation.

This variable can then be used in another LILA expression as follows:

    select part_name
    from item
    where weight_units = !avg_wu

The value of a variable may be displayed via the list_values command as follows:

    ? list_values !avg_wu

The user may then retrieve all parts containing the average value, using the print command.

3.2.2  <u>Retrieval of Information About Database Constituents</u>

The data model (=schema) may be accessed by privileged users. The operations available are listed in 2.2.2.

3.2.3  <u>Retrieval of System Performance Data</u>

Some monitoring data, such as the names of active concurrent users, is available to privileged users (see 2.2.2).

### 3.2.4    Report Generation

The LINUS print command provides a default format. It also allows the user to specify the character width of each printed column and to alter the maximum number of rows of data to be printed. If there are more than the maximum number of rows to be printed, the user is queried as to whether the remaining rows are to be printed. It also allows for a user-defined heading to be printed.

There also exists a create list command which directs retireved data to a Multics word processing file, which may then be manipulated and formatted using standard word processing commands. (An application program using MRDS may also create a Multics word processing file.)

If more complex reporting of retrieved output is desired, the report command directs the retrieved output to the Multics Report Program Generator, which then processes the output according to a predefined report definition. (An application program using MRDS may also use the Multics Report Program Generator.)

### 3.2.5    Constraints and Limitations

(Not Applicable)

### 3.2.6    Additional Aspects of Retrieval and Presentation

(Not Applicable)

### 3.3    ALTERATION

The delete and modify facilities operate in conjunction with a selection expression, just as does the retrieval facility. The insert facility does not utilize a selection expression.

### 3.3.1    Insert Facilities

The insert facility in MRDS and in LINUS is provided by the store operation. Tuples may be stored into one relation at a time. Values must be provided for every attribute defined in the base relation. If the user desires a non-key attribute value to be null, the null value must be explicitly provided. Uniqueness of tuples within a relation is enforced through the concatenated values constituting the primary key.

### 3.3.1.1 MRDS

The first attempt to store a tuple into a relation must specify the relation name and the values to be stored in the same order and number as the associated attributes appear in the data model (=schema) or submodel (=view). In this case, the submodel (=view) must contain all the attributes contained in the model (=schema) for this base relation, although they may be renamed and reordered.

After the first call to store a tuple in a relation has been executed, subsequent calls may specify "-another" in place of the relation name.

Example in PL/1:

```
call dsl_$store (db_index,
                 "order",
                 5553,
                 3133,
                 200,
                 status_code);
o
o
o
do while (status_code = 0);
call dsl_$store (db_index,
                 "-another",
                 5662,
                 2970,
                 350,
                 status_code);
o
o
o
end;
```

### 3.3.1.2 LINUS

LINUS allows tuples to be stored into a relation in several ways. The values to be stored may be specified in one of three ways: (1) directly within the command line, (2) intractively in response to prompting for each attribute, or (3) by placing a set of new values in a Multics file and providing the name of the file within the command line.

If (1) or (2) is used, the user has the option of visually verifying the values prior to their actual placement into the database. If (3) is used, the user can specify the delimiter character used to separate the values on the file to be stored from.

Examples (underscore indicates system generated output):

(1)  ? store order 5553 3133 200 -brief

(2)  ? store order 5665 4210 150
     supplier_number = 5665
     part_number = 4210
     quantity = 150

     OK? yes

(3)  ? store order -brief
     supplier_number? 3030
     part_number? 2970
     quantity? 59

## 3.3.2  Delete Facilities

The delete facility in MRDS and LINUS is provided by the delete operation. The delete operation is used in conjunction with the selection expression (see 3.1). The only constraints are that the select list must not reference more than one relation and must not contain any set operators (union, inter or differ). Other relations can be referenced in the where-clause. All selected tuples in the referenced base relation are deleted. Thus, if the base relation from which tuples are to be deleted is being referenced via a data submodel (=view), then all attributes defined in the base relation must also be defined in the data submodel (=view).

MRDS Example:  (Delete all orders which refer to bolts).

```
call dsl_$delete (db_index,
    "-range (o order) (i item)
    -select o
    -where ((i.part_name = "Bolt") &
            (o.part_number = i.part_number)),"
            status_code);
```

LINUS Example:  (Delete all orders which refer to bolts).

The LILA expression is -
```
select *
from order
where part_number = {select part_number
                        from item
                        where part_name = "Bolt"}
```

The LINUS command is -

```
delete
```

### 3.3.3    Modify Facilities

Relations can be altered by modify operations. The modify operation is used in conjunction with the selection expression (see 3.1). The select list must not reference more than one relation although other relations may be referenced in the where-clause. Primary keys cannot be modified. Any attempt to do so will result in an error status code. All attributes specified in the select list are modified for each tuple selected.

### 3.3.3.1   MRDS

Modification is performed on all selected tuples. It is possible to retrieve a tuple using the retrieve operation and then apply the modify operation using the "-current" parameter in place of the selection expression. This allows one-tuple-at-a-time modification.

MRDS Example:    (Change to 500 the quantity of parts #9391 on order from supplier #4444).

```
call dsl_$modify (db_index,
    "-range (o order)
    -select o.quantity
    -where ((o.supplier_number = 444) &
            o.part_number = 9391))", 500,
    status_code);
```

### 3.3.3.2   LINUS

Modification is performed on all selected rows of data. Data to be modified must be contained within one table, and key columns cannot be modified. New values may be specified within the request line, or they may be entered interactively, in response to LINUS prompting. In both cases, the user is asked to verify the new values before the modification takes place, unless the -brief control argument is specified. A processed LILA expression must be available before the modify command is entered, followed by the new values.

If the -brief argument is not provided, then LINUS displays a list of selected column names, together with the column_values as entered by the user, and requests that the user verify the correctness of the column values before the modification operation proceeds. If the verification is negative, the modification does not take place. The user may reenter the modify request without again specifying the associated LILA expression.

New column_values may be specified in two forms: (1) as constants or as LINUS variables which have previously been set, or (2) as arithmetic expressions combining constants, LINUS variables, and possibly the names of columns that have been selected for modification.

The select-clause of the associated LILA expression must specify columns from only one table, and only non-key columns may be selected. The select-clause associated with a modify request must not contain arithmetic expressions, but is restricted to simple or qualified column names. Also, no set operators (union, inter, or differ) may appear in the LILA expression.

LINUS Examples:

(1)  LILA expression:

    select      quantity
    from        order
    where       supplier_number = 4455

To increase the quantity of all parts on order from the selected supplier by 10 percent, do:

    ? modify (quantity + .10 * quantity)
    quantity = (quantity + .10 * quantity)
    OK? yes

(2)  LILA expression:

    select      weight_units
    from        item
    where       part_name = "Bolt"

To correct the designated weight unit of bolts, do:

    ? modify -brief
    weight_units? 19

## 3.3.4    Commit and Undo Facilities

(Not Applicable)

## 3.3.5    Additional Alteration Facilities

(Not Applicable)

## 3.4    ADDITIONAL FUNCTIONAL CAPABILITIES

## 3.4.1    Arithmetic and String Operations

(See 2.6.2)

3.4.2    <u>Sorting</u>

Sorting is not directly supported. Selected data may be sorted within the Multics Report Program Generator. It may also be written to a file and sorted using the Multics sort command.

3.4.3    <u>Library Functions</u>

(See 2.6.2)

3.4.4    <u>User-Defined Functions</u>

User-defined functions can be created for use by MRDS or LINUS. They may be written in any language that accepts and processes a standard Multics argument list. The function name is made known to MRDS or LINUS by the declare operation. LINUS accommodates set (i.e., aggregate) functions and scalar functions. MRDS accommodates only the latter (See 2.6.2).

3.4.5    <u>Transactions</u>

MRDS and LINUS support concurrent access to a database. This is accomplished by opening a database using the open operation and specifying either the retrieval or update mode. (Shared usage is implied by these modes. If the user wishes non-shared access to the database the exclusive_retrieval or exclusive_update mode must be specified.)

If the database is opened in one of the shared modes, then it is incumbent upon the user to declare a scope of access prior to referencing the data. This is done by use of the set_scope and dl_scope (i.e., delete scope) operation. When setting a scope, the user specifies, for each relation, the action (retrieve, store, delete, modify or null) that is being requested as well as the action (retrieve, store, delete, modify, or null) which other users are to be prohibited from performing. This scope of access, once granted, cannot grow but it can shrink. That is, the user may delete part of the scope. The user is not allowed to declare another scope of access until all the current scope of access has been deleted. The user may also specify the maximum time to wait for a set_scope request to be honored.

MRDS Example:

```
call dsl__$set__scope (db__index, "item", 1, 14,
    "supplier", 15, 15, 60, status_code);
o
o
o
call dsl_$dl_scope_all (db_index, status_code);
```

Note: In the set__scope operation the third argument indicates that the caller wishes to retrieve from the item relation. The fourth argument indicates the user wishes everyone else to be denied update privileges. Argument 6 indicates that the caller wishes to both read and update the supplier relation. Argument 7 indicates that the user wishes to prevent anyone else from reading or updating the supplier relation. The parameter 60 indicates the user wishes to wait no more than 60 seconds for the request to be granted.

LINUS Example:

To accomplish the same thing in LINUS, do as follows:

? set_scope item r sdm supplier rsdm rsdm

Note: The default wait time is 30 seconds; sdm signifies store, delete and modify.

? del_scope *

### 3.4.6   Multi-Tuple Alterations

The modify and delete operations allow multiple tuples of one relation to be altered using some tuples of another relation as arguments to the operation (see 3.3.2 and 3.3.3).

### 3.4.7   Grouping

Not Applicable)

### 3.4.8   Exception Handling Mechanisms

MRDS and LINUS rely on the exception handling mechanisms provided by the Multics operating system.

### 3.4.9    Additional Functional Capabilities

MRDS and LINUS support a snapshot view capability allowing users to define temporary relations (temporary tables in LINUS). The operation is called define_temp_rel (or define_temp_table). A temporary relation cannot be altered. It can be refined by creating another temporary relation. It can also be queried using the retrieve operation.

The define_temp_rel is executed in conjunction with a selection expression (see 3.1). The one variation is that in MRDS at least one of the attribute names specified in the select list must be followed by an asterisk (*) to denote it as a primary key component. Upon creation, it is assigned an index value which is returned to the user. This value is then used as an identifier of the temporary relation, for reference within subsequent operations.

MRDS Example:

```
call dsl_$define_temp_rel (db_index,
    "-range (i item)
    -select i.color_type i.part_name*
    -where (i.city_name = "London"),
    temp_rel_index,
    status_code);
```

In LINUS the primary key is specified in the define_temp_table command.

LINUS Example:

LILA expression:

```
select      color_type part_name
from        item
where       city_name = "London"
```

Then execute the command:

```
? define_temp_table London_parts part_name
```

### 4.0    DEFINITION, GENERATION AND ADMINISTRATION FACILITIES

The main components of an MRDS database are:

1.  The data model (this corresponds roughly to the internal schema in the ANSI/SPARC model).

2.  The data submodel (this corresponds roughly to the external schema in the ANSI/SPARC model).

3.    The database itself.

The creation, generation and administration of the data model are considered database administrator functions. The creation of the data submodel and its administration are viewed as Database Administrator functions if the database is secure or as user functions if the database is not secure.

4.1      DEFINITION FACILITIES

4.1.1    Constituents of a Database Definition

The MRDS (or LINUS) database definition consists of a definition of the:

o     Domains
o     Attributes
o     Relations
o     Indexes
o     Data Model
o     Data Submodel (optional for databases that are not secure)

The definitions of domains, attributes, relations and indexes (the secondary indexes which serve as quick-access paths to tuples) are placed in a text file.

(For an example, see 3.1).

4.1.2    The create__mrds__db command creates an unpopulated database and a data model (=schema) based on the definitions found in a text file (see 4.1.1).    The database name is a parameter of this command.

The maximum number of relations in a database is 256.

4.1.3    Relation Definition

A relation is defined in the text file referenced by the create__mrds__db command.    The relation definition consists of:

o     A relation name
o     The attribute names in a relation
o     An indicator as to which attribute names are primary key components

The referenced attribute names must appear in a domain or attribute statement.

For Example (see 3.1):

        order (supplier_number* part_number* quantity)

4.1.4    <u>View Definition</u>

Data submodels are one type of view defined for MRDS.

Data submodel definition is accomplished with the create_mrds_dsm command. It allows the user to rename relations and attributes, omit relations and attributes, reorder attributes within a relation and assign security restrictions to relations and attributes. (It does not allow for the redefinition of a data type, but this is allowed in the declaration of the receiving variable in the application program using MRDS.) The data submodel definition is placed in a text file, the name of which is a parameter of the create_mrds_dsm command. Submodel relations cannot span more than one base relation.

Example:

        default attribute access:  read_attr;

        relation: co=Company (city sno = supplier_number);

        relation access: co (append_tuple, delete_tuple);

        attribute access:
            city in co (read_attr, modify_attr);

In this example, the company relation is renamed to "co". The co relation contains two attributes: (1) city (which is not renamed) and (2) sno (which is the new name defined for supplier_number). All attributes are given a default access of read if no explicit access is given. The city attribute has explicit access of read and modify. The co relation has explicit access of append (store) and delete. (See 6.1)

For defining the other type of view (i.e., temporary relation), see 3.4.9.

4.1.5    <u>Tuple Definition</u>

Tuples are implicitly defined as tuples of a relation (in MRDS) or rows of a table (in LINUS). There is no explicit tuple definition.

4.1.6    <u>Attribute Definition</u>

Attributes are defined in the text file referenced by create_mrds_db. They are defined by default with names identical to each domain name and may also be explicitly defined to range over a specified domain. In this case the attribute definition consists of the attribute followed by the associated domain name. (For example, see 3.1 and 4.1.3)

        attribute: city_name    character;

### 4.1.7 Domain Definition

Domains are defined in the text file referenced by create_mrds_db. Domain definitions consist of:

o   The domain name
o   The data type (see 2.7.1)
o   An optional name of a data integrity checking procedure
o   An optional name of a data encoding procedure
o   An optional name of a data decoding procedure
o   An optional data type for the decoded value

For example (see 3.1):

```
domain:  name char (32)
        -check_proc valid_name_routine
        -encode_proc encode_routine
        -decode_proc decode_routine
        -decode_dcl float bin (72)
```

### 4.1.8 Definition of Additional Database Constituents

Secondary indexes may be defined for any attribute in any relation. The index is defined in an index statement contained in the text file referenced by create_mrds_db. Each secondary index must consist of no more than one attribute.

For example (see 3.1):

```
index:  company (city supplier_name)
```

### 4.2 GENERATION FACILITIES

### 4.2.1 Constituents of a Database Generation

The create__mrds__db command creates an unpopulated database with the components defined in the referenced text file. If the text file containing the definition discussed in 4.1 is named sample_db.cmdb, the command to create a database named new_db would appear as follows:

```
create_mrds_db  sample_db.cmdb  new_db
```

This would create a Multics directory named new__db.db. Immediately subordinate to this directory are a number of files and another directory.

o    The database control file (db.control) contains information necessary to control concurrent access to the database.

o    The database model file (db__model) contains data model information common to the entire database, such as descriptions of all the domains and a list of all relation names.

o    The secure.submodels directory will be used to store all submodels that the Database Administrator wishes to be used with a secured database.

o    For each relation, there is created a relation model.  The relation model contains data model information unique to each relation, such as the relation definition and the attribute definitions.

o    For each relation there is created a null (or empty) file which may be populated using the store function (see 3.1.1).

The create__mrds__dsm command creates a data submodel which may reside separate from the database for unsecure databases.  It contains database location information and alias information.

4.2.2    Generation of Database Constituents

The database files (i.e., relations) are populated using the store function (see 3.3.1).

4.3      DATABASE REDEFINITION

4.3.1    Renaming Database Constituents

Database relation names and attribute names can be renamed by creating a temporary database using the new definition and then using standard Multics facilities to replace the original file model and affected file name with the new file model and file name in the database. The domain names can be renamed by replacing the original db_model file with the new db_model file using standard Multics facilities.  Databases may be renamed by using the Multics rename command on the database directory as long as the directory retains a ".db" as the last component of the name.  In a similar manner, data submodels may be renamed as long as they retain a ".dsm" as the last component of their name.

Data submodels must be modified to reflect such renaming, but application programs using the data submodels remain unaffected.

**4.3.2**     <u>Redefining Database Constituents</u>

Constraints on domains can be added, removed or changed
by copying a new data model file.

**4.4**       DATABASE REGENERATION AND REORGANIZATION

**4.4.1**     <u>System-Controlled</u>

(Not Applicable)

**4.4.2**     <u>DBA-Controlled</u>

(Not Applicable)

**4.5**       DATABASE DICTIONARY

The database dictionary information is maintained in the
db_model file and in the relation model files.

**5.0**       <u>INTERFACES AND DBMS ARCHITECTURE</u>

**5.1**       <u>System Information Architecture</u>

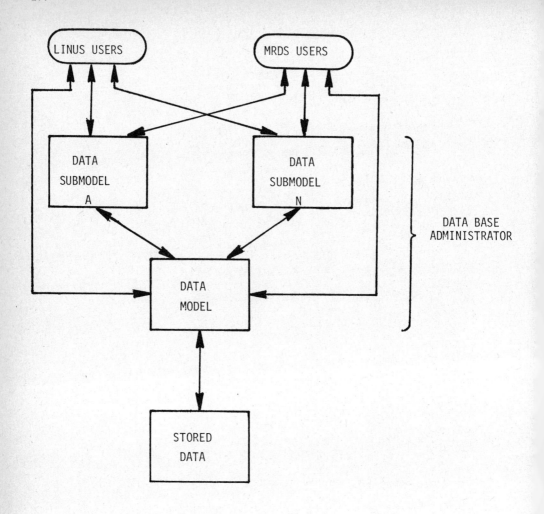

INFORMATION ARCHITECTURE

5.2       INTERFACE DESCRIPTIONS

5.2.1     MRDS_Data_Sublanguage

The MRDS data sublanguage provides a CALL-level
interface for application programs to access an MRDS
database.   This data language can be used in any
language supported by Multics which supports the CALL
statement provided the language supports data types that
the database data types may be converted to using the
PL/1 conversion rules.   Specifically it can be used in
COBOL, PL/1, FORTRAN.   Data is transmitted to the
program in piped mode, a tuple at a time, from the set
of data specified by the user's selection expression
(see 3.2.1).   All status information is transmitted via
a status return code in each CALL statement.   Security
is provided by Multics access control lists applied to
the database and files, by access control lists applied
to the data submodel, and by security restrictions
within the data submodel.   Recovery is provided by the
normal Multics operating system features.   For more
details, see the MRDS descriptions in Sections 2, 3, and
4.

5.2.2     LINUS

LINUS provides an interactive interface to a MRDS
database.   Data is transmitted as a table of rows and
columns (see 3.2.1.2).   Abnormal status information is
presented to the user as English language messages on
the terminal.   For security and recovery features, see
5.2.1.   For more details see the appropriate LINUS
descriptions in sections 2, 3 and 4.

5.2.3     Administrative_Interfaces

The administrative interfaces are provided by a set of
interactive commands.   They include the following
commands (each command is followed by a comma and a
short form of the command name):

adjust_mrds_db, amdb
        reinitializes a database concurrent access control
        file (db.control).

create_mrds_db, cmdb
        creates an unpopulated MRDS database.

create_mrds_dm_include, cmdmi
        builds a PL/1 include file of structure
        declarations where the level 1 names are those of
        the model/submodel relations, and where the level 2
        declarations match those of the attributes in each
        relation.

create_mrds_dm_table, cmdmt
    provides a picture, or graphic display of the data
    model/submodel structure.

create_mrds_dsm, cmdsm
    creates a data submodel definition file (provides
    an alternate description of the database).

display_mrds_db_access, dmdba
    displays the current access to relation data in a
    MRDS database.

display_mrds_db_population, dmdbp
    displays population statistics of relations in a
    MRDS database.

display_mrds_scope_settings, dmss
    displays the opening modes and scope settings for
    all of the MRDS databases that a user's process has
    opened.

display_mrds_db_status, dmdbs
    displays the open and concurrent access users of a
    database.

display_mrds_temp_dir, dmtd
    displays the directory used for temporary storage
    during a database opening.

display_mrds_db_version, dmdv
    displays    the    version    of    an    MRDS    data
    model/submodel.

display_mrds_dm, dmdm
    displays specified information from the data model.

display_mrds_dsm, dmdsm
    displays    specified    information    from    the    data
    submodel and optionally displays related data model
    information.

display_mrds_open_dbs, dmod
    displays a list of pathnames and opening indexes of
    all    currently    opened    databases    in    the    user's
    process.

quiesce_mrds_db, qmdb
    places the database in a quiescent (non-active)
    state for such purposes as dumping, etc.

secure_mrds_db, smdb
    secures or unsecures a MRDS database or displays
    the current security state.

set_mrds_temp_dir, smtd
sets the directory for temporary storage for a
database opening.

unpopulate_mrds_db, umdb
deletes all of the data from a MRDS database.

update_mrds_db_version, umdbv
updates the database model version to the newest
version.

## 6.0    OPERATIONAL ASPECTS

## 6.1    SECURITY

Two different levels of database security are provided
by MRDS:    relation level security and attribute level
security.

A secure database cannot be referenced by a user other
than a Database Administrator via the data model or via
a data submodel that does not reside under the
secure.submodels directory of the database.  A Database
Administrator may reference the database via the data
model or a data submodel regardless of the security
state of the database.

### 6.1.1    Relation Level Security

This level of security does not provide any data model
security in that there is no restriction on the amount
of information about the data model (relation and
attribute descriptions) that the user may obtain.  Any
user may access the database via either the data model
or a data submodel.

By setting the access control lists on the relation
model file and the relation data file, the Database
Administrator can restrict a user, or group of users, so
that the relation may be read but may not be updated by
that user, or group of users, or so that the relation is
not accessible at all by that user, or group of users.

### 6.1.2    Attribute Level Security

To use attribute level security the database must not
only be secured but there must also be at least one
secured submodel containing specifications for the data
access permissions on both the relations in the view
defined by the submodel and the attributes in those
relations.

The access permissions that may be set in the submodel are:

relation access:

| | |
|---|---|
| append_tuple | allows tuples to be stored into the relation |
| delete_tuple | allows tuples to be deleted from the relation |
| null | allows no activity on the relation |

attributes access:

| | |
|---|---|
| read_attr | allows the attribute value to be read |
| modify_attr | allows the attribute value to be modified |
| null | allows no activity on the attribute |

The only restriction on the attribute access permissions is that null access cannot be specified with any other access.

There are several restrictions on which access can be set on the relations.

1.  null relation access permission cannot be specified with any other access permissions.

2.  append_tuple and delete_tuple can only be set if the submodel relation is a full view of its corresponding model relation. A full view implies that the submodel relation contains all the attributes in the model relation.

3.  append_tuple can only be set on a relation if read_attr access is also set on all of the primary key attributes in that relation. If this restriction were not applied then it would be possible to store tuples until the duplicate key error was generated, at which point the values of the primary key attributes would be known.

Any user who can read the data submodel file, as determined by associated access control list, will be granted the access specified in the data submodel.

The access control list requirements of relation level security are also enforced on a secured database and take precedence over the permissions granted in the submodel, i.e. if the access control lists indicate that a user may only read data from a relation's data file and the data submodel indicates that the user may store tuples, the user will be unable to store any data.

6.2     PHYSICAL INTEGRITY

6.2.1   Concurrency Control

Deadlocks are prevented and concurrency control is provided through use of the "set scope" and "delete scope" functions (see 3.4.5).

6.2.2   Recovery and Restart

The quiesce_mrds_db command allows the administrator to force a database into a quiescent state. The database can then be saved using normal Multics facilities. If it is necessary to restore a database after a crash, this saved copy can be restored using normal Multics facilities in conjunction with the quiesce_mrds_db command.

6.3     OPERATING ENVIRONMENT

6.3.1   Software Environment (Operating System)

MRDS and LINUS utilize Multics system features to a great degree. The data is stored in the Multics storage system hierarchy. Report generation is provided by the Multics Report Program Generator (MRPG).

6.3.2   Hardware Environment (CPU, Memory, Peripherals)

Not applicable, since MRDS and LINUS run in a virtual memory dynamic paging environment.

7.0     ESSENTIALLY RELATIONAL SOLUTIONS FOR GENERALIZED DBMS PROBLEMS

MRDS and LINUS are simpler and easier to use than other non-relational database management systems. The power of the data selection language allows users to retrieve what is wanted with one command without having to worry about coding complex procedures to retrieve the desired data.

MRDS and LINUS provide a significant degree of data independence by removing access path information from the user interface. Additional data independence is achieved through use of the data submodel which allows users to reference data using aliases and user specific views. Through use of the data submodel views, databases can be restructured without impacting MRDS application programs or LINUS queries.

MRDS and LINUS optimize each query according to storage considerations (such as secondary indexes) and progress is being made in optimizing on dynamic characteristics (such as the number of tuples in a relation).

The non-procedural aspect of MRDS allows application programmers to ignore many representational details, such as storage structures.

The high level interface provided by MRDS and LINUS is ideal for adaptation to a database machine facility and contributes toward the eventual distribution of databases.

8.0 DATABASE APPLICATIONS USING THE SYSTEM

1. Library Catalog Application

2. Statistical Analysis

3. Seismic Data Collection

4. Patent Querying Application

5. End User Facility Development

6. Database Concepts Teaching Application

7. Auto Tracking Application

3.6  Feature Analysis Of MRS

MRS
System Evaluation

by
J.Z. Kornatowski
I. Ladd
C.M. Robertson

Computer Systems Research Group
University of Toronto
121 St. Joseph Street
Toronto, Ontario
Canada M5S 1A1

October 1980

# 1 INTRODUCTION

## 1.1 Identification

MRS is a relational database management system for mini and micro computer applications. It was designed and implemented by the Database Project of the Computer Systems Research Group, University of Toronto, under the direction of Prof. D. Tsichritzis.

## 1.2 Status

### 1.2.1 System

MRS was released in July 1979. It is available from the Computer Systems Research Group, University of Toronto, for a distribution fee. The current version has been distributed to over 50 installations worldwide. (See 8.1.)

### 1.2.2 Applications

MRS is a general-purpose Database Management System suitable for applications involving small databases (to approximately 1 megabyte). It is not suitable for statistical databases due to limited built-in arithmetic capabilities.

There are two main restrictions: 1) it can support no more than 30,000 tuples per relation; and 2) it can support a maximum of 70 attributes per relation.

Example:

The following is an example of a simple application from the MRS User's Manual, which will be used throughout this analysis to illustrate features of

MRS. It consists of a database storing information on movies, directors, and actors -- a small film library. This database consists of two relations: **movies** and **actors**. **Movies** stores the name of the movie, the year it was made, and the name of its director. **Actors** also stores the movie's name, as well the names of as its stars. Any one movie would have only one entry in **movies**, but might have several in **actors** if it had more than one star. Sample entries for **movies** and **actors** are shown below.

********** movies **********

| movie_name (char) | year_made (numeric) | director (char) |
|---|---|---|
| Coming Home | 1979 | Hal Ashby |
| Heaven Can Wait | 1978 | Warren Beatty |
| Superman | 1979 | Richard Donner |
| Love and Death | 1976 | Woody Allen |

********** actors **********

| actor_name (char) | film (char) |
|---|---|
| Jane Fonda | Coming Home |
| John Voight | Coming Home |
| Warren Beatty | Heaven Can Wait |
| Julie Christie | Heaven Can Wait |
| Woody Allen | Love and Death |

## 1.3 <u>System Background</u>

MRS is a member of the SQL database management family. It is written in the "C" programming language and is implemented on the LSI-11/PDP-11 family of computers under the Mini-UNIX/UNIX operating systems. MRS was originally designed as a workstation in a distributed database management system by I. Ladd, J. Kornatowski, and R. Hudyma. This prototype was subsequently redesigned and implemented by. J. Kornatowski and I. Ladd to become a practical standalone database management system. This is the version presently distributed by the Computer Systems Research Group. Due to the widespread acceptance of MRS and ongoing user demands, the redesigners have produced a new, supported and enhanced commercial product called MISTRESS that is downward-compatible with MRS at the query language level.

## 1.4 <u>Overall Philosophy</u>

The philosophy of MRS is a small system that is simple in its design, flexible in its abilities, usable by the ordinary person, and runnable on a wide family of mini and microcomputers. MRS is integrated with the operating system under which it runs. It complements and interacts with the operating system utilities. It does not duplicate the function of the system utilities. MRS fulfils the need for a practical small Database Management System, and many of its features and developments are a direct consequence of user feedback. It provides a suitable working environment for the rapid development of protoype applications.

## 1.5 Essentialy Relational Characteristics

MRS is a relational Database Management System modelled on "System R". The Query language based on SQL implements many of the most common commands and adds a number of practical features demanded by users.

## 1.6 Interfaces

The query language/operating system interface in MRS allows for the following capabilities:

* Database Schema Definition
* Query Language
* Database Altering
* Database Generation
* Data Entry
* Database load and dump
* Definition of indices

The Interactive Subsystem interface in MRS allows for the following:

* interactive insertions
* interactive updates
* interactive deletions

## 1.7 Documentation

J. Kornatowski (1979). The MRS User's Manual, University of Toronto Press.

I. Ladd (1979). A Distributed Database Management System Based on Microcomputers, MSc Thesis, University of Toronto.

R. Hudyma, I. Ladd, and J. Kornatowski (1979). Implementing a microcomputer database management system. Computer Systems Research Group Technical Report, University of Toronto.

R. Hudyma (1978). Architecture of Microcomputer Distributed Database Systems. M.Sc. Thesis, University of Toronto.

## 1.8 General System Description

MRS is a useful tool for relational applications. It is a small, powerful, integrated tool for real databases.

## 2 <u>DATABASE</u> <u>CONSTITUENTS</u>

### 2.1 <u>General</u> <u>Description</u>

| System Term | Feature Catalogue Term |
|---|---|
| database | database |
| relation (table) | relation |
| tuple | tuple |
| attribute | attribute |
| attribute name | attribute name |
| attribute type | attribute type |

### 2.2 <u>Database</u>

### 2.2.1 <u>Database</u> <u>Structure</u>

A database is described by the name of the operating system directory in which it resides. It consists of the data directory, the relations and their associated indices.

## 2.2.2 Database Operations

The following operations are available for dealing with a database: create a database directory; list the names of all relations in a database; perform backup and recovery via single commands; and change the security (access) to the database.

These are performed by "mkmrsdb", "display", "backup", "restore", and "protect", respectively.

Examples:

```
mkmrsdb DATA      (create an MRS database directory called DATA)
display table;    (list all relations in the database directory)
backup DATA       (perform backup)
restore DATA      (perform restore)
protect DATA      (make the database totally private)
```

## 2.2.3 Database Constraints

Constraints are not supported.

## 2.2.4 Additional Database Properties

## 2.3 Relation

### 2.3.1 Relation Structure

A relation is identified by a (unique) entry in the data directory of the database.  Alias names are not allowed.  A relation is a collection (table) of tuples; duplicate tuples are allowed.  The order of attributes is used only on database queries which do not specify an alternate order.

### 2.3.2 Relation Operations

The following operations are available for dealing with relations:  defining and creating a relation;  deleting a relation;  displaying the attributes of a relation; qualified or unqualified selection from a relation;  performing joins; and performing "bulk" insertion, updates, and deletion.

Examples:

```
create table movies
            (movie_name char(30),year_made numeric,director char(20))
create table actors
            (film char(30), actor_name char(20));
drop table movies;
display table movies;
select from movies;
select from movies where year_made > 1978;
select director,year_made from movies,actors
            where movie_name=film  and actor_name=director;
insert intomovies from 'moviefile';
update movies set year_made=1979;
delete from movies where movie_name='Superman';
```

2.3.3 <u>Relation</u> <u>Constraints</u>

2.3.4 <u>Additional</u> <u>Properties</u> <u>of</u> <u>Relations</u>

2.4 <u>Views</u>

Views are not supported.

2.4.1 <u>View</u> <u>Structure</u>

2.4.2 <u>View</u> <u>Operations</u>

2.4.3 <u>View</u> <u>Constraints</u>

2.4.4 <u>Additional</u> <u>Properties</u> <u>of</u> <u>Views</u>

2.5 <u>Tuple</u>

## 2.5.1 Tuple Structure

A tuple is a collection of attribute values.


## 2.5.2 Tuple Operations

The following operations are available for dealing with tuples: inserting; updating; and deleting. Implicit operations are available for existence testing and equality testing.

Examples:

> **insert into** movies: ['Coming Home',1978,'Warren Beatty'];
> update movies **set** director='Warren Beatty';
> delete from movies **where** year_made <= 1970;


## 2.5.3 Tuple Constraints


## 2.5.4 Additional Properties of Tuples

There is an exclusive tuple-oriented interface, the interactive subsystem. Tuples are addressed implicitly.

Examples:

> MRS prompts are in **boldface**; entries by the user are in roman type.
>
> insert into movies;
> **movie_name:** Coming Home
> **year_made:** 1979
> **director:**        Hal Ashby
> **>>>READY** .e
>
> **movie_name:** Heaven Can Wait
> **year_made:** 1987
> **director:** .↑
> **year_made:** 1987 1978
> **director:** Warren Beatty

```
>>>READY   .d
movie_name: Heaven Can Wait
year_made: 1978
director: Warren Beatty
>>>READY   .e

movie_name: New York
year_made: 1980
director:        Woody Allen
>>>READY   .>movie_name
movie_name: New York Manhattan
>>>READY   .e

movie_name: .q

Number of tuples entered = 3
*update movies set movie_name,year_made
              where movie_name = 'Manhattan';

movie_name: Manhattan
year_made: 1980 1979
>>>READY   .e
Number of tuples updated = 1
*
```

## 2.6 Attribute

### 2.6.1 Attribute Structure

An attribute is a component of a relation identified by a  (unique)  name  and
domain.   An  attribute  value  is  a component of a tuple with a value of the
corresponding domain.   Alias names cannot be defined.   The attribute names are
inserted   into   the   data   directory   at   the time the relation is defined and
created.

## 2.6.2 Attribute Operations

The following attribute operations are available:

> < <= = >= > ¬=
>
> MATCH    (full pattern matching)
>
> Inclusion in sets of values derived from other relations
>
> COUNT, MAX, MIN, UNIQUE

There are no coersion rules.  Attribute operations are only allowed on  attributes of the same domain.

Examples:

```
select from movies
            where year_made>= 1975;
select max year_made from movies;
select count frommovies;
select min year_made from movies,actors
            where movie_name=film and
            actor_name='Jane Fonda' ;
select unique film from actors;
```

## 2.6.3 Attribute Constraints

2.6.4 <u>Additional</u> <u>Properties</u> <u>of</u> <u>Attributes</u>

2.7 <u>Domain</u>

2.7.1 <u>Domain</u> <u>Structure</u>

Two domains are supported: the NUMERIC domain of integers; and the CHAR domain
of variable-length character strings.  A NULL value is a special value in each
of these domains.

Examples:

**create table** movies
                (movie_name **char**(30), director **char**(20), year_made **numeric**));

2.7.2 <u>Domain</u> <u>Operations</u>

2.7.3 <u>Domain</u> <u>Constraints</u>

2.7.4 <u>Additional</u> <u>Properties</u> <u>of</u> <u>Domains</u>

## 2.8 <u>Additional</u> <u>Database</u> <u>Constituents</u>

An additional database consitituent is the index, a  mechanism  for  improving
the performance of some database operations.  An  index on an attribute may be
created or deleted by the user with a single command, but its physical  structure, maintenance, and use by the database management system is entirely transparent to him.

Examples:

```
create index years on movies (year_made);
create index films on actors(films);
```

## 3 <u>FUNCTIONAL CAPABILITIES</u>

### 3.1 <u>Qualification</u>

The qualification is an English-like predicate calculus expression with predicate joined by AND and OR connectives. The expression is applied to each
tuple in the specified relations.

Examples:

>     **where** year_made=1978 **or** year_made=1980;
>     **where** year_made=1979 **and** director='Hal Ashby';

### 3.1.1 <u>Restriction</u>

Restrictions are expressed by predicates which are comparisons of attributes
to constants or attributes to attributes. The standard six conditionals are
used (< <= = >= > ¬=), as well as ¢match' which is a general pattern matching
conditional. Only values of the same type may be compared.

Examples:

>     **select from** movies
>                 **where** year_made=1978 **or** year_made=1980;
>     **select from** movies
>                 **where** year_made=1979 **and** director='Hal Ashby';

## 3.1.2 Quantification

Quantification is implicit in that the qualification is applied to each tuple in the specified relations.

## 3.1.3 Set Operations

## 3.1.4 Joining

Two relations can be joined at the same time, but a relation is not allowed to be joined to itself. Joining attributes need not have special properties. Joining is implicit with the qualification operating on more than one relation. The truth-valued expression in this case is applied to each tuple in the Cartesian product of the relations. The general Cartesian product is restricted to the required join by including a predicate in the expression relating attributes from each of the two relations. This mechanism allows a general join including equi joins and natural joins.

Examples:

```
        select actor_name from movies,actors
                    where movie_name=film and year_made > 1975;
        select year_made,actor_name from movies,actors
                    where movie_name=film
                    and actor_name match 'Warren Beatty';

        select from movies,actors where
                    movie_name = film and actor_name = 'Jane Fonda';
```

### 3.1.5 Nesting and Closure

A third type of predicate is used for nesting. This compares an attribute to a set of values of the same type obtained by a projection on the qualified tuples of a relation. The comparison is whether the attribute value is in the obtained set or not.

Examples:

```
where movie_name in select movie_name  from  movies
           where director match 'Hal Ashby';
```

### 3.1.6 Additional Aspects of Qualification


### 3.2 Retrieval and Presentation


### 3.2.1 Database Queries

Queries are expressed by SELECT statements. They allow projection and functional operations on qualified tuples.

Examples:

```
select from movies;
```

produces output of the form:

| movie_name | year_made | director |
|---|---|---|
| Coming Home | 1978 | Hal Ashby |
| Superman | 1979 | Richard Donner |
| Heaven Can Wait | 1978 | Warren Beatty |

```
select year_made from movies;
```

produces output of the form:

year_made

```
1978
1980
1979
1980
1979
1975
1978
1977
1980
```

**select unique** year_made **from** movies;

produces output of the form:

year_made

```
1977
1978
1980
```

## 3.2.2 Retrieval of Information About Database Constituents

The DISPLAY TABLE command allows the user to find out the names of all relations in the database. It also allows him to find out attribute names,
tuples, and other relevant information for a named relation. In general, this
command interacts with the other facilities through the mechanism of operating
system commands and files.

Examples:

**display table;**

produces the output:

******* TABLES *******

    movies
    actors

**display table movies;**

produces the output:

******** movies ********       LENGTH =  16     FIELDS = 3

movie_name      CHAR (30)

```
year_made      NUMERIC
director       CHAR (20)
```

### 3.2.3 Retrieval of System Performance Data

### 3.2.4 Report Generation

### 3.2.5 Constraints and Limitations

### 3.2.6 Additional Aspects of Retrieval and Presentation

## 3.3 Alteration

### 3.3.1 Insert Facilities

The insertion operation adds a tuple to a relation. All unspecified attribute values are set to NULL. A given attribute value must match the specified type for that attribute. There are two modes of insertion. The English-like insert allows the direct insertion of a tuple without prompting. The interactive insert allows for the successive insertion of multiple tuples. It prompts for each attribute value with the name of the corresponding attribute, and requests the user to confirm the insertion. It incorporates many useful features, such as the ability to back up to the last attribute value entered and alter it, display the attribute values before entering, change any named attribute value, and re-promt on errors.

Examples:

English-like insertion:

**insert into** movies:

```
                        ['Coming Home',1978,'Hal Ashby'];
        insert into movies (year_made,actor_name)
                        [1978,'Jane Fonda'];
```

Interactive (the prompt is <u>italic</u>):

```
*insert into movies;
movie name: 'Coming Home'
year made: 1978
director: 'Hal Ashby'
>>>READY: .e

movie name: 'Heaven Can Wait'
year made: 1987
director: 'Warren Beatty'
>>>READY: .>year_made
year made: 1987 1978
>>>>READY:  .d
movie name: Heaven can Wait
year made: 1978
director: Warren Beatty
>>>>READY  .e
```

## 3.3.2 <u>Delete</u> <u>Facilities</u>

The deletion operation deletes qualified tuples from a relation. There are two modes of deletion. The English-like delete allows the direct deletion of a set of qualified tuples without prompting. The interactive delete (update) presents each attribute value of each qualified tuple with the name of the corresponding attribute and requests the user to confirm the deletion.

Examples:

English-like delete:

```
delete from movies where
                director match 'Warren Beatty';
```

Interactive:

```
update movieswhere director match 'Warren Beatty';
movie name: Heaven Can Wait
year made: 1978
director: Warren Beatty
>>>>READY   .x
```

<u>Number of tuples deleted</u> = <u>1</u>

### 3.3.3 Modify Facilities

The update operation updates qualified tuples of a relation. There are two modes of update. The English-like update allows the direct update of a set of qualified tuples by storing, without prompting, the specified attribute values into the corresponding attributes. The interactive update prompts for each attribute value of each qualified tuple with the name of the corresponding attribute, as well as the original value, and requests the user to confirm the update.

Examples:

English-like update:

**update** movies **set** year_made = 1978
                    **where** actor_name **match** 'Warren Beatty';

Interactive:

**update** movies;
<u>movie name</u>: <u>Heaven Can Wait</u>
<u>year made</u>: <u>1987</u>   1978
<u>director</u>: <u>Warren Beatty</u>
>>> <u>READY</u>: <u>.d</u>
<u>movie name</u>: <u>Heaven Can Wait</u>
<u>year made</u>: <u>1978</u>
<u>director</u>: <u>Warren Beatty</u>
>>> <u>READY</u>: <u>.c</u>

<u>Number of tuples updated</u> = <u>1</u>

### 3.3.4 Commit and Undo Facilities

### 3.3.5 Additional Alteration Facilities

### 3.4 Additional Functional Capabilities

### 3.4.1 Arithmetic and String Operations

### 3.4.2 Sorting

A general-purpose sort capability is available using the MRS/operating  system interface.  The order will be preserved until the next alteration operation.

Examples:

```
into 'movie_list' select director,year_made from movies;
do 'sort movie_list';
```

### 3.4.3 Library Functions

The following functions are supported:

MAX       selects the largest value of the specified attribute

MIN       selects the smallest value of the specified attribute

COUNT     shows how many tuples satisfied the selection

UNIQUE    sorts tuples and removes duplicates

Examples:

```
select max year_made from  movies;
```

produces the output:

**Maximum value = 1980**

```
select min year_made from movies;
```

produces the output:

**Minium value = 1971**

```
select count from movies;
```

produces the output:

**Number of tuples retreived = 8**

```
select unique year_made from movies;
```

produces the output:

**year_made**

```
1971
1975
1978
1979
1980
```

3.4.4 <u>User</u>-<u>Defined</u> <u>Functions</u>

3.4.5 <u>Transactions</u>

3.4.6 <u>Multi</u>-<u>Tuple</u> <u>Alterations</u>

3.4.7 <u>Grouping</u>

3.4.8 <u>Exception</u> <u>Handling</u> <u>Mechanisms</u>

If a command is in error, MRS rejects it and preserves the state of the database.  User-defined triggers are not supported.

3.4.9 <u>Additional</u> <u>Functional</u> <u>Capabilities</u>

## 4 DEFINITION, GENERATION AND ADMINISTRATION FACILITIES

### 4.1 Definition Facilities

There are no separate facilities for the definition and generation of database constituents.  Defining a shema automatically results in creation, and creation automatically results in definition.

### 4.1.1 Constituents of a Database Definition

A database definition consists of a series of commands defining the  relations in  a  database and the indices for these relations.  Each relation definition defines the attributes and domains.  The database definition is stored in  the database directory.

### 4.1.2 Database Definition

Examples:

```
        create table movies
                (movie_name char(30),
                year_made numeric,
                director char(20));

        create table actors
                (film char(30),
                actor_name char(20));

        create index years on movies(year_made);
        create index actors on actors(actor_name);
```

There are no inherent limits to the number of relations.

### 4.1.3 Relation Definition

A relation is defined by the "create table" command.

Examples:

```
create table movies
        (movie_name char(30),
         year_made numeric),
         director char(20));
```

There are no inherent limits to the number of attributes and the order of definition. Keys are not supported.

### 4.1.4 View Definition

### 4.1.5 Tuple Definition

A tuple is defined by its relation. See 4.1.3.

### 4.1.6 Attribute Definition

An attribute is defined at relation definition time when it is given a name and a domain. See 4.1.3.

### 4.1.7 Domain Definition

There are two domain types:

> CHAR(n)
>
> and
>
> NUMERIC

See section 4.1.3.

### 4.1.8 Definition of Additional Database Constituents

### 4.2 Generation Facilities

### 4.2.1 Constituents of a Database Generation

All constituents of a database may be created, destroyed, added, or deleted dynamically. A database is generated when the relations comprising it are defined. The database directory, which is initialized by a separate process, is automatically updated.

## 4.2.2 Generation of Database Constituents

The database directory is generated with the "mkmrsdb" command. Relations, attributes, and domains are generated with the "create table" command. Indices are generated with the "create index" command. Tuples may be loaded with a bulk insertion command.

Examples:

```
mkmrsdb DATA                creates database directory called "DATA"
create table movies(...)    creates relation,attributes, domains
create index years
    on movies(year_made)    creates index on relation "movies"
insert into movies
    from 'movie_list'       bulk insertion of tuples from prepared list
```

## 4.3 Database Redefinition

All constituents of a database can be dynamically re-defined by  deleting  the old  definition  and creating a new one.  Tuples may be dumped into a file and reloaded.

## 4.3.1 Renaming Database Constituents

### 4.3.2 <u>Redefining</u> <u>Database</u> <u>Constituents</u>

### 4.4 <u>Database</u> <u>Regeneration</u> <u>and</u> <u>Reorganization</u>

See section 4.3.

### 4.5 <u>Data</u> <u>Dictionary</u>

A data dictionary (data directory) is maintained for each database.  It stores
the  database schema, relations, attributes, and domains.  It supports queries
on the schema.

# 5 INTERFACES AND DATABASE MANAGEMENT SYSTEM ARCHITECTURE

## 5.1 System Architecture

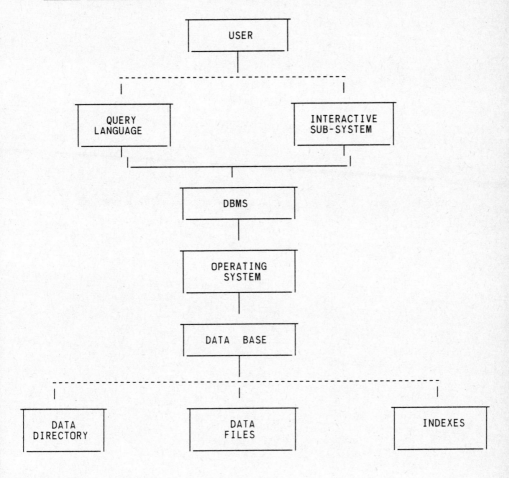

## 5.2 Interface Descriptions

1.      Query Language / Data Base

2       Interactive Subsystem / Data Base


### 5.2.1 Query Language

The query language is based on SQL and designed for use by users of minimal experience. The user perception of the database is a set of tables.

### 5.2.2 Interactive Subsystem

The Interactive subsystem is based on user tastes and designed for use by users with no experience. The user perception of the database is one tuple of a relation at a time. The subsystem allows manipulation of attribute values within a tuple.

# 6 OPERATIONAL ASPECTS

## 6.1 Security

### 6.1.1 Access Control

MRS uses the capabilities of the file protection/access scheme provided by the operating system. In general, relations are readable but non-modifiable by others. A user may change any database or relation belonging to him to be modifiable (full access), or non-readable (full security) by others, or any combination.

### 6.1.2 Capabilities

## 6.2 Physical Security

### 6.2.1 Concurrency Control

### 6.2.2 Crash Recovery

The database may be backed up and restored at the user's command.

### 6.3 Operating Environment

### 6.3.1 Software Environment (Operating System)

MRS has been designed as an integrated tool within the operating system environment. It makes use of the operating system, its utilities, and other programs to enhance its capabilities.

MRS is written in the "C" language with the Query Language parser written in "YACC". It is portable within Mini-UNIX and UNIX environments.

### 6.3.2 Hardware Environment (CPU, Memory, Peripherals)

As MRS is portable within the Mini-UNIX and UNIX family, it has been run on many combinations of PDP-11 processors and disks.

CPU:        LSI-11, LSI-11/23, PDP-11/05, PDP-11/10,  PDP-11/34,  PDP-11/40,
            PDP-11/44, PDP-11/45, PDP-11/50, PDP-11/70, etc.

Disk:       From double-density, dual drive floppy disks up  to  large  hard
            disks.

# 7 ESSENTIALLY RELATIONAL SOLUTIONS FOR GENERAL DATABASE MANAGEMENT SYSTEM PROBLEMS

## 7.1 Advantages

Since it is based on sets, the query language is easily understood by non-database people. We have trained many such in a remarkably short period of time. The query language is reasonably clear in its concepts and may be used as the basis of many forms of interaction with the database.

The query language allows commands to be packaged and executed as a unit, thus creating a custom high-level user-oriented command based system. The natural "table-like" format can be easily integrated with other programs to build pro-totypes and applications with speed and flexibility.

## 7.2 Disadvantages

A single table has been found to be a natural concept for many "non-computer" users. However, the concept of a join and the various join operations are a much more difficult set of concepts. Users in general prefer to deal with only one table rather than using joins. Thus, applications have been packaged to look like a single table, even if the underlying structure consists of several tables and joins.

## 8 <u>DATABASE</u> <u>APPLICATIONS</u> <u>USING</u> <u>THE</u> <u>SYSTEM</u>

MRS has been distributed internationally to over 50 Universities, Colleges, and commercial organizations (see 8.1). its extensive distribution,abases, it has become impossible to keep track of all applications. However, some typi-cal uses at the University of Toronto include:

ATHENIANS:    Historical/Social database of noted ancient Athenians

CRABS:        Computerized Reprint and Bibliographic System

DISTRIB:      Records of software distributions

MES:          Mark Entry System -- extensive system for keeping track of stu-dent marks

MRS has been closely involved in other research projects at the Computer Sys-tems Research Group, and has become an integral part of such packages as OFS (Office Form System), for form manipulations, and TLA, an office procedure specification and information package with a form system interface. OFS and TLA are also distributed by C.S.R.G.

3.7   Feature Analysis Of NOMAD


Feature Analysis of Relational Concepts,
Languages and Systems for
NOMAD and NOMAD2 (*)


by
Daniel R. Ries


Computer Corporation of America
575 Technology Square
Cambridge, Massachusetts 02139


October 1980


(*) Prepared  while  the  author  was  at  Lawrence  Livermore
Laboratory.

Feature Analysis of Relational Concepts, Languages and Systems for

NOMAD$^{TM}$ and NOMAD2$^{TM}$

Prepared by:

Daniel R. Ries
October, 1980

FORWARD

This report was prepared for inclusion in a Feature Catalogue of Relational Concepts, Languages and Systems being prepared by the Relational Database Task Group of ANSI/X3/SPARC - Database Systems Study Group. The format and content of the report are based on the Working Paper RTG-80-81 of the relational database task group. This report compares NOMAD/NOMAD2 to the terms and definitions of that paper and not to other commercial products.

NOTICE

$^{TM}$NOMAD and NOMAD2 are registered trademarks of National CSS, Inc.

.0    INTRODUCTION

    1.1    Name of System:  NOMAD, Release 6

           Available From:  National CSS, Inc.
                          187 Danbury Road
                          Wilton, Connecticut 06897

    1.2    Status

        1.2.1  System

             Current System:  NOMAD, Release 6 has been available since

             May 1978.

             NOMAD2 is available in July, 1980.

        1.2.2  Applications

             NOMAD is suitable for and used in an extremely wide
variety of applications.  There are no inherent limitations
on the total size of the applications except the machine
limitations on the System NOMAD is running on.

    1.3    Database System Background

             The NOMAD database management system was initially released
in 1974.  The system is independent of any particular class of
systems and is not based on any other particular system.

    1.4    Overall Philosophy

             NOMAD was developed to provide users of National CSS, Inc.'s
timesharing services with a database management system.  The creators
of the system saw a strong need for a report writer which could
produce reports from different records.  Both hierarchial and
normalized records could be combined using relational joining type
operators.  Furthermore, the developers of the system saw the need

to allow the output of such reports to be stored in a format
suitable for further reports in the database.

## 1.5 Essentially Relational Characteristics

NOMAD can be used as a fully relational system.  It supports
a data sublanguage which can perform the functions of the relational
algebra without using iteration or recursion.  NOMAD supports several
different join operators.  Note that in the data sublanguage, a sequence
of high level, set oriented commands may have to be used to achieve the
power of the relational algebra.  In particular, the 'join' commands
cannot be arbitrarily nested.  Instead these commands can be used to
create other relations which can then be used in subsequent commands.
The details on the nesting are described in Section 2.1.5.

NOMAD does support other features which allow the user to
define some database constituents which are not purely relational.
For example, hierarchial records are permitted and table-lookup
operations dependent on an access method can be defined.  Note that
users are allowed to design and use a database  without using any of
the hierarchial features.

## 1.6 Interfaces

NOMAD supports three interfaces to the database:

1)  Command Level Interface - A command at a time is
    interactively entered to the system.

2)  Procedure Interface - The above commands can be combined
    with conditional and looping instructions.

3)  Programming Language Interface.  The NOMAD database can
    be referenced from FORTRAN, COBOL, PL/1 or BAL programs
    through a subroutine call mechanism.

The first Interface is the most general and supports the following capabilities:

(1)  Data Schema Definition

(2)  Query Language

(3)  Database Altering

(4)  Constraint Definition

(5)  Database Generation and Regeneration

(6)  Database Schema Redefinition and Re-naming

(7)  Report Generation

(8)  Data Entry

(9)  Database Security

(10)  Database Utilities

(11)  Storage Structure Definition

(12)  Database Dictionary

(13)  A special purpose language

The Procedure and Programming Language interface can issue all of the commands in the command level interface and can thus perform all of the capabilities mentioned above.  The distinctions between the three interfaces are discussed in Section 5.0.  In Sections 2., 3. and 4., only the command level interfaces will be discussed.  Note that interfaces can be used in on-line or batch modes.

1.7   Documentation

1)  NOMAD Reference Manual

Form 1004-2, November, 1979

2)  "NOMAD2 features and capabilities"

Form 1004Y, May, 1980

3)  "Examples of NOMAD As a Relational Database System"
Daniel D. McCracken, April 17, 1979

1.8   General System Description

NOMAD is available through National CSS, Inc.'s time sharing
service.  Alternately, customers can obtain NOMAD on IBM compatible
computer systems that run National CSS Operating Systems and on
National CSS's mini-computers.

Some of the features available in NOMAD2 that are not in NOMAD
include statistical analysis routines that take data from the database,
perform analysis and optionally return that data in a form usable by
NOMAD.  In addition, basic data types such as arrays are allowed.

2.0   DATABASE CONSTITUENTS

The NOMAD system does not put bounds on what is considered 'one'
database.  Instead, NOMAD uses the term 'Database' to refer to a single
relation or a set or relations defined at one time.  Note that the relational operators can be used across these 'Databases' by having several
open databases.  In the discussion, a 'set of databases' will mean what is
normally meant by a relational database.

2.1   General Description

The constituents of a NOMAD 'set of databases' are:

1)  Databases - contain one or more, possibly unnormalized
or hierarchial relations called 'MASTERS'.

2)  Masters - contain one or more 'segments'.  If multiple
segments are present in a Master, they must be arranged
in a hierarchy.   Only the top level segments are called
'MASTERS'.

3)  Segments - contain one or more attributes which are called
'items'.

4)  Master/Segment Instance - One tuple with values in some

of the items.

     5)   Item - the attributes of a Master/Segment.

NOMAD does not support the basic concept of user defined Domains except
as the fundamental types supported by the system (See Section 2.6).
However, a 'member' constraint (see Section 2.6.1) can be used to
restrict the set of possible values of an item.  In addition, the 'limit'
constraint (see Section 2.6.3) can be used to restrict the range of
possible values of an item.

## 2.2   Database

### 2.2.1  Database Structures

At the schema level, relations can be added to the set
of databases by using a 'SCHEMA' command.  A schema can be
named and can include other schemas and one or more hierarchial
or normalized Masters.  Note that the "Set of Databases" is
unnamed.  The 'DBADD' command can be used in a SCHEMA to logically
group a set of related databases into one SCHEMA.

### 2.2.2  Constraints

The database schemas can be defined with zero or more
passwords to control access to the database.  These passwords
are combined with schema procedures to control access to con-
stituants within a database.

## 2.3   Master (=F.C. Relation)/Segment (=F.C. Relation)

### 2.3.1  Master Structure

A master is thought of as a hierarchial or normalized
relation.  A master is named and can have an access method
specified.  If the master is hierarchial, it is composed of
segments which are composed of items.  If the master is normalized,
it is composed directly of items.  An alias name can be given
as a master or a segment.

2.3.2  Master Operations

Masters can be created in two ways.  A Master can be created by defining a schema.  Secondly, a Master can be dynamically created and populated as the output of selection, projection and joining operations on other Masters.  Such implicitly created Masters can be used in retrieval operations, but cannot be updated via NOMAD commands.  Note that operations on a hierarchial Master are made equivalent to the normalized expansion of the segments, (i.e. the items in higher level segments are repeated).

2.3.3  Master Constraints

Masters (and Segments) can be constrained in several ways.  A key can be declared for the Master as for each segment and that key can be given a Unique/Not unique parameter. NOMAD enforces the uniqueness.

Retrieval procedures (RPROCs) and Update Procedures (UPROCs) can be used to define a boolean expression which must be true for the Master/Segment instances in the database. The boolean expression can contain items in the master and reference a password number which indicates that a given password must have been used to allow instances to be retrieved or updated. Note that items in a segment can be defined across database and master boundries so that the logical expression can in fact involve many masters.  Violations on these constraints are treated as errors and simply reported to the user.

2.4  Views

Views are not explicitly supported in NOMAD.  However, new schemas and subschemas can be defined which have masters based on items from other masters, creating in effect a dynamic view.  Also, new databases can be created from selection, projection and joining operations and these new databases are in effect, static views.

## 2.5   Master/Segment Instances (=F.C. tuple)

### 2.5.1   Tuple Structure

The definition of a tuple is given in the definition of a Master/Segment.  Missing values are allowed in attributes and are given the default value 'NOT AVAILABLE'.  Note that NOT AVAILABLE is different than zero or blank.

### 2.5.2   Master/Segment Instance Operations

Individual instances of a Master/Segment can be obtained with logical and directional comments.  The logical commands are LOCATE (with a boolean expression) and KEYED.  Directional commands include NEXT, PREVIOUS, FIRST, LAST. STEP, TOP.  The logical and directional commands can be freely intermixed. Instances in the database can be inserted, deleted, modified and printed.

### 2.5.3   Tuple Constraints

Constraints are defined with the Master/Segment.

## 2.6   Item (=F.C. Attribute)

### 2.6.1   Item Structure

Items can be named, with aliases, and must be one of the primary internal data types:  4 byte   Real, 8 Byte Real, 2 byte integer, 4 Byte integer, 1 to 256 byte character field, 1 to 15 byte packed decimal field.  In addition, a variety of 'NAME' and 'DATE' types are supported.

Items are defined with a display format, and optionally a heading and internal format.

Items can be defined with table look-up options to extract values for printing (DISPLAY), store values (ENCODE) and check for membership (MEMBER) using values in other Masters in the same schema.  The use of these table look-up options are restricted to keyed fields in other Masters.

Items can also be dynamically defined to be an expression involving other items in the Master.

### 2.6.2  Item Operations

Items can be compared if they are either numeric or alpha numeric for equality, not equality, less than, etc. Dates can also be compared.  Character strings can be operated on with substring and other string manipulation operators. Numeric values can be operated on with the normal arithmetic operators.  Special functions are provided to add/subtract months and years to dates.

### 2.6.3  Item Constraints

The Master/Segment constraints can be used to constrain items.  In addition, Limits and Character String templates or masks can be specified when defining items.  In addition, ENCIPHER options are provided to encode/decode data based on user specified keywords.

## 2.7  Domain

Not applicable.

## 3.0  FUNCTIONAL CAPABILITIES

In this section, four Masters will be used to illustrate the functional capabilities on NOMAD.  The Masters are:

1)  S     -   the supplier with items

   SNO   -   the supplier number

   SNAME -   the supplier name

   STATUS

   CITY

2) P        -     the parts with items

   PNO      -     the part number

   PNAME    -     the part name

   COLOR

   WEIGHT

   CITY

   COST

3) SP       -     the supply with items

   SNO      -     the supplier number

   PNO      -     the part number

   QTY      -     the quantity

4) C        -     the components with items

   PNO      -     the part number

   ICMP     -     the immediate components of PNO

In NOMAD commands, the names of items can be used by themselves if the names are unique in the database (or 'open databases'). If the names are not unique, a 'FROM mastername' can precede the item names.

3.1   Qualification

The NOMAD qualification is calculus oriented and the results of the qualification are broken into 'By-items' and 'Object-items'. The By-items dictate the sorting and grouping of the Object-items. The results of the qualifications are either the automatic input to the next command, a printed report, or a new database master file.

3.1.1  Restriction

NOMAD supports the following simple conditionals:

$<$, $>$, $=$, $<=$, $>$, $=$, $>>$, $><$, $>=$.  Mnemonic equivalents

(LT, GT, etc) can also be used.  Items (Attributed) can be compared with constants, expressions and other Items.

These comparators can be used between all numeric types (automatic coercion), between alphanumeric types, between date types and/or name types.

Special comparators include: AMONG, BETWEEN and CONTAINS. The first two can be used on either numeric or alphanumeric data.  The last operator can be used only on alphanumeric data. Arithmetic operators can also be used on date data types.

NOMAD supports the following logical connectors:  AND, OR, XOR, NOT, IMPLIES, EQUIVALENCE.

These operators are combined to form a logical expression which  is applied  to each tuple in the master.  Projection is done automatically by naming items in the By-items or Object-items.  Selection in NOMAD has three flavors:

1)    SELECT logical-expression.  This command applies
      a restriction to the tuples in a MASTER which will
      be considered in the following NOMAD commands.
      For example,

          SELECT FROM S STATUS = 10

          COMMAND1

          COMMAND2

      would cause COMMANDs 1 and 2 to apply to S tuples
      which had a status of 10.  Note SELECTS can be cleared,
      reset and/or nested.  Also note that the 'FROM S' command
      is optional since 'STATUS' is a unique item name in the
      database.

2)    WHERE logical-expression.  The where clause is used to
      restrict tuples that are being listed or output to
      another master.  For example:

List . . . where COLOR = 'RED' would list
only the red part.  The 'where' condition is in
effect only for the duration of the command.

3)     IF logical-expression.  The If clause is very
similar to the where clause.  The distinction
is not relevant to this analysis.

## 3.1.2  Quantification

NOMAD does not explicitly support universal quantification.
Instead 'COUNT' and group by operators can be used to obtain
the quantification results.

## 3.1.3  Set Operations

1)     UNION between two masters can be achieved by
creating an 'external' NOMAD file from one of
the masters and loading that file into the other
master.  For example:

```
CREATE FROM MASTER:  ITEM1...ITEMN ON FILE1
LOAD MASTER2 READ FILE1
```

2)     INTERSECTION, DIFFERENCE, AND EXTENDED CARTESIAN
PRODUCT are achieved through the joining operations
described in Section 3.1.4.

## 3.1.4  Joining

NOMAD supports six flavors of joining operations.  We
first review these operators and then discuss NOMADs solutions
to the joining of a relation with itself.

The format of a NOMAD join is as follows:

{BY by-items} object-items $\left[\begin{array}{l} \text{EXTRACT} \\ \text{SUBSET} \\ \text{REJECT} \\ \text{MERGE} \\ \text{EXTRACT ALL} \\ \text{SUBSET ALL} \end{array}\right]$ {MATCHING m-items} object-items

These matching (joining) operations are basically 'equijoins' based on equal values between the by-items of one MASTER (=RELATION) and the m-items of the other MASTER (=RELATION). The six operations are discussed in turn for the following command:

$\left[\begin{array}{l} \text{LIST} \\ \text{CREATE} \end{array}\right]$ BY FROM P PNO PNAME    OP    MATCHING FROM SP PNO QTY....

=EXTRACT    -    This command results in each tuple in P together with the first (if any) tuple from SP with a matching PNO. Those tuples in P with no corresponding tuple in SP are included in the result but with a 'not available' value for QTY.

OP=SUBSET    -    This command results in the same tuples as 'EXTRACT' except that only the tuples from P that have corresponding SP tuples are included. Note that each tuple in P can still occur at most once in the result.

OP=REJECT    -    For this clause, the item QTY should not
be present.  The results of the create are
all of the tuples in P that have no corresponding tuples in SP, i.e. the parts that
aren't supplied.  Note that this operator
can be used to implement a set difference
operator.

OP=MERGE     -    This operation creates one tuple for each
tuple in P as does the EXTRACT operator.
In addition, each tuple in SP that has no
corresponding tuple in P generates one
tuple in the result.

OP=EXTRACT ALL - This operation is similar to the EXTRACT.
Each tuple in P contributes to one or more
tuples in the output master.  If $n(\geq 1)$
tuples in SP correspond to a tuple in P,
the tuple in P appears n times, each time
with the appropriate QTY.

OP=SUBSET ALL  - This operation corresponds to the mathematical
definition of a relational join.  Tuples
appear in the output master if and only if
the joining value is in both P and SP.

Notes:

1)    The 'by-items' are all included in the output
Master.  The 'matching-items' are not.  If there
are name conflicts in the object lists, a 'NAMED'
clause can be used to rename the item.

2)    A MASTER can be joined with itself.  For example,

LIST BY PNO FROM C REJECT MATCHING ICMP;

Lists those parts that have components but are
not themselves components.

3) The internal type of a 'by-item' must be the same
as the internal type of the corresponding 'matching-
item'.  However, a temporary new-item can be
defined by:

DEFINE IN MASTER NEWITEM AS FORMAT EXP = ITEM;

the new-item format can be used to control the
internal type and new-item can be used as a by or
matching item.

4) Multiple items can be specified as by-items and
matching items by repeating the key words 'BY'
and 'MATCHING' respectively.

5) One LIST or CREATE command can have multiple
matching operators if all of the joins are to be
done on the same matching items.  For example:

CREATE (BY PNO FROM SP SUBSET MATCHING PNO FROM P

PNAME) SUBSET ALL MATCHING ICMP PNO NAMED FRED;

will join these relations since the join between
any two relations is on the same item.

However, if one wanted to join S, SP, P with SNO
being the linking item between S and SP and
PNO being the link between SP and P; two commands
would have to be used:

                    CREATE BY SNO FROM S SNAME CITY SUBSET ALL

                         MATCHING SNO FROM SP PNO ON TEMP1;

                    CREATE BY PNO FROM TEMP1 SUBSET ALL MATCHING PNO

                         FROM P PNAME CITY NAMED PCITY;

### 3.1.5  Nesting and Closure

Projects and Selects that are within individual MASTERS
can be nested between the 'joining' operators.  However,
as illustrated in the previous section, the joining operators
cannot be arbitrarily nested.  Instead 'CREATES' must be
used to create intermediate masters.

All of the operations are closed though, in that a
CREATE can be used with any of the operators to generate a
new master (= relation).

### 3.1.6  Additional Aspects of Qualification

A 'LOCATE' or 'KEY' command can be used to move to a
particular record in the MASTER based on values in the MASTER.
This 'logical' movement through a MASTER is useful if the
MASTER is hierarchical in nature or in order to examine and/or
update individual MASTER records.  Note that these operations
can be issued through the command level interface.

## 3.2  Retrieval and Presentation

### 3.2.1  Database Queries

Queries are expressed by using the keyword 'LIST' together
with the qualification operators.

### 3.2.2  Retrieval of Information about Database Constituents

An SLIST (Schema List) command produces a schema like
description on masters, items, defined items, selects currently
in effect, user defined variables, and certain attributes of
named constituents.  The results of an SLIST can be stored

in a file and used with the selection and joining clauses.

3.2.3  Retrieval of System Performance Data

A utility DBCHK is provided which gives the storage utilization and blocking factors to indicate when a database should be reorganized.  Such reorganization is primarily for garbage collection of disk space created by deleting instances of MASTERS/SEGMENTS.

3.2.4  Report Generation

NOMAD has an extensive report generation facility.  The general format is:

LIST  [By-item1 By-item2...][object-item1 object-item2...]

The report is ordered by the BY items.  Sorting precedence is determined by the order of the items in the BY-list.  Column headings and formats are defined at schema definition time but can be over-ridden at command time.

The report writer supports the following features:

- Retrieval, sorting and automatic formatting of the report

- Report functions such as sums, averages, maximums, minimums.

- Totaling and subtotaling

- User-controlled formatting

- Computations in the report

- ACROSS (horizontal listing)

- Titling, footings, group headings

- Screening and selection of data to be included in the report.

- Disjoint reports for non-related items

- Joining of databases with relational operators

3.2.5 Constraints

See the MASTER and item constraints defined in Section 2.

## 3.3 Alterations

The Alterations to the data base are either through the command Language interface one tuple at a time, or through a bulk 'LOAD' facility. Note that either method can also be initiated through the procedural or programming language interfaces. Note that for 'LOAD' commands, 'file' can be a user created file or the output of a CREATE.

3.3.1 Insert Facilities

New masters can be inserted into the database by issuing new 'SCHEMA' commands. New items (=Attributes) can be inserted into a MASTER(=Relation) with a 'SCHEMA REORG' command.

New instances of a MASTER(=Tuples) can be inserted in several ways:

1) INSERT name item1= . . . item2= . . . ;
   to individually insert instances.

2) PROMPT name; NOMAD prompts for values for each item.

3) LOAD name READ file; to LOAD multiple instances.

If some of the items are not given values, they default to N/A (Not Available). If a violation of a 'UNIQUE KEY' defined in the schema occurs, the instance is not added and an 'ON UNIQUE' condition is raised. The user can specify the action to take if certain conditions arise.

### 3.3.2  Delete

Masters can be deleted from the database by deleting their definition in the containing schema.  Items can be deleted with a 'SCHEMA REORG' command.

Instances of a MASTER (= tuple) can be deleted by three methods:

1)    Position to a particular instance through a LOCATE, KEY, or directional statement.  Then DELETE name.

2)    SELECT logical expression.  Then DELETE name deletes all of the instances where the logical expressions were true.

3)    LOAD name ONMATCH delete READ file;  This command deletes all instances in name that have matching Key values in file.

### 3.3.3  Modify

Master and item definitions can be modified by a 'SCHEMA REORG' command.

Instances of MASTERS can be changed by three methods:

1)    Position to a MASTER.  CHANGE item1 = expression item2 =   .;  To change one instance.

2)    SELECT logical expression.  CHANGE item1 = expression ...  To change all of the tuples for which the logical expression is true.

3)    LOAD name ONMATCH CHANGE item1 item2...READ file. This command changes all instances in name that have matching KEY values in file.

### 3.3.4  Commit and UNDO

The system allows the user to issue the COMMAND SAVE

(=COMMIT) and/or RESTORE (=UNDO) a series of database alterations since the last SAVE or RESTORE. This feature can be bypassed with a 'SAVE ON' command or initiated with the 'SAVE OFF' command.

## 3.4 Additional Functional Capabilities

### 3.4.1 Arithmetic and String Operations

See Section 2

### 3.4.2 Sorting

During the SCHEMA definition time, KEYS can be specified for MASTERS and the MASTER is kept in sorted order on these keys.

During a LIST or CREATE, a 'BY clause' specifies the order of the tuples.

### 3.4.3 Library Defined Functions

AVERAGE, COUNT, NUMBER, FIRST, LAST, MAX, MEDIAN, MIN, STDDEV, SUM, UNIQUE, VAR are all supported.

### 3.4.4 User Defined Functions

The user can write FORTRAN or assemble functions which can be called from NOMAD. These functions can be used in derived item definitions.

### 3.4.6 Multi-tuple Alterations

These are supported. See Section 3.3

### 3.4.7 Grouping

The By-items in LIST and CREATE can be used to group instances of a MASTER. The BY items can be used with the Library functions to generate average salary by dept., etc.

### 3.4.8 Exception Handling Mechanisms

In the command level interface, the exceptions are reported to the terminal and/or to a file.

In the procedural interface, an 'ON condition' statement can be used to either generate a MESSAGE or execute a sequence of statements.

## 4.0 DEFINITION, GENERATION AND ADMINISTRATION FACILITIES

### 4.1 Definition Facilities

To define the sample database used in [DATE77], the following SCHEMA COMMAND can be given:

```
SCHEMA CJDATE;
MASTER SUPPLIER INSERT = KEYED(SNO, A);
        ITEM SNO        A2 ;
        ITEM SNAME      A5 ;
        ITEM STATUS     A2 ;
        ITEM SLOC       A6 ;
MASTER PART INSERT = KEYED(PNO, A);
        ITEM PNO        A2 ;
        ITEM PNAME      A5 ;
        ITEM COLOR      A5 ;
        ITEM WEIGHT     A2 ;
        ITEM PLOC       A6 ;
MASTER SHIPMENT INSERT = KEYED(SUPPNO, A, PARTNO, A);
        ITEM SUPPNO     A2 ;
        ITEM PARTNO     A2 ;
        ITEM QTY        99 ;
END;
```

### 4.1.1 Constituents of a Database Definition:

One NOMAD database, three MASTERs (= RELATION) and 12 items (= Attributes) are defined in the above schema.

4.1.2 Database Definition

The above example defines one database. Existing databases can be incorporated into this database at RUN time or
SCHEMA definition time by a 'DBADD' command. All master
names must be unique within one database.

4.1.3 MASTER (= RELATION) Definition

There are no specific limits on the number of items
permitted for one MASTER. Item names must be unique within
each segment in a MASTER. Thus if the MASTER is normalized
item names must be unique.

The 'KEYED' clause specifies that a MASTER will be
maintained in sorted order according to the values in the key.
Optionally, the key can be declared 'UNIQUE'.

Options for MASTERS include:

1)     ACCESS = opt - to specify whether READ/CREATE/
       CHANGE/DELETE can be used.

2)     ALIAS = name

3)     INSERT = Position

                   or

           KEYED (item1 $[^A_D]$,..., itemn $[^A_D]$, $[^{unique}_{notunique}]$)

4)     RPROC = rname
              :
       rname $\doteq$ logical expression

       to control read and insert access to a MASTER.

5)     UPROC = uname
              :
       uname $\doteq$ logical expression to control alterations

       of a MASTER.

4.1.4  View Definition

Dynamic views, where no actual Data is stored can be defined by the DEFINE command.

Creates two dynamic items in SUPPLY based on items in other MASTERS.  Note that PARTS and SUPPLIER must be KEYED and that only the 'First' SNAME for a given SNO would be used.  Thus this view mechanism does not allow the full power of the relational Algebra.

Static views can be generated by a 'CREATE' command and can thus use the full power of the NOMAD joining operators. See Section 3.1.4.

4.1.6  MASTER Instance (= Tuple) Definitions

See Section 3.3

4.1.7  Item  (= Attribute) Definition.

The general format of an item definition is:

ITEM item1 display-format [options];

The options include:

1) DISPLAY 'item2  FROM master1' to provide a table look up function using the value of name for outputing the item.  The MASTER must be 'KEYED' on item1, although the name can be different.

2) ENCODE 'item2 FROM master1' to provide a table look-up function on inputing values into the Relation.

3) MEMBER 'Master1' when a value is internal for item1, it is checked to make sure there is an instance in Master1 with a key equal to the value.

4) ALIAS = name.

5) LIMITS = n:m or (a, b, c, n:m, z) - for alphanemeric,

numeric, date, or name data types.

6) MASK = 'Literal' to specify a template for a character string.

i.e. MASK = 999-99-9999 for a Social Security Number.

7) ACCESS = options to specify READ/WRITE access permissions.

8) ENCIPHER/DECIPHER.

## 4.2 Generation Facilities

The SCHEMA commands can be given at any time from any of the interfaces. They can be intermixed with other NOMAD commands. For population of the database see Section 3.3.

## 4.3 Database Redefinition

### 4.3.1 Renaming Database Constituents

Item names, Aliases, and display formats, headings, limits, etc. can be changed with a 'SCHEMA CHECK' command.

### 4.3.2 Redefining Database Constituents

The internal formats of items, the number of items, the number of MASTERS can be changed with a 'SCHEMA REORG' option. Items can be added or deleted to MASTERS with this option. MASTERS can be added or deleted from a database with this option.

## 4.4 Database Regeneration and Reorganization

See Section 4.3.2. In general, reorganization is controlled by the user not the system.

## 4.5 Database Dictionary

An SLIST (Schema List) produces (prints as to a database readable file) descriptions of the database constituents:

mastername

itemname

MASTERS

DEFINES

SELECTS

SLIST can be used in the procedural interface to find the

schema definitions of an item.

5.0    INTERFACES AND DBMS ARCHITECTURE

5.1    <u>System Architecture</u>

NOMAD supports three interfaces as shown in Figure 1.

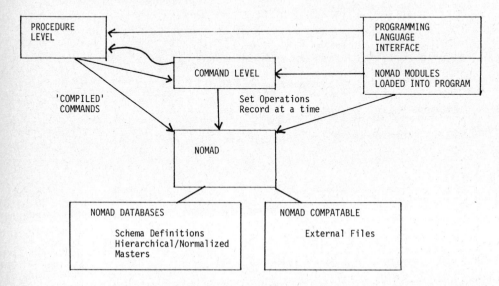

Figure 1.  System Architecture

5.2    <u>Interface Descriptions</u>

5.2.1  Command Level Interface

This interface has been described in detail in Sections

2., 3., and 4.0.

## 5.2.2 Procedure Level Interface

Procedures are invoked with a 'NOMAD filename' command.

This interface is very similar to the command level interface with the following additions:

1) Flow of control constructs include:

'IF...THEN...ELSE'...' constructs, where a boolean condition can be specified and a different series of NOMAD commands can be executed depending on the TRUE/ FALSE value of the boolean condition. These 'IF' statements can be nested.

'GO TO...' and LABELS.

'FOR Statement' to go through a loop a fixed number of times (NOMAD2).

2) Exception handling constructs:

'ON condition [message][commands]' allows the user to specify a set of NOMAD commands to be executed on a specific error condition. The error conditions can be a LIMIT, MASK, UPROC, UNIQUE violation.

'Command1 OTHERWISE [commands]' allows the user to specify a set of commands to be executed if Command1 fails.

3) System Variables: (This feature is actually available at the COMMAND Level interface but is more useful in this interface). A variety of system variables are set when commands are executed. These variables fall into three catagories: variables used for tracking exception conditions, variables used to indicate counts for changes, deletes, inserts, etc., and variables containing NOMAD parameters which in fact can be modified temporarily by

each user.  These variables can all be used in 'if tests' to control the flow of the procedure.

4)   Miscellaneous:  In addition, procedures can be built into modules, compiled, traced and be switched into a conversational mode.

5.2.3  Programming Language Interface:  NOMAD commands and procedures can be called through subroutine linkages from COBOL, PL/1, FORTRAN or BAL.  Data from individual items or entire segments can be retrieved into user specified variables in the program. The system variables mentioned above can also be retrieved. A special command is provided to allow the program to query the data dictionary.

## 6.0   OPERATIONAL ASPECTS

### 6.1  Security

The security facilities were discussed with the constraints in Section 2.

### 6.2  Physical Integrity

#### 6.2.1  Concurrency Control

Only one user is allowed to access a database at one time and use the SAVE/RESTORE commands.  Multiple users can use the same database, but in that made, the affects of each command are realized immediately.

#### 6.2.2  Crash Recovery

Note stated.

### 6.3  Operating Environment

#### 6.3.1  Software Environment

NOMAD runs on the NCSS operating system.

#### 6.3.2  Hardware Environment

NOMAD (and the NCSS operating system) require a minimum
of 256K bytes of memory on an IBM plug compatable mainframe.
Those mainframes can be IBM 370/Model 138 and larger.
In addition, NCSS will provide their own 3200 system to run
NOMAD.

7.0    ESSENTIALLY RELATIONAL SOLUTIONS FOR GENERALIZED DBMS PROBLEMS:

NOMAD illustrates the following advantages: simplicity, permits
optimization, high level interfaces, efficient storage and retrieval potential,
security and flexible data modeling.  The realization of those advantages has
been described in Sections 1-6 and is not repeated here.

The following features are also significant advantages of NOMADs
Relational Model:

1)    Normalization of a Hierarchy.  This feature allows hierarchies to be
      used as though they were relations.

2)    The concept of system variables as a method to communicate multiple
      results of set operations is useful.

3)    The different joining operators add power to a relational system.

4)    A consistent approach to missing values is attempted.  The effects
      of missing values in joining is controlled by the user through the
      selection of the joining operator.

Two limitations of NOMAD should also be pointed out:

1)    'CREATE' only creates NOMAD compatable external files.  These files
      can be used for subsequent retrieval but cannot be updated with NOMAD
      commands.

2)    Data Independence.  NOMAD allows considerable data independence from
      the physical representation of the data and from the access paths.
      However, the default item naming conventions can restrict the logical
      data independence.  Under that convention, an item name can be used

without naming the MASTER if the item name is unique within the database.  Suppose the item name 'FRED' was unique and used by 300 procedures.  If a user adds a new MASTER with the name 'FRED' to the database, all 300 programs would have to be rewritten; note that none of the 300 programs needs to be concerned with the new master.

## 8.0    DATABASE APPLICATIONS

It is estimated that NOMAD is used by over 2000 users on NCSS timesharing service for over 200 applications and another 2000 - 2500 users on in-house dedicated systems for another 50 applications.  Sales order entry, inventory control, environmental management, market research, sales analysis, personnel management, project control, resource allocation, project costing; securities tracking, budget tracking and analysis, portfolios analysis and management, investment analysis, acquisition and divestment analysis, cash management, insurance risk analysis, and state government bill tracking.  It is interesting to note that most of the applications are analysis and management aids rather than some of the basic business systems such as payroll and general ledger.

One of the larger databases is about 200 megabytes and has over 50 Masters.  Other databases have from 5 to 15 Masters.  It is estimated that 75% of the applications make use of the relational-like table look-up facilities and that almost 50% of the applications regularly use the relational 'matching' commands.

The user experience with NOMAD and NOMAD2 was generally very favorable.  One user indicated that the company's primary NOMAD application used a hierarchical database design.  That application made extensive use of the table look-up facilities, but very rarely used the join or matching operators.

A user at a different site reported that most of the applications used normalized relations. Non-computer professionals were able to use these Masters and the joining operators after being shown or given a few standard procedures. For this site, NOMAD's flexibility was its most important feature. The latter user also commented that the 'MERGE MATCHING' and 'REJECT MATCHING' joining operators were the most heavily used.

ACKNOWLEDGEMENTS

Representatives of National CSS, Inc., several users of NOMAD, and another member of the RTG study group have aided in the preparation of this report. The technical expertise and responsiveness of Rolf Lie, Francine Forseth, and Brad Whitlock of National CSS were greatly appreciated. The insights of John McCall of Lawrence Livermore National Laboratory and Robert Wiley of Standard Oil of California in the user experience with NOMAD were also very useful. Finally, several valuable observations were made by Harrison R. Burris of TRW, Inc. on an earlier draft of this report.

3.8  Feature Analysis Of ORACLE

Feature Analysis
of
ORACLE (*)

by
B.H. Driver

Technology Services Company
8401 Corporate Drive, Suite 210
Landover, Maryland 20785

December 1980

(*) Prepared while the author was at PRC  Information  Science
Company, McLean, Virginia.

Preface

All examples in this feature analysis are based on the data base below:

| S# | SNAME | STATUS | CITY |
|----|-------|--------|------|
| S1 | Smith | 20 | London |
| S2 | Jones | 10 | Paris |
| S3 | Blake | 30 | Paris |
| S4 | Clark | 20 | London |
| S5 | Adams | 30 | Athens |

| P# | PNAME | COLOR | WEIGHT |
|----|-------|-------|--------|
| P1 | Nut | Red | 12 |
| P2 | Bolt | Green | 17 |
| P3 | Screw | Blue | 17 |
| P4 | Screw | Red | 14 |
| P5 | Cam | Blue | 12 |
| P6 | Cog | Red | 19 |

| J# | JNAME | CITY |
|----|-------|------|
| J1 | Sorter | Paris |
| J2 | Punch | Rome |
| J3 | Reader | Athens |
| J4 | Console | Athens |
| J5 | Collator | London |
| J6 | Terminal | Oslo |
| J7 | Tape | London |

SPJ

| S# | P# | J# | QTY |
|----|----|----|-----|
| S1 | P1 | J1 | 200 |
| S1 | P1 | J4 | 700 |
| S2 | P3 | J1 | 400 |
| S2 | P3 | J2 | 200 |
| S2 | P3 | J3 | 200 |
| S2 | P3 | J4 | 500 |
| S2 | P3 | J5 | 600 |
| S2 | P3 | J6 | 400 |
| S2 | P3 | J7 | 800 |
| S2 | P5 | J2 | 100 |
| S3 | P3 | J1 | 200 |
| S3 | P4 | J2 | 500 |
| S4 | P6 | J3 | 300 |
| S4 | P6 | J7 | 300 |
| S5 | P2 | J2 | 200 |
| S5 | P2 | J4 | 100 |
| S5 | P5 | J5 | 500 |
| S5 | P5 | J7 | 100 |
| S5 | P6 | J2 | 200 |
| S5 | P1 | J4 | 1000 |
| S5 | P3 | J4 | 1200 |
| S5 | P4 | J4 | 800 |
| S5 | P5 | J4 | 400 |
| S5 | P6 | J4 | 500 |

From C. J. Date, 1977; An Introduction to Database Systems, Reading, Mass.: Addison-Wesley Publishing Company, pg 105.

# TABLE OF CONTENTS

# 1. Introduction

## 1.1      Identification

ORACLE is an RDBMS marketed by Relational Software Incorporated, Menlo Park, California, that uses SQL, a query language developed by IBM.

## 1.2      Status

### 1.2.1      System

A prototype of ORACLE (Version 0) was released in 1978 under U.S. government contract. Two copies of ORACLE, Version 1, were delivered in June 1979. Version 2 of ORACLE is now installed in 20 sites. RSI's emphasis has been on performance. A summary of features promised for future releases is presented in Figure 1-1.

Figure 1-1

**Capabilities Announced for Future Releases of ORACLE**

Near-term

On-line monitor of system resources

Restart

Rollback

Privacy control

Limited closure capability on hierarchic relationships

Forms-transaction processing

Concatenated keys

Usage statistics

User-controlled clustering in physical storage

Aliases for attribute names

Comments on attribute definitions in data dictionary

"date" data type

Long-term

Trigger

Assertion

Snapshot

Word-processing

1.2.2        Applications

ORACLE is intended to be a system for naive users requiring a flexible DBMS. RSI promotes ORACLE as especially suitable for applications requiring security granularity (to be implemented in future releases) or a DBMS that runs on several mainframes. Applications under development include several defense-oriented data bases.

At present, RSI is looking for customers who are familiar with the relational model and willing to tolerate the inconveniences of using a new product. For marketing reasons RSI is anxious to attract large customers and OEM customers. At the same time, RSI is interested in the single-user market.

## 1.3 System Backround

RSI began development of ORACLE in 1977 and demonstrated a prototype relational system in 1978. The first copy of the system was delivered in June 1979. External interfaces to ORACLE resemble those of System R; however, ORACLE employs a different internal structure.

## 1.4 Overall Philosophy

RSI states that "The ultimate objective of a data base system is to manage all the data which encompasses the related activities of an organization while remaining flexible and easy to use."

## 1.5 Essential Relational Characteristics

Currently, attributes used to join relations must be indexed; RSI has announced that this restriction will be relaxed in a future release.

In addition, the set operators union, intersection, difference and extended cartesian product are not supported; updates cannot be performed on user views; and semantic integrity constraints are not supported.

The following capabilities are promised for future releases: set operators, semantic integrity constraints, i.e., assertions and triggers, and updates using views.

## 1.6          Interfaces


|      Interface Type          | ORACLE Interface |
|------------------------------|------------------|

        Interface Type                            ORACLE Interface

(1) Database schema definition       Definition statement in SQL

(2) Query language                SQL, mapping-oriented language
based on relational calculus

(3) Database altering            SQL; Interactive Application Facility

(4) Constraint definition        None implemented at present

(5) Database generation and
    SQL regeneration

(6) Database schema redefinition   EXPAND TABLE, ADD COLUMN, and
    and renaming               EXPAND COLUMN statements in SQL

(7) Report Generation           ORACLE Report Writing

(8) Data entry                    Separate Load utility; Interactive
Application Facility interface

(9) Security definition, monitoring  SQL
    control

(10) Database Control (utility):
                load    }
                dump   }        IMPORT/EXPORT utilities
                backup  }
                restore }       Promised for future release
                recovery }
                monitoring }

(11) Definition of storage structure,  SQL
    index and access paths

(12) Database dictionary        System-maintained, queried
using SQL

(13) Special purpose language     FTP

## 1.7      Documentation

Documentation for ORACLE consists of the ORACLE USERS GUIDE, containing the following manuals:

ORACLE INTRODUCTION

SQL LANGUAGE REFERENCE

SQL LANGUAGE EXAMPLES

HOST LANGUAGE INTERFACE

TERMINAL INTERFACE

INTERACTIVE FORMS PROCESSOR

UTILITIES

MESSAGES AND CODES

ORACLE INSTALLATION GUIDE

2. Database Constituents

2.1        General Description

The constituents of an ORACLE database consist of the  database,  relations
(also  called  tables),  views,  tuples  (also  called  rows  and  records), and
"domains" (also called columns and fields).    Individual  data  items  within  a
logical record are called "attributes".  ORACLE does not have a term for domains
as  used  in  the  feature  catalog.  In this document, however, "attribute" and
"domain" are used with the same meaning as in the feature catalog.

These constituents are related as follows.  A relational database  consists
of  relations  of  possibly  different  types.  A relation consists of tuples of
identical type.  A view is derived from  one  or  more  relations  by  means  of
projection  and  qualification  operations.    A tuple consists of item values of
possibly different types.  A domain is defined in terms of a  user-defined  data
type.

## 2.2 Database

### 2.2.1 Database Structure

An ORACLE database consists of a set of relation definitions, which are stored in system-maintained relations, a set of stored tuples for each relation, and a set of views (virtual relations defined on base relations). A data base is named by assigning the desired name to the file when the data base is created.

### 2.2.2 Database Operations

### 2.2.3 Database Constraints

At present no capability for database constraints is implemented. Global assertions and triggers have been announced for future versions of ORACLE.

## 2.3 Additional Database Constituents

## 2.4 Relation

### 2.4.1     Relation Structure

A relation is defined as a two-dimensional table of data items, thus the predominant perception of a relation is as a table of rows and columns. Relations within a database are assigned unique names at the time of definition.

Duplicate tuples are permitted, although the system will enforce a uniqueness requirement for a primary key if it is specified in the definition. Attribute order is significant. Aliases for relation names can be assigned in view definitions.

### 2.4.2     Relation Operations

Not applicable

### 2.4.3     Relation Constraints

ORACLE supports a uniqueness requirement for any attribute the user wishes to use as a key. Primary keys must be indexed. In addition, the system will reject NULL values in inserted or updated tuples.

The first attribute defined for a relation must be assigned a value when a tuple is inserted.

2.5        Views

2.5.1        View Structure

Views are defined as dynamic virtual tables comprising a  selected  portion
of  the  database.  Views are defined by assigning a name to a stored retrieval
command.  Views are derived by selecting  qualified tuples from base  relations.
Keys are inherited from base relations.

2.5.2        View Operations

Views are defined in a view definition statement that can include any valid
retrieval  and selection operations.  They may be referenced like base relations
in retrieval commands; at present, update operations may not reference views.

2.5.3        View Constraints

Views can be used to implement access control on the  basis  of  access  to
columns  and/or  to selected tuples.  Views also provide a means for restricting
type of access.

2.5.4        Additional Properties of Views

## 2.6        Tuple

### 2.6.1        Tuple Structure

A tuple in ORACLE is defined implicitly by the relation definition. It consists of a set of values and/or nulls corresponding to the relation definition. Unique key values may be used for identifying tuples, but are not required.

### 2.6.2        Tuple Operations

Tuple structure is implicitly defined by relation definition statements. An instance of a record consists of a set of associated stored values for the attributes named in the relation definition. A tuple may be required to have a unique key. Tuples may be retrieved one at a time using the FETCH command in the Host Language Interface.

### 2.6.3        Tuple Constraints

The first attribute defined in the relation must always be valued. A uniqueness constraint can be imposed on tuples by specifying a uniqueness requirement for an attribute in the definition (concatenated keys are not presently supported). Constraint violations result in rejection of the insert or update command.

2.6.4       Additional Properties of Tuples


2.7       Attribute


2.7.1       Attribute Structure

An attribute (column) is defined as a field in a relation for values of a specified data type.

Attributes are assigned unique names within the relation when the relation is defined. Alias capabilities for attribute names are promised for future versions of ORACLE. Aliases will be assigned in view definitions. The only distinguished attribute values in ORACLE are nulls.


2.7.2       Attribute Operations

Attributes can be manipulated in selection and retrieval operations using the relational comparison operators, arithmetic operators, and aggregate functions; arithmetic operators and aggregate functions can also be used in insertion and update operations. Attributes have the same compatibility requirements as the primary data types.

### 2.7.3        Attribute Constraints

Not applicable


### 2.7.4        Additional Properties of Attributes

Not applicable


### 2.8        Domain


### 2.8.1        Domain Structure

ORACLE supports domain definition only as specification of a field size and pre-defined data type from the set of available data types. The following external data types are available: variable-length alphanumeric string and floating-point decimal.


### 2.8.2        Domain Operations

Not applicable


### 2.8.3        Domain Constraints

Not applicable

## 2.8.4      Additional Properties of Domains

Not applicable

3. Functional Capabilities

3.1        Qualification

Qualification in ORACLE is calculus-oriented.  Qualification results may be thought of as a relation populated with qualified rows.

Qualification can be used with retrievals, update and deletions, e.g.,

```
    SELECT  SNAME
    FROM    S
    WHERE   CITY = 'PARIS';
    /

    UPDATE  S
    SET     STATUS = 10
    WHERE   CITY = 'PARIS';
    /

    DELETE  S
    WHERE   S# = 'S7';
    /
```

### 3.1.1   Restriction

The following operators can be used in simple conditions:

| SYMBOL | DEFINITION |
|---|---|
| = | the equal comparison operator |
| ~= | the not equal comparison operator |
| > | the greater than comparison operator |
| >= | the greater than or equal comparison operator |
| < | the less than comparison operator |
| <= | the less than or equal comparison operator |
| BETWEEN | the range comparison operator |
| | (The range is specified as a pair of constants, expressions or attributes connected by AND.) |
| IN | the set inclusion operator.  IN tests a field for inclusion in a set of values. |
| AND | the boolean operator AND |
| OR | the boolean operator OR |
| X... | true for the string beginning with X |
| NULL + $(exp_1, exp2)$ | if value of $exp_1$ is null, use value of exp2 |

Stored values, constants, and nested expressions can be used in selection criteria.  NULL can be specified to test for an unvalued field.

The truth tables used for evaluation of logical expressions are:

```
AND | T F ?      OR | T F ?      NOT |
----+------      ---+------      ----+----
 T  | T F ?       T | T T T       T  | F
 F  | F F F       F | T F ?       F  | T
 ?  | ? F ?       ? | T ? ?       ?  | ?
```

Nulls cause arithmetic expressions to be evaluated as false unless an alternate treatment for NULLs has been specified. Expressions can be combined into boolean expressions using AND and OR, e.g., "Print the number and names of all suppliers who supply project in quantities greater than 500".

```
SELECT   S#,SNAME

FROM     S, SPJ

WHERE    SPJ.S#=S.S#

AND      QTY > 500;

/
```

3.1.2          Quantification

ORACLE supports neither universal nor absolute quantification. Universal quantification is planned for a future release.

3.1.3          Set Operations

Set operations are not directly supported; they can be accomplished using combinations of other SEQUEL operators.

### .1.4       Joining

Joins in ORACLE are handled by means of restriction in selection criteria subject to the following constraints:

- o   Reflexive joins required using a different table name for each table reference to the base relation.

- o   At present items used for specifying joins must be indexed.

- o   Up to 255 relations can be joined

Only equi-joins are supported. Outer-joins are supported.


### 3.1.5       Nesting and Closure

Logically, selection in ORACLE produces a relation populated with qualified tuples. (Retrieval and alteration operations also produce relations.)

Simple qualification criteria can be nested to express more complex iteria, e.g., "Find the parts that come in either red or blue and have a ght less than 15."

```
SELECT PNAME

FROM P

WHERE (COLOR = 'RED' OR COLOR = 'BLUE')

      AND WEIGHT <15;

    /
```

The result of one qualification can be further qualified. This is expressed by embedding a projection in a WHERE clause, e.g., "Find the names and cities of suppliers who are located in cities where there are projects."

```
SELECT SNAME, CITY

FROM S

WHERE S.CITY IN

    SELECT J.CITY

    FROM J;

    /
```

Closure capabilities for hierarchical relationships are available.


### 3.1.6 Additional Aspects of Qualification

Not applicable


### 3.2 Retrieval and Presentation


### 3.2.1 Database Queries

A retrieval is perceived to return a table populated with qualified tuples. Retrievals may result in any number of tuples, i.e., all qualified tuples are retrieved. Retrieved tuples may be sorted before they are displayed. When selection criteria are combined with OR, a tuple that meets each condition is operated on twice, unless UNIQUE is specified in the projection (SELECT) clause.

User-defined arithmetic operations and ORACLE-supplied functions may be used with retrieved values.

### 3.2.2    Retrieval of Information about Database Constituents

Schema information, stored as system-maintained tables, can be retrieved using SQL retrieval commands, e.g., "Print the names of attributes in the SPJ table."

```
SELECT *
FROM COL
WHERE TABLE = 'SPJ';
/
```

### 3.2.3    Retrieval of System Perfomance Data

No system performance data is provided by ORACLE at present. Monitoring capabilities have been announced for a future release.

### 3.2.4    Report Generation

Report-writing facilities are available with a word processor. RSI is developing an easier-to-use report writer.

3.2.5      Constraints and Limitations

Elimination of duplicate copies of a single tuple and collection of usage statistics have been announced for future releases.


3.3        Alteration


3.3.1      Insert Facilities

Inserted data are perceived as new rows in a stored table.    Single   tuples (complete and incomplete) can be inserted into ORACLE base relations, using SQL, e.g.,

        INSERT INTO SPJ:   <S2, P6, J3, 500>;

        /

        INSERT INTO SPJ (S#, P#):   <S2, P6>;

        /

Attribute  names   must   be   specified  when   a   value   is not supplied for every attribute in the relation.    The leftmost attribute in the relation  definition, however,  must   always   be   valued.  NULLs are not accepted when an attribute is defind as NONULL.


The results of a query can be used in an insert operation, e.g., "Create  a tuple  in S for any supplier who supplies a part to a project and is not already listed in S."

```
      INSERT INTO S (S#):

SELECT UNIQUE S#

FROM SPJ

WHERE SPJ.S# NOT IN

SELECT UNIQUE S#

FROM S;

/
```

Inserts can also be done using the Forms Transaction Processor.


3.3.2          <u>Delete Facilities</u>

Tuples can be deleted from a base relation, e.g., "Delete from the S
relatio n any supplier who does not supply a part to a project."

```
          DELETE S

          WHERE SPJ.J3 NOT IN

SELECT J#

FROM J;

/
```


3.3.3          <u>Modify Facilities</u>

One or more attributes in a stored tuple may be modified. Either a
constant or the result of an arithmetic expression can replace a  stored  value,
e.g., "Change the minimum quantity for all parts supplied to projects to 200."

```
          UPDATE SPJ
```

```
SET QTY = 200

WHERE QTY < 200;

/
```

NULL may be substituted for a stored value.

User-supplied parameters are perceived as individual values for named attributes in SQL commands or FTP commands.

It is not currently possible to use the results of a retrieval from a different tuple to modify a value.

### 3.3.4 Commit and Undo Facilities

None available.

### 3.4 Additional Functional Capabilities

### 3.4.1 Attribute and String Operations

ORACLE supports addition, subtraction, multiplication, and division in selection, retrieval, and modify operations.

### 3.4.2    Sorting

Retrieved tuples can be sorted before they are displayed, using a total concatenated sort field of up to 255 characters. Each field within the sort field can be sorted in ascending or descending order.

### 3.4.3    Library Functions

ORACLE supports the aggregate functions MIN, MAX, COUNT, SUM, AVERAGE.

### 3.4.4    User-defined Functions

User-defined functions are not supported at this time.

### 3.4.5    Transactions

Transaction capabilities are available. Locking can be specified for tables or rows.

### 3.4.6    Multi-tuple Operations

All tuples meeting selection criteria can be modified with a single command; likewise, all qualified tuples are deleted with one command. Insertions that copy one or more tuples from one relation to another are supported.

### 3.4.7    Grouping

Tuples can be grouped by value for one or more items for use with aggregate functions.

### 3.4.8    Exception-handling Mechanisms

ORACLE notifies the user of errors or exceptional conditions by means of return codes in the Host Language Interface and error messages in the self-contained interface.

## 4. Definition, Generation, and Administration Facilities

### 4.1 Definition Facilities

The following definition is used in the discussion below.

```
CREATE TABLE S
    S# (CHAR (6) IMAGE),
    SNAME (CHAR (15)),
    STATUS (NUMBER),
    CITY (CHAR (15));
    /
CREATE TABLE J
    J# (CHAR (6) IMAGE),
    JNAME (CHAR (15));
    CITY (CHAR (15));
    /
```

```
CREATE TABLE P

    P# (CHAR (6) IMAGE),

    PNAME (CHAR (15)),

    COLOR (CHAR (8)),

    WEIGHT (NUMBER);

    /

CREATE TABLE SPJ

    S3 (CHAR (6) IMAGE),

    P# (CHAR (6) IMAGE),

    J# (CHAR (6) IMAGE),

    QTY (NUMBER);

    /

DEFINE VIEW PROJSUPP AS

    SELECT UNIQUE J.J#, J.JNAME, S.S#, S.SNAME

    FROM J, S, SPJ

    WHERE J.J# = SPJ.J#

      AND S.S# = SPJ.S#

    ORDER BY J.J, S.S#;

/
```

### 4.1.1          Constituents of a Database Definition

A database definition consists of relation definitions, which contain attribute definitions, and view definitions.

### 4.1.2          Database Definition

A database may have any number of relations.

### 4.1.3          Relation Definition

A base relation is defined by assigning it a unique name and defining each of its attributes. A relation may have up to 255 attributes, any of which may be key (no unique key is required). The first defined attribute is treated by the system as a primary key; it must be defined as NONULL and it must be indexed. Current maximum field width is 255 characters; the maximum width for all attributes in a tuple is 64K characters.

### 4.1.4          View Definition

Views are defined by assigning view status and a view name to a retrieval command, which may or may not include selection criteria. The only restrictions on view definition are restrictions on retrievals. Views may be referenced like other relations in retrieval operations, but cannot be used in alteration operations.

Future releases will permit users to assign alias attribute names in views.

## 4.1.5 Tuple Definition

Properties of tuples are implicitly defined in the relation definition.

## 4.1.6 Attribute Definition

Attributes are defined in relation definitions. Attribute names must be unique within a relation. Domains are defined as part of the attribute definition by specifying maximum field width (up to 255 characters) and character type. The definition may include a specification that the attribute be valued for every tuple. A uniqueness requirement may also be specified.

## 4.1.7 Domain Definition

Domains can only be defined in terms of the picture specified in an attribute definition. ORACLE supports alphanumeric and floating point decimal date types.

## 4.1.8 Definition of Additional Database Constituents

Not applicable

### 4.1.9       Generation Facilities

Once a file is created, ORACLE automatically generates a relation when the relation is defined.

### 4.2       Database Redefinition

### 4.2.1       Renaming Database Constituents

No renaming capability is supported.

### 4.2.2       Redefining Database Constituents

Relation definitions can be expanded to include additional attributes; attribute field widths will be subject to expansion in future releases.

New views may be defined at any time. No other redefinition capabilities are provided. Definition changes entail modification of the dictionary tables; however, no restructuring of the database is required as a result of definition changes.

### 4.3       Database Regeneration and Reorganization

4.3.1        System-Controlled

ORACLE dynamically reuses space and re—organizes portions of  the  database
as  alterations to the database are processed.  No complete restructuring of the
database is ever initiated.


4.3.2        DBA-Controlled

No DBA control over database reorganizaton or regeneration is provided.


4.4          Database Dictionary

The  ORACLE  data  dictionary  consists  of system--maintained base
relations  and  views.                      The tables are:

| Table Name | Type | Attribute |
|---|---|---|
| SECURITY | Base relation | KEY, ENTITY, COLUMN, GRANTOR, OWNER, ACCESS |
| XREF | Base relation | NAME, TABLE |
| VIEWDEF | Base relation | VIEW, LINE, TEXT |
| DICTIONARY | Base relation | NAME, TYPE, OWNER |
| COLUMNS | Base relation | TABLE, COLUMN, DATATYPE, LENGTH, IMAGE, NONULL, COLID |
| TAB | View | NAME, TYPE, CREATOR, GRANTEE |
| COL | View | COLUMN, TABLE |
| TABLES | View | TABLE |
| USER | Base relation | NAME, ID, PASSWORD, GRANTOR |
| DBS | Base relation | NAME, EXTENTS, SIZE, SECFLAG, OWNER |
| EXTENT | Base relation | DB NAME, FILE, EXTNUM, SIZE |
| DTAB | Base relation | TABLE, COMMENT |
| DTABLES | View | TABLE, TYPE, CREATOR, GRANTEE |
| DCOL | View | TABLE, COLUMN |
| PRIVS | View | TABLE, COLUMN, GRANTOR, ACCESS |
| COLDEF | View | TABLE, COLUMNS, DATATYPE, LENGTH, IMAGE, NONULL |
| VIEWS | View | VIEW, TEXT |

| VIEW XREF | View | VIEW, TABLE |
| USERS | View | USER, OWNER |
| GRANTS | View | TABLE, COLUMN, GRANTEE, ACCESS |

The VIEWDEF table contains the SQL commands defining the view. The user can query the dictionary using SQL retrieval commands, e.g., "List the definition of columns in the PROJ table."

```
SELECT      COLUMN, DATATYPE, LENGTH, IMAGE, NONULL
FROM        COLUMNS
WHERE       TABLE = 'PROJ';
/
```

| PROJNO | NUMBER | 8 | UNIQUE | YES |
| PNAME | CHAR | 10 | NON-UNIQUE | NO |
| BUDGET | NUMBER | 8 | | NO |
| EMPCNT | NUMBER | 8 | | NO |

## 5. Interface and DBMS Architecture

### 5.1 System Architecture

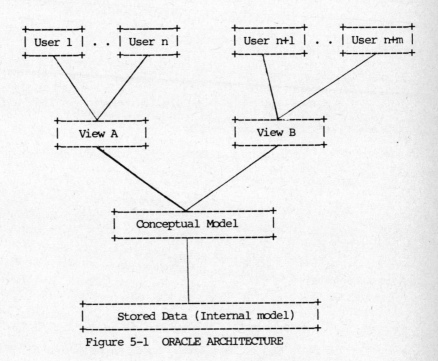

Figure 5-1   ORACLE ARCHITECTURE

## 5.2        Interface Description

### 5.2.1        SQL

SQL is a self-contained language for data definition, selection, query, and update.   It  can be used to define relations and attributes, to insert, modify, or delete tuples,  and  to  retrieve  relations  or  projections  on  relations. Relations are treated as tables.

SQL  commands  are  linear  and use English keywords.  Selection is based on the relational  calculus,  with  criteria  specified  in  a  WHERE-clause.   The language is user-driven and is intended for ad hoc query and update.  SQL can be used  on  a stand-alone basis; SQL commands can also be embedded in user-written programs.

### 5.2.2        Interactive Application Facility (IAF)

Interactive Application Facility is a system-driven fill-in-the-blank  type of  interface  for  tuple  insertion  update,  and queries.  It can be used on a stand-alone basis.  The DBA defines forms which are presented to  the  user  for keyboard input.

### 5.2.3 Host Language Interface

ORACLE interfaces to host language by means of program calls, using SQL statements embedded in a host programming language as a data sublanguage. Programs log on to ORACLE, open data bases, pass SQL statements to ORACLE, execute those statements, close data bases, and exit. Communication takes place via a LOGON Data Area defined in the user program and specified in the logon call. Programs may substitute program variables into SQL statements.

When data is delivered to a program one tuple at a time, ORACLE places a return code in the cursor data area after each call. A single user program may have multiple SQL cursors open at one time.

### 5.2.4 User Friendly Interface

The User Friendly Interface (UFI) is the interface between a terminal user and ORACLE. UFI handles communications with the DBMS, routing of output and scheduling for printing, and writing SQL commands to a file. UFI also provides a very limited line-oriented text-editing capability.

# 6. Operational Aspects

## 6.1　　　Security

### 6.1.1　　　Access Control

Privacy control is maintained by means of password and views. Thus, access could be limited to any set of values in the data base that can be specified in a SQL command. The person defining a base relation or a view can grant or revoke the following privileges to other passwords: read, insert, delete, update, add columns, create indexes, define assertions or triggers, execute compiled programs, and grant privileges to other users. Access to a view is constrained by authorization for underlying relations.

Any user can define and maintain private relations. The person defining a relation can perform any operation, on that relation, including granting and revoking privileges.

## 6.2 Physical Integrity

### 6.2.1 Concurrency Control

The lowest concurrency granularity is at the row level. That is, as SQL statements are executed, rows are only locked while they are being actually operated upon.

If a user wishes to read or update consistent data, he can issue the following command

$$\text{BEGIN TRANSACTION} \langle \text{table name} \rangle \begin{Bmatrix} \text{READ} \\ \text{UPDATE} \end{Bmatrix} , \langle \text{table,} \rangle \ldots$$

Each table specified will be locked until the END TRANSACTION command is issued. The READ modifier is issued by someon who wishes to read consistent data. The UPDATE modifier is issued by someone who wishes to update a table(s) and wishes to block other updates.

Release 3 will allow roll back recovery to tne beginning of a transaction.

### 6.2.2 Crash Recovery

No automatic crash recovery capabilities are provided. The user can back up and restore a database manually, using the IMPORT/EXPORT utility; however, no logging or undo capability exists.

Audit capabilities are promised for a future release.

## 6.3 Operating Environment

### 6.3.1 Software Environment

ORACLE is relatively independent of executive, control, or operating systems. The operating system is used only for interfacing to peripherals, such as secondary storage.

### 6.3.2 Hardware Environment

ORACLE can be used on the following hardware:

```
IBM
  Memory Requirement:
  CPU's
      System 360 (model 40 and above)
      System 370 (all models)
      303X (all models)
      4300 (all models)
  Operating Systems
      VM
      MIS, SVS, OS/MVT
      OS/VSI, OS/MFT
      DOS/VSE, DOS/VS, DOS

DEC
  Memory requirements:  80K words
  CPU's
      PDP-11 series (model 23 and above)
```

VAX-11 series (all models)

Operating Systems
RSX-11M, IAS, UNIX and others
VAX/VMS, VAX/UNIX


ORACLE also requires secondary storage (disk space) and terminal or batch input and output facilities.

3.9   Feature Analysis Of PASCAL/R


Feature Analysis of the

PASCAL/R

Relational System

by
J.W. Schmidt
M. Mall
W.H. Dotzek


Fachbereich Informatik
University of Hamburg
Schlueterstrasse 70
D-2000 Hamburg 13
West Germany

February 1982

# 1. Introduction

## 1.1 Identification

PASCAL/R is a relational DBMS involving the programming language PASCAL/R, an extension of PASCAL. PASCAL/R is an ongoing research and development product at the Fachbereich Informatik, Hamburg University (principal investigator: J. W. Schmidt).

## 1.2 Status

### 1.2.1 System

PASCAL/R is operational since 1978. It is currently (spring 1982) active at the University of Hamburg, at the ETH Zurich, at NBS in Washington D.C., at DEC in Maynard, Massachusetts, at the University of Toronto, at the University of Kiel, and at PCI, London.

### 1.2.2 Applications

- Database Research and Development

- Implementation of Database Systems and Languages

- Teaching of Database Concepts

- Database Design

- Database Applications

## 1.3  System Background

The PASCAL/R system development started as an  extension  of  a  PASCAL  compiler  and its runtime system. The query evaluation subsystem is based on an  algorithm  proposed  by  F.Palermo  (IBM San Jose). Proposals similar to the PASCAL/R approach are, e.g.,  PLAIN  (T.  Wasserman), RIGEL  (L.  Rowe),  THESEUS (J.  Shopiro),  ASTRAL (T.  Amble et al.). PASCAL/R is implemented on a DECsystem-10  under the operating system TOPS 10.

The PASCAL/R system is written in PASCAL.

## 1.4  Overall Philosophy

PASCAL/R considers a database as an (external)  variable  that  can  be  accessed by (compiled or interpreted) programs.

The PASCAL/R language  provides  the  data  structure relation,  operations and control structures for relations and full standard PASCAL. The major  design  objective  of PASCAL/R  is  to  integrate relation structures and PASCAL data and control structures as closely as  possible.  This effort seems worth-while for two reasons.

Firstly, many programming tasks may benefit  directly from  the  new set-like data structuring facility, from its general content-based selection and test  mechanisms,  and from  its  altering  operators.  Secondly, since database models concentrate on  data  structuring,  querying,  and alteration they are, in general, not "algorithmically complete".  Therefore,  both  programming  tools,  database models  and  programming  languages,  have  to  be applied cooperatively to solve database-intensive applications.

The PASCAL/R system is considered to be a framework within which the essential concepts of programming languages and database models can be taught and studied with respect to their interaction, trade-off, and implementation effort.

## 1.5   Essential Relational Characteristics

PASCAL/R is "relationally complete".  It supports

- the structural aspects of the relational model, including the domain concept;

- insert, update, and delete operations; and

- a calculus-oriented data selection language.

## 1.6   Interfaces

The interfaces to the PASCAL/R system provide the following capabilities :

- Database Schema Definition including (limited) Constraint Definition

- Interactive Interface to Database Querying and Altering Facilities

- Database Generation

- Definition of Access and Storage Structures

- Database Dictionary

- Database Utilities: Save, Restore, Reorganize

- The High Level Programming Language PASCAL/R

- Report Generator

- Screen Definition Facilities

## 1.7 Documentation

J.W. Schmidt: 'Some High Level Language Constructs for Data of Type Relation', ACM Transactions on Database Systems, Vol 2, No 3, (September 1977).

J.W. Schmidt, M. Mall: 'PASCAL/R Report', Bericht Nr. 66, University of Hamburg, W. Germany (January 1980).

W. Lamersdorf, J.W. Schmidt: 'Specification of PASCAL/R', Berichte Nr. 73 and Nr.74, University of Hamburg, W. Germany (July 1980).

M. Jarke, J.W. Schmidt: 'Query Processing Strategies in the PASCAL/R Relational Database Management System', Proc. ACM/SIGMOD Internat. Conf. on Management of Data, Orlando (June 1982).

## 1.8 General System Description

The PASCAL/R Relational Database System provides the following capabilities:

- definition of relations, relation keys, domains;

- generation of relational databases, i.e. collections of relations;

- a calculus-oriented query mechanism and a specific key-based selection mechanism for relation element (=tuple) selection;

- an interactive interface;

- an interface to PASCAL and to PASCAL/R, an extension of PASCAL by a data structure relation, relation-valued and quantified expressions, relation altering operators and a control structure controlled by relations;

- utility programs for the definition of access paths and the analysis and reorganization of databases.

## 2. Database Constituents

### 2.1 General Description

Term translation table:

<u>System</u> <u>Term</u>                                                      <u>Feature</u> <u>Catalogue</u> <u>Term</u>

| | |
|---|---|
| database | database |
| relation | relation |
| relation element | tuple |
| (relation element) component | attribute |
| (relation element) component identifier | attribute name |
| (relation element) component type | attribute type<br>= domain |

A relational database consists of relations of possibly different type. A relation consists of relation elements (=tuples) of identical type. A relation element consists of relation element components (=attributes) of possibly different type. Relation element components are denoted by component identifiers; component types (=domains) define the set of legal component values and operators; component values are considered to be atomic, i.e., they can not be further decomposed by database operations.

### 2.2 Database

## 2.2.1  Database Structure

A structure of type database consists of a fixed collection of (base) relations and is identified by its name.

## 2.2.2  Database Operations

Databases can be defined (schema definition), generated, and reorganized. A database is defined by a PASCAL/R type definition; a database is generated and reorganized by privileged utility programs.

## 2.2.3  Database Constraints

Database constraints are defined on the relation, relation element (=tuple), and element component (=attribute) level.

## 2.3  Relation

## 2.3.1  Relation Structure

A structure of type relation consists of elements (=tuples) of identical type.

A relation may be perceived as an array-like structure with a key-based selection mechanism for relation elements; a relation may also be perceived as a set-like structure with first-order predicates for subset selection.

The value of a relation is always a subset of the Cartesian product of the component types defining the relation element components.

The relation constraints (see 2.3.3, relation key) does not permit the existence of two or more elements in a relation with identical values for the key components.

Relations have fixed identifiers; Relation names can be redefined by the formal/actual parameters of PASCAL/R.

## 2.3.2  Relation Operations

Operations defined on relations are those for qualification (see 3.1), querying (see 3.2) and altering (see 3.3).

Major design goals for the operations were:

- formal rigor and uniformity:

  relational structures and operations are defined in terms of first-order predicate calculus and set theory.

- conceptual soundness:

  relational concepts are defined in terms of programming language concepts (data structures, selectors, types, variables, Boolean and relational expressions etc.).

The elements (=tuples) of a relation are not ordered.

However, an order on the relation elements (=tuples) is induced by the order on the key value set (as defined by the type of the key component); in case of a composite key a lexicographic order on the key values is assumed. This order can be exploited by a set of relation handling procedures (see 3.2.1(1)).

## 2.3.3  Relation Constraints

A relation is constrained by its key. The key is defined by one or more relation element component identifiers. The system enforces that there are no two or more

elements in a relation with the same value for the key
components. In other words, the key constraint guarantees
that every relation element can be identified uniquely by
its key value.

Altering the value of a relation variable must not
violate the relation type, i.e. the relation element type
and the key. PASCAL/R tries to detect as many type violations as possible at compile time; possible type violations that cannot be eliminated at compile time are indicated by a warning and are resolved by standard runtime
actions (see 3.4.8).


## 2.4  View


A PASCAL/R database does not support views.

However, within a PASCAL/R program local relations
can be defined that may have certain properties of static
views. Local relations can be manipulated by the qualifying (see 3.1), querying (see 3.2), and altering (see 3.3)
capabilities defined for relations.


## 2.5  Tuple


### 2.5.1  Tuple Structure


In the current version of PASCAL/R, relation element
(=tuple) types have to be defined by the data structure
record (only "flat" records without variants are allowed).
The data type record is a structure consisting of a fixed
number of components, possibly of different type.

Keys are defined at the relation level.

There exists a selection mechanism for unique relation element (=tuple) qualification, based on key values (see 3.1.1).

## 2.5.2  Tuple Operations

PASCAL/R provides a test operation to check whether an element (=tuple) with a given value exists in a relation or not (see 3.2.1 (3)).

The value of a relation element (=tuple) can be changed by an assignment operation. Depending on the value of the relation element and on the value of the expression assigned the effect of an assignment operation is equivalent to an update, insert, or delete operation on relations (see 3.3).

The general selection mechanism selects each relation element (=tuple) that fulfills a given predicate; a selection may also be used to control a for-statement (see 5.2); thus, selected elements (=tuples) can be accessed and processed one-at-a-time by the body of the for-statement.

## 2.5.3  Tuple Constraints

The type of a relation element (=tuple) is given by the relation element type definition. A selected relation element (=tuple), e.g., rel[kval], inherits the additional constraint that the value of its key component, e.g., k, must not be altered.

The relation element (=tuple) constraints are part of the relation element type definition; constraint violations are regarded as type violations.

## 2.6 Attributes

### 2.6.1 Attribute Structure

A component (=attribute) of a relation element (=tuple) is perceived as an object of unstructured type (=domain) and is identified by a name (component identifier (=attribute name)).

### 2.6.2 Attribute Operations

The operations on element components (=attributes) are defined by the component type (=domain) (see 2.7.2).

### 2.6.3 Attribute Constraints

The constraints on element components (=attributes) are defined by the component type (=domain) (see 2.7.3).

## 2.7 Domain

### 2.7.1 Domain Structure

Component types (=domains) are identified by names and have the structure of sets of unstructured values.

The following basic value sets are provided : integer, real, Boolean, character, ascii, strings of fixed length. New value sets may be defined by enumerating their elements.

No distinguished domain values like null, unknown etc. are defined.

### 2.7.2  Domain Operations

The assignment operator is defined for each component type (=domain); additionally, the following operators are defined:

- for string, char, ascii, Boolean, integer, real, enumeration, and subrange: comparison operators ( = , <> , <= , >= , < , > ),

- for Boolean: logical operators (and, or, not),

- for integer and real: arithmetic operators (+, -, *, /, div, mod) and additional functions provided by PASCAL.

Component types (=domains) are the basis of compatibility for relation element components (=attributes): only components defined by component types with identical names are compatible.

### 2.7.3  Domain Constraints

Constraints on integer value sets and enumeration value sets can be defined by upper and lower bounds (subrange types).

## 3.  Functional Capabilities

### 3.1  Qualification

PASCAL/R  mechanisms  for  selections  are  content-oriented.  Relation  elements  are  selected  by  means  of selection  predicates  that  have  to  be  fulfilled  by  the value  of  the  selected  elements.

PASCAL/R  has  a  specific  selection  mechanism  that  is based  on  the  equality  of  key  values;  it  leads  to  unique elements  and  fits  best  in  an  array-like  perception  of relations.

PASCAL/R  also  has  a  general  selection  mechanism  that is  based  on  first-order  predicates;  it  leads  to  a  variable number  of  selected  elements  and  fits  best  into  a  set-like perception  of  relations.

Selection  predicates  usually  have  relation  elements amongst  their  operands,  and,  thus,  have  to  correspond  with the  type  definition  of  relation  elements.

Example of a Database Type (=Schema) Definition
==================================================

{see C.J. Date : An Introduction to Database Systems,
    2nd Edition, page 52}

```
type cityname        = packed array of [1..15] char;
     suppliername    = packed array of [1..20] char;
     partname        = packed array of [1..20] char;
     quantity        = integer;
     creditstatus    = 0..999;
     weightunits     = 0..9999;
     colortype       = (red,blue,yellow,green,black);
     suppliernumber  = 1..99999;

     company         = record snr: suppliernumber;
                              sname: suppliername;
```

```
                                    status: creditstatus;
                                    city: cityname
                          end;

   item            =     record pnr: integer;
                                 pname: partname;
                                 color: colortype;
                                 weight: weightunits;
                                 city: cityname
                          end;

   order           =     record snr: suppliernumber;
                                 pnr: partnumber;
                                 qty: quantity
                          end;
   companies       =     relation <snr> of company;
   items           =     relation <pnr> of item;
   orders          =     relation <snr,pnr> of order;

   business        =     database suppliers: companies;
                                  parts: items;
                                  shipments: orders
                          end;
```

Example of a Database Declaration
==================================

```
var  mybusiness     : business;
```

### 3.1.1  Restriction (=Selection)

Free variables can be defined to denote the elements
of (range) relations. The scope of a free variable, i.e.,
the context in which it is known, is a subsequent Boolean
expression (selection predicate). Free variables, e.g., r,
and selection predicates, e.g., p, form selections, e.g.
### each r in rel : p(r) ### that select those elements
of the relation, rel, that fulfill the selection predicate.

Any Boolean expression containing free variables,
PASCAL expressions, comparison or logical operators (see
2.7.2) (or quantified expressions, see 3.1.2.) is a legal

selection predicate.

Given its key value, e.g., kval, any element of a selection, e.g., rel, can be selected by an index-like selection mechanism, e.g., rel[kval].


Example:
```
    ... mydatabase.parts[4711] ...
    ... with mydatabase do     {with-statement see 5.2}
        begin
                ... parts [ 46*100 + 111 ] ...
                ... shipments [ 100, 4711 ] ...
                ... each p in parts : (p.pname = 'cardreader') or
                                      (p.weight >= 10)  ...
        end
```


## 3.1.2  Quantification


Existentially and universally quantified variables can be defined to denote the elements of (range) relations. The scope of a quantified variable is the subsequent Boolean expression (matrix predicate). Provided r denotes an element variable and p is a matrix predicate, then some r in rel ( p(r) ) and all r in rel ( p(r) ) are legal quantified expressions that evaluate to a Boolean value indicating whether or not the predicate p holds for at least one or for all elements of the (range) relation, rel.

Any Boolean expression constructed out of quantified variables, PASCAL expressions, comparison or logical operators, or quantified expressions forms a legal matrix predicate. Quantified expressions can also be used as selection predicates (see 3.1.1.).

Absolute quantification is not supported (there is, however, a counting function size(re), see 3.2.1).


Example:
```
  with mydatabase do
      begin ...
      ...    each p in parts : ( p.color = blue ) and
             some sp in shipments ( sp.pnr = p.pnr ) ...
      end
```

### 3.1.3  Set Operations

For set-like operations see 3.2 and 3.3.

### 3.1.4  Joining

Since quantified expressions can be used as selection predicates a relation can be restricted dependently upon data in another, possibly different, relation (see example 3.1.2.). For the construction of new relations by joining relations, see 3.2. .

### 3.1.5  Nesting and Closure

A quantified predicate (see 3.1.2) can be used as the matrix of another predicate (see 3.1.1 and 3.1.2), and a relation expression (see 3.2.1) can be used as a range relation. Therefore, quantified and relational expressions, i.e., predicates and queries can be nested arbitrarily (see however 3.2.5).

## 3.2  Retrieval and Presentation

### 3.2.1  Database Queries

The selection mechanisms of section 3.1 form the basis of the PASCAL/R query facilities.

The result of a query against a PASCAL/R database is

either

1. a single relation element ( 1-element query ), or

2. a relation value containing a number of relation element (=tuple) values ( N-element query ), or

3. a Boolean value ( Boolean query ).

1. 1-Element Queries:

A selected relation element, rel[kval], is a variable and can therefore be regarded as a (simple) expression evaluating to the value of the selected element.

Example:
```
    var thispart: item;   ...
    with mydatabase do
    begin   ...
         thispart := parts[4711] ;  ...
    end
```

Five relation handling procedures (low, next, this, high, prior) select at most one relation element from the relation variable, e.g., rel, given as the first procedure parameter. If the element exists, it is assigned to a second parameter, e.g., relem, and a Boolean standard function, eor(rel), becomes false; if the element does not exist, the Boolean function eor(rel) becomes true and relem remains unchanged.

| | |
|---|---|
| low (rel,relem) | selects the element of the relation variable which has the lowest key value. The order on key values is given by the order on the value set underlying the key component type; in case of a composite key a lexicographic order on the key values is assumed. |
| next (rel,relem) | selects the element of the relation variable which has a key value next highest to the current key value in the variable relem. |
| this (rel,relem) | selects the element of the relation variable which has the key value equal to the current key value in the variable relem. |

| high (rel,relem) | selects the element of the relation variable which has the highest key value. |
| prior (rel,relem) | selects the element of the relation variable which has the key value next lowest to the current key value in the variable relem. |

Example:
```
   var thispart: item;   ...
   with mydatabase do
   begin   ...
        thispart.pnr := 4711;
        next ( parts, thispart ) ;   ...
   end
```

2. N-Element Queries:

The relation elements selected by the general selection mechanism, each r in rel : p(r) , can be converted into the relation (-valued) expression, [ each r in rel :  p(r) ] .  The value of this expression is equal to the subrelation of rel that fulfills the selection predicate, p.

Relation expressions are generalized to provide :

```
Projection :        [ <r.f,...r.g> of each r in rel : p(r) ] ;
Cartesian Product: [ <rl.f,...rn.h> of each rl in rell, ...
                     each rn in reln : p(rl,...rn) ]
Union :             [ each rl in rell : pl(rl),...,
                      each rn in reln : pn(rn) ]
```

In the latter case, the relation element types of rell,...reln have to be compatible. (For a different use of the general selection mechanism see 5.2)

Example:
```
   var shipped parts: items;   ...
   with mybusiness do
   begin   ...
        shipped_parts := [ each p in parts :
                           some sp in shipments
                           (sp.pnr = p.pnr) ] ;      ...
```

```
      end
```


Example:
```
    var local_supply: relation <sname,pname> of
                      record sname: suppliername;
                             pname: partname
                      end ;        ...
    with mybusiness do
    begin   ...
    local_supply := [ <s.name,p.name> of each s in suppliers,
                      each p in parts : s.city = p.city ]
    end
```


## 3. Boolean Queries:

Quantified expressions return Boolean values.


Example:
```
    var all_squares_are_red :  Boolean ;   ...
    with mybusiness do
    begin   ...
        all_squares_are_red := all p in parts
        ( (p.color = red) or not (p.shape = square) ); ...
    end
```


Note, that this Boolean query is equivalent to
```
    all_squares_are_red :=
        all p in [each p in parts: p.shape = square]
            ( p.color = red ) ;
```


The element test operator, in, tests whether or not a given element exists in a relation; the set-like operators =, <>, >, >=, <=, < test relation equality or inclusion.


Example:
```
    var thispart: item;
        thispart_exists: Boolean;   ...
    with mybusiness do
    begin   ...
        thispart_exists := thispart in parts ;   ...
    end
```

Note that this Boolean query is equivalent to
```
    thispart_exists := parts [ thispart.pnr ] = thispart ;
```
and to
```
    thispart_exists := some p in parts (p = thispart) ;
```
It differs, however, from
```
    thispart_exists := parts [ thispart.pnr ] in parts ;
```
The latter query is equivalent to
```
    thispart_exists := some p in parts (p.pnr = thispart.pnr);
```

Example:
```
  var theseparts: items;
      these_parts_exist: Boolean;   ...
  with mydatabase do
  begin   ...
          these_parts_exist := theseparts <= parts;   ...
  end
```


PASCAL/R's query facility is considered to be relationally complete.

Absolute quantification is not directly supported; there exists, however, a function, size(re), counting the number of elements in a relation expressions, re.


Example:
```
  var three_red_parts :  Boolean ;   ...
  with mydatabase do
  begin   ...
      three_red_parts :=
          size ( [each p in parts : p.color = red ] ) = 3
  end .
```


## 3.2.2  Retrieval of Information About Database Constituents


The database schema is stored in a data dictionary organized as a PASCAL/R relational database. Privileged users (e.g. the DBA) are allowed to access the dictionary in order to retrieve and partially alter schema information.

### 3.2.3   Retrieval of System Performance Data

Information about the physical organization is stored
in the dictionary, e.g.  on

- storage utilization  (allocated  vs.  utilized  storage
  space),

- access paths and storage structures,

- distributions of relation component values (see 4.4.1),

and can be accessed by privileged users (e.g. the DBA).


### 3.2.4   Report Generation

Relation expressions can be listed  on  printers  and
displays.

Example:
```
   list ( [ <s.name,p.name> of each s in suppliers,
            each p in parts: s.city = p.city ] ) ;
```
This list command may produce the output
```
   abel      axe
   abel      bolt
    :         :
   zille     wrench
```

Standard programs for output  formatting  (report  generation) exist.


### 3.2.5   Constraints and Limitations

The current implementation is restricted to

- five (free and quantified) variables per expression

- 15 subexpressions, e.g.,
```
        ... and ( s.city = p.city )  ...
```

within relation expressions and quantified expressions.


### 3.2.6  Additional Aspects of Retrieval and Presentation

Facilities for automatic screen layout exist.


### 3.3  Alteration


Altering operators on relations are considered as generalized assignment operators.

In the array-like perception an altering operation replaces the value of a relation element by a new value specified as an expression of the relation element type.

In the set-like perception an altering operation replaces the value of a relation by a new value specified as a relation expression.


### 3.3.1  Insert Facilities

Relations can be altered by insert operations.

In the array-like perception a single element is inserted by assigning a (record) expression to a relation element that is not yet inserted.

```
Example:
  with mybusiness do
    if not parts[4711] in parts
    then parts[4711] :=
          < 4711, 'cardreader', blue, 20, 'washington' > ;
```

The above PASCAL/R expression constructs a record value of type item from its component values using the PASCAL/R record constructor <...> .

In the set-like perception elements are inserted into
a relation by assigning a (relation) expression to a relation variable.


Example:
  <u>var</u> insparts: item;   ...
  <u>with</u> mybusiness <u>do</u>
  <u>begin</u>
     parts := [ <u>each</u> p <u>in</u> parts : true ,
                <u>each</u> i <u>in</u> insparts :
                  <u>not</u> <u>some</u> p <u>in</u> parts (i.pnr = p.pnr) ]
  <u>end</u>


The Value of the above relation expression is the union of
the  old value of the relation variable and the set of new
elements to be inserted.

    An equivalent shorthand  notation  using  the  insert
operator, :+, reads


Example:
  <u>var</u> insparts: item;   ...
  <u>with</u> mybusiness <u>do</u>
  <u>begin</u>   ...
     parts :+ insparts ;
  <u>end</u>


Using the insert operator the insertion of a  single  element reads


Example:
  <u>with</u> mybusiness <u>do</u>
    parts :+ [ <4711,'cardreader',blue,20,'washington'> ] ;




3.3.2  Delete Facilities


    Relations can be altered by delete operations.

    In the array-like  perception  a  single  element  is
deleted by assigning the "void" (record) expression (i.e.,
the empty  record  constructor,  < >  )  to  an  existing

relation element.

Example:
  <u>with</u> mybusiness <u>do</u>
    <u>if</u> parts[4711] <u>in</u> parts
    <u>then</u> parts[4711] := < >  ;


In the set-like perception elements are removed from a relation by assigning a (relation) expression to a relation variable.

Example:
  <u>var</u> delparts: item;   ...
  <u>with</u> mybusiness <u>do</u>
  <u>begin</u>  ...
    parts := [ <u>each</u> p <u>in</u> parts : <u>not</u> <u>some</u> dp <u>in</u> delparts
                ( p.pnr = dp.pnr ) ]
  <u>end</u>


The value of the above relation expression is the set difference of the old value and the set of elements to be deleted.

    An equivalent shorthand notation using the delete operator, :-, reads


Example:
  <u>var</u> delparts: item;   ...
  <u>with</u> mybusiness do
  <u>begin</u>  ...
    parts :- delparts
  <u>end</u>


Using the delete operator for the deletion of a single element reads

Example:
  <u>with</u> mybusiness <u>do</u>
      parts :- [ parts[4711] ] ;

## 3.3.3  Modify Facilities

Relations can be altered by modify operations.

In the array-like  perception  a  single  element  is modified  by assigning a (record-) expression to an existing relation element.


Example:
  with mybusiness do
    if parts[4711] in parts
    then parts[4711] :=
         < 4711, 'parfume', yellow, 1, 'cologne' > ;


Note, that individual components of relation elements  can be modified


Example:
  with mybusiness do
    if   parts[4711] in parts
    then parts[4711].weight := 2;


In the set-like perception relation elements are  modified by  assigning  a (relation) expression to a relation variable.


Example:
  var modparts: item;   ...
  with mybusiness do
  begin   ...
    parts := [ each p in parts :
                  not some mp in modparts (p.pnr = mp.pnr),
               each mp in modparts :
                  some p in parts (mp.pnr = p.pnr) ]
  end


The value of the above relation expression is  defined  by set difference and set union.

An equivalent shorthand  notation  using  the  modify operator, :&, reads

```
var modparts: item;   ...
with mybusiness do
begin   ...
      parts :& modparts
end
```

Using the modify operator the modification of a single element reads

Example:
```
  with mybusiness do
  parts :& [ < 4711, 'parfume', yellow, 2, 'cologne' > ];
```

## 3.4  Additional Functional Capabilities

### 3.4.1  Arithmetic and String Operations

The arithmetic operators are presented in 2.7.2 .

Because strings are defined as arrays of characters, PASCAL/R has (limited) facilities for manipulating strings.

### 3.4.2  Sorting

Relation elements are not sorted. However, through the relation handling procedures low, next, high, prior (see 3.2.1(1)) the order defined by the key values can be exploited to gain an ordered access to relation elements.

### 3.4.3  Library Functions

PASCAL/R provides the PASCAL standard functions and a function 'size' counting the number of elements of a relation-valued expression.

### 3.4.4  User Defined Functions

Within the PASCAL/R language environment the user can define any kind of private functions; libraries can be built up by means of external procedures and functions.

### 3.4.5  Transactions

The PASCAL/R system is a single-user system. A new version that allows concurrency through "transaction" procedures with (selected) relations as read and read/write parameters is under development.

### 3.4.6  Multi-Tuple Alterations

The relation altering operators, :=, :+, :& (see 3.3.1 to 3.3.3) may alter more than one relation element (=tuple) at a time.

### 3.4.7  Grouping

### 3.4.8  Exception Handling Mechanisms

The PASCAL/R compiler tries to detect  as  many  type
violations  (=exceptions)  as possible. In case a decision
cannot be made without runtime  information  warnings  are
generated at compile time.

A specific class of runtime type violations occurs if
the  value  of  a relation expression does not fulfill the
key constraint defined on a left-hand-side relation  variable.   A collision of this kind is resolved by a standard
coercion mechanism: The system selects one element out  of
every  multiplicity  of  elements  of  the right-hand-side
relation expression that has the same  value  in  what  is
defined to be the key of the left-hand-side variable.  The
fact that a coercion between relation expression and relation variable occurred is reported to the user through the
standard status variable, coerced.

# 4. Definition, Generation And Administration Facilities

## 4.1 Definition Facilities

### 4.1.1 Constituents of a Database Definition

A PASCAL/R database definition (=schema definition) contains the definition of the

- database type,

- relation types,

- relation element (=tuple) types, and

- relation element component (=attribute) types (=domains).

This information is stored in a database dictionary (logical part).

In addition, a PASCAL/R database definition contains information about

- the (primary) indexes to be maintained for relations,

- the blocksize of the files implementing relations,

- expected and actual distribution of component values (see 4.4).

This information is stored in the database dictionary (physical part).

## 4.1.2  Database Definition

A database type (=logical schema) definition associates a database type identifier with a database type. A
database is defined by the PASCAL/R data structure database and specifies for each database component (=relation)
its type and a component identifier.


Example:
```
{ type (=Schema) definition }
 type business = database suppliers :  companies;
                          parts      :  items;
                          shipments  :  orders
             end;
```


Technically, a database is defined by a utility program that reads a database type (=logical schema) definition from a text file and initializes the logical part of
a database dictionary.

A database type definition is not completely defined
until the constituting relation types (e.g., companies)
are defined.

A database type definition does not require the
introduction of type identifiers for the relation types.


Example:
```
 type business = database
                 suppliers : relation ... end ;
                 parts     : relation ... end ;
                 shipments : relation ... end
             end ;
 (see example 4.1.3)
```


## 4.1.3  Relation Definition

A relation type definition associates a relation type
identifier with a relation type. A relation type is
defined by the PASCAL/R data structure relation and specifies the relation element type as well as the relation
key.

```
type
   companies = relation < snr > of company;
   parts     = relation < pnr > of item;
   shipments = relation < snr,pnr > of order;
```

A relation type is not completely defined until the constituting relation element (=tuple) type (e.g. item) is
defined.

A relation type definition does not require the
introduction of type identifiers for the relation element
(=tuple) types.

Example:
```
   type companies = relation < snr > of record ... end ;
        parts     = relation < pnr > of record ... end ;
        shipments = relation < snr,pnr > of record ... end ;
```
(see example 4.1.5).

## 4.1.4  View Definition

A PASCAL/R database definition defines base relations
only.

## 4.1.5  Tuple Definition

A relation element (=tuple) type definition associates a relation element type identifier with a relation
element type.

The relation element type is defined by the PASCAL
data structure record (only "flat" records without variants and with unstructured components are allowed), and
specifies for each relation element component (=attribute)
its type and a component identifier.

Example:
```
type item = record pnr     : integer;
                    pname   : partname;
                    color   : colortype;
                    city    : cityname
             end
```

The relation element type is not completely defined  until
the  constituting  component types (=domains) (e.g. color-
type) are defined.

The relation element  type  definition  requires  the
introduction  of  type identifiers for the component types
(=domains); a component type identifier  is  either  user-
defined  (see 4.1.7) or it is one of the built-in identifiers integer, real, Boolean, char, ascii.


## 4.1.6   Attribute Definition


A relation element component (=attribute) is  defined
as  part  of  the  relation  element  type definition (see
4.1.5). The component  definition  specifies  a  component
(=attribute)  type  (=domain,  see  4.1.7) and a component
identifier.


## 4.1.7   Domain Definition


A relation element  (=tuple)  component  (=attribute)
type  (=domain)  definition  associates  a  component type
identifier  with  a  component  type.  A  component  type
(=domain)  is  defined  by  a  PASCAL "simple type", i.e.,
either by

- a standard type, i.e., integer,  real,  Boolean,  char,
  ascii
  Example:
```
        type quantity = integer;
```

- a scalar type, i.e., an ordered set of values given  by
  an  enumeration  of  the identifiers which denote these
  values
  Example:
```
        type colortype = ( red, blue, yellow, green, black );
```

- a <u>subrange</u> <u>type</u>, i.e., a subrange of a scalar type, or of the types integer or char given by the indication of the first and last value in the subrange.
Example:
      <u>type</u> creditstatus = 0..30;


## 4.1.8 Definition of Additional Database Constituents

Technically, a database is defined by means of an interactive utility program that reads the logical part of a data dictionary (i.e., the database type definition) and asks the (privileged) user for information about access paths and storage structures (see 4.1.1) to be stored in the physical part of the data dictionary.


## 4.2 Generation Facilities

A PASCAL/R database is generated by a utility program that accesses a database dictionary and creates an empty database according to the schema, access paths, and storage structures as defined in the dictionary.

An identifier is associated with the database.


## 4.3 Database Redefinition


## 4.3.1 Renaming Database Constituents

Within a PASCAL/R program the identifier for the database, the database type, the database relation types, the relation element types, and the element components can be redefined.

### 4.3.2 Redefining Database Constituents

An existing database can be redefined only with respect to its access paths.

### 4.4 Database Regeneration and Reorganization

### 4.4.1 System-Controlled

The database system maps string values that exceed an implementation-dependent length into code numbers of fixed length. This mapping is order preserving and may lead to collisions, i.e., depending on the actual distribution of string values different strings may be mapped into the same code number. Collisions of this kind are resolved by system- controlled recoding. The user does not realize how data are represented.

### 4.4.2 DBA-Controlled

A database can be regenerated to provide new or to cancel existing access paths. A database can be reorganized to minimize the amount of storage occupied. A database may also be reorganized by redefining the mapping between string values and code numbers (see 4.4.1) to achieve a desired distribution of code numbers. The DBA can ask for reports on the physical status of the database.

## 4.5  Data Dictionary

The database definition is stored in a database dictionary.  The database dictionary is perceived as a
PASCAL/R database and can be accessed by privileged users.

## 5. Interfaces and DBMS Architecture

### 5.1  System Architecture

The <u>Relation</u> <u>Selection</u> <u>System</u> (RSS) evaluates N-element and Boolean Queries. RSS optimizes query evaluation by scanning a (range) relation only once and by minimizing the size of intermediate results; basically, this is achieved by rearranging the order in which subexpressions and quantifiers are evaluated.

The <u>Relation</u> <u>Access</u> <u>System</u> (RAS) performs the 1-element access using existing access paths.

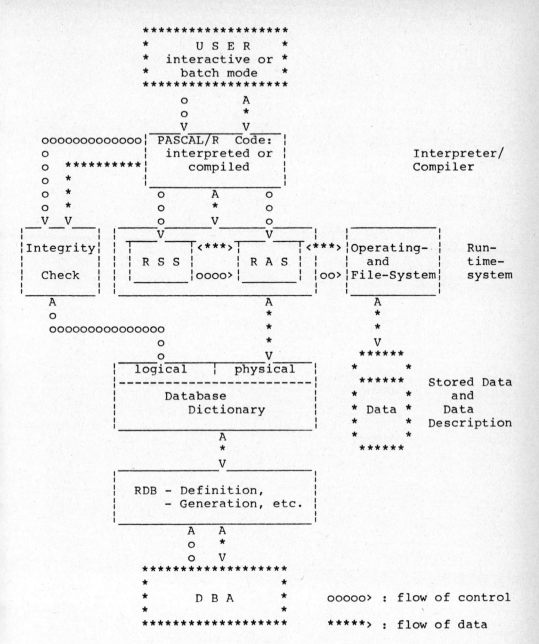

Figure 5.1   PASCAL/R System Architecture

## 5.2  Interface Descriptions

The PASCAL/R system provides three user interfaces:

1. Database / PASCAL/R-program

2. Database / interactive user

3. Database / privileged user (DBA) .

1. PASCAL/R-programs:

The program parameter mechanism binds a PASCAL/R database as a global variable to a PASCAL/R program.

Example:
```
  program copyitems ( mybusiness, orderlist ) ;
  type   ... { see 3.1 }
        item     = record ... end ;  ...
        business = database ... ;
                          parts : relation <pnr> of item;
                  end;
  var  mybusiness : business ;
        orderlist : file of item ;
  begin    ...
        rewrite (orderlist) ;
        with mydatabase do
        for each p in parts : some sp in shipments
                (p.pnr = sp.pnr) do begin orderlist↑ := p;
                                          put (orderlist)
                                  end
  end .
```

PASCAL/R extends the programming language  PASCAL
essentially by

- a data structure relation,

- the  operations  introduced  above  for  (database)
  relations,

- a control structure controlled by the general relation selection mechanism.

The only difference between  PASCAL/R  database  relations  and  PASCAL/R  program  relations  is  their

lifetime. Database relations are explicitly generated and dropped by a privileged user (DBA); the lifetime of program relations is determined by the lifetime of the PASCAL/R block in which they are declared. Treating database and program relations alike means in particular:

- Expressions over database variable constituents can be assigned to program variables (database queries);

- Expressions over program variables can be assigned to database relations (database alterations).

- Boolean queries can control program statements (if..then..else..; while..do..; repeat...until..;)


Example:
```
     var thispart: item;    ...
     with mydatabase do
     begin  ...
         if not some sp in shipments
                ( sp.pnr = thispart.pnr )
         then parts :- [ thispart ]
     end
```
Example:
```
     var theseparts : items ;    ...
     with mydatabase do
     begin  ...
       if not some sp in shipments
                ( some tp in theseparts (sp.pnr = tp.pnr) )
       then parts :- theseparts
     end
```

An essential construct of PASCAL/R is a for control structure controlled by a relation element selection, each r in rel : p(r) (see 3.1). That way the elements can be processed one at a time by any PASCAL statement.

Example:
```
var max_weight_shipped : weightunits ;
begin ...
   max_weight_shipped := 0 ;
   with mydatabase do
      for each p in parts :
         some sp in shipments (p.pnr = sp.pnr)   do
      if   max_weight_shipped <  p.weight
      then max_weight_shipped := p.weight ;
end
```

The with-statement of PASCAL is generalized so that database relations can be denoted without prefixing them by the database identifier, e.g.,

Example:
```
with mybusiness do
begin ...  parts  ... end;
```

is equivalent to

```
mybusiness.parts
```

Relations can also be declared as local variables in PASCAL/R procedures; they can be passed as (read and read/write, i.e., value and reference) parameters; so, procedure statements can be used to form compound database query and altering operations.

Example:
```
procedure average_weight ( parts: items;
                           var avg: weightunits );
   var a: weightunits;
   begin    a := 0;
      for each p in parts : true   do
         a := a + p.weight;
      avg := a div size(parts)
   end
```

# 6. Operational Aspects

## 6.1 Security

### 6.1.1 Access Control

Currently, access to a PASCAL/R database is controlled only through the standard feature of the operating system.

## 6.2 Physical Security

### 6.2.1 Concurrency Control

The PASCAL/R system is a single-user system. The system guaranties that no two users access a database in parallel.

Extensions to a multi-user system are under development.

## 6.2.2 Crash Recovery

The current version of PASCAL/R provides no restart and no recovery capabilities.

## 6.3 Operational Environment

PASCAL/R is implemented on the DECsystem-1o.

## 6.3.1 Software Environment (Operating System)

The PASCAL/R system operates under the TOPS 10 operating system. It makes use of the file system in the same way standard PASCAL does, with the addition of direct block access.

Index structures are part of the Relational Access System (RAS, see 5.1).

The PASCAL/R system (Compiler, RSS, RAS, Utilities) is coded in PASCAL, except about one page of MACRO10 assembler code.

Portability problems are caused mainly by the PASCAL/R compiler; it is a one-pass compiler and the code generation is scattered all over the compilation process. However, the portation effort is reduced significantly if a PASCAL compiler exists on the target machine.

## 6.3.2 Hardware Environment (CPU, Memory, Peripherals)

```
CPU         : KA, KI, or KL processors for the DECsystem-1o.
Main Memory : for compilation:
                        32 K words  for code
                                    (1 word = 36 bit)
                + min. 13 K words  for data.
              typically 45 K words.
```

```
        for execution:
            ca. 7..15 K words   system code
            + min.  1 K words   program code
            + min.  1 K words   for data
            + min. 2x128 words  buffer size

Peripherals : discs
```

## 7. Essentially Relational Solutions For Generalized DBMS Problems

In the PASCAL/R Project particular emphasis has been put on the following two issues :

1. design of a <u>linguistic</u> <u>form</u> (i.e. language) <u>that</u> <u>fully</u> <u>supports</u> <u>the</u> <u>relational</u> <u>model</u> as originally defined by Codd.  Additionally language design goals are :

   - economy of concepts,

   - orthogonality,

   - generality.

   The syntax and semantics of the language are defined informally  and formally (PASCAL/R Report and PASCAL/R Denotational Semantics Definition, see section 1.7).

   A particular goal of the language design effort was  to study interfaces between programming languages and database models, and between compilers and database systems.

2. <u>data</u> <u>independence</u> <u>and</u> <u>system</u> <u>optimization</u>. The logical and physical definition of data is strictly separated. Thus, only the system (RSS and RAS, see section 5.1) can  access and utilize information about the physical properties of data, e.g. quantity, access paths, storage structure.  Within the PASCAL/R Project there is a strong tendency to use a subset of  PASCAL/R to implement the  language's full relational functionality.

# 8. Database Applications Using The System

Currently, PASCAL/R is used for

- Database Research:
    Principles of Database and Transaction Design;
    Maryland, Hamburg, Zuerich, Toronto.

- Implementation of Database Systems and Languages:
    Hamburg, Toronto.

- Teaching of Database Concepts:
    Hamburg, Zuerich.

- Database Development and Use:
    Hamburg.

The biggest PASCAL/R database developed at Hamburg University holds oceanographic data and biological and survey data on antarctic fish (Krilldb). Krilldb is under development since about 18 months and ran through three iterations; currently, it holds approximately 60 Mbyte of (primary) data in 50 relations and has been used by some 35 fish biologists. The procedure library for Krilldb has about 8000 PASCAL/R statements. Krilldb is used to store and evaluate data collected by the "First International Biomass Expedition" (FIBEX). Data collected by previous expeditions were kept and evaluated separately by means of file systems. Data conversion turns out to be a minor problem: small PASCAL/R programs read data from files of various formats, test the data on plausibility and integrity, and insert it into Krilldb.

3.10  Feature Analysis Of PRTV

Feature Analysis of the
Peterlee Relational Test Vehicle (*)

by
Peter Hitchcock

British Columbia Systems Corporation
112 Fort Street
Victoria, British Columbia
Canada V8W 2Y2

November 1980

(*) Prepared while the author was at the Department of Computer Science, University of Victoria, Victoria, British Columbia.

# 1.0  INTRODUCTION

## 1.1  IDENTIFICATION

The Peterlee Relational Test Vehicle (PRTV) was developed at
the IBM UK Scientific Centre in Peterlee, County Durham,
England.

## 1.2  STATUS

### 1.2.1  SYSTEM

PRTV was a research system with the objectives of being a
test bed for relational ideas, providing a suitable database
subsystem for other projects and as a framework for
performing database experiments.  The project has been
concluded and PRTV is no longer active.

### 1.2.2  APPLICATIONS

PRTV was designed to be a query oriented database subsystem.
The accessing language, ISBL (Information System Base
Language), was intended as a language that a more user
friendly front end would compile into, although in some
applications it was used directly.

Five applications of PRTV have been documented mostly
involving queries against databases that remained fairly
static in content.  Databases of 110 Megabytes and relations
containing 11-1/2 million tuples were handled
satisfactorily.  The final evaluation of PRTV (14), found
that real world queries often ran into many hundreds of
relational statements. The end users were not capable of
writing such programs, instead they accessed the system
through a parameter driven programs which invoked the PRTV
system.  Writing these programs was eased by a macro
processor and a flexible way of defining extensions to the
system.

## 1.3  SYSTEM BACKGROUND

Four distinct systems were developed in the period
1970-1978.  IS/1.0 was operational by the end of 1971.  It
implemented the basic relational algebra but was found
deficient in its end user language features and its overall
performance.  IS/1.1 improved the language features through
the use of a macro processor, MP/3.  In 1973/74, the
performance issues were addressed by IS/1.2 adopting a new
architecture and end user language.  IS/1.2 was renamed PRTV
in 1975 following the incorporation of facilities for end
user extensions.

Use of the prototype in live applications was a major aspect
of the research activity.

## 1.4  OVERALL PHILOSOPHY

PRTV did not attempt to provide the full requirements of an
integrated database management system.  Limited resources
and work being done elsewhere directed the projects
activities towards interactive query and problem solving
applications.  It was intended that PRTV be appropriate as:

*    a stand alone query/problem solving system

*    a database component of a specialized application

*    a relational front end to a conventional database
     management system.

The need to extend easily the functions provided by the
system was stressed throughout.

## 1.5  ESSENTIALLY RELATIONAL CHARACTERISTICS

PRTV does not support the insert, update and delete rules of
Codd 1979, but has all the other characteristics of a
relational system.  It does not support semantic integrity
constraints.

## 1.6  INTERFACES

 1. Database Schema Definition:  not implemented directly

2. Query Language:  ISBL

3. Database Altering:  ISBL

4. Constraint Definition: ISBL

5. Database Generation and Regeneration:  utilities

6. Data schema redefinition and re-naming:  not implemented

7. Report generation:  not implemented

8. Data Entry:  utility, or user written function

9. Security Definition, Monitoring and Control:  ISBL used
   to define logon password and the relations seen by other
   users.

10. Database Control (utilities):  no special language

11. Definition of Storage Structure, Indexes and Access
    Paths:  no user interface

12. Database Dictionary:  ISBL can be used to give
    properties of relations in the database

13. Interface to Programming Language:  ISBL can be passed
    to PRTV from PL/I.  Results are returned in relational
    files accessible to PL/I.  Likewise relational files can
    be created in PL/I and passed to PRTV where they are
    turned into relations and stored.

    User extensions to PRTV are written to a certain
    protocol using PL/I.


## 1.7  DOCUMENTATION

1. P.A.V. Hall, P. Hitchcock and S.J.P. Todd, An Algebra of
   Relations for Machine Computation, Conference Record of
   the second ACM symposium on Principles of Programming
   Languages, Palo Alto, Calif., January 1975.

2. A. Hansel, A Formal Definition of a Relational Database
   System, IBM UK Scientific Centre Report No. 80, 1976.

3. S. Mandil, The MP/3 Macroprocessor, IBM UK Scientific
   Centre Report No. 44, 1973.

4. P. Hall, Optimisation of a Single Expression in a
   Relational Database System, IBM Journal of Research and
   Development, 20 3, 1976, 244-257.

5.  S. Todd, Relational Database Research at the IBM UK
    Scientific Centre.  Peterlee: A Survey, IBM UK
    Scientific Centre Report No. 93, 1977.

6.  B. Aldred, S. Huyshe, A. Storey, Information Systems for
    Agricultural Crop Research, IBM UK Scientific Centre
    Report No. 103, December 1978.

7.  B. Aldred, B. Smedley, UMS Technical Overview, IBM UK
    Scientific Centre Report No. 50, May 1974.

8.  Swedish Environment Protection Board and IBM Sweden, An
    Experiment using Database Techniques in Environment
    Research, IBM Sweden, November 1972.

9.  B.K. Aldred, B. Smedley, An Urban Management System – A
    General Overview, IBM UK Scientific Centre Report No.
    81, 1976.

10. R.N. Stamper, The LEGOL Project, a Survey, IBM UK
    Scientific Centre Report No 81, 1976.

11. O. Bertrand, NLS, A Generator and Interpreter of User
    Languages, Proc. of IBM International Conference on
    Relational Database, Bari 1976.

12. M. Tibuya, Practice of Noun Phrase Model, Proc. of IBM
    International Conference on Relational Database, Bari
    1976.

13. R.A. Storey, M. Bunzel, N. Ourusoff, W. Trebeljahr,
    Report of the World Health Organisation Information
    Systems Programme and IBM UK Scientific Centre Study on
    the Design of Information Systems, IBM UK Scientific
    Centre Report No. 105, January 1979.

14. R.A. Storey, An Evaluation of the Peterlee Relational
    Test Vehicle, IBM UK Scientific Centre Report No. 106,
    August 1979.

15. PRTV User Manual, IBM UK Scientific Centre Technical
    Note, No. 34.

16. S. Todd, The Peterlee Relational Test Vehicle – A System
    Overview, IBM Systems Journal, 15 4, 1976.

17. A. Storey, World Health Organisation/ IBM UK Scientific
    Centre Joint Study Report on the Design of Information
    Systems, IBM UK Scientific Centre Report No. 105,
    January 1979.

18. C. Jardine, J. Owlett, Applying a Relational Database
    System to Historical Data, IBM UK Technical Note No. 74,
    1979.

19. P. Hitchcock, User Extensions to the Peterlee Relational Test Vehicle, Proceedings of the Conference on Very Large Data Bases II, Brussels, September 1976, North Holland 1976.

20. M.G. Notley, On the Design of a Graphic Display Language for Interrogating a Large Data Base, UKSC 4, June 1971.

21. M.G. Notley, Extensibility in Information Systems, Symposium on Extensible Languages, Grenoble, September 1971.

22. M.G. Notley, A Model of Extensible Language Systems, UKSC 22, March 1972.

23. M.G. Notley, The Peterlee IS/1 System, UKSC 18, March 1972.

24. J. Owlett, Deferring and Defining in Databases, Architecture and Models in Data Base Management Systems (ed. G.M. Nijssen), North Holland 1977.

25. R.A. Storey and S.J.P. Todd, Performance Analysis of Large Systems, Software Practice and Experience, vol. 7, no. 3,pp. 363-369, June 1977.

26. S.J.P. Todd, Implementation of the Join Operator in Relational Data Bases, IEE/IERE Colloquium on Information Structure and Storage Organisation, London, April 1974.

27. J.S.M. Verhofstad, The PRTV Optimizer: the Current State, TN 41, UKSC 83, May 1976.

28. J.S.M. Verhofstad, An Evaluation of the PRTV Optimiser, UKSC 91, in preparation.

29. IBM Corporation, IBM Interactive Management and Planning System under IMS/VS - User Guide, SB11-5220, December 1978.

## 2.0  DATABASE CONSTITUENTS


### 2.1  GENERAL DESCRIPTION

Term Translation Table

| PRTV Term | Feature Catalogue Term |
|---|---|
| database | database |
| workspace | - |
| relation | relation |
| tuple | tuple |
| selector name | attribute name |
| component | attribute value |
| domain | domain |


#### 2.1.1  RELATIONAL VIEW

The constituents of a user´s view of a PRTV database are:
DB (= database), WS (= workspace), R (= relation), T (=
tuple), S (= selector = attribute = rolename), C (=
component = object), D (= domain).

These constituents are related as follows:

A relational DB consists of R´s of possibly different types.
A WS consists of R´s of possibly different type.  An R
consists of a set of T´s of identical type.  A T is a set of
S, C pairs with each C taken from a named domain D whose
underlying type is character or numeric.  The type of a
relation or tuple is a set of S:D pairs.


#### 2.1.2  RELATIONAL FILE VIEW

The constituents of the view of PRTV seen from a PL/I
program are those of the relational view except that a
relation is presented and accepted as a relational file (=
RF).  An RF is an ordered stream of T´s.

T´s do not appear directly as PL/I structures, rather the
individual objects in a tuple are read by giving the
appropriate selector name.  An implicit cursor is used to

step through a relational file using a get next command.

When a relational file is written it could contain duplicate T´s.  These duplicates are removed when the file is closed, converted to a relation and stored in the WS or DB.

## 2.2  DATABASE

### 2.2.1  DATABASE STRUCTURE

A database is a set of named relations.  These names are partitioned into sets, not necessarily disjoint, which represent those relations that can be seen by each user of the database system.  The database has no further structure from the point of view of PRTV.

### 2.2.2  DATABASE OPERATIONS

Database operations are part of ISBL.  The commands are:

1. Create relation <rname>: adds an identifier to the set of relations.

2. Destroy relation <rname>: removes an identifier from the set.

3. Put <rname>: copies a relation from WS to the DB relation.  Any relation may be copied to WS provided that a DB relation with the right name exists.

4. Get <rname>: copies a relation from DB to WS and enters its name in the WS.

5. Keep <rname>: When an assignment is made to a relation, the result is not realised immediately but is kept in the form of a definition.  The PUT command would copy this definition into the database. The KEEP command evaluates the definition and stores the result in the database. This is intended as an optimization feature to avoid multiple evaluations  of a common expression. The user would see a difference only if the assignment involved values which referred to a relation by name, rather than by value.

6. Pass relation <rname><user name><status>: gives another user the right to access a relation.

## 2.2.3  DATABASE CONSTRAINTS

No mechanism is implemented.


## 2.3  RELATION


### 2.3.1  RELATION STRUCTURE

A relation is a set of tuples.  The order of the tuples is
arbitrary, as is the order of the components of a tuple.
There are no duplicate tuples in a relation.

The type of a relation is a set of S, D pairs.  All the S
names of a relation must be distinct, although the D names
need not be.

Base relations have their type defined when they are entered
into the DB or WS.  Relations, which appear on the left-hand
side of an assignment statement, inherit their type from
that of the relational expression on the right-hand side.
DB relations when created by Create Relation have a name but
no type.  This type is inherited from the corresponding WS
relation when the Put Relation command is executed.  It was
felt that this _interpretive_ style, cf APL, was better suited
to the query environment.


### 2.3.2  RELATION OPERATIONS

ISBL has the six operations of the relational algebra i.e.
selection, projection, union, intersection, difference and
join.  Additional operations are the renaming of selectors,
the calculation and concatenation of a new component to each
tuple in a relation, and glumping (or grouping).  The
division operator is not implemented.  The result of any
operation is itself a relation and so complex expressions
can be built up without restriction.  The compatibility
requirements of the operands will be discussed with each
operator.


### 2.3.3  RELATION CONSTRAINTS.

Not implemented.

## 2.3.4 ADDITIONAL PROPERTIES OF RELATIONS

None.


## 2.4 VIEWS


### 2.4.1 VIEW STRUCTURE

Views in PRTV are implemented in terms of relations which
may be passed to other users. Their value is given by a
relational expression. These views are essentially read
only, in that there is no general mechanism which will
reflect updates back to the underlying relations in whose
terms the view is defined. Views can be defined and passed
at any time.


### 2.4.2 VIEW OPERATIONS

Views are defined as relational expressions using the
relational operations defined earlier. Names in the
expressions may be bound in two ways, by value, or by name.

Binding by value is the default binding, the current value
of the named relation is found and inserted in the
expression. Any subsequent changes to the original relation
are not reflected in the value of the view.

If binding by name is specified, the named relation is not
evaluated at the time of definition of the view, but is
evaluated every time the value of the view is used. If the
underlying relation is changed in value, then these changes
are seen in the view.

There are no restrictions on the use of views. If they are
updated, this is seen as a redefinition of the relation
which held the view, rather than a change to the underlying
relations in whose terms the view was defined.

Views behave exactly as other relations and so may be stored
in the database using the PUT operator and retrieved using
the GET operation. In the case of a view defined in terms of
relations bound by name, the view is not materialized,
rather the view definition is stored. Views are only
materialized when the value of the relation is required. See
however the later section on optimization. Care is needed to

ensure that the base relations referred to in such stored
views do not have their type changed, or are not deleted.


## 2.4.3  VIEW CONSTRAINTS

None.


## 2.4.4  ADDITIONAL PROPERTIES OF VIEWS

None.


## 2.5  TUPLE


## 2.5.1  TUPLE STRUCTURE

A tuple is specified in ISBL as a set of selector : domain :
object triples.  The ordering of objects within a tuple is
immaterial.   Selector names must be unique within a tuple.
ISBL then treats the tuple constant as a relation containing
one tuple; it can then be used by the relational operations
in a natural fashion.


## 2.5.2  TUPLE OPERATIONS

None.


## 2.5.3  TUPLE CONSTRAINTS

Object values must agree with the data type of the domain.


## 2.5.4  ADDITIONAL PROPERTIES OF TUPLES.

Tuples are also presented to the user via the relational
file interface.

## 2.6  ATTRIBUTES


### 2.6.1  ATTRIBUTE STRUCTURE

Attribute name is the feature analysis term for the selector
names of PRTV.

Selector names distinguish the individual ´columns´ of a
relation.  The selector names of a relation can be changed
by the project operator.  They must be unique within a
relation.

Within a tuple the selector identifies an object which takes
its value from a named domain.


### 2.6.2  ATTRIBUTE OPERATIONS

The objects in a tuple which are selected by selectors can
be combined into expressions, called selector expressions,
according to the basic underlying datatype of the domain.
The basic arithmetic operations are:  +, -, *, / and
POWER(N1,N2).  The character operations have names similar
to PL/I.  They are:  SUBSTR(S1,S2,S3), CONCAT(S1,S2),
INDEX(S1,S2), VERIFY(S1,S2) and LENGTH(S).  STREQU(S1,S2)
compares two strings for equality when they are formed as
the result of expressions.

It was a design feature of PRTV that it should be easy to
add new functions should they be required.

Objects selected can also be compared if they come from the
same domain.  The comparison operations are =, ^=, >, >=, <,
<=.  Only = and ^= are applicable to character domains.

The use of selector expressions will be found under the
individual relation operations.


### 2.6.3  ATTRIBUTE CONSTRAINTS

None.


### 2.6.4  ADDITIONAL PROPERTIES OF ATTRIBUTES

None.


## 2.7 DOMAIN


### 2.7.1 DOMAIN STRUCTURE

A domain is a set of possible values whose underlying
datatype is numeric or character.  Domains cannot be defined
so that this set of possible values is restricted in some
way.  Domains are used to provide some compatibility
checking for the relational operations.


### 2.7.2 DOMAIN OPERATIONS

The usual character and arithmetic operations are
applicable, via selector expressions, to domains of the
appropriate type.


### 2.7.3 DOMAIN CONSTRAINTS

None.


### 2.7.4 ADDITIONAL PROPERTIES OF DOMAINS

None.


## 2.8 ADDITIONAL DATABASE CONSTITUENTS


### 2.8.1 WORKSPACE

The intent of the WS is that relations can be manipulated
and changed without affecting the database. WS operations
are part of ISBL.  Get and Put transfer relations to and
from the workspace and database. The assignment statement of
ISBL creates and gives values and types to new relations in

the workspace.


## 2.8.2  RELATIONAL FILES


An alternative view of a relation as a flat file is possible
when the database is accessed via a PL/I program. See
section 2.1.2

## 3.0  FUNCTIONAL CAPABILITIES


### 3.1  QUALIFICATION


#### 3.1.1  RESTRICTION

Selection (:) acts on a relation and results in a new
relation of the same type.  This new relation is a subset of
the old, each of its tuples satisfying some criteria called
a _filter_.  Filters contain comparisons between the objects
in a tuple or between the objects and constants.  The
results of the comparisons, which can involve selector
expressions, can be combined with the usual Boolean
operators, |, ^, &, or (,).

Comparison is only allowed between objects from the same
domain.

Example:

        S1: (SNAME = ´SMITH´|STATUS = 20)

Projection (%) acts on one relation to produce another.  For
each tuple in the original, the result contains a tuple with
the selectors renamed, or only some objects present.  A
_projection_ _list_ specifies selection of components and their
new names.  It contains selector names from the input
relation, each optionally qualified by a new name for the
corresponding component in the result relation.  This
qualification is done using the _rename_ (->) operator. To
rename some components and to leave the remainder unchanged,
a list is given of the selectors to be changed with their
new names, followed by ,... (meaning and so on).

Example:

S% CITY -> TOWN, COLOR    yields the relation

```
+---------+---------+
| TOWN    | COLOR   |
+---------+---------+
| London  | Red     |
| Paris   | Green   |
| Rome    | Blue    |
+---------+---------+
```

SP% QTY -> AMOUNT,... yields a relation having type
(S#,P#,AMOUNT).

Only selector names are changed by the rename operator.  The
domains remain unchanged.

Any duplicate tuples in the resulting relation are purged.

It is an error if the selector names in the relation are no
longer distinct.


## 3.1.2  QUANTIFICATION

PRTV is not calculus oriented, and so the existential and
universal quantifiers do not appear explicitly. However such
queries can be answered in the algebra based systems and the
glumping operator is useful in this regard.


## 3.1.3  SET OPERATIONS

Union (+) operates on two relations to produce a relation
which is the set union of the two.  The types of the two
relations must be the same, and this is the type of the
result relation.  Any duplicate tuples are purged.

Intersection (.) produces the intersection of two relations
of the same type.

Difference (-) has been generalised to work on two relations
which may be of different types, but which have some
selector; domain pairs in common.  The result is a set of
tuples in the first relation for which there are no tuples
in the second relation which have equal values on the common
components.  If the types of the two input relations is the
same, then we have the conventional set difference.  The
type of the result is the type of the first relation.

Example:

Those parts not currently supplied is given by the expression

    P - SP.

which has type (P#, PNAME, COLOR, WEIGHT, CITY).


3.1.4  JOIN


Join has been generalised in the same way as difference.

The join operator (*) accepts two operand relations to produce a new relation.  The type of the join is dictated by the selector names that each relation has in common.  At one extreme, if there are no selector names in common, then every tuple in the first relation is paired with every tuple in the second.  Each pair is concatenated to give a tuple in the result relation.  This is the full quadratic join or cross product.

If some selector names match, tuples are put into the result relation only if the values for the common selectors in each of the contributing tuples also match.  This is a join on common selectors or an equi-join over several domains.

If the two relations have the same type, then join degenerates into an intersection.

Example:

    A = (S*P)%S#,P# is an equijoin on CITY, and gives potential local suppliers of parts.

    The expression, SP - A, gives information about things which are not supplied locally.

The _rename_ extension to the project operator was introduced so that the right type of join could be described.

An example of this would be a reflexive join.

Consider the relation PP:(super:part,sub:part). It has selector names ´super´ and ´sub´ which serve to describe the relationship between a part and the parts that make it up. To expand the parts explosion by one level, we must join the relation to itself.This is achieved by taking the ´sub´ selector of the first relation and the ´super´ selector of the second relation and renaming them to the selector ´link´. The join will now take place over this common

selector name resulting in a relation with selectors
´super´, ´link´ and ´sub´. The ISBL expression follows:

(PP % super,sub->link) * (PP % sub,super->link)


### 3.1.5  NESTING AND CLOSURE

The result of any relational operation in PRTV is itself a
relation.  Complete nesting of relational expressions is
allowed.


### 3.1.6  ADDITIONAL ASPECTS OF QUALIFICATION.

None.


## 3.2  RETRIEVAL AND PRESENTATION


### 3.2.1  DATABASE QUERIES

Database queries are expressed as relational expressions.
The result of a query is a relation which may be stored or
listed.  The query facility is relationally complete in the
sense of DSL Alpha.

The design of PRTV made it easy to add user defined
functions to the query language.


### 3.2.2  RETRIEVAL OF INFORMATION ABOUT DATABASE CONSTITUENTS

PRTV contains the following expressions which give
information about the results of relational expressions.
This information is returned as a relation, and so can
subsequently be used in queries.

DEGREE (expression) - gives the degree, (no. of selectors),
of the relational expression.

CARD (expression) - gives the cardinality of the relational
expression.

DOMAINS (expression) - gives the domain names and selector names of the specified expression.

PRTV also contains the commands:

LIST RELATIONS - gives the relations accessible to this user, together with their domain and selector names.

LIST DOMAINS - gives the domain names known to this user with their underlying data type of character or number.

LIST USERS - gives the logon identifiers of all the authorized users/of this particular database.


## 3.2.3  RETRIEVAL OF SYSTEM PERFORMANCE DATA

None beyond that supplied by querying the operating system.


## 3.2.4  REPORT GENERATION

Not implemented as part of PRTV.  The intent was that this would be supplied via the PL/I interface.


## 3.2.5  CONSTRAINTS AND LIMITATION.

No limitation.


## 3.2.6  ADDITIONAL ASPECTS OF RETRIEVAL AND PRESENTATION

A PL/I program accesses a relation as a relational file. Any ISBL command can also be issued from a PL/I program. There are also PL/I procedures to obtain information about database constituents.


## 3.3  ALTERATION

Relations in the workspace  may have their values changed by the assignment of a relational expression. PRTV adopts an APL-like approach to this assignment. The relation on the

left hand side takes it type from the type of the expression
on the right hand side. This type is always well defined.
This means that the type of a relation may be change by
assignment. New selectors could be added, or the type
changed completely.

New relations in the workspace may be created by assignment
by virtue of their appearance on the left hand side of an
assignment statement.

Relations in the database have their value changed by using
the PUT operation to replace the old value with the
corresponding one from the workspace.


### 3.3.1   INSERT FACILITIES

For relations a change relation is built up and the union
operator used.  A change relation may be built from tuple
constants or from a user defined function.  To change the
database structure Create Relation, Create Domain are used.


### 3.3.2   DELETE FACILITIES:

Similar to insert, except that set difference is used.  To
change the database structure,  Destroy Relation, Destroy
Domain, and Drop may be used.

No constraints are implemented.  This is dangerous because
of defined relations.


### 3.3.3   MODIFY FACILITIES.

Usually performed as a combination of insert and delete
operations.


### 3.3.4   COMMIT AND UNDO FACILITIES

PRTV supports the idea of a workspace.  Relations may have
their values changed in the workspace.  These changes can
subsequently be committed to the permanent database.

3.3.5  ADDITIONAL ALTERATION FACILITIES

Concatenation operator.

The concatenation operator (#) allows the concatenation of new objects to a tuple.  The value of this object is defined in terms of the existing objects in the tuple by the means of Selector expressions.  The selector name and domain name of the new object must be defined.

Example:  Abbreviate part names to three characters

A = P#ABBREV(PNAME) <- SUBSTR(PNAME,1,3)

P = A%(P#,ABBREV -> PNAME,COLOR,WEIGHT,CITY).

3.4  ADDITIONAL FUNCTIONAL CAPABILITIES

3.4.1  ARITHMETIC AND STRING OPERATIONS

See selector expressions

3.4.2  SORTING

Because of the way PRTV is implemented, relations are presented so that they are ordered on the first domain and within the first, on the second etc.  This is not guaranteed as part of the data model.  The order of domains can be changed by the projection operator.

3.4.3  LIBRARY FUNCTIONS

There are some builtin functions such as SUBSTR, INDEX which are used in selector expressions. The builtin function SUM is used in association with the glumping operator to formulate the functions of COUNT, TOTAL, AVERAGE etc. PRTV was designed in such a way that it is very easy to include and use user defined functions, making a special library of builtin functions unnecessary.

### 3.4.4   USER DEFINED FUNCTIONS

Tuple at a time extensions can be defined through selector
expressions.  Library functions are added by writing a PL/I
procedure to a certain protocol and relinking the system.

Full user defined functions are defined using the relational
file interface and the CALL statement.

### 3.4.5   TRANSACTIONS

Not implemented.

### 3.4.6   MULTI-TUPLE ALTERATIONS

Nothing special was implemented.

### 3.4.7   GROUPING

PRTV implements the glumping operation.  This is a class of
queries which have the following general structure.

  1. First partition the set of tuples into groups.

  2. Act on each group to produce one (or zero) tuples which
     form a new relation.

The ISBL takes the form

    Relational expression $(control fields)(selector(domain)
    <- outer selector expression...)

where $ represents the glumping operator, control fields
represent those fields on which grouping is defined, and the
outer selector expression represents a constant, SUM (inner
expression), or any selector expression.  An inner
expression may be a constant or a field which is not a
control field.

Example:

Find the average weight of parts from each city.

```
P $(CITY)(TOTAL PARTS(N) <- SUM(1)
            TOTAL WEIGHT(N) <- SUM(WEIGHT)
            AVG WEIGHT(N) <- TOTAL WEIGHT/TOTAL PARTS.)
```

The result is a relation with selectors

        CITY, TOTAL PARTS, TOTAL WEIGHT, AVG WEIGHT.


3.4.8  EXCEPTION HANDLING MECHANSISMS


Nothing special was implemented.


3.4.9  ADDITIONAL FUNCTIONAL CAPABILITIES


None.

## 4.0  DEFINITION, GENERATION AND ADMINISTRATION FACILITIES.

These are not separated from the language which has already been described and which is available to all users.  The way that it should be used in practice is the following. Starting with an empty database a special user, the database administrator, is created.  He creates and loads the appropriate relations, creates additional users, and passes relations or views of relations to them.

There are system utilities to reorganize the database.

## 5.0   INTERFACES AND DBMS ARCHITECTURE

### 5.1   SYSTEM ARCHITECTURE

PRTV was designed as a database subsystem.  It is accessed
through the language ISBL either directly by the user at a
terminal, or through the relational file interface from the
host language PL/I.

### 5.2   INTERFACE DESCRIPTIONS

#### 5.2.1   ISBL

This language is the data sublanguage used directly by an
end user, compiled into by a particular user front end, or
called from a PL/I program.  The language is a linear text
stream.  It is used to access all the constituents named
earlier.  ISBL is based on the relational algebra.
Relations are manipulated as sets, but the results are
presented as tables.  User extensions, which are written in
PL/I can be invoked by a CALL statement or by their use in
selector expressions.

#### 5.2.2   INTERFACE FROM PL/I

ISBL statements can be passed to PRTV by using a PL/I call
statement.  The results are passed back to PL/I through the
relational file interface.

# 6.0 OPERATIONAL ASPECTS

## 6.1 SECURITY

### 6.1.1 ACCESS CONTROL

Simple password protection at logon time. No logging or
audit trails. Each user sees his own set of relations, some
of which may be views of relations held by others.

## 6.2 PHYSICAL INTEGRITY

### 6.2.1 CONCURRENCY CONTROL

No concurrent access.

### 6.2.2 CRASH RECOVERY

Not implemented.

## 6.3 OPERATING ENVIRONMENT

### 6.3.1 SOFTWARE ENVIRONMENT

PRTV runs under CMS or TSO, and uses the basic file access
methods.

### 6.3.2 HARDWARE ENVIRONMENT

PRTV was implemented on IBM 370/145 and requires a 1
Megabyte virtual machine under CMS or an 896K byte virtual

partition under OS.

PRTV consists of about 17,000 lines of PL/I and 4,000 lines of Basic Assembler Language. The executable module occupies about 400K bytes.

## 7.0  ESSENTIALLY RELATIONAL SOLUTIONS FOR GENERALIZED DBMS PROBLEMS

### 7.1  GLUMPING OR GROUPING

Although it is possible to specify any operation on relations using the tuple at a time interface into PL/I, there is an important class of extensions which can be considered separately within the relational framework. These have the general structure: first partition the set of tuples into groups, and then act on each of the groups to produce one (or zero) tuples which form a new relation. This corresponds to producing relations which are not in first normal form, (elements of tuples can themselves be a set of tuples or a relation), and then acting on each of these sub-relations. The PRTV designers decided that the user should not be allowed to store and manipulate relations which were not in first normal form and so the partitioning and the corresponding actions were coalesced together into one glumping operation. The primitive builtin function SUM, allows for the definition of the more general operations such as SUBTOTAL etc. in a more general way. This approach does not extend to grouping hierarchies of more than two levels, nor does it allow glumped relations to be loaded or displayed, both of which might be useful presentations for end users. For an example of glumping see the earlier section on grouping

### 7.2  SELECTOR RENAMING

The problem addressed here is the one of closure. The result of any relational expression is itself an expression whose type must be known. It was felt that the conventional algebraic join definitions that were known in 1974 did not make the type of the result sufficiently clear if the domains being joined had different selector names. Often this was resolved by assignment to a relation of a known type or by a reliance on column ordering. Both these techniques were thought to be unsatisfactory and the definition of join based on common names was implemented. This forced the designers to implement a renaming operation, which was found to be quite usable in practice.

### 7.3  OPTIMIZATION

The use of relations and their set oriented operations meant
that sophisticated solutions could be found to the database
optimization problem. The underlying implementation
technique used was to delay the evaluation of a relation or
a relational expression until that result was needed.  This
is the case if the result is to be listed, turned into a
relational file or stored in the database using the KEEP
operation.  Instead a table is built up which associates
each relation name with the expression which is to be
evaluated to find its value. These      expressions are not
exactly the same as the original, some compilation has been
done to resolve names where necessary, a syntax check has
been done etc. When the relation is subsequently referred
to, this expression is used to build up a more complex
expression for the result. This deferred evaluation of
intermediate results continues until the expression must be
evaluated. Optimization techniques can then be used to
change the order of evaluation, to recognize common subexpressions etc. More detail can be found in (4,27,28).
When evaluation does take place it happens in a stream
fashion.  Tuples are requested one at a time from the top of
the evaluation tree. These requests filter down to the base
relations at the bottom, where they are recovered from the
database again a tuple at a time.  This means that a wrong
result could be rejected by a user before the complete
relation has been realised. In practice, this idealised
evaluation is not always possible, it may be necessa/ry to
have a break point in the evaluation tree so that the
intermediate result can be sorted. The optimization
techniques try  to delay this as long as possible so that
the size of the set to be sorted is as small as possible.

It is interesting to note that this idea of deferred
realisation has very little effect on the user language. The
only place where it is exposed is the necessity for the KEEP
operation which forces realisation of an expression before
it is stored in the database.  Deferred realisation and the
mechanism for views are clearly very similar.

The large scale evaluation of PRTV (14) found that, although
in theory the user is not aware of optimization, performance
considerations meant that he should have some notion of what
was going on.

## 8.0  DATABASE APPLICATIONS USING THE SYSTEM

PRTV was developed as an experimental tool to investigate
relational techniques.  It has now been evaluated (13,14)
and is no longer in use.

There are six major applications of PRTV in the public
domain.

The first was a joint project in 1972 between the Swedish
Environmental Protection Board and IBM Sweden, studying the
effect of thermal pollution by nuclear power stations using
the Baltic Sea for cooling water (8).

The second was a joint project with the Greater London
Council in urban planning and used an early version of PRTV
as a database subsystem.  It made use of the extensibility
features to enhance calculation and report generation
facilities and in particular introduced facilities for the
processing of geographic data.  The database size was
approximately 60 Megabytes (9).

The third application, LEGOL (10), provided a formal
framework for describing statute law, PRTV being used to
store both the legal rules and precedents.  A partricular
characteristic of the LEGOL application was that a large
number of relational operations (e.g. 60) were carried out
on small data volumes (e.g. relations with 10 tuples).  PRTV
was principally designed to carry out fewer operations on
substantially larger relations.

In the fourth application (11,12), PRTV was used in natural
language and user oriented query systems, where the main
research was directed towards problems of language
interpretation.

The fifth application was a major evaluation of PRTV,
conducted as a joint project with the World Health
Organization (WHO), (13,14).  The database was large, 108
Megabytes, with one relation containing 11-1/2 million
tuples.  To improve performance, this relation was reduced
to 500,000 tuples by storing some fields as repeating
groups.  Some of the queries required of the order of 100
ISBL statements for their solutions.  To make the system
more accessible to the end users, a parametric intertace was
written for certain classes of query.  The flexibility of
the architecture made this and other links to support
functions such as report generation and complex statistical
analysis very easy.

Functionally, the system covered most of the applications which were running on the previous COBOL based system and indeed, the scope of the application was broadened because of the extensibility inherent in PRTV. Many queries were answered which could not have been answered by the existing system.

The major difficulties were performance related arising from the volumes of data. Some of these problems had been addressed in the optimizer component of PRTV, but in practice, it was not possible to shield the end user entirely from such things as the best sequence for operations, etc.

Finally, IBM has announced an International Field Program called Interactive Management Planning System or IMPS (29). IMPS is a relational system which aslo allows a read only view of IMS data.The external syntax of IMPS is not the same as that of PRTV, although the function is very similar. The underlying relational access methods upon which it is built are those of PRTV.

3.11   Feature Analysis Of QBE

Feature Analysis of
Query-by-Example

by
C.J. Bontempo

IBM Corporation
Systems Research Institute
205 East 42nd St., 7th Floor
New York, New York 10017

December 1980

Feature Catalog of Query-By-Example
(December 1980)
by
C. J. Bontempo
IBM Corp.-System Research Institute

(This is a preliminary document subject to change.  It does not
constitute a representation of Query-By-Example by the IBM Corporation)


1.0 Introduction


1.1   Identification

QUERY-BY-EXAMPLE.  The system was introduced by the IBM
Corporation as an Installed User Program (IUP) in September
1978.  QUERY-BY-EXAMPLE was originally a research project at
the T. J. Watson Research Lab in Yorktown, N. Y.  The principal architect of the language is Dr. Moshe' Zloof, IBM
Research, Yorktown.

1.2   Status

1.2.1   System

The system is currently an Installed User Program, a product
of the IBM Corporation Data Processing Division.  This description is restricted to the current IUP version of QBE.  It is
also being used as the nucleus of a research (experimental)
project in office automation at Yorktown.  The extended system
is called Office procedures By Example (OBE) which involves not
only tables but text, reports and charts as well as the ability
to distribute these objects according to several criteria.

1.2.2   Applications

QBE can be used in support of a broad range of applications such
as accounting, finance, inventory teaching, sales, oil and chem-
ical analysis and personnel.  It is useful as an application
development tool as well as an interactive  query processor.  The
system runs under VM-CMS.  The maximum size database is 226 megabytes.

1.3   System Background

As noted in 1.1, the system was originally experimental.  It
underwent revisions and extensions before its release as a
product; many of these were made as a result of human factors
experimentation.

## 1.4   Overall Philosophy

Query-By-Example's outstanding characteristic is probably
its usefulness to non-programmers and those with only limited
programming skills.  Users can create base relations, insert,
delete and modify relations, create snapshots (derived static
relations), and query against relations using a language as
powerful as the relational calculus.

The user thinks in terms of tables, rows and columns and
performs database operations by making appropriate entries in
skeleton tables.  The system provides a comprehensive range of
authorization and security facilities.  In addition, a programming interface is provided by which QBE can be called from
PL/I or APL.

The philosophy behind Query-By-Example is to provide the end-
user a powerful tool to define, query, update and control a
relational database with the perception of manual manipulation
of tables.  This is achieved by programming directly on two-dimensional skeletons of tables thus using a metaphor familiar to
the user as opposed to a linear string programming language,
(although a linear syntax is also available).  It is important
to stress that users can define their own tables, thus setting
up their own applications, without the aid of professional
programmers.  In general, the system seeks to facilitate user
interface through a uniform table oriented language for major
database processing functions.

## 1.5   Essentially Relational Characteristics

QBE processes relations represented as two-dimensional tables.
There are no external links among tables that are perceptible
to the user.  There are no order dependencies among tuples or
attributes; no essential insert, delete, update dependencies;
and no index dependencies for data access.

Indeed, there is a real sense in which the relational data model
has been captured and extended to the user interface insofar as
query and database modification functions are expressed through
the use of two-dimensional tables.  Union, Intersection,
Difference, Projection, and Join can be expressed in the language.
Insert, delete and update rules as specified in CODD's later
work are not supported on a predeclared basis; but the query
language can be used to specify referential integrity as a
part of an update transaction.  Specifically, query-dependent
insert, delete and update statements can be used to enforce
CODD's Rule 2.

## 1.6   Interfaces

Query-By-Example has two language forms:  tabular (self-contained) and linear (program embedded).  The first makes use
of two-dimensional tables as the vehicle thru which the user
(1) requests information from the database (2) specifies changes
to tables (3) specifies changes to the database.  The objectives

of this technique is to allow users to express various functions in tabular format, thus capitalizing on the tabular form of data organization which the system employs. Simply, since the user thinks of data as stored in tables, the system allows the user to express queries and other functions in the same way. The user specifies what information is desired by making entries in appropriate columns of relevant tables. An example illustrates this technique against a table, called PART.

Display (or print) the names of green parts.

| PART/ | P# | / | PNAME | / | COLOR | / | WEIGHT | / | CITY | / |
|-------|----|---|-------|---|-------|---|--------|---|------|---|
| / | | / | P.__ROD/ | | GREEN | / | | | / | / |

The entries for the query show the two basic concepts involved in QBE query formulation (1) constant elements and (2) example elements. In this case GREEN is the constant element entered by the user under COLOR. __ROD is an example of a possible answer. Since the user wants to see elements of this sort, this example element is preceded by P., for print (or display). From the simple, basic notions of example element, constant element, and tables, extremely complex queries can be constructed. This language form is provide for interactive terminal users. It constitutes a self-contained language form.

A linear syntax is also provided for use with PL/I and APL. This one-dimensional syntax can be used to define tables as well as specify queries embedded in the two host languages mentioned. There are no known limitations to the expressive power of this format for query as compared to the tabular format. That is, any query that can be formulated in the two-dimensional screen format can be expressed in the linear format.

Find the names of green parts.

```
PART(PNAME/COLOR)
(/P.__ROD/GREEN)
```

The linear representation of a query is entered within a PL/I application program or an APL workspace. QBE processes the query when invoked from the program or workspace. Linear queries can be stored in CMS files and executed via a CMS terminal session.

In both modes, queries can be stored for subsequent execution. Both linear and two-dimensional forms use a small set of keywords.

Interfaces for specific functions are as follows:

1. Database schema definition: QBE
2. Query: QBE
3. Alteration: QBE
4. Constraint definition: QBE
5. Database generation and regeneration: bulk loader, LQBEDB. IMS extract from a DL/I database.

6. Database schema redefinition and renaming: QBE
7. Report generation: the system provides images of multiple tables as output; table names and column names can be customized for output; column width for output is under user control through QBE.
8. Data entry: insertion via QBE or utilities as in 10 below.
9. Monitoring: the user who creates a table has complete control over its use.
10. Database control (utilities): bulk loader from any normalized file; IMS extract; dump (CMS facility used to record disk image) and interactive dump through QBE snapshots; backup through CMS utility (CMSDDR); restore through log. Recovery using normal CMS facilities.
11. Definition of storage structure: automatic system function; indices: user can request column inversions; access path selection: automatic system function.
12. Data dictionary: limited dictionary with entries retrievable through QBE.
13. Special purpose language: none.

## 1.7 Documentation

1. Zloof, M. M. (1977). "Query-by-Example: A Data Base Language". IBM Systems J., vol. 16, no. 4.

2. Zloof, M. M. (1975). "Query-by-Example". AFIPS Conf. Proc., National Computer Conf. 44, pp. 431-438.

3. Zloof, M. M. (Sept. 22-24, 1975). "Query-by-Example: The Invocation and Definition of Tables and Forms". Proc. of the Int'l. Conf. on Very Large Data Bases, Boston, Massachusetts, pp. 1-24.

4. Zloof, M. M. (1975). "Query-by-Example" Operations on the Transitive Closure". IBM Research Report RC 5526, IBM Thomas J. Watson Research Center, Yorktown Heights, New York.

5. Zloof, M. M. (1976). "Query-by-Example: Operation on Hierarchical Data Bases". AFIPS Conf. Proc., National Computer Conf. 45, pp. 845-853.

6. Zloof, M. M. (Feb. 7, 1978). "Security and Integrity Within the Query-by-Example Data Base Management Language". IBM Research Report RC 6982, IBM Thomas J. Watson Reearch Center, Yorktown Heights, New York.

7. Query-by-Example Terminal User's Guide, IBM Manual SH20-2078

8. Query-by-Example Program Description/Operations Manual, IBM Manual SH20-2077

9.  Zloof, M. M. (1980).  "A Language for Office and Business
    Automation", IBM Research Report RC 8091, Thomas J. Watson
    Research Center, Yorktown Heights, N.Y. (appears in Pro-
    ceedings of NCC Office Automation 1980, March 3-5, 1980,
    Atlanta, Georgia).

## 2.0 Database Constituents

## 2.1 General Description

### 2.1.1 Term translation table

| Feature Catalog Term | QBE Term |
| --- | --- |
| Database | Database |
| Relation | Table |
| View | Snapshot |
| Tuple | Row |
| Attribute | Column |
| Domain | Domain |

In addition, a value of a specified attribute for a given table (i.e., the component of a row) is a DATA ELEMENT. The primary key of a relation is a table KEY.

## 2.2 Database

### 2.2.1 Database Structure

A database is a collection of tables defined by one or more users, or, by the DBA, and system tables as follows:

        TABLE   table
        DOMAIN  table
        PROGRAM table
        AUTHORITY  table

The TABLE table contains the names of the tables in the database and the owner of each table. The DOMAIN table contains all previously defined domains with their names, ATTRIBUTES (QBE term for data characteristics such as data type, image, minimum and maximum input column width), and owners. The PROGRAM table contains the names of stored queries or programs. It contains query name, owner and descriptive comments. The AUTHORITY table contains table names and the identities of users authorized to access them on a selective basis i.e., access to: print, update, delete and insert.

At the schema level, a database consists simply of table names and column names for the collection of tables in the database associated with a user identification. That is, all tables a user is authorized to access. At the instance level, the database consists of all rows of all tables which a particular user is authorized to access.

## 2.2.2  Database Operations

The only significant database operations are those used to
display the names of tables and columns in the database.

The P.  operator is used to obtain the names of all tables
in the database.  This operator is entered by the user in the
left-most column of a skeleton table.

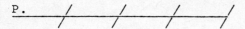

The system response is a display of all user-defined tables
and system tables.

The P.P. yields all table and column names.  It constitutes a
user's DATA BASE DIRECTORY.

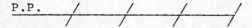

## 2.2.3  Database Contraints

Authority over user tables is controlled by the user who defines
and creates the table.  System tables are created and maintained
by the system.  Authority to see and update system table contents
can be granted to users only by the DBA.  The DBA has unlimited
access to all user defined tables.  Since preparation of  external
storage areas for all user defined tables can be accomplished
only under the DBA identification, the DBA has ultimate authority
over all table creation.

A database cannot exceed 226 megabytes.

## 2.3  Relation

### 2.3.1  Relation Structure

A relation, defined as a set of ordered n-tuples whose components consist of elements from n-domains (not necessarily distinct), is represented as a two-dimensional table of columns and rows.  A table is the only perception of a relation which the user has.  Duplicate tuples are not allowed; attribute order is insignificant.

### 2.3.2  Relation Operations

Important operations on relations are as follows:

1.  I.table name I. - defines a table with the given table and column names i.e. insert the named table into the database directory of tables (TABLE table)

2.  D.table name    - deletes the named table from the database directory; all tuples of the named table must be deleted prior to this operation

3.  table name$_1$ U. table name$_2$ - Changes the name of the table from table name$_1$, to table name$_2$

These operations are performed on displayed skeleton tables. Thus, to insert a new table name with related column names the user would key the I. operator and the table and column names into the skeleton table as follows:

| I. SUPPLY I. | S# | SNAME | STATUS | CITY |
|---|---|---|---|---|
| | | | | |

4.  P. - This operator displays or prints all rows of a table.  To this end it is used as a row operator.

Display the entire SUPPLY table

| SUPPLY | S# | SNAME | STATUS | CITY |
|---|---|---|---|---|
| P. | | | | |

The user keys in the 'P.' operator under the table name.

5.  D. - deletes all rows of a table

    Delete all information about suppliers

    | SUPPLY | S# | SNAME | STATUS | CITY |
    |--------|----|-------|--------|------|
    | D.     |    |       |        |      |

6.  I. column name - used to add a new column to
    the definition of a table
    already defined to the system.

    | SPJ | S# | P# | J# | I.QTY |
    |-----|----|----|----|-------|
    |     |    |    |    |       |

7.  D. column name - deletes a column from the def-
    inition of a table already
    defined to the system.

    | SPJ | S# | P# | D.J# | QTY |
    |-----|----|----|------|-----|
    |     |    |    |      |     |

    Result:

    | SPJ | S# | P# | QTY |
    |-----|----|----|-----|
    |     |    |    |     |

8.  Describe - creates table and domain definitions
    needed by the bulk loader; used when
    saving a table for subsequent return
    to the database.

9.  Disk - creates data elements and column defini-
    tions needed by the bulk loader; used
    when saving a table for subsequent return
    to the database.  This command and
    DESCRIBE can only be used by the DBA.

10.  I. table name I., P. - these operators can be
    used in conjunction to
    create a SNAPSHOT, i.e.,
    a static derived view
    from one or more tables.

11.  AUTH - used to specify authority over a user
    created table.  This operator is used
    in conjunction with I. (grants author-
    ity), D. (withdraws authority) and U.
    (changes authority).

Grant authority to CODD to print SNAME and STATUS
in the SUPPLY table.

| | SUPPLY | / S# | / SNAME | / STATUS | / CITY/ |
|---|---|---|---|---|---|
| I. | AUTH(P.)CODD | | N | M | |

## 2.3.3. Relation Constraints

Only authorized users of tables can delete, print/display,
or create a snapshot of those tables.

Every table must have a KEY column to insure uniqueness
of rows.

A column can be added to a table that contains data only
by creating a SNAPSHOT of that table.

A table cannot have more than 100 columns.

Tables must be 1st normal form relations.

## 2.3.4.

Design considerations at the gross logical DB design level
involve answers to the following questions:

1. What will the tables contain?
2. What makes each table unique?
3. What does the data in each column look like?
4. What columns will the user need to compare,
   either in the same or in different tables.

## 2.4 Views

The system supports static views, but does not support
dynamic views. The system term for the former is SNAPSHOT.
There is no difference in the structure of a SNAPSHOT and
other tables.

Snapshots are created as user defined tables using the I.
(insert) operator and the full facilities of the query language to define the new relation. The naming mechanism is
the same as the mechanism used to create the source relations.

Keys are inherited from source relations, but users can over-
ride this automatic key propagation.

The following example indicates how snapshots are named and
derived.

Create a SNAPSHOT of those suppliers who supply project J1.

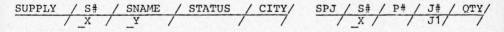

| SUPPLY | / S# | / SNAME | / STATUS | / CITY/ | SPJ | / S# | / P# | / J# | / QTY/ |
|---|---|---|---|---|---|---|---|---|---|
| | / X | / Y | / | / | | / X | / | / J1/ | / |

```
I.SSUPP I / S#  / SNAME /
   I.    / _X /  _Y  /
```

SSUP is the SNAPSHOT consisting of rows of suppliers who satisfy the query.

### 2.4.2.  View Operators

Any operation valid for base relations can be used on SNAPSHOTS.

### 2.4.3.  View Constraints

Any user authorized to read a base relation can create a snapshot using that relation.  Otherwise, no other constraints found.

### 2.4.4.  Additional Properties of Views

SNAPSHOTS can be useful in creating and manipulating subsets of a base table as "private files".  They are also useful in creating back-up copies of a table prior to modification of the table.

## 2.5  Tuple

### 2.5.1

A tuple is a row in a table.  It consists of attributes defined over domains.  A row is implicity defined when the table is defined.  Tuples are also created dynamically as the results of queries.  Keys are defined at the relation level.  Unique tuple identification is achieved through a table KEY which consists of one or more column names (attributes).

### 2.5.2  Tuple Operations

Tuples may be inserted, deleted, updated or retrieved.  New tuples can be formed from tuples or components of tuples in one or more tables.  This formation of new tuples may be based on matching values of a common domain.  Normally, redundant tuples are not retrieved, but the ALL. operator can be used to return duplicates when desired.

Query-dependent inserts, deletes and updates can be specified.  For example, a tuple insertion can be dependent upon the outcome of a query.

Tuples are not ordered; order can be requested for display or other output.  Tuples must be unique.  The system rejects attempts to violate uniqueness and notifies the user by message.

## 2.5.4. Additional Properties of Tuples

Tuples are treated as elements of a set or rows in a table.

## 2.6 Attributes

An attribute is a COLUMN NAME. Attributes are defined based on domains (defined at data definition time). Multiple attributes can be defined over a single domain.

Attributes are defined as a part of table definition. After the table column names have been entered in the skeleton table (see section 2.3.2), the system displays the following table:

| SUPPLY | S# | SNAME | STATUS | CITY |
|--------|--------|--------|--------|--------|
| KEY | Y(DEF) | Y(DEF) | Y(DEF) | Y(DEF) |
| DOMAIN | - | - | - | - |
| TYPE | - | - | - | - |
| IMAGE | - | - | - | - |
| ICW | 2(DEF) | 5(DEF) | 6(DEF) | 4(DEF) |
| OCW | - | - | - | - |
| POSITION | 1 | 2 | 3 | 4 |
| INVERSION | Y(DEF) | Y(DEF) | Y(DEF) | Y(DEF) |

At this point, the system has assumed a default option of 'yes' for KEY in every column. Similar defaults are assumed for other data characteristics (system name is ATTRIBUTE). The user can accept the defaults or modify the table as appropriate, thus overriding the defaults. The meanings of the keywords provided in the left-most column is as follows:

KEY
- Yes or No

DOMAIN
- The user may reference a previously defined domain or create a new domain. The domain "definition" consists of domain name and TYPE, IMAGE, ICW and OCW as defined below. When a previously defined domain is referenced, these four characteristics are inherited.

TYPE
- Character, numeric (fixed or float), date, or time.

IMAGE
- Defines output image for all data except character. This is an edit (for display or print) that includes space for dollar sign, decimal point, plus or minus, credit symbol or exponent. Leading zeros can be replaced by blanks or asterisks. Date components can be defined, e.g., day, month, year, as well as time, e.g., hour, minute, second.

ICW
- Maximum number of characters or numbers that can be input to this column without widening the column.

```
OCW       -  Width of character data for output (display).
POSITION  -  The sequence of columns when the system
             produces column headings, that is, unless
             dynamically modified by the user.
INVERSION -  Index created for the column.  (Y or N)
```

Tuples can be manipulated with the standard comparison operators $=, >, <, \neg =, > =, < =$. Arithmetic operators are as follows

```
+ (Add), - (Subtract), *(Multiply),
/ (Divide), **(Raise to a power (A² ))
```

The following aggregation functions are available as built-in functions:

```
FUNCTION                          MEANING

CNT.         Count the number of items.
SUM.         Add the items together;
             may be used only with numeric data.
AVG.         Find the average of the items;
             may be used only with numeric data.
MAX.         Find the maximum (largest) value.
MIN.         Find the minimum (smallest) value.
UNQ.         Use unique values only (omit
             duplicates).
```

The unique function can be used with the count, sum, or average functions. Thus, CNT.UNQ. means count only the unique values.

For all of these operations, data must be of the same type.

2.7   Domain

2.7.1   Domain Structure

A domain is defined as the set of values from which the
values (system term is DATA ELEMENT) in an attribute (COLUMN)
are drawn.   Domain data types are:

> Character
> Fixed
> Float
> Date
> Time

2.7.2   Domain Operations

Domain names, IMAGE, TYPE, OCW, ICW can be read from the
DOMAIN table.

2.7.3   Domain Constraints

Domain values are variable length not exceeding 3200 bytes.
Maximum column width for output is 75.   Data which exceeds
the maximum is folded automatically.

2.8   Additional Database Constituents

Transactions, Database Directory (system tables).

## 3.0  Functional Capabilities

### 3.1  Qualification

The basic framework within which retrieval (identification and selection) is achieved in QBE has already been
presented in Section 1.7 of this report.  The fundamental
selection operators are:

P.                  - selects a column or row for display
                       or print.
example element - provides an "example" of the data
                       to be selected; can be used to link
                       data in two or more tables i.e., as
                       a linking example element.
constant            - qualifies selection to some subset of
                       the rows in a table.

Example

    Select all rows of the SUPPLY table.

| SUPPLY | S# | SNAME | CITY | STATUS |
|--------|----|-------|------|--------|
| P. | | | | |

    Select all data elements (values) of the
    CITY column (attribute).  (Projection)

| SUPPLY | S# | SNAME | CITY | STATUS |
|--------|----|-------|------|--------|
| | | | P.__N.Y. | |

### 3.1.1  Restriction

Restriction is performed through the use of example elements
with the P. operator.

Example

    Find all the rows which have suppliers in
    New York City.

| SUPPLY | S# | SNAME | CITY | STATUS |
|--------|----|-------|------|--------|
| P. | | | N.Y. | |

(Projection has already been shown in 3.1.)

Restriction and projection can be combined as follows:

Print the part numbers and weights of red parts that
are less than 10 lbs.

| PART | P# | PNAME | COLOR | WEIGHT |
|------|----|-------|-------|--------|
| | P.__COG | | RED | P. $<$ 10 |

Tuple attributes (columns) can be compared to other tuple attributes as well as to constants.

### 3.1.2 Quantification

Existential quantification is implicit in those operations that result in the selection of one or more rows of a table. It is also implicit in the use of a LINKING EXAMPLE ELEMENT.

Example

> Find the supplier names for suppliers who supply Project J4.

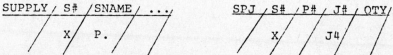

Universal quantification is supported indirectly through the use of the Count, CNT. operator.

### 3.1.3 Set Operations

Set operations are supported and can be expressed explicity as follows:

UNION:

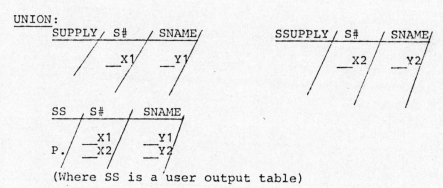

(Where SS is a user output table)

INTERSECTION:

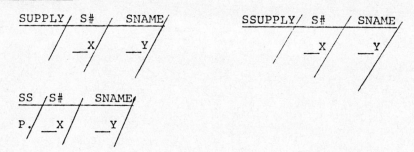

426

DIFFERENCE:

EXTENDED CARTESIAN PRODUCT:

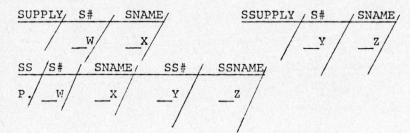

## 3.1.4  Joining

Joins are expressed by specifying the same LINKING

EXAMPLE ELEMENT in multiple tables.

Find the names of suppliers for the part with P#=P5.

| SUPPLY | / S# | / SNAME / |
|---|---|---|
| / | __X / | P. / |

| SP | / S# | / P# / |
|---|---|---|
| / | __X | / P5 / |

Result:

| / SNAME / |
|---|
| / / |

(Result contains the names of suppliers for which the
expression is true.)

A table can be joined to itself.  Up to 12 tables can be
joined in a single query.  Equi-join, Hi-join, Lo-join and
natural join are supported.  Join columns must be of the
same data TYPE.

## 3.1.5  Nesting and Closure

Queries are easily extended.  Queries can be nested and saved.

## 3.1.6  Additional Aspects of Qualification

The language supports partial qualification on a search
value.  For example:

Find any supplier whose name begins with 'X'.

| SUPPLY | / S#/ | SNAME /.../ |
|---|---|---|
| / | / | P.'X'_Y/ / |

Joins can be performed based on partial qualification.

## 3.2  Retrieval and Presentation

The result of any query can be printed or displayed with
column headings and column widths under user control.  Output
can be selected from multiple tables.  Column order and sort
order can be modified dynamically for output.

## 3.2.1  Database Queries

Queries can be saved and nested.

The result of any query is a relation. **The language is relationally complete insofar as the required algebraic operations are expressible.**

### 3.2.2  Retrieval of Information about Database Constituents

System tables may be queried. Data is retrievable from all such tables using the normal query facilities.

### 3.2.3  Retrieval of System Performance Data

Nothing found.

### 3.2.4  Report Generation

The system will print table images of any output.

### 3.2.5  Constraints and Limitations

The only constraints are imposed by a DBA or by the user who created a table through the authority mechanism.

## 3.3  User perception of data for all alteration operations is tabular.

### 3.3.1  Insert Facilities

Table definitions and user created tables can be altered by insertion. The user perceives constituents as tables.

Insertion of tables and columns has been described in prior sections of this report (See Section 2 ).

Tuple insertion - simple

Insert a new row in the SUPPLY table.

| SUPPLY | S# | SNAME | STATUS | CITY |
|--------|-----|-------|--------|------|
| I. | S4 | AJAX | | N.Y. |

Key columns (attributes) must be unique. Non-KEY columns can be null. Any blank column entry is interpreted as null.

Query-dependent insertion

Insert into PART a part whose number is P7 which has the same name, color and weight as part P4.

| PART | P# | PNAME | COLOR | WEIGHT |
|------|-----|-------|-------|--------|
| | P4 | _X | _Y | _Z |
| I. | P7 | _X | _Y | _Z |

Insertion into one table can be dependent upon a query against another table. See, for example Section 3.3.2.

3.3.2 Delete Facilities

Table contents and tuples of user created tables can be deleted.

Simple deletion - the operation can be performed selectively on a row basis.

Delete all data on red parts.

| PART | P# | PNAME | COLOR | WEIGHT |
|------|-----|-------|-------|--------|
| D. |  |  | RED |  |

Query dependent deletion -

Delete all suppliers from the SUPPLY tables who supply any part weighing less than 10 lbs.

| SUPPLY | S# | SNAME | ... |
|--------|-----|-------|-----|
| D. | _X |  |  |

| SPJ | S# | P# | J# | QTY |
|-----|-----|-----|-----|-----|
|  | _X | _Y |  |  |

| PART | P# | PNAME | COLOR | WEIGHT |
|------|-----|-------|-------|--------|
|  | _Y |  |  | $< 10$ |

### 3.3.3 Modify Facilities

Simple update –

Update the supplier city for S4 to N.Y.

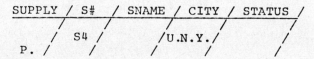

Note: The P. requests the system to display the table after the change is made.

Query – dependent update

Increase the weight of all red parts by 10%.

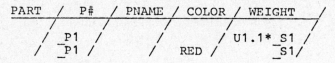

### 3.3.4 Commit and Undo Facilities

As described in 3.4.5 when a transaction is not committed, it is backed out.

### 3.4.1 Arithmetic and String Operations

Already covered in Section 2. Also, the system supports text search on columnar data including facilities for "don't care" or "universal match" logic.

### 3.4.2 Sorting

Both ascending and descending sorts with up to 12 sort "keys" are possible in a single query. Sorting occurs for presentation of data only.

### 3.4.2 Library Function

MIN, MAX, CNT, SUM, AVG.

Count unique (UN.) and count every (ALL.) are supported.

### 3.4.4 User Defined Functions

Higher level functions are defined as queries. This takes the form of:

I. query

The query is executed via an X. query command, and can be updated with screen contents using the U. query command.

### 3.4.5  Transactions

A transaction terminates when it is committed by the user.
A SAVE command can be used explicitly to force an end of
transaction for stored queries.

### 3.4.6  Multi-attribute Alterations

Multiple tuple alterations are supported along with query-
dependent alteration as noted in previous sections.

### 3.4.7  Grouping

Grouping is supported.

> Print the number of each supplier and the total quantity
> of parts supplied by each.

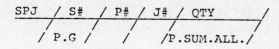

### 4.0 Definition, Generation and Administration Facilities

## 4.1 Definition Facilities

Data definition for all database constituents is part of a single uniform mechanism as described in prior sections.

### 4.1.1 Constituents of a Database Definition

Tables, Columns, Data Characteristics (system term=attributes), snapshots, stored queries, database directory.

### 4.1.2 Database Definition

Already described in prior sections of this report.

### 4.1.3 Relation Definition

As described in prior sections.

### 4.1.4 View Definition

As described in prior section 2. No query or update con-straints on operations performed on snapshots.

### 4.1.1 - 4.1.8

As described in prior sections.

### 4.2.1 Constituents of a Database Generation

Database, tables (relations), columns (attributes), rows (tuples), domains.

### 4.2.2 Generation of Database Constituents

QBE load program (bulk loader), IMS extract program, and facility for developing static views, SNAPSHOTS.

## 4.3 Database Redefinition

The databases and their constituent tables can be redefined dynamically.

### 4.3.1 Renaming Database Constituents

Changes to table names and column names can be performed dynamically as already described in previous sections. (Changes to domain characteristics can also be performed dynamically. These changes are automatically posted to system tables by the system).

### 4.3.2  Redefining Database Constituents

New columns (attributes) can be added to unpopulated tables dynamically.  Tables already populated with data can be expanded by defining a new, static view (SNAPSHOT).

Table names must be unique.  Column names need not be unique.

## 4.4  Database Regeneration and Reorganization

### 4.4.1  System-controlled

Except for updates to the system tables already noted, none known.

### 4.4.2  DBA-controlled

The DISK and DESCRIBE commands and the bulk loader already described are the only facilities found.

## 4.5  Database Dictionary

The system supports limited directory facilities as already described.  Constituents of this directory are updated automatically by the system.  Users can read entries on any database constituents they are authorized to read.  Other changes to the directory are under system/DBA control.

The language for querying the dictionary is the same as for querying other database constituents.

## 5.0   Interfaces and DBMS Architecture

### 5.1   System Architecture

The DBA is sensitive to and has ultimate authority over all tables.   One can say, therefore, that the DBA view corresponds to the conceptual view of the data.

User views correspond roughly to external views.

### 5.2   Interface Descriptions

At the logical level the primary interface is QBE, either tabular or linear syntax as already described.   All database constituents are available and all database processing functions are expressible.   The tabular language is interactive and is user driven.   This self-contained language is complete in the sense already noted.

### 6.0   Operational Aspects

6.1

### 6.1.1   Access Control

The user gains access to the system through a user I.D.
and password.  (This is the CMS protocol).  Once the user
is logged on, QBE corroborates the I.D. which implies
authorization to see various database constituents.  Private
relations can be defined as snapshots and supported as
"private" through the normal authorization mechanism.

### 6.1.2   Capability

Security is supported to the column level and can be value
based.  Any valid QBE qualifier can be used to define authorization.

The user specifies constraints as queries against tables
by keying the keyword AUTH in the TABLE NAME column.  Options
are:

> Print authority
> Update authority
> Delete authority
> Insert authority

Authority can be granted on a column basis and can be value
based.

## 6.2 Physical Integrity

Concurrent reading of the database is supported. Only a single user has write access to a database at any given time.

### 6.2.2 Crash Recovery

QBE uses a transactions concept in which copies of old and new data are both maintained until transaction completion time. This assures that system failure will not leave the data base in a state of partial modification.

Facilities exist for periodic backup of the QBE data base. In addition, all storage modification activity is separately logged and available for QBE recovery in the event of data base damage.

### 6.3.1 Operating Environment

When used interactively Query-By-Example statements go through a screen manager which sends to the parser a linear string mapping of the 2-Dimensional syntax. The parser in turn passes control to the data base processor which evaluates the queries dynamically to optimize the search. Thus the Data Base processor is an interpreter. The access module of Query-By-Example is the IBM Cambridge Scientific Center XRAM, which maintains indices dynamically.

QBE executing under control of IBM Virtual Machine Facility /370 using facilities of Control Program (CP) and Conversational Monitor Program (CMS). VM/CMS requirements include the System Extensions Program Product 5748-XB1 of the Basic System Extension Program Product 5748-XX8. If remote 3277 terminals are used, the VM/370 control program must include the fix for APARS VM07289 and VM08338.

Since part of QBE was written in PL/I, execution requires access to the PL/I Transient Library (IBM Program Product Number 5734-LM5).

### 6.3.2 Hardware Environment

The system runs on IBM S/370 MOD-135 and up. For tabular language input, the system requires the IBM 3277-II. Any teletypewriter terminal supported by VM-CMS can be used for linear (string) input. File media is disk. VM-CMS is required.

7.0

The system appears to exhibit:

1. Simplicity –            Data objects are always relations and
                           functions are basically based on the few
                           operations of the relational algebra,
                           although the language is, in general, best
                           viewed as a relational calculus language.

2. Uniformity –            A single language supports data definition,
                           database changes, retrieval and authoriza-
                           tion.

3. Data independence –     The language is highly data independent and
                           non-procedural.  The user is virtually
                           totally free of constraints of representation
                           at the storage level except, as has been
                           noted, where data TYPE must be known.

4. Symmetry –              The system appears to take advantage of
                           the symmetry of the relational model.

5. Security –              Security constraints are specified using
                           the power of the QBE qualifying expressions.

3.12   Feature Analysis Of RAPID

RAPID
Feature Analysis

by
R. Hammond
S. Hobbs
M. Jeays

Systems Development Division
Statistics Canada
Ottawa, Ontario
Canada K1A 0T6

January 1981

RAPID - Feature Analysis

R. Hammond, S. Hobbs, M. Jeays
Systems Development Division
Statistics Canada, Ottawa, Canada  K1A 0T6

RAPID is evaluated using the "Feature Catalogue of Relational Concepts, Languages and Systems", Working Paper RTG-80-81 of the Relational Database Task Group of ANSI/X3/SPARC - Database System Study Group, May 1980.

-----------------------

440

Contents:

# 1 INTRODUCTION

## 1.1 Identification

RAPID is a database management system (DBMS), by which is meant a set of software that provides tools to describe, create, control and access data files in a direct access environment. The name "RAPID" is an acronym: Relational Access Processor for Integrated Databases, which reflects the essential aspects of the system.

"Relational" refers to the theoretical data model on which the system is predicated. This model was first popularized by E.F.Codd of IBM and since has been well discussed in the literature (see particularly C.J.Date: An Introduction to Database Systems: Addison Wesley). The "relational" approach differs from others primarily in the simplicity of its basic file structures and the fact that relationships are defined dynamically at the time of retrieval of data rather than when the data is stored.

"Access Processor" defines the primary function of the software. It provides a simple means of access to data for the user of utilities as well as the application programmer and designer of customised software.

"Integrated Databases" are the object of, and the product of any DBMS. The words have become commonly misused in the recent past so we shall state our understanding of the terms. By "integrated" we mean that RAPID manages both data descriptions (meta-data) and the application data itself. It provides access to this information by a consistent set of facilities which ensure the integrity between the data and its description. By "database" we mean any collection of RAPID files which are seen by the user as being related in some way. A database evolves as new application functions are added or as separate databases are integrated (connected) into a common application.

Thus RAPID performs the function of the storage model upon which a variety of query processors have been built. The most important feature of RAPID is that it does not presume to be a system with integrated query languages etc. as assumed by the RTG-80-81 paper. It is simply a system that supports a wide variety of query processors. This feature has allowed RAPID to be interfaced with a number of commercially available report-writers and statistical packages, and will allow it to support relational languages as they become available.

To fully comply with the RTG-80-81 guidelines, Sections 2, 3, and 4 of this document would have to be completed for each query processor listed in Section 1.6. This is an onerous task, and not particularly relevant to the purpose of RAPID. Thus, the facilities provided by the RAPID nucleus to support the query processors will be described in Sections 2, 3, and 4. Query processors use different subsets of the facilities to provide languages and higher level functions appropriate to the user group for which they are intended.

## 1.2 Status

### 1.2.1 System

RAPID has been operational since 1975 and is installed in various government agencies in Canada, United States, Sweden, Brazil, East Germany and Hungary. The United Nations, through CELADE (Centro Latinoamerica de Demografia) which is part of the Economic Commission for Latin America, has installed RAPID at its headquarters in Santiago, Chile and in Costa Rica. RAPID is not available to the private sector.

The nucleus of RAPID is stable, with most development being done in the area of interfaces and utility packages. RAPID is fully supported by Systems Development Division of Statistics Canada.

### 1.2.2 Applications

There are about 9,000 Megabytes of data currently stored in RAPID relations at Statistics Canada. RAPID has been used in a variety of applications, but its primary use has been in databases subject to frequent statistical queries which access few attributes and many tuples (often millions).

A benchmark of RAPID against ADABAS and TOTAL in 1979 showed RAPID to be:

| STRONG | COMPARABLE | WEAK |
|---|---|---|
| sequential retrieval | data compression | random updates |
| database loading | record deletion (keys) | |
| sequential update | keyed retrieval | |
| field additions | | |
| record deletion (no keys) | | |
| access path creation | | |
| size limitations | | |

RAPID places some limits on the size of its relations:

```
2,147,483,647 tuples per relation
  536,870,811 attributes per relation
       65,536 tracks per relation (BDAM)
4,294,967,296 bytes per relation (VSAM)
           19 relations open at one time per user
```

1.3 System Background

RAPID evolved from a tabulation system (STATPAK) used at Statistics Canada since 1971 where data was stored in an essentially relational form as transposed files (each attribute was a direct access dataset) with inherent maintenance problems. The transposed file concept was married with ideas for self documenting data and database technology in the development of "String Files for TOTAL" in 1973.

"String" files were used to process several applications, including the 1974 Test Census of the Population of Canada. Analysis of that application showed that the concepts were sound, but that performance was a major factor in processing statistical queries (millions of tuples for few attributes). RAPID was developed in 1975 in response to anticipated performance problems in an environment with an abundance of practical experience, statistical methodology, database theory, research facilities, skillful programmers, and good management.

The first major application of RAPID was to process the 1976 Census of the Population of Canada (1100 Megabytes of data). Analysis of the processing characteristics on large relations led to a major update of RAPID software in 1977 to improve performance and to prepare for a virtual storage environment.

## 1.4 Overall Philosophy

The most important criterion in the development of RAPID was to separate the data storage mechanism from the query processors. Query processors include all those commercial and home-made report writers, statistical tabulators, and interactive browsing mechanisms that are currently installed or might be installed at Statistics Canada. In the developers' opinion, a relational query processor can be built on a hierarchical data storage mechanism only with restrictions, but a hierarchical query processor can be built on a relational storage mechanism without restriction.

Other objectives included:

1. Flexibility - the system must support a variety of different views of the data.

2. The separation of relations such that independently designed relations can be JOIN'ed based on data content.

3. The ability to provide high performance access for statistical queries (many tuples - few attributes). Very good performance would be needed for informational queries (medium subset of tuples and attributes), and performance for operational queries (few tuples - many attributes) could be sacrificed if needed.

4. The ability to have self-documenting files that can be used on a stand alone basis without access to a data dictionary. (Hammond's Postulate: any pair of datasets will get out of step in todays operating systems.)

5. To allow for dynamic (by applications during execution) creation and deletion of attributes, tuples, and access paths without any need for reorganization. This includes adding additional space as needed to the datasets.

6. To provide data compression, particularly for attributes whose domains have a small range with little ability to identify (qualitative) such as sex, marital status, credit status, etc.

7. To provide a single interface with execution time binding of all applications (including query processors) to the database software.

8. To provide open time binding of applications to the database with options of read only, update, or update with logging for each relation.

9. To support user specified data representations for all common data types.

10. To provide an external data dictionary for query processors and other high level functions. This dictionary must not be required for the nucleus to function.

## 1.5 Essentially Relational Characteristics

RAPID supports the structural aspects of the relational model and provides facilities for insert, update, and delete operations, as well as the data access facilities needed to build or interface to a data sub-language. Primitives are defined for manipulating relations, while JOIN's and other inter-relational operations are not implemented in the RAPID nucleus.

Various data-manipulating systems have been built using RAPID, and each uses a subset of the relational algebra operators.

It is significant to note that JOIN's have been done without any restriction (cycles, JOIN's to the same relation and more than one JOIN between two relations).

## 1.6 Interfaces

RAPID provides a host language interface which is used by both application programs and RAPID utilities. Because of this common interface, a number of programs developed for specific application systems have been adopted as RAPID utilities.

RAPID commands may be invoked from any host language which supports the CALL facility. Currently, facilities are available to simplify and standardize usage from PL/I and COBOL. Users of other host languages follow the COBOL instructions.

The interface between RAPID and PL/I is different in that it uses compiler and execution facilities not supported by any other host language.

In the following classification of interfaces, the primitive commands which one would normally use in the programming of such an interface are listed first and those packages which supply the function to higher level users are briefly described. This paper will not go into detail on any of these packages as to do so would require excessive space and would not provide a true understanding of what we feel is the essential nature of RAPID. Later sections will describe the primitives in more detail and for convenience an index is given in Section 1.8 of available commands and their function.

### 1.6.1 Database Schema Definition

Commands: $DEFN, $KYDF, $WTUA, $WTVL

MDM        - Meta-Data Memory - data dictionary

### 1.6.2 Query Language

Commands: $DEFQ, $DELQ, $FIND, $KYRT, $SCAN

DREAM      - Direct RElational Access Method - online relation browsing

RML        - Relational Manipulation Language - online/batch utility for manipulating relations

### 1.6.3 Database Altering

Commands: $STOR

LOADGEN    - generate subroutines for custom programs

RAPMERGE   - merge sequential files onto relations

RAPUPD     - online updates

### 1.6.4 Constraint Definition

RML        - Relational Manipulation Language

### 1.6.5 Database Generation and Re-generation

Commands: $REFM

INITRELN  - allocate and format disk space

### 1.6.6 Database Schema Redefinition and Renaming

Commands: $RNAM

### 1.6.7 Report Generation

Commands: $RETR, $SEQR

DREAM     - online query processor for browsing relations

EASYTRIEVE - vendor product plus interface

EXTRACTO  - vendor product plus interface

PATTERN   - frequency distribution of values in attribute

SAS       - vendor product plus interface

SPSS      - vendor product plus interface

STATPAK   - batch tabulation system

TPL       - Table Producing  Language - U.S.  Bureau of  Labor Statistics
            package plus interface (under development)

### 1.6.8 Data Entry

None.

### 1.6.9 Security Definition, Monitoring and Control

Commands: $FCTL, $STPR

AUDIT     - detects alterations to data by attribute

### 1.6.10 Database Control

UNLOAD    - dump relation to sequential dataset

RELOAD    - restore relation from UNLOAD'ed dataset

TRANSFER  - physical copy from relation to relation

BACKOUT   - restore relation to beginning of log file

RECOVER   - restore relation to a checkpoint

TRAMP     - online execution of primitive commands

### 1.6.11 Definition of Storage Structure, Indexes and Access Paths

Commands: $INDX, $KYDF, $KYAD, $KYDL

KEYGEN     - generate/delete access path

### 1.6.12 Database Dictionary

Commands: $RDMD

MDMUPDT    - online/batch dictionary update

MDMREAD    - online browsing of dictionary

MDMPRNT    - batch formatted display of dictionary

### 1.6.13 Special Purpose Language

Because of RAPID's self-documenting files, many application systems have been built with tailor-made languages for retrieval, tabulation, updating and other functions.

## 1.7 Documentation

1. "Database File Design," Systems Development Division, Statistics Canada, Ottawa, June 1976.

2. "RAPID DBMS," Systems Development Division, Statistics Canada, June 1978.

3. "RAPID Language Reference Manual," Systems Development Division, Statistics Canada, Ottawa, May 1978.

4. "RAPID Meta-Data Memory," Systems Development Division, Statistics Canada, Ottawa, June 1978.

5. "RAPID Database Creation," Systems Development Division, Statistics Canada, Ottawa, June 1978.

6. "RAPID Programmer's Guide," Systems Development Division, Statistics Canada, Ottawa, May 1978.

7. "RAPID Retrieval," Systems Development Division, Statistics Canada, Ottawa, June 1978.

8. "RAPID Utilities," Systems Development Division, Statistics Canada, Ottawa, June 1978.

9. "Database Performance Manual," Systems Development Division, Statistics Canada, Ottawa, October 1978.

10. "ADABAS/RAPID Demonstration Database," Systems Development Division, Statistics Canada, Ottawa, June 1978.

11. Podehl, W. M. "STATPAK - General Concepts and Facilities," Systems Development Division, Statistics Canada, Ottawa, 1972.

12. Turner, M. J. "A New File-Type for TOTAL or How and Why Statistics Canada Has Widened the Scope of the TOTAL DBMS," Systems Development Division, Statistics Canada, Ottawa, December 1972.

13. Turner, M. J. "The Impact of Data Bases on Statistical Agencies," Systems Development Division, Statistics Canada, Ottawa, January 1974.

14. Turner, M. J. "Data Management at Statistics Canada," Systems Development Division, Statistics Canada, Ottawa, March 1975.

15. Turner, M. J. and Podehl, M. "GSS Plans For a Generalized Database Management System," Systems Development Division, Statistics Canada, Ottawa, October 1975.

16. Turner, M. J. and Hammond, R. and Cotton, P. "A DBMS for Large Statistical Databases," Systems Development Division, Statistics Canada, Ottawa, September 1979. VLDB5 pg 319-327.

## 1.8 <u>General</u> <u>System</u> <u>Description</u>

Each primitive command has a five character name beginning with "$".
They will be referenced by name frequently throughout the rest of this
document and are summarized below. These are commands available from the
various host languages, e.g. PL/I and COBOL.

Environment commands:

```
$CLOS  -  close a relation
$DQUE  -  release resources
$DUMP  -  dump control blocks
$FCTL  -  retrieve file control information
$OPNx  -  open a relation
$QIES  -  create recovery point
$REFM  -  delete all attributes and tuples
$STPR  -  display performance statistics
```

Meta-data commands:

```
$DEFN  -  define attribute
$DELS  -  delete attribute or access path
$KYDF  -  define access path
$RDCD  -  retrieve attribute description
$RDMD  -  retrieve meta-data from relation or dictionary
$RDUA  -  retrieve user area
$RDVL  -  retrieve domain
$RNAM  -  rename attribute or access path
$WTUA  -  write user area into attribute meta-data
$WTVL  -  write domain into attribute meta-data
```

Data manipulation commands:

```
$DEFQ  -  define query for future use by $FIND
$DELI  -  delete index value(s)
$DELQ  -  delete query previously defined
$FIND  -  find next index at which query specified by $DEFQ is true
$INDX  -  allocate index value(s)
$KYAD  -  add new key/index couplet
$KYDL  -  delete key/index couplet
$KYRT  -  retrieve key/index couplet
$RETR  -  retrieve data cell(s) for specified index
$SCAN  -  find next index with exact match on specified element value(s)
$SEQR  -  retrieve data cell(s) for index beyond specified index
$STOR  -  store data cell(s) for specified index
```

Program facility commands:

```
$CDED  -  create data element descriptor
$CELM  -  convert data element
$DEFR  -  define logical record
$DELR  -  delete logical record definition
```

## 2  DATABASE CONSTITUENTS

### 2.1 General Description

As mentioned in Section 1, a RAPID database and its constituents are more a characteristic of an application program or query processor than the storage model. For example, the STATPAK system usually views its data as a hierarchy of geographic areas which contain zero or more households which contain zero or more persons. As an intelligent processor, it also knows that there are three relations, and when processing a query that only involves some attributes of persons for all tuples it ignores the heirarchy and views only the specified attributes of the "person" relation.

For ease of explanation to non-data processing oriented users, the following terms are frequently used:

CELL       - the value for a particular tuple for a particular attribute.

COLUMN    - an attribute.

CURSOR    - a synonym for INDEX.

DATABASE - the collection of relations currently being accessed.

DOMAIN    - the collection of values that may appear in an attribute.

FILE      - relation.

INDEX     - an arbitrary pointer to a tuple, maintained by RAPID to force uniqueness among tuples. See also CURSOR.

KEYTREE   - an access path used for performance in direct access of tuples by data values in attributes.

RECORD    - the set of values for a subset of attributes being viewed for a particular tuple in a particular relation.

ROW       - tuple.

## 2.2 Database

### 2.2.1 Database Structure

This is left completely to the application, although each relation is maintained as a self-documenting entity in an O/S dataset.

### 2.2.2 Database Operations

This is generally left to the application, but there are two database commands:

$QIES - flush all RAPID buffers and (optionally) place a recovery point record on the log file.
$DQUE - close all relations (optional recovery point) and release all RAPID resources.

### 2.2.3 Database Constraints

RAPID stores data in a variety of formats, and sizes within formats. When a query processor navigates between relations, it is responsible for ensuring appropriate data conversions.

### 2.2.4 Additional Database Properties

Application dependent.

## 2.3 Relation

### 2.3.1 Relation Structure

A RAPID relation is a collection of tuples and attributes whose existence
is maintained independently; if it has neither it is considered empty and
not available for read-only access. When a new attribute is defined on a
relation with existing tuples, access to the new cells returns null
values although they do not physically occupy space. Similarly, new
tuples automatically have null values for all attributes. "Duplicate"
tuples are allowed, as each is assigned an arbitrary, unique, INDEX value
which is used during access. Attribute order is not significant, except
that a list of attribute names is used to define a RECORD during
processing, and retrieve/store accesses maintain the defined order.
Alias attribute names are not allowed, and duplicate attribute names are
allowed in a RECORD, and on different relations.

### 2.3.2 Relation Operations

A relation is created and its disk space formatted with the INITRELN
utility. Additional disk space may be added at any time with the EXPAND
utility, and excess space freed back to the operating system with the
RAPRLSE utility. Attribute descriptions may be moved between relations
and the data dictionary through a copy command in the data dictionary
processor. RAPID primitive commands at the relation level include:

    $OPNx - open relation for processing in read-only, update, or update
            with logging mode.
    $CLOS - terminate processing and release resources.
    $FCTL - determine status of a relation, including counts of tuples and
            attributes.
    $RDMD - retrieve a list of names and descriptions of attributes.
    $DEFQ - define a query which will be used to locate tuples. The query
            specifies names of attributes, relational operators, constant
            values, etc.
    $FIND - locate a tuple which satisfies the query.
    $DELQ - delete a query definition.

### 2.3.3 Relation Constraints

A KEY is a set of data values which must exactly match the cells of the
associated attributes to identify a tuple. This is a dynamic process, so
there may be duplicate keys; thus a KEY/INDEX couplet is required to
uniquely identify any given tuple. In some processes, the INDEX alone is
used as the key.

In RAPID, KEY/INDEX couplets may be stored in a special type of column
(attribute?) where they are kept in ascending sequence of data value and
accessed by binary and sequential searches ($KYAD - add key, $KYDL -
delete key, and $KYRT - retrieve key). Keytrees are defined with $KYDF,
and deleted with $DELS. The names of the member attributes may be
retrieved with $RDVL. These "keytrees" are easily generated at any time
with the KEYGEN utility application, based on any attribute or
combination of attributes.

Due to RAPID's transposed organization, keytrees are only needed for random access against very large relations, as the $SCAN command (search for exact match of data values) is very efficient.

### 2.3.4 Additional Properties of Relations

Experience at Statistics Canada has shown:

1. That users perceive themselves as data processing specialists.
2. That they most readily understand "flat files" (relations in at least first normal form).
3. That they would like to view data as a hierarchy.
4. That a variety of hierarchies must be imposed on the same data.

The last point is the key to the advantages of the relational storage model. A wide variety of hierarchies can be supported without duplication of data, just as it is in the "real world".

## 2.4 Views

### 2.4.1 View Structure

Just as a database is the collection of relations being accessed, a VIEW is a subset of attributes and tuples with their navigation paths within the database. Views are very dynamic, and may be data dependent (e.g. MARRIED FEMALES). The difference between views may be as subtle as a different data format (e.g. SALARY as FIXED DEC(11,5) or FLOAT DEC(6)).

With RAPID, the nature and limitations of views depends on the application or query processor, but the primitive commands supply a number of facilities for views within a relation.

### 2.4.2 View Operations

The meta-data commands may be used to determine the feasibility of a view and navigation paths. Within a relation, a number of RECORD's may be defined ($DEFR) which name the attributes and data formats in which the cells are to be materialized. Tuples may then be stored from or retrieved into a program work area matching the definition.

### 2.4.3 View Constraints

Each execution of a command results in a status being returned to the application which may then be interpreted for its meaning in a particular logical circumstance. For example, if a program which is looking at old data views SALARY as a FIXED DEC(5) value and the attribute has a 7 digit domain, a warning will be issued by $DEFR; but data may be retrieved until a value of more than 5 digits is encountered, when a value of null and a further message will be returned.

### 2.4.4 Additional Properties of Views

It is easy to define views on a single relation, as demonstrated by most commercial products dealing with flat files. Products supporting multi-relation DYNAMIC views with simple syntax are not readily available. Is the concept of VIEW is more complex than it seems, or is the technology just in its infancy?

## 2.5 Tuple

### 2.5.1 Tuple Structure

A tuple is a row which currently exists when a relation is viewed as a table with rows and columns. It seems meaningless, but tuples may exist even if no attributes exist. As mentioned earlier, each tuple has an INDEX or cursor for unique qualification.

### 2.5.2 Tuple Operations

Tuples are allocated and freed with the $INDX and $DELI commands; and assume a null value for all existing attributes when first allocated. The INDEX of a tuple may be determined with the $FIND, $SCAN, $KYRT, and $SEQR commands. Actual cells in a tuple are retrieved and stored with the $RETR, $SEQR and $STOR commands.

### 2.5.3 Tuple Constraints

Tuples are not ordered (except by INDEX) and may not appear unique. RAPID's lack of constraints on tuples places a burden on query processors. Some utility applications (RAPMERGE for example) insist on a unique key on some combination of attributes.

### 2.5.4 Additional Properties of Tuples

In a transposed organization, for performance, it is often preferable to determine the tuples in a set to be viewed as a list of INDEX's, sort the list in ascending INDEX order, retrieve the data cells (tuples) in INDEX order, and re-sort as needed as a flat file for ordered processing.

## 2.6 Attribute

### 2.6.1 Attribute Structure

An attribute is a column, when a relation is viewed as a table with columns and rows, and attributes exist independently of tuples. Each attribute has a domain which is one of its characteristics along with data type, size, precision, etc. The name of an attribute (limited to 8 characters) is specified when it is allocated, and alias names are not supported.

### 2.6.2 Attribute Operations

Attributes are allocated and freed with the $DEFN and $DELS commands. At the time of definition, its physical characteristics of data type, size and precision are specified, yielding a default domain. Each cell (row/column intersection) for the attribute assumes a null value until updated with a $STOR command. The characteristics are partially used for data compression in RAPID. For example, FIXED BIN(3) is a two byte value when viewed from PL/I, but is stored by RAPID in 4 bits. Other commands allow the user to further restrict the domain ($WTVL) and store application oriented meta-data about the attribute ($WTUA). A number of commands are available to retrieve attribute meta-data.

Systems programmer commands are available to access segments of columns (a large number of tuples for a particular attribute). This is used mostly for boolean operations in the application between columns defined as LOGICAL (each cell occupies one bit).

Attribute descriptions are normally moved between relations and the data dictionary through a copy command in the data dictionary processor.

Other attribute operations are an application function of the query processor in use, typically operating at the tuple level.

### 2.6.3 Attribute Constraints

Attribute constraints are limited to ensuring that a value to be stored is within the domain of the attribute. Violations result in a status message, and the storing of a null value.

### 2.6.4 Additional Properties of Attributes

Ideally, attribute characteristics should be defined only in terms of their domain. Unfortunately, characteristics such as FIXED, FLOAT, BINARY, DECIMAL, CHARACTER, CHARACTER VARYING with appropriate SIZE and PRECISION values are needed to communicate with todays host languages.

## 2.7 Domain

### 2.7.1 Domain Structure

In RAPID, a domain is the set of values that may be stored in a particular attribute. The default domain is the range of values allowed by the data type and size of the attribute. The user may further restrict the domain by supplying ($WTVL) a list of values (or ranges of values) which is stored with the attribute's meta-data. A value of null will always be found as part of the domain specification.

RAPID has two special attribute types, LOGICAL and CODED. A LOGICAL attribute is a single bit wide, and has an implicit domain of TRUE and FALSE where FALSE is also null. A CODED attribute's domain is an ordered list of value names. A CODED attribute's values are stored as unsigned binary numbers in a minimum number of bits and used as an index into the list to return the value name (data compression).

### 2.7.2 Domain Operations

The only domain operations are the meta-data commands used for their storage and retrieval.

### 2.7.3 Domain Constraints

Value names are limited to 16 characters, and all values are constrained by the data type of the associated attribute. In the data dictionary, attributes of different type and size may share the same domain (CODESET), and keywords are used to represent boundary values (e.g. MAX - the highest positive number the data type will allow).

The domain is used by the $STOR command to ensure that only valid values are stored on a relation. Violations result in the storing of a null value in the cell and the returning of a status indicator.

### 2.7.4 Additional Properties of Domain

Some data types are better than others at supporting the null value concept. For example, FLOAT allows more than one representation of zero so that null can be identified from zero, but FIXED does not allow such luxury.

## 2.8 Additional Database Constituents

None.

## 3  FUNCTIONAL CAPABILITIES

### 3.1 Qualification

As expressed earlier, the functional capabilities to be described in this
section apply more to a query processor or other application program than
to the storage model. There are a number of such processors used with
RAPID, and the only capabilities that will be discussed are those
primitive commands used in their development.

### 3.1.1 Restriction

The $DEFQ command is used to specify a restriction on a relation,
followed by $FIND commands to locate the tuples which satisfy the query.
The queries are named, so that many queries can exist concurrently for
the same relation. If the query is coded as a literal, the maximum
length of the literal string is 256 characters, but when specified as a
program variable, there is no limit on the length of the character
varying variable.

The query string is composed of query elements combined with the "&" and
"|" boolean operators. Each query element is coded in one of the
following formats:
    (i)    Attribute1 OP Constant
                or
    (ii)   Attribute1 OP Attribute2
                or
    (iii) Attribute1 or ¬Attribute1
where "Attribute1" and "Attribute2" are attributes on the relation,
"Constant" is a numeric or character constant, and "OP" is one of the
following comparison operators:
    =,  >,  >=,  <,  <=,  ¬=,  ¬>,  ¬>=,  ¬<,  ¬<=
In case (i), the constant must conform in type to the attribute.

Fixed-point numeric constants (RAPID types "FB" and "FD") are written as
an optional "+" or "-" sign followed by one or more decimal digits
containing an optional decimal point. The number of digits following the
decimal point should be the same as specified by the precision of the
attribute (see $DEFN). If not, digits following the decimal point are
truncated or padded with zeroes as necessary according to the precision
of the attribute.

Floating-point numeric constants (RAPID types "EB" and "ED") are written
as a fixed-point numeric constant followed by the letter E, followed by
an optionally signed decimal integer exponent.

Character constants (RAPID types "CH" and "CV") are contained in either
single quotes or double quotes (the double quote character ") with no
imbedded quotes of the same type. Character constants may also be
specified in hexadecimal by coding X' followed by a sequence of
hexadecimal digits, with each group of two representing a byte, followed
by ' (end quote). Since PL/I also uses the single quote as a delimiter
in character strings, all single quotes within the query string must be
doubled if it is coded as a PL/I literal.

Coded constants (RAPID type "CD") must be specified as the 16 byte
character code value. Coded attributes must have standard domains as
created by the MDM copy command.

Logical constants (RAPID type "LO") may be represented as either quoted
character strings "TRUE" and "FALSE" or numeric 1 and 0. Only the "="
and "¬=" comparison operators are valid in query elements involving
logical attributes.

In case (ii), the respective attributes to be compared must be of the
same type and scale, although not necessarily of the same length (i.e.
the RAPID types must be identical). Coded attributes are handled
internally using the character code value and may be compared with
character attributes. When comparing character attributes of different
lengths, the shorter character value is padded to the right with blanks
before comparison.

In case (iii), "Attribute1" must be a logical attribute (i.e. it must
have a RAPID type of "LO"). These two formats, respectively, are simply
shorthand ways of writing: Attribute1 = "TRUE" and Attribute1 = "FALSE".

The "&" and "|" boolean operators apply between two query elements or
groups of query elements enclosed in parentheses. Normally the query
string is evaluated left to right with no priority of operator. However,
groups of query elements may be enclosed in parentheses to define
priority of evaluation. The group of query elements enclosed in
parentheses is evaluated as a unit prior to applying the logical result
of this unit with the adjacent query element. A "¬" boolean operator may
be specified before a left parenthesis to reverse the logical result of
the following parenthesized expression.

Evaluation of the query string follows the normal rules of boolean
algebra (except that there is no priority of operator). Query elements
which have no bearing on the result of the query are not evaluated (e.g.
if the accumulated logical result of the query is true and the current
boolean operator is an |, evaluation of the next query element is
skipped). Hence, the query string can be optimized if the query elements
which best determine the truth of the entire expression are placed near
the beginning of the query string.

The syntax of the query string is essentially free format. Blanks are
not significant except within character constants.

Examples

```
$DEFQ FILE('RELN') NAME('QUERY1')
      QUERY('PROJECT="RAPID" & LRECL>=BLKSIZE');

$DEFQ FILE('RELN') NAME('QUERY2')
      QUERY('RECFM="FB" & (OWNER="XYZ" | OWNER="ABC")');

$DEFQ FILE('RELN') NAME('QUERY3')
      QUERY('TEST & ¬(RECFM="FB" | LRECL<80)');

$DEFQ ('RELN','QUERY4','FLOATCOL < .3E-2 & OWNER = "O''BRIAN"');
```

### 3.1.2 Quantification

This is normally accomplished by a series of $FIND or $SCAN commands. The INDEX is used to start at the "top" of the relation and proceed toward the logical end of file at which time a special status is returned.

### 3.1.3 Set Operations

Application function.

### 3.1.4 Joining

Application function.

### 3.1.5 Nesting in Closure

Application function.

### 3.1.6 Additional Aspects of Qualification

The highest level of qualification is specification of the relations. With RAPID, the user connects (through JCL or TSO command) the dataset name and DDNAME. The DDNAME is then connected to the RAPID file name through the $OPNx command.

## 3.2 Retrieval and Presentation

### 3.2.1 Database Queries

The $FIND command returns the INDEX of a tuple which satisfies a query definition ($DEFQ - Section 3.1.1). A special case of that facility exists in the $SCAN command with which the user supplies a workarea containing the exact match values for the attributes which will satisfy the query. The $SEQR command may be used to retrieve the INDEX's of tuples in their arbitrary physical sequence, and the $KYRT command may be used to retrieve the INDEX's in logical ascending order for a direct access path.

### 3.2.2 Retrieval of Information about Database Constituents

Information about database constituents is known as meta-data in RAPID. Some of the meta-data commands are:

$FCTL - count of tuples, attributes, date of last update, etc.
$RDMD - access meta-data from either a data dictionary or a relation. Includes list of attribute names, their characteristics, domains, etc.
$NXTK - answers the question "Does a particular attribute exist?" without physical access to meta-data.
$RDUA - retrieve application oriented meta-data (user area) about an attribute.

### 3.2.3 Retrieval of System Performance Data

The $STPR command may be used to display current processing statistics for use in performance evaluation. This command may also be issued by the $CLOS, $DQUE and $QIES commands. The $FCTL command returns some statistical data and the amount of free space currently available.

### 3.2.4 Report Generation

Stand-alone packages with interfaces to RAPID include EASYTRIEVE, EXTRACTO, SAS, SPSS and soon TPL. STATPAK is a major home-made statistical tabulation package which functions only with RAPID. DREAM is an example of a generalized application program which has become a RAPID Utility. It is intended as a query processor for online browsing, but is frequently used for batch reporting.

### 3.2.5 Constraints and Limitations

Application function.

### 3.2.6 Additional Aspects of Retrieval and Presentation

There are a number of commands which return the INDEX of a tuple, but actual retrieval of data values is done only by $RETR, and $SEQR using a supplied INDEX value. This anomaly exists in RAPID commands because many queries are satisfied by knowledge that something exists without need of retrieval, a performance benefit in a transposed structure.

## 3.3 Alteration

### 3.3.1 Insert Facilities

A view in RAPID is a transient entity which is attached to the application and exists only between its definition ($DEFR command) and its explicit ($DELR) or implicit ($CLOS; etc.) deletion. Attributes, domains, and tuples may be added at any time ($DEFN, $WTVL, and $INDX).

### 3.3.2 Delete Facilities

In RAPID, every allocation command has a corresponding deletion command. Thus views, attributes domains and tuples may be dynamically deleted. The $REFM (reformat) command is available to instantly delete all attributes and tuples. Space freed by the delete commands is automatically reused by later insert commands.

### 3.3.3 Modify Facilities

As described earlier, the cells of data initially have null values. They are updated with the $STOR command. The application meta-data associated with an attribute may be retrieved ($RDUA) modified and replaced with the $WTUA command.

### 3.3.4 Commit and Undo Facilities

A checkpoint may be taken at any time, and the RECOVER utility used to restore the database to a specified checkpoint.

### 3.3.5 Additional Alteration Facilities

A functional deficiency of RAPID is that the access paths (keytrees) are not automatically maintained when $STOR updates a data cell. Some applications have turned this "deficiency" into a feature with which they create application dependent special access paths.

## 3.4 Additional Functional Capabilities

Application function.

# 4  DEFINITION, GENERATION AND ADMINISTRATION FACILITIES

## 4.1 Definition Facilities

### 4.1.1 Constituents of a Database Definition

A RAPID database is dynamic, composed of the set of relations currently being viewed, and a subset of attributes and tuples within the relations.

### 4.1.2 Database Definition

Implicit, by opening a relation for processing:

```
$OPNL FILE('S') NBUF(4);
```

### 4.1.3 Relation Definition

A RAPID relation is essentially a repository for attributes and tuples. Foreign keys are frequently used with RAPID, and may be defined ($KYDF) but typically accessed through the $SCAN command. See Section 4.1.6.

### 4.1.4 View Definition

See Section 2.4.

### 4.1.5 Tuple Definition

See Section 2.5. To allocate a single tuple, a variable is needed for the INDEX value which will be returned:

```
DCL  CSR   FIXED BIN(31) INIT(-1);
$INDX FILE('S') INDX(CSR) RANGE(1);
```

### 4.1.6 Attribute Definition

Normally, users create a RELATION description in the MDM (data dictionary) and use its copy command to define the attributes and their domains on a relation. The MDM processor is simply a generalized application using the host language interface being described here. See Section 2.6. To allocate the "SNAME" attribute on relation "S":

```
$DEFN FILE('S') NAME('SNAME') TYPE('CV') SIZE(100);
```

### 4.1.7 Domain Definition

See Section 4.1.6. This is supported by the $WTVL command which is almost never used outside of generalized software. It can be coded as follows:

```
DCL   1     VALTAB,
          5   (ENTRY_CNT      INIT(03),
               ENTRY_LEN      INIT(18),
               KEY_LEN        INIT(16),
               KEY_POS        INIT(01)) FIXED BIN(31),
          5    ELEMENTS(3),
           10 VALU_NAME       CHAR(16)
                              INIT('BLUE','GREEN','RED'),
           10 VALU_CODE       FIXED BIN(15)
                              INIT(1,2,3);
     $WTVL FILE('P') NAME('COLOUR') FROM(VALTAB);
```

### 4.1.8 Definition of Additional Database Constituents

Primary and secondary (foreign) access paths may be defined with the $KYDF command:

```
     $KYDF FILE('S') NAME('$KEYPRIM') CLMS('S#,END.');
```

### 4.2 Generation Facilities

### 4.2.1 Constituents of a Database Generation

To generate a database, an application must allocate relations that do not currently exist, and possibly a data dictionary.

### 4.2.2 Generation of Database Constituents

Allocation of space for the example relations would typically be done in a TSO session:

```
     RAPSTART
     INITRELN S
     INITRELN P
     INITRELN SP
```

Since there is a small volume of attributes and tuples, the RAPUPD Utility would typically be used to define attributes, tuples, and populate the relations. Other Utilities for populating a relation include:

```
     RAPMERGE - loading from a flat file.
     RAPCOPY  - copy complete relations.
     RML      - project a view of a relation onto a new relation.
```

## 4.3 Database Redefinition

### 4.3.1 Renaming Database Constituents

All users must be aware of name changes. Each relation is an O/S dataset, and may be renamed with standard system functions.

To rename an attribute, the $RNAM command may be used:

    $RNAM FILE('P') OLDNAME('COLOUR') NEWNAME('COLOR');

### 4.3.2 Redefining Database Constituents

The ability to create and delete attributes, tuples and to some degree domains has been described elsewhere. Redefinition typically involves creating the new, copying from the old, deleting the old and renaming. Programs which properly define their view are insulated from most changes as described in Section 2.4.3.

Additional space may be added to relations (EXPAND utility) and excess space released (RAPRLSE) without moving or reorganizing data.

## 4.4 Database Regeneration and Reorganization

### 4.4.1 System-Controlled

Not required.

### 4.4.2 DBA-Controlled

In general, there is no need to reorganize a properly normalized relational database. The DBA may need to change the physical characteristics of relations, for example, when moving relations (datasets) to new devices. This is supported by the RAPCOPY utility, and such changes are transparent to all users.

## 4.5 Database Dictionary

RAPID has, in effect, a distributed database dictionary. Information normally starts off in the MDM (Meta-Data Memory) and is COPYed to relations so that changes to the MDM will not impact existing data. MDM is long overdue for replacement, but its' simplicity and flexibility make it hard to replace. In simplified terms, the user defines sets of entities (RELATION, FILE, CODESET, STUBSET, etc.). Instances of the entities are named, and contain a list of elements, each with a comment. Some standard entity sets have specific formats (e.g. RELATION). This meta-data may be accessed by programs using the $RDMD command.

The example could be stored in MDM as follows:

```
RELATION  P           KEY(P#)
          P#           CHAR(2)          PART NUMBER
          PNAME        CHAR(10)         PART NAME
          COLOUR       CODED(COLOUR)    COLOUR OF PART
          WEIGHT       FIXED BIN(23,2)
          CITY         TEXT(50)


VALUESET  COLOUR
          RED
          GREEN
          BLUE
```

## 5  INTERFACES AND DBMS ARCHITECTURE

### 5.1 System Architecture

All utilities and application programs  access relations through a common
system interface with  two entry points ($INTER using  the PL/I execution
environment, RAPLNK which simulates  a partial PL/I environment  for non-
PL/I users).

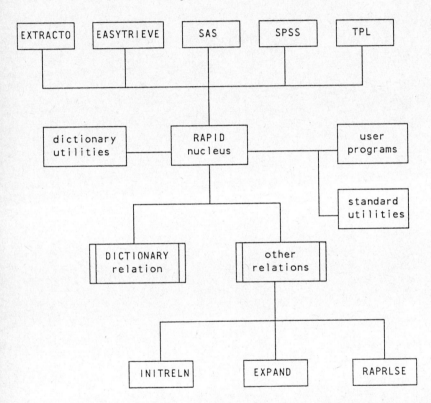

Stand-Alone Packages with RAPID Interfaces

Space Management Utilities

## 5.2 Interface Descriptions

### 5.2.1 PL/I Interface

The PL/I pre-processor facilities are used  to provide a set of statement macros that simplify and standardize the use of RAPID primitive commands. The commands are expanded  into a CALL statement to a  common entry point to the RAPID nucleus, followed by the testing of the returned status code as needed.  For example, a command coded as follows:

```
$RETR FILE('reln') CLMS('alpha,beta,gamma,end.')
      INDX(csr) INTO(workarea);
```

is expanded to the following form:

```
DO;
   $OP='$RETR';
   $FILE='reln';
   CALL $INTER($OP,$STAT,$FILE,csr,
                 'alpha   beta    gamma   end.    ',workarea);
   IF SUBSTR($STAT,1,1)¬='*' THEN
       SIGNAL CONDITION($ERROR);
END;
```

NOTE: Lower case was used to demonstrate the macro expansion and
      is not used normally.

### 5.2.2 COBOL Interface

All RAPID  primitives can  be invoked  from a  COBOL (or  other language) program, through the CALL statement. The  parameters are defined so as to be  identical to  the corresponding  PL/I CALL  statement.  Checking  the returned status  code is  the  responsibility of  the  application program. Data  is  communicated through  work  areas  defined in  the  application program.

# 6  OPERATIONAL ASPECTS

## 6.1 Security

### 6.1.1 Access Control

RAPID does not contain security mechanisms. In practice, the operating system password facility is used to protect relations (which are contained as one relation per O/S dataset) where necessary. This can be done at the WRITE PROTECT or READ/WRITE PROTECT level. If a dataset is password protected to prevent WRITE access, a security violation is recorded if any attempt is made to open the relation in update mode ($OPNU or $OPNL). At Statistics Canada, such events are passed to the security office for attention.

### 6.1.2 Capability

As described above, each relation can be protected at the O/S dataset level if required. Thus, relations are considered to be security domains in this context.

## 6.2 Physical Integrity

### 6.2.1 Concurrency Control

RAPID makes no provision for concurrency while updating because of the limited need to update statistical databases, and the significant cost of concurrency to readers. Application programs and utilities require exclusive control of relations being updated.

### 6.2.2 Crash Recovery

Backup and restore utilities (UNLOAD, RELOAD, RAPSYNC) are available which operate on single relations.

RAPID provides "before image" logging for relations opened in logging mode ($OPNL). Database checkpoints may be taken with the $QIES command, but restarting of program logic is the responsibility of the application.

Utilities are available to undo updates to a particular checkpoint (RECOVER) and to restart by recovering to the beginning of the log file (BACKOUT). These operations may become primitive commands at some future date.

## 6.3 Operating Environment

### 6.3.1 Software Environment

RAPID requires an IBM operating system such as MVS, VS1, MVT, or the equivalent. TSO (Time Sharing Option) is required for interactive execution of the RAPID Utilities. The RAPID nucleus is coded in re-entrant assembler and makes use of BDAM (and soon VSAM) access methods for relations and BSAM for logging. It makes few other demands on the operating system. RAPID utilities are for the most part coded in PL/I with some assembly language subroutines.

At execution time, RAPID will make use of PL/I transient routines for dynamic space allocation and message IO transmitters, sharing such with the application PL/I host. This sharing of the PL/I environment has led to simplified debugging of both application programs and the RAPID nucleus.

### 6.3.2 Hardware Environment

RAPID requires an IBM 370 or compatible CPU. No firm measurement of memory requirements can be given, but 32K plus RAPID internal buffers is a guideline. In general, RAPID becomes more efficient as more storage is given for internal buffers (it pages data to and from disk using sophisticated algorithms) and it is not uncommon to see RAPID applications using 500K to more than 1M of storage.

RAPID relations may be stored on any direct access device supported by the operating system.

Logging requires an additional sequential file, and this may be either tape or disk.

# 7  ESSENTIALLY RELATIONAL SOLUTIONS FOR GENERALIZED DBMS PROBLEMS

## 7.1 Simplicity

In RAPID each relation is seen as a two dimensional matrix of rows (tuples) and columns (attributes). The greatest advantage this has given is that all segments of the data processing community understand the data concepts.

## 7.2 Uniformity

No comment.

## 7.3 Data Independence

RAPID emphasizes the importance of data independance, both in the implementation and the written guidance provided with it. In particular, the self-documenting feature of RAPID files is of great importance in providing robustness to RAPID application systems.

## 7.4 Permits Optimization

The combination of a relational storage model and transposed organization have allowed RAPID to transfer only the needed data between the application and database. This limits response time to the speed of the cpu, which is unusual in a database system. For example, a STATPAK tabulation which accessed two attributes for nearly 25 million tuples executed in five minutes on an Amdahl V6. In RAPID applications, optimization of queries and the navigation between relations has been left to the application system designers. The logical independence of normalized files provides substantial opportunity to ensure that the design of application systems can permit future optimization, as "hard" linkages are seldom built into code.

## 7.5 Basis for High-level Interfaces

At present, relatively little has been done to build high-level, multi-, relational generalized programs. Experience with single relation utilities and soft-coded application systems which process many relations, has shown the ease with which future developments can take place. In particular, RAPID's use of self-documenting files and dynamic database definition facilities have provided much needed tools for system builders.

## 7.6 Natural

Once explained, normalization of files is usually understood by most people to be a worthwhile simplification, and as such, normalized files are seen as a "natural" representation of data.

## 7.7 Efficient Storage and Retrieval Potential

RAPID was designed for processing of very large statistical databases. Most queries tend to address relatively few columns, and very many rows. The transposed file design of RAPID is directed towards this environment. The storage of meta-data with the attributes allows the system to provide effective data compression transparent to the user. Somewhat surprisingly, performance compares _very_ favourably with several commercial record-oriented DBMS packages, except in random update mode in particular circumstances.

## 7.8 Multiple Views of Data

Within a relation, RAPID supports selective processing of the various attributes without regard to other attributes that may be present. Automatic data conversion facilities which permit an application program to operate independently of the physical storage definition used, will soon be released. Since each relation is independent and self-documenting, databases can be formed as the user requires.

## 7.9 Advantages for Distributed Databases

RAPID is not to be considered for use in a distributed environment, other than as a base from which subsets are transferred to and from local systems.

## 7.10 Security

Access restrictions are not supported in RAPID. Physical security is simple and effective.

## 7.11 Basis for Database Semantics

We are planning a major development at Statistics Canada, which will begin with a machine-readable catalogue of surveys, publications, data files and so on. The relation will be a fundamental unit of data to be described within this catalogue, and will thus be the cornerstone of an overall organization of data. This catalogue will evolve into a conceptual schema describing the bureau's data processing applications.

## 7.12 Strong Theoretical Foundation

The advantages of working with normalized files has been stressed throughout this evaluation, and should need no further emphasis at this point.

# 8  DATABASE APPLICATIONS USING RAPID

## 8.1 Applications at Statistics Canada

### 8.1.1 Census of Population

RAPID was used for the processing of the Canadian Census of Population in 1976, and will be used again for the 1981 Census. The Census database consists primarily of two very large relations; one with 24 million tuples, each one corresponding to an individual, and a second with about 8 million tuples, each one corresponding to a household. The editing and imputation is performed by a generalized processor known as CANEDIT, against sections of the database known as work units. Update activity ceases once the editing is complete.

The Census database is used extensively in read-only mode for the production of a very large number of tabulations designed both for publication and for internal use. The majority of these tabulations are produced by the semi-generalized package known as STATPAK. This utility is designed around the known structure of the database, but can accept very generalized specifications of the tabulations required. The transposed file design of RAPID contributes to the efficient processing of this large number of tabulations.

### 8.1.2 Intercorporate Ownership

This database contains information about the mutual and foreign ownership of business corporations within the Canadian economy. It consists of a pair of relations; the first containing one row for each corporation above a defined size, and a second in which each row describes a directed ownership link between a pair of corporations.

Various application programs can then follow ownership chains that may be of any degree of complexity. In particular, many-to-many linkages, and even loops occur, and can be processed effectively.

It is interesting to note that the logical design of this database was highly confused until a decision was made to normalize the file design. At that point, most of the logical difficulties disappeared, and the revised design was seen to be much "cleaner" and more understandable to all personnel assigned to the project.

### 8.1.3 Consumer Price Index

The C.P.I. is an important measure of the performance of the Canadian economy. The database consists of one main relation containing the time-series data in a matrix form with the time dimension mapped into the attribute names and the city and item dimensions mapped onto the tuples. Other relations describe the cities, items, and imputation rules. It is estimated that this particular file design using RAPID provides a fifty fold gain in performance in critical areas of the application when compared to the original design using TOTAL.

The monthly phases of production are: priced data loading, imputation, aggregation, and retrievals. Currently, data from January 1974 is kept online in a database requiring 100 Megabytes of disk storage, but provision is made to archive and reload any number of months of the oldest data on the database.

Items, cities and their aggregate structures may be updated as necessary with the only limitation being that no more than 1052 items may be defined. This limit was chosen as a further optimization so that the data for each city on the main relation does not straddle RAPID segment boundaries and cause excessive paging by the RAPID buffer management algorithms. The aggregate structures of items and cities are maintained in keytrees on the respective relations. This non-standard use of what is meant to be an access path is tolerated by the RAPID nucleus and eliminated the need for what would have been two very trivial relations.

### 8.1.4 Record Linkage

Considerable progress has been made towards a generalized record linkage utility that uses RAPID as an intrinsic part of its internal processing mechanism. This package has been used to link disease incidence files with mortality records to determine statistical information such as survival rates.

Much more work in this area is anticipated in the future.

## 8.2 Applications Outside of Statistics Canada

### 8.2.1 CELADE

Centro Latinoamerica de Demografia is part of the Economic Commission for Latin America, a United Nations subsidiary. CELADE installed RAPID in 1978 and developed the SPSS (Statistical Package for the Social Sciences - SPSS Inc., Chicago) interface.

The WFS (World Fertility Survey) has been conducted in 35 countries, and data for 5 countries has been loaded on RAPID databases. The data typically involves over 500 attributes and 5000 tuples per country. End users process the data directly through SPSS, typically through the batch facilities of OS VS1 on IBM 148 machines.

### 8.2.2 Census of Population in Brazil

Fundacao Instituto Brasileiro de Geografia E Estatistica (the Brazilian statistical office) is using the RAPID/STATPAK combination for the tabulation of their recent Census of Population in the same way as they were used in Canada.

### 8.2.3 U.S. Bureau of Labor Statistics

The Bureau of Labor Statistics is currently developing an interface with their very powerful Table Producing Language (TPL) package. There is some hope that this combination will eventually replace the use of STATPAK at Statistics Canada.

### 8.2.4 Agriculture Canada

The Canada Soil Information System has several RAPID databases composed of some 30 relations. One of the databases is accessed from coast to coast through a service bureau network.

3.13  Feature Analysis Of RAPPORT

Feature   Analysis
of
RAPPORT

by

Michel Lacroix
Philips Research Laboratory
2 Avenue Van Becelaere
1170 Bruxelles
Belgium

Alain Pirotte
Computer Corporation of America
575 Technology Square
Cambridge, Massachusetts 02139
USA

Wolfgang Dotzek
University of Hamburg
Fachbereich Informatik
Schlueterstrasse 70
D-2000 Hamburg 13
West Germany

September 1981

# Feature Analysis of RAPPORT

## Abstract

The RAPPORT database management system is described using the "Feature catalogue of relational concepts, languages, and systems", Working paper RTG-80-81 of the Relational Database Task Group of the ANSI/X3/SPARC Database System Study Group.

## Acknowledgement

We gratefully acknowledge comments and suggestions about a previous version of this paper by C.F. Banfield of Logica Ltd., London.

## Contents

# 1. Introduction

## 1.1 Identification

RAPPORT is a database management system based on the relational model. It was designed by LOGICA, a British software house (64 Newman Street, London W1A 4SE).

## 1.2 Status

### 1.2.1 System

Used in-house by LOGICA since 1977. Released as a product in October 1979. Second release in July 1980. Some features are still being implemented.

MICRO RAPPORT was released in November 1980 : it is a subset of RAPPORT installed on a Z80-based microcomputer system. MICRO RAPPORT supports the retrieval and updating commands provided by RAPPORT. Backup and recovery, data security and other RAPPORT options are not implemented in MICRO RAPPORT.

### 1.2.2 Applications

Existing applications include: financial planning, computer aided design, stock control, project management, scientific analysis.

## 1.3 System Background

## 1.4 Overall Philosophy

See Section 1.8.

## 1.5 Essentially Relational Characteristics

RAPPORT provides file (= relation) definition, an embedded and a stand alone data manipulation language with update operations. It does not support the so-called "insert-update-delete" rules referred to in the feature catalogue.

The stand alone language is not relationally complete and the embedded language relies on the power of the host language (FORTRAN, COBOL or CORAL) for reaching the power of the relational algebra. Remarkably, RAPPORT does not have a dedicated join operation. It is thus not "fully relational".

## 1.6 Interfaces

The interfaces to RAPPORT offer the following capabilities:

- database definition at the logical level and at the physical level (storage structure, indexes, access paths);
- database interactions (retrieval and updating) via an embedded language and via a stand alone interactive

language;
- database generation;
- multi-user access and data integrity through a  locking
  scheme;
- data security by passwords and encryption
- utilities:
    . backup and recovery
    . statistics gathering on usage  of  database  and  of
      storage structures
    . fast loading and unloading of data

## 1.7  Documentation

Logica documents include :

- Introduction to RAPPORT
- RAPPORT designing and using a database
- RAPPORT user manual
- RAPPORT interactive query language user manual
- RAPPORT system managers manual

## 1.8  General System Description

RAPPORT is a portable DBMS for applications  in  FOR-
TRAN,  COBOL  or CORAL environments on mainframe, mini and
micro computers.

RAPPORT is a flat file  system,  which  provides  the
power  of  relational operations through relatively simple
languages.

RAPPORT probably lies at the borderline of  what  can
really be called "relational".

Interesting aspects of RAPPORT appear to be its relative  simplicity,  portability  and physical data independence.

## 2. Database Constituents

### 2.1 General Description

Term Translation Table

| Rapport term | Feature Catalogue term |
|---|---|
| file | relation |
| record | tuple |
| field | attribute |
| field name | attribute name |

A RAPPORT database consists of a collection of named files (=relations). A file consists of a collection of records (=tuples) of identical type. A record consists of a collection of fields (=attributes) of possibly different types. A field is denoted by a name (=attribute name). A field type (=attribute type) can be a FORTRAN standard type (_real_ or _integer_) or a one-dimensional array thereof.

### 2.2 Database

#### 2.2.1 Database Structure

A database is a collection of files (=relations) whose structure is defined in a schema (RAPPORT Database Definition File). A database does not have a name.

### 2.2.2  Database Operations

Operations are provided for defining and generating a database.  Some  database reorganizations are supported by utility programs.  Files and indexes  can  be  defined  or deleted after database generation.

There is no direct RAPPORT command to destroy a data-base.

### 2.2.3  Database Constraints

Database constraints are defined on the file  (=rela-tion)  and  on the field (=attribute) level.  They consist essentially in the definition of keys.

### 2.2.4  Additional Properties

### 2.3  Relation

### 2.3.1  Relation Structure

The predominant perception of a relation is as a flat file  of  records of identical structure or as a table.  A file is identified by a name.  Duplicate  tuples  are  not allowed.  Attribute order is insignificant.

## 2.3.2  Relation Operations

The operations on files (=relations) are:

- retrieval of a record (=tuple) given a  conjunction  of simple conditions on its fields (=attributes);
- group retrieval within loops (see Section 3.2.1);
- updating of one or several records (=tuples) in a  file (=relation);
- insertion of one record (=tuple) at a time  in  a  file (=relation);
- deletion of one or several or all records (=tuples)  in a file (=relation).

There is no command for removing a relation from  the schema.

## 2.3.3  Relation Constraints

Primary keys must be specified for each file  (=relation).   Primary  key violations result in run-time errors in application programs: insertion or update of  a  record (=tuple)  that  would lead to the duplication of a primary key value in a file (=relation) is not executed.  (In  the host  language  interface,  this  error  is  signaled by a return code associated with the insertion or update operation;  in the stand alone interactive language, this error is signaled by a message).

## 2.3.4  Additional Properties of Relations

## 2.4  Views

RAPPORT does not support views.  However, it is  possible  to  give  particular users access to only a part of the database.  Such a database part has to be a whole file (=relation).

## 2.5   Tuple

### 2.5.1   Tuple Structure

- A record (=tuple) consists of a collection of named
  fields (=attributes).
- Field names (=attribute names) must be unique within
  the whole database. (At the FORTRAN programming interface a tuple appears as a collection of FORTRAN variables).
- A mechanism exists to select individual tuples for read
  and write purposes (see the FETCH command in Section
  3.2.1 and the STORE command in Section 3.3.1).
- Keys are defined by tagging one or more fields in the
  file definition as defining the primary key.

### 2.5.2   Tuple Operations

From the point of view of the update and retrieval
operations, tuples are treated as records in a file. However, neither the host language interface nor the stand
alone interactive language provide operations for handling
a tuple as a single entity.

At the embedded language interface, a tuple is
represented by a collection of variables (one for each
attribute). There is exactly one such "tuple" per database relation, acting as a data buffer between the application program and the DBMS. Reading, updating and writing a tuple in a relation is made via this buffer. RAP-
PORT provides a loop construct for enumerating all the
tuples satisfying a Boolean condition in a relation; at
each execution of the loop body, a new tuple value is made
available in the relation buffer. Notice that this tuple
value is associated with a relation and not with a particular loop; thus nested loops on the same relation share
the same buffer.

## 2.5.3 Tuple Constraints


## 2.5.4 Additional Properties of Tuples

In the manual "RAPPORT : designing and using a data-base", it is stated that a record (=tuple) usually describes some entity (the fields of the record describing the attributes of the entity).

However, a database design philosophy based on an entity-relationship also seems to be advocated in this manual : such a design philosophy more naturally leads to represent entities as relational domains.

Anyhow no design strategy is actually privileged or supported by the system.


## 2.6 Attributes


## 2.6.1 Attribute Structure

Attributes have a type and a name (=attribute name). The type of fields (=attribute types) are FORTRAN types (integer, real, or a one-dimensional array thereof). Alias field (=attribute) names can be defined for the use in the stand alone interactive language.

It is possible to indicate that an integer field or array is to hold a character string for use in the stand alone language.

### 2.6.2  Attribute Operations

The relational comparison operators can be used for comparing fields (=attributes) of records (=tuples) possibly from different files (=relations). Comparisons can be combined to form conjunctions. No compatibility check is done for the embedded language, and the FORTRAN rules for coercion (or type conversion) apply; in the stand alone interactive language, a comparison of two fields (=attributes) is allowed only if both fields are defined on the same underlying type.

There is no direct operation to drop, add or remove a relation attribute.

### 2.6.3  Attribute Constraints

Using the embedded language, field (=attribute) names have to be unique within the whole database, whereas field names in the interactive environment only have to be unique within the file (=relation) they are defined in.

Size constraints can be defined indirectly on an integer field by specifying in the database schema that the field is to be packed into n bits. An attempt to store an integer that cannot be represented in n bits results in a run-time error. (For the treatment of run-time errors, see Section 3.4.8).

In a RAPPORT schema, one can specify that the key of a file (=relation) is a single integer field ranging from 1 to N. Attempts to store a record (=tuple) with a key value outside the defined interval results in a run-time error.

### 2.6.4  Additional Properties of Attributes

If an entity is viewed as a tuple, then the relational attributes describe properties of the entity (see Section 2.5.4).

## 2.7 Domain

User-defined or application-dependent domains are not supported.

Field (=attribute) types are constrained to be one of the FORTRAN standard types (see Section 2.6.1.).

Null, unknown and undefined values are not supported : they are the responsability of users.

## 2.8 Additional Database Constituents

## 3. Functional Capabilities

The facilities for selecting and manipulating data-base constituents are available in two kinds of languages:
- embedded languages with FORTRAN, COBOL or CORAL as a host language;
- a stand alone interactive query language.

The capabilities of both kinds of interfaces are in general very similar. Their main difference is that the embedded languages always return an error test variable after execution of a RAPPORT command which can be used afterwards by control statements in the programming language environment. (In the following this variable is named ITEST). The interactive query language does not provide that facility. The subsequent presentation concentrates on the FORTRAN embedded language. Local dissimilarities with the stand alone interactive language are mentioned when applicable. All examples refer to the RAPPORT file definitions as stated in Section 4.1.2.

### 3.1 Qualification

Records (=tuples) satisfying some Boolean condition are delivered one at a time in a loop (SEARCH loop) or by repeated execution of a FETCH statement.

The retrieved values (field of the records) can be further used in other selection operations. The selection mechanism is thus procedural or navigational.

### 3.1.1 Restriction

The comparison operators that can be used for restricting fields of records are: =, >=, >, <=, <, <>. A field can be compared with a FORTRAN, COBOL or CORAL expression (including a field of another record). In the stand alone interactive language, only comparison with a constant or a field of another record is allowed. Note that the comparison between two fields of the same record (theta-restriction) is not allowed (or at least may not produce the intended result). The simple comparisons described above can be combined into a conjunction. Disjunction, negation and parentheses are not allowed.

## Example of Selection

The tuples of the relation P(PPNUM, PPNAME, COLOR, WEIGHT, PCITY) where COLOR='GREEN' and WEIGHT is less or equal to 10 can be selected by the following SEARCH loop.

```
SEARCH P(COLOR .EQ. 'GREEN'; WEIGHT .LE. 10)

    {the selected tuples can be processed one at a time
     in the body of this loop}

ENDSEARCH (ITEST)
```

### 3.1.2 Quantification

No explicit quantifiers are available.

### 3.1.3 Set Operations

The power is there but they are not explicitly available.

### 3.1.4 Joining

Joining must be expressed procedurally with embedded SEARCH loops. There is no dedicated join operation.

Example: the join of SP(SPSNUM, SPPNUM, QTY)
                 with   P(PPNUM, PPNAME, COLOR, WEIGHT, PCITY)
                 on matching partnumbers can be expressed as
                 follows.

```
SEARCH SP
```

```
SEARCH P(PPNUM .EQ. SPPNUM)

     {the "joined tuples" are available one at a time
     in the body of this loop}

ENDSEARCH (ITEST1)

ENDSEARCH (ITEST2)
```

In the host language interface, there is no constraint on the compatibility of the join attributes; in
the stand alone interactive language, the attributes must
have the same representation.

A relation cannot directly be joined with itself in
nested loops because only one buffer is statically allocated by RAPPORT for every database relation. In the host
language interface, the desired effect can however be
achieved by using host language statements for copying the
relevant fields of the buffer into program variables.

### 3.1.5  Nesting and Closure

Despite the limitations mentioned in Sections 3.1.1
to 3.1.4, any qualification can be expressed using nested
SEARCH loops, and the storage and control structures of
the host language.

The stand alone language is not relationally complete
and the embedded language relies on the power of the host
language for reaching the power of the relational algebra.

### 3.1.6  Additional Aspects of Qualification

## 3.2   Retrieval and Presentation

### 3.2.1   Database Queries

The facilities for defining queries essentially consist of the capabilities for qualification described in
Section 3.1. The predominant perception of retrieval
operations is as follows: the records (=tuples) of a file
(=relation) satisfying a Boolean condition can be accessed
one at a time inside a loop; the values of these records
(=tuples) can also be used for retrieving records of
another file (=relation) in a nested loop. RAPPORT provides facilities for one-record-at-a-time queries as well
as for queries that result in a variable number of records
(=tuples). Record-at-a-time queries can be expressed by
using the FETCH command, specifying uniquely the primary
key in the conditions.

<u>Example</u>

        FETCH S ( ITEST ; SSNUM = 100 )

        IF ( ITEST .NE. 1 ) GOTO 1

        {code for handling the record fetched}

        STOP

    1   {exception handling procedure, e.g., if
        record is not found}

For queries that result in a variable number of
records (=tuples) SEARCH loops are appropriate (see for
example Section 3.1.1).

The tuples selected in a SEARCH can be delivered in
the loop body in any user-defined ascending or descending
lexicographic order. The required order is indicated by
an optional ORDER clause prefixed to a SEARCH loop.

As described above, the result of a qualification
operation is produced tuple by tuple. The output of these
tuples is to be programmed by the user with the standard
host language output statements. A special WRITE

statement is available in the stand alone interactive language (see Section 3.2.4).

There is no Boolean-valued qualification operation.

The embedded language has the power of relational completeness, but this power relies on control structures and temporary storage provided by the host language.

The stand-alone interactive language is not relationally complete. Its power can be roughly characterized as follows. Nested SEARCH loops on different relations can denote the Cartesian product of these relations (available tuple by tuple in the body of the innermost loop). The conditions in the arguments of the SEARCH loop are equivalent to a limited form of theta-restrictions on this Cartesian product (see limitations on the conditions of the SEARCH in Sections 3.1.1 and 3.1.4). Projection on the desired attributes of this restricted Cartesian product can be achieved by writing only the values of the desired attributes in the innermost loop.

### 3.2.2   Retrieval of Information
####          About Database Constituents

In the interactive language, the HELP command can be used to retrieve the names of relations and their attributes.

### 3.2.3   Retrieval of System Performance Data

Commands of the embedded language are available for printing statistics about
- the physical dispersion of data within the database files
- the performance of accesses to each database relation by all the application programs during a given period (the number of logical retrieval operations and the number of physical read operations on disk per logical retrieval).

A detailed presentation of these statistics is not given here, since their understanding would require a presentation of the internal structure of RAPPORT, which falls outside of the scope of the Feature Catalogue.

This interface is not relational and is thus independent from the qualification capabilities described in Section 3.1.


### 3.2.4 Report Generation


RAPPORT does not have a real report generator. The form of the output document has to be specified procedurally.

Example of a program in the RAPPORT interactive language for printing as a table the name and status of the London suppliers:

```
WRITE ('----------------------------')

WRITE ('| SUPPLIER NAME | STATUS | ')

WRITE ('----------------------------')

SEARCH S WHERE ( CITY = LONDON )

WRITE ('| ',SUPPLIERNAME,' | ',STATUS,' |')

LOOP

WRITE ('----------------------------')

EXECUTE
```


Typical output of this program:

```
----------------------------

| SUPPLIER NAME | STATUS |

----------------------------

| SMITH         | 20     |

| CLARK         | 20     |

----------------------------
```

## 3.2.5   Constraints and Limitations

Limitations were mentioned in Sections 3.1.1,   3.1.4, and 3.2.1.

## 3.2.6   Additional Aspects of Retrieval
and Presentation

## 3.3   Alteration

The altering facilities of RAPPORT are  very  similar to  the traditional operations of insertion or update of a record in a file.  A deletion facility  for  removing  all the records of a file satisfying some Boolean condition is provided.  Using the interactive query  language,  altera- tions are expressed as transactions. A transaction appears as a sequence of commands preceded by TSTART and  followed by TEND (see Section 3.4.5).

## 3.3.1   Insert Facilities

Field (= attribute) values for  a  record  (=  tuple) which  is  to  be  inserted  in a file are assigned in the record buffer which is associated to that file,  and  then stored  in  the  database  with the INSERT statement.  The record buffer is filled by FORTRAN  assignment  statements or  by  previous database retrieval operations on the file to which the buffer is associated.

Example fragment of a program inserting
a new tuple in the SP relation

SPSNUM = 547

SPPNUM = 4711

QTY    = 2

```
INSERT SP (ITEST)

IF (ITEST .EQ. 0) GO TO 1

    {here should come some code for treating exceptions
    occurring during INSERT, e.g., for handling the
    situation where a record with the same key already
    exists in the SP file}

1 ...
```

As it appears in the example above, exceptional conditions (e.g., a violation of a key constraint) are signaled by the DBMS to the application program by setting a
user-defined test variable ITEST to a given error code.

In the interactive language, a SET assignment statement is provided for setting fields of the record buffer
associated to a file to a constant value or to the value
of a field of another record.

Example using the interactive query language for
inserting the same tuple as above.

```
  TSTART

      SET SP-SUPPLIERNO TO 547

      SET SP-PARTNO     TO 4711

      SET SP-QUANTITY   TO 2

      INSERT SP

  TEND

  EXECUTE
```

RAPPORT also has a STORE statement. It acts like an
INSERT statement if the pre-specified values for the primary key of the record (=tuple) to be inserted do not
already exist in the file (=relation). Otherwise STORE
has the same effect as the UPDATE statement (see Section
3.3.3).

### 3.3.2 Delete Facilities

Records in a file that satisfy a Boolean condition (similar to that associated to a SEARCH loop) can be deleted.

<u>Example</u> delete all the records in SP where
          PNUM is 4711

          DELETE SP (N; SPPNUM .EQ. 4711)

This form of delete is the only truly set-oriented operation in RAPPORT.

The number of records which are actually deleted is returned as the value of the first argument (here variable N).

There is no distinction between unique record deletion by providing the key, and multiple record deletion.

<u>Example</u> delete the record of SP whose key is
          SPSNUM=547, SPPNUM=4711

          DELETE SP(N;SPSNUM .EQ. 547; SPPNUM .EQ. 4711)

All the records in a file can be deleted by the CLEAR statement. The result is an empty file, not a modified schema.

<u>Example</u> delete all records of SP

          CLEAR SP(N)

### 3.3.3 Modify Facilities

Individual records in a file can be modified. The key values and all the other fields (updated or not) of a record to be modified must be present in the record buffer associated with the file before the UPDATE statement can start executing. This means in practice that the update of a record must be preceded by a retrieval of this record.

An update operation on a record (=tuple) identified by a key value that does not exist in a file (=relation) is an error. If a user is not sure whether or not a given key value exists in the file (=relation), he or she can use the STORE command. It results in an update if the key value exists and in an insertion if the key value does not already exist (see also Section 3.3.1).

Example update the city of supplier 50 to London

FETCH S (ITEST; SNUM .EQ. 50)

IF (ITEST .NE. 1) GO TO 1

SCITY(1) = 'LOND'

SCITY(2) = 'ON'

UPDATE S (ITEST)

IF (ITEST .NE. O) GO TO 2

...

STOP

1     {code for handling the case of a record not found

or other exceptions}

...

2     {code for handling exceptions in update}

...

## 3.3.4  Commit and Undo Facilities

All updates in a transaction (see Section 3.4.5) can be "undone" before the end of the transaction by using a single BACKOUT command. In the stand-alone language, "COMMIT" is implicit at the end of a transaction. In the embedded language interface, "COMMIT" marks the end of a transaction.

### 3.3.5   Additional Alteration Facilities

## 3.4   Additional Functional Capabilities

### 3.4.1   Arithmetic and String Operations

The embedded language relies on the operations of its host language (FORTRAN, COBOL or CORAL).

The stand-alone interactive language does not have arithmetic or string operations (see however Section 3.4.3).

### 3.4.2   Sorting

The order (ascending or descending) in which the records (=tuples) are to be delivered in a SEARCH loop (in the embedded as well as in the stand-alone language) can be specified in an ORDER clause prefixed to a SEARCH loop.

### 3.4.3   Library Functions

The stand-alone language supports the functions MIN, MAX, SUM and AVERAGE. These functions can be applied to numeric fields of the records of a database file (= relation) or to a subset of records selected by Boolean conditions similar to those available to write SEARCH loops.

The function operates on all the values of a numerical field, and the result is put in the field with the same name in the buffer.

Example retrieval of the average weight of all screws in the file P (interactive mode)

        AVG P ( PARTNAME EQ 'SCREW' )

        WRITE ( "AVERAGE WEIGHT OF SCREWS IS ",WEIGHT )

        EXECUTE


Additionally, the stand-alone interactive language provides the function COUNT, which returns the number of records (=tuples) in a file (=relation) satisfying a specified condition. If the condition is omitted, the total number of records (=tuples) in a file (=relation) is returned.

There is no facility for duplicate control and for repeated function application (grouping).


### 3.4.4  User - Defined Functions

User-supplied FORTRAN functions can be invoked from the interactive language. These "functions" can access the current values of the record buffer associated with each database file, modify these values, or produce other side-effects such as printing.

These functions are "global" to all the users of a database and the DBMS does not support authorization mechanisms for modifying these functions.


### 3.4.5  Transactions

A transaction is dynamically determined by the TRANSACT and COMMIT statements (TSTART and TEND in the stand-alone language). The DBMS automatically sets locks (preventing concurrent write or concurrent read) on the database files as soon as they are accessed in a transaction.

The user is aware of the concurrency of transactions in the sense that a transaction can be backed out ("undone") by the DBMS in the case of a deadlock.

### 3.4.6  Multi-tuple Alterations

Only a version of delete (see Section 3.3.2) operates on several tuples.  Insert operates on one tuple at a time.

### 3.4.7  Grouping

There is no facility for partitioning sets of tuples, e.g. for repeated function applcation.

### 3.4.8  Exception Handling Mechanism

In the embedded language, the outcome of each database manipulation command is signaled to the application program in a variable which is passed as an argument of the command.  The application program then has the responsibility to test this return code and take the appropriate exception handling decisions.

In the stand alone interactive language, each run-time error results in a message displayed to the user and generally also in aborting the execution of the current command.  (Notice that the decision to undo the updates that have previously been performed in the current transaction unit is left to the interactive user.)

# 4. Definition, Generation, and Administration Facilities

## 4.1 Definition Facilities

### 4.1.1 Constituents of a Database Definition

A RAPPORT database definition (=schema definition) is specified by a special Database Definition File. It comprises definitions on the logical and physical level and specifies:
- the names of files (=relations);
- the names of fields (attributes);
- the type of fields;
- the primary key;
- the maximum number of records (=tuples) in a file (=relation);
- various physical information:
  - on access paths (relative addressing and hashing, declaration of secondary indexes including their expected selectivity);
  - on the mapping of relations and indexes on "physical" files (i.e., files known by the operating system);
- information on certain aspects of the system behavior.

### 4.1.2 Database Definition

A database is defined by a sequence of file (=relation) definitions (see Section 4.1.3). Special DBMS features can be invoked by an OPTION clause.

<u>Example</u>

OPTION

LIST; SORT

{a listing of the preprocessed program will be
produced and sorted retrieval is allowed}

Restrictions on the number of constituents, such as
the maximum number of files, of fields per file, of
indexes etc., have to be set up at DBMS installation time,
but they can be changed by the database administrator.

<u>Simplified</u> <u>Example</u> <u>of</u> <u>File</u> <u>Definition</u>

This example shows how the files corresponding to the
relations P(PPNUM, PNAME, COLOR, WEIGHT, PCITY), S(SSNUM,
SNAME, STATUS, SCITY) and SP(SPSNUM, SPPNUM, QTY) could be
described in a RAPPORT Data Definition File. The example
is simplified in the sense that all access paths and physical aspects of the definition are omitted.

FILE P

FIELDS

PPNUM; PKEY; 'PARTNO'

PNAME(3); 'PARTNAME'; CHARS

COLOR(2); 'COLOR'; CHARS

WEIGHT; 'WEIGHT'

PCITY(2); 'CITY'; CHARS

FILE S

FIELDS

SSNUM; PKEY; 'SUPPLIERNO'

SNAME(3); 'SUPPLIERNAME'; CHARS

STATUS ; 'STATUS'

SCITY(2) ; 'CITY'; CHARS

FILE SP

FIELDS

      SPSNUM; PKEY; 'SUPPLIERNO'

      SPPNUM; PKEY; 'PARTNO'

      QTY ; 'QUANTITY'


Annotations:
- the default type for the field is one FORTRAN _integer_;
- the numbers between parentheses indicate the dimension of the fields (number of _integer_ or _real_ locations);
- PKEY indicates that field is part of the primary key of the file;
- the strings between quotes rename the fields for use in the interactive language;
- CHARS indicates to the interactive language processor that an _integer_ field in fact holds a character string.


### 4.1.3  Relation Definition

    The definition of a file (=relation) states the file name and the maximum number of records (=tuples) in the file. It is followed by some optional definitions regarding physical properties and by the definition of the record fields (=attributes). Additionally, secondary indexes can be defined.

Example

    FILE P

        {file name is P}

    RECORDS 1000; CHANNEL 2

        {maximum number of records in file P is assumed to be

        1000; the file will reside on disk file 2}

    FIELDS

        {followed by field definitions}

    INDEX

{followed by the definition of the indexed fields}


## 4.1.4  View Definition

A kind of view definition (see however 2.4) is achieved by omitting definitions of certain files (=relations) in the Data Definition File. (There are physical restrictions which are not mentioned here.)


## 4.1.5  Tuple Definition

In the RAPPORT system, records (=tuples) are perceived as a collection of fields (=attributes) (see 4.1.3)


## 4.1.6  Attribute Definition

Field (=attribute) definition associates a field name with a field type.  No user defined field types can be defined.  Therefore field types are restricted to FORTRAN types (see 2.6.1 and 4.1.2). Additionally, information on the physical level can be specified and it can be stated whether or not the field is part of the primary key.  For use in the stand-alone language additional definitions are required (see 4.1.2).


## 4.1.7  Domain Definition

User-defined domains are not supported. The possible field (=attribute) types are the FORTRAN standard types.

### 4.1.8  Definition of Additional Database Constituents

### 4.2  Generation Facilities

A database is generated in two steps.  First the Data Definition File (=schema) is processed; then the result of this processing is used for generating the database physical files (that will contain the relations and their indices).

None of these facilities are "relational in nature".

### 4.3  Database Refefinition

#### 4.3.1  Renaming Database Constituents

Not explicitly supported.

#### 4.3.2  Redefining Database Constituents

The database relations can be individually redefined by modifying the database schema, selectively regenerating the physical files that are to hold them, and writing ad hoc programs for performing the reorganization (filling new relations from old ones).

## 4.4  Database Regeneration and Reorganization

Utility programs are provided for unloading, copying and loading files after the relations have been redefined.

## 4.5  Database Dictionary

Not supported.

# 5.   Interfaces and DBMS Architecture

The functional capabilities listed in Section 1.6 are supported by the architecture described below. This architecture is described in terms of relationships between programs (system modules and utilities, application programs) and files (user supplied data such as the system representation of the compiled schema and the files constituting the database). System programs include :

- A utility for compiling a Database Definition File (see Section 4) into a Common File. The Common File is used by the Preprocessor and the run-time database handler (the RAPPORT Nucleus).

- A Security Structure Processor for compiling a Security Structure File (see Section 6.1). This utility also accesses the Database Definition File (see Section 4) and produces the Security Common File, which is used by the RAPPORT run-time Nucleus (the database handler).

- A New Password Processor for setting and modifying the passwords for access authorization and for encryption. It produces a new Security Common File. If encryption passwords are modified, the database is also accessed for performing the necessary re-encryption.

- A utility for (1) establishing the correspondence between RAPPORT logical files (=relations) and files known to the host operating system, and (2) specifying the maximum populations for each RAPPORT logical file.

- A Preprocessor translating the embedded database language into host language (e.g. FORTRAN) code and calls to the RAPPORT Nucleus (run-time database handler). The preprocessor accesses the Common File.

- The RAPPORT Nucleus, which satisfies the database manipulation requests issued by the application programs and the Interactive Query Language Processor and those interactively entered by the Database Administrator (requests for statistical informations, dumping, logging, recovery and roll-forward operations).

- The Interactive Query Language Processor

- Utility programs for initializing, physically reorganizing, copying, loading or unloading database files.


  The diagram summarizes the architecture  of  RAPPORT.
There are 3 types of nodes in the diagram :

1) Users (application programmers, Database Administrator)

2) Files (e.g. database schema, stored database files)

3) Processors (e.g. translators, database handler, application programs)

Arcs denote flows of data between the nodes.

  The following are not included in the diagram :

- the utility programs

- the log files, the dump files

- the interactions of the Database Administrator with the Nucleus for requesting statistics, backup dumps, logging, recovery, roll-forward operations

- the file in which the Interactive Query Language Processor stores Stored Command Sequences

- the files holding the application program in various forms (source, object, linked).

# Sketch of the Overall Architecture of RAPPORT

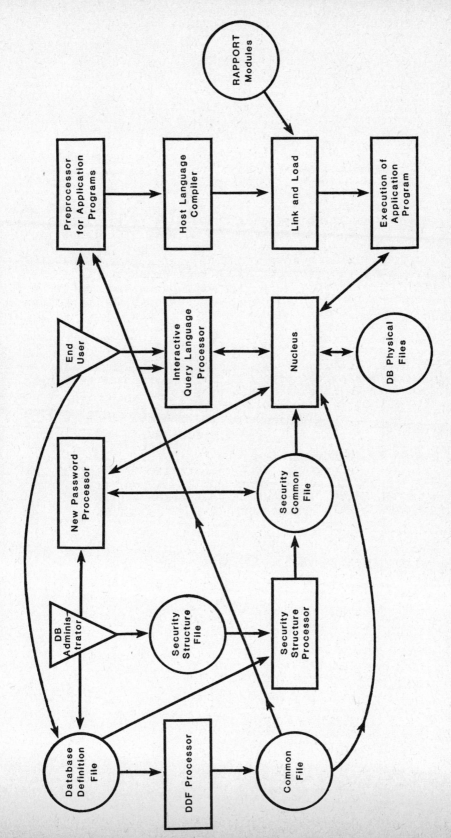

# 6. Operational Aspects

## 6.1 Security

Access authorization can be controlled by passwords. Read and read/write authorization are offered.

The individual fields (= attributes) of records and also the subset of records of a file determined by the value of a field can subjected to authorization control.

The system also features a data encryption mechanism. The permission to decrypt and encrypt/decrypt data is controlled by passwords. Prime key attributes and attributes on which secondary indexes are defined cannot be protected by encryption.

Operational aspects :

- The specification of data to be protected by passwords and encryption constitutes the Security Structure File. This file is processed by a utility program (the Security Structure Processor) into data used at run-time by the RAPPORT Nucleus (= database handler) for authorization control and encryption/decryption.

- The Database Administrator can interactively initialize and modify passwords through a utility program (the New Password Processor). Modification of encryption passwords results in the re-encryption of the data concerned (see also Section 5.1).

## 6.2  Physical Integrity

### 6.2.1  Concurrency Control

Concurrency control is handled by locking whole files. Two levels of locks are available:
- <u>read</u> <u>locks</u> : the file can be read but not modified by other users;
- <u>write</u> <u>locks</u> : the file cannot be accessed by other users.

Locks are automatically set by the DBMS in a transaction (see Section 3.4.5) as soon as a read or write operation is encountered in the transaction.

Locking of files can be done explicitly at the beginning of a transaction (LOCK statements are provided to that effect).

Deadlocks are detected by the DBMS and are resolved by backing out one of the deadlocked transactions.

Read-only operations can be performed without protection (i.e., without setting locks) outside a transaction.

### 6.2.2  Crash Recovery

In the case of a single-user access to the database, an application program can create dump copies of the database at checkpoints. In the case of multi-user access to the database, this function can only be performed centrally via a dialogue with the run-time Nucleus of the DBMS.

Before- and after-images of updates can be logged, giving the possibility to recover from a crash up to the most recent transaction completed.

## 6.3 Operating Environment

### 6.3.1 Software Environment

RAPPORT is a portable DBMS that can run in an environment which supports FORTRAN and direct access disk I-0. Minimum requirements for the host operating system include a message-passing or shared data mechanism between the run-time DBMS Nucleus and the different user programs.

### 6.3.2 Hardware Environment

RAPPORT is compact enough to run on small minicomputers, occupying typically 64K bytes at run-time. There is a version for micro-computers requiring only 46K bytes.

# 7. Essentially Relational Solution
   for Generalized DBMS Problems

RAPPORT relies on the data structuring tool of the relational model, viz. relations.

Relations appear as flat files in RAPPORT. The operations on these files do not explicitly refer to access paths, thus allowing the modification of these access paths without having to modify the application programs.

This <u>data</u> <u>independence</u> allows a limited form of program performance improvement by mere access paths modifications. RAPPORT does not however follow the "relational ideal" requiring that the formulation of requests to a database be completely separated from efficiency considerations. The RAPPORT data manipulation language is procedural and the requests involving more than one file necessarily embed an access strategy (specifying essentially the order in which the files are accessed). In addition to the modification of data independent access paths mentioned above, performance tuning during the life of a database thus implies the modification of the database access strategies embedded in the application programs.

## 8. Database Applications Using the System

Existing applications include: computer aided design, industrial process control, scientific data processing, management information systems, financial planning, market research, configuration management, simulation and modelling, exploration data analysis.

3.14   Feature Analysis Of SYSTEM R

Feature Analysis
of
SYSTEM R

by
K.C. Kinsley

Computer Science Department
University of Central Florida
Box 25000
Orlando, Florida 32816

December 1980

Preface

All examples in this feature analysis are based on the database below:

| S# | SNAME | STATUS | CITY |
|----|-------|--------|------|
| S1 | Smith | 20 | London |
| S2 | Jones | 10 | Paris |
| S3 | Blake | 30 | Paris |
| S4 | Clark | 20 | London |
| S5 | Adams | 30 | Athens |

| P# | PNAME | COLOR | WEIGHT |
|----|-------|-------|--------|
| P1 | Nut | Red | 12 |
| P2 | Bolt | Green | 17 |
| P3 | Screw | Blue | 17 |
| P4 | Screw | Red | 14 |
| P5 | Cam | Blue | 12 |
| P6 | Cog | Red | 19 |

| J# | JNAME | CITY |
|----|-------|------|
| J1 | Sorter | Paris |
| J2 | Punch | Rome |
| J3 | Reader | Athens |
| J4 | Console | Athens |
| J5 | Collator | London |
| J6 | Terminal | Oslo |
| J7 | Tape | London |

SPJ

| S# | P# | J# | QTY |
|----|----|----|-----|
| S1 | P1 | J1 | 200 |
| S1 | P1 | J4 | 700 |
| S2 | P3 | J1 | 400 |
| S2 | P3 | J2 | 200 |
| S2 | P3 | J3 | 200 |
| S2 | P3 | J4 | 500 |
| S2 | P3 | J5 | 600 |
| S2 | P3 | J6 | 400 |
| S2 | P3 | J7 | 800 |
| S2 | P5 | J2 | 100 |
| S3 | P3 | J1 | 200 |
| S3 | P4 | J2 | 500 |
| S4 | P6 | J3 | 300 |
| S4 | P6 | J7 | 300 |
| S5 | P2 | J2 | 200 |
| S5 | P2 | J4 | 100 |
| S5 | P5 | J5 | 500 |
| S5 | P5 | J7 | 100 |
| S5 | P6 | J2 | 200 |
| S5 | P1 | J4 | 1000 |
| S5 | P3 | J4 | 1200 |
| S5 | P4 | J4 | 800 |
| S5 | P5 | J4 | 400 |
| S5 | P6 | J4 | 500 |

From C.J. Date, 1977;  An Introduction to Database Systems, Reading, Mass.: Addison-Wesley Publishing Company, pg. 105.

# 1.0 INTRODUCTION

## 1.1 Identification

System R is a relational DBMS involving the language SQL (Structured English Query Language). SQL (also called SEQUEL II) is an English-like relational data sublanguage that is the main external interface supported by System R.

Developed by: IBM Research Laboratory

San Jose, California

## 1.2 Status

### 1.2.1 System

System R is in current use with implementation of the prototype system now essentially complete, at the IBM Research Laboratory in San Jose, California on an IBM 370. The system is experimental in nature.

### 1.2.2 Applications

All software for System R was developed as a research tool in relational data base and is not generally available outside of the IBM Research Division.

## 1.3 System Background

System R is an experimental database management system, based on the relational model, which has been under development at IBM Research Laboratory in San Jose, California since 1975. The prototype system was completed in 1979. System R currently supports the high level relational user sublanguage SQL.

The original version of SQL, called SEQUEL, was based on an earlier

language called SQUARE (Specifying Queries As Relational Expressions).
SQL is more English-like than SQUARE. Controlled experiments involving
college students were carried out to test SEQUEL's usability. Based on
the results of that study, the present SQL was designed. SQL is intended
for the non-specialist in data processing as well as the professional
programmers and is designed to allow easy definition and access of
databases. This is because the user specifies only what is desired,
not how to obtain it.

Since SQL's original version, it has been expanded to include a data
manipulation facility which permits insertion, deletion, and update of
tuples, a data definition facility which allows definition of relations
and alternate views of relations and a data control facility which
enables each user to authorize other users to access of his data. In
addition ,facilities have been added to permit coupling with a high level
programming language.

1.4 Overall Philosphy

The developers of System R state the philosphy in the architectural
update as follows: "Perhaps the greatest impediment to the use of
computerized data management systems is the cost and complexity of
understanding and installing such systems. At present, installation
of a database management system requires a staff skilled in telecommunications,
operating systems, data management and in the application area. System R is
a relational database management system designed to address this problem.
System R is designed to allow easy definition of databases and of the
applications which use them while still providing the function and
performance available in most commercially available systems."

The goals of System R are as follows ( Section 1.7.5):

(a)  to provide full capability of DBMS in realistic operating environment.

(b)  to provide high level of data independence by isolating end user from underlying storage structure.

(c)  to support two different types of processing against database, i.e., ad-hoc queries and updates and canned programs.

(d)  to allow easy definition of databases and the applications which use them.

## 1.5  Essentially Relational Characteristics

System R satisfies all the requirements of a fully relational system, as specified by CODD (TODS Vol. 4, No. 4, Dec. 1979).

## 1.6  Interfaces

System R contains the SQL user language, contained in the Relational Data Interface (RDI) and the Relational Storage Interface (RSI), an internal interface for accessing tuples in base relations.  SQL provides capability for scheme definition, quering, database altering, constraint, definition, database generation, and data entry.  RSI supports space management, index and link management, concurrency control and recovery. RSL is not concerned with normal relation operations - further discussion will be made in Section 5.

## 1.7  Documentation

1.  Astrahan, M.M., et. al.  System R:  Relational Approach to Database Management.  ACM Transactions on Database Systems, Vol. 1, No. 2, June 1976, pp. 97-137.

2.  Chamberlin, D.D., et. al.  Sequel 2:  A Unified Approach to Data Definition, Manipulation, and Control.  IBM J. Res. Dvlp., Vol. 20, No. 6, Nov. 1976, pp. 560-574.

3.  Boyce, Raymond F., Chamberlin, Donald D.  Using A Structured English Query Language as A Data Definition Facility.  IBM RJ 1318 (#20559) Dec. 10, 1973, pp. 1-15.

4.  Chamberlin, D.D., et. al.  Data Base System Authorization, IBM RJ 2041 (28513) July 18, 1977, pp. 1-14.

5.  Blasgen, M.W., et. al.  System R:  An Architectural Update. IBM RJ 2581 (33481) July 17, 1979, pp. 1-36.

6.  Selinger, P.G., et. al.  Access Path Selection in a Relational Data Base Management System.  IBM Research Report RJ 2429 Jan. 1979.

7.  Chamberlin, D.D., et. al.  Support for Repetitive Transactions and Ad-Hoc Query in System R.  Research Report RJ 2551, IBM Research Laboratory, San Jose, California, May 1979.

8.  Astrahan, M.M., et. al.  Evaluation of the System R Access Path Selection Mechanism.  IBM Research Report IBM RJ2797 (35713), April 10, 1980.

9.  Astrahan, et. al.  A History and Evaluation of System R. IBM Research Report RJ2843 (36129), IBM Research Laboratory, San Jose, California, June 12, 1980.

## 1.8  General System Description

System R adopts a relational data model and supports the language SQL for defining, accessing, and modifying multiple views of stored System R provides the capability for SQL programs to run in two different modes.  A user may work with the system interactively using pure SQL commands, or in batch mode by imbedding SQL statements into a PL/I or COBOL program.  Programs wirtten in PL/I or COBOL with imbedded SQL statements go through a precompiler, XPREP, in which SQL statements are replaced by host-language calls to the access module.

The access module is stored in the System R database to protect
it from unauthorized modification.

Interactive SQL is supported by a user interface (UFI) which controls
dialog management and the formatting of the display terminal. Because
the UFI is executing SQL statements that are not known in advance, the
access module must be generated dynamically.

Both the UFI and the user's object program are submitted to the
Execution-time System (XRDI). The XRDI interacts with the access
module security before the database is accessed.

The access module for either batch or interactive mode calls the
Research Storage System (RSS). RSS is a special multi-user access
method facility for locking, logging, recovery, and index maintenance.
RSS performs the actual accessing of the database.

## 2.0 DATABASE CONSTITUENTS

### 2.1 General Description

The constituents of the SYSTEM R database are:

DB  (= Database)

R   (= Table)

V   (= View)

T   (= Row)

C   (= Column)

D   (= Domain)

The DB consists of R's of possibly different types.  Any one R consists of T's of identical type.  A v is an R derived from one or more R's by use of qualifications.  A T consists of C values of possibly different type.  C's are defined in terms of a D.  D's are implicitly defined by the particular C's (column) definition.

### 2.2 Database

#### 2.2.1 Database Structure

A SYSTEM R database consists of independent snapshots (static derived relations), views (dynamic derived relations) and tables (base relations).  In addition, two system tables are maintained for the relations' definition.

#### 2.2.2 Database Operations

A database is defined and generated through the definition and generation of its base and derived relations.

#### 2.2.3 Database Constraints

Nothing found.

2.3  Relation

   2.3.1  Relation Structure

      The system term for a relation is a table.  A relation is
perceived as a table of rows and columns.  All relations have
unique character names.  A relation is comprised of tuples of
the same type.  Duplicate tuples are allowed.  A row consists
of attributes of possibly different types.  Attribute order
is insignificant.  The name of a table may be qualified by
the name of the user who created it.  Alias names can be defined
using the keyword SYNONYM.

   2.3.2  Relation Operations

      The basic operation on a SQL relation is the mapping.  A mapping
returns a collection of values from the key phrase:

```
SELECT  (attribute(s))
FROM    (relation(s))
WHERE   (qualification(s)) ;
```

An omitted attribute list returns all columns of the relation.
An omitted qualification list returns all the rows.
In addition, relations can be created, deleted, linked with
another relation, revised by adding columns, modified by
inserting or deleting rows, joined.  The set operations of
union, intersection and difference are supported in SYSTEM R.
Relations in these set operations must be union compatible.

   2.3.3  Relation Constraints

      All relations must be in first normal form.  Inter-relational
and intra-relational constraints can be made using assertions
about the integrity of data in the relation.  An assertion is

a SQL predicate which evaluates to TRUE or FALSE.  If a
modification to a tuple in the relation is issued which
violates an assertion, the modification is rejected and
a violation code with the names of the violated assertions
is returned.

A trigger can be defined to be executed at the occurrence
of reading or modification of a tuple of a relaxation.
The trigger, which consists of one or more SQL statements,
is executed immediately after the read or modification is
completed.

### 2.3.4  Additional Properties Of Relations

Additional attributes can be added to a table via the
keyword EXPAND.  Tables can be dynamically created and
deleted using the keywords CREATE TABLE and DROP TABLE.
A row can be uniquely identified by the image command
which creates an index for each tuple.  A link between
two relations which match in the given attribute may be
defined.

## 2.4  Views

### 2.4.1  View Structure

A user can define both static and dynamic derived relations.
The system uses the term and keyword VIEW to define a dynamic
derived relation.  A view's structure is a portion of an
overall relation.  A view is dynamically defined by a user as
a mapping of an existing relation(s) and views.  Each view has
a unique character name.  Static derived relations are created
via the assignment statement.  The result of the query is copie

into the database.

### 2.4.2 View Operations

Once a view has been defined, its operations are the same as those of a table. Queries may be issued against it and other views may be defined in terms of it. However, some modification operations may not be allowed. (Section 2.4.3). Snapshots may be updated, queried or processed in the same way as tables.

### 2.4.3 View Constraints

Updates may be made via a view only if each tuple of the view is associated with exactly one tuple of a stored relation. An update must not apply a built-in function such as AVG or SUM to a view field which itself is defined by a built-in function (AVG, MAX, MIN, SUM or COUNT); i.e., updates are not permitted for views which involve joining, grouping or duplicate elimination.

## 2.5  Tuple

### 2.5.1 Tuple Structure

The system name for tuple is row. System constraints are the only limit on the number of tuples allowed. Attributes differ in a tuple, but different tuples have the same corresponding attributes (and therefore domains). No key is required. A key may be defined by specifying a unique image (index) on a relation. A tuple type, i.e., tuple structure is defined implicitly when a relation is defined.

### 2.5.2 Tuple Operations

Tuples may be modified via the keyword UPDATE. Single tuples or a set of tuples may be inserted in or deleted from a relation.

Tuples from two relations can be grouped together on pages of memory.  This is intended to make access to many-to-one relationships efficient because it limits the number of pages that must be brought into main memory in response to a query.

Links can be used to connect a tuple in one relation to tuples in another relation with the same value in specified attributes.

### 2.5.3  Tuple Constraints

By using the assertion feature, constraints can be imposed by the user on tuples inserted, deleted or updated within a relation.  Examples of this are asserting that values of specified attributes are within a certain range (such as salary), asserting that each employee in a department is also in the payroll roster, and asserting that a new salary is larger than an employee's  former salary.  If a tuple does not meet the constraint specified in the assertion, the update is not completed and a violation code with error messages are returned.

## 2.6   Attribute

### 2.6.1  Attribute Structure

The system term for attribute is column.  An attribute's domain is defined at time of relation creation.  Attributes are given unique names within their relation.  When a relation is defined, the attribute names are specified.  Null values are allowed by specifying NULL or NONULL for attributes that are not part of keys.

### 2.6.2 Attribute Operations

Attributes can be relationally compared or arithmetically manipulated. The aggregate functions AVG, MAX, MIN, SUM, COUNT are available.

### 2.6.3 Attribute Constraints

See Section 2.5.3

## 2.7 Domain

### 2.7.1 Domain Structure

The system has no term for domain. Domains are implicitly defined when the attributes of a table are declared. Basic data types are character, integer, decimal and floating point.

### 2.7.2 Domain Operations

Operations defined on domains are string, integer and real comparisons with logical "and", "or" and "not". Domains are the basis of compatibility of relation element components. Arithmetic operations (add, subtract, multiply, divide) are defined on integers and reals with set functions (AVG, MAX, MIN, SUM and COUNT) defined on appropriate domains.

### 2.7.3 Domain Constraints

Nothing found.

## 2.8 Additional Database Constituents

SQL allows a group of modifications to be placed in a transaction block, using BEGIN TRANSACTION

.

.

.

END TRANSACTION

A trigger can be defined to be executed at the occurrence of some modification of a tuple.  The trigger is executed immediatetly after the tuple update is completed.

Assertions are supported by SYSTEM R.  To users with control privileges on a table (e.g. a DBA) when an assertion is issued, the system static assertions can be made about individual tuples in a relation or about one or more relations.  Transistion assertions are enforced either upon completion of a statement or upon completion of a transaction.

## 3.0 FUNCTIONAL CAPABILITIES

### 3.1 Qualification

SQL mappings are used for n-element selection on the basis of a mapping. In general, a mapping returns a collection of values, i.e., the selected attributes of the tuples that satisfy the WHERE clause.

An example of qualification for an attribute through the WHERE clause:

```
SELECT  * (* is SYMBOL for all)
FROM    S (RELATION)
WHERE   CITY = 'LONDON';
```

Duplicate values are not eliminated from the returned set unless the user requests unique values. The result of a query is returned in system-determined order unless the user requests an ordering. The result of a query is a relation.

### 3.1.1 Restriction

All operators ( < ,>, ≤, ≥,=,≠)can be used in the qualification. The qualification may appear as a constant, another attribute or another nested query (SELECT). Boolean expressions can be composed using AND, OR and NOT can be included.

The truth value of the WHERE clause is computed using two-valued logic to evaluate ANDs and ORs. The tuple is considered to satisfy the WHERE clause if the overall truth value of the clause is TRUE but not if the overall truth value is FALSE. An exception to the above rules is made in the case of predicates that search for null values explicitly. In these predicates, the null value is treated like any other value.

The projection command is represented by a vertical subsetting.
Again, duplicate tuples are only eliminated if the user so specifies.
The SQL projection command has no WHERE clause.  Essentially, all
tuples are selected.

### 3.1.2 Quantification

Not supported.

### 3.1.3 Set Operations

System R supports the set operations INTERSECT, UNION and MINUS.
The following is an example of set difference return suppliers
supplying no parts:

```
SELECT   S#
FROM     S
MINUS
SELECT   S#
FROM     SP;
```

A query may contain several set theoretic operations, with parentheses
used as needed to resolve ambiguities.  Duplicate tuples are
eliminated from the operands before performing the set operation.
A special built-in function called SET is provided that evaluates
a set of values for a particular attribute which is present in a
given group.  This set of attributes may then be compared with other
sets.  Set equality, set inequality, set inclusion and set non-inclusion
operations exist in the SQL language.

### 3.1.4 Joining

SQL supports the join operation.  Joins can be made over several
relations as well as over one relation.  The user must be careful
in multiple relation joins to properly qualify each attribute name.
Conceptually, the Cartesian product of these relations is formed

and then filtered by the predicates in the WHERE clause. Both the equi-joins and the natural join are available.

```
SELECT   S#,P#
FROM     S,P
WHERE    S.CITY = P. CITY ;
```

### 3.1.5 Nesting and Closure

A predicate in a WHERE clause may test an attribute for inclusion in a set. It is possible to use the result of a mapping in the WHERE clause of another mapping. This is called nested mapping. Multiple levels of nesting are allowed in qualifications. The inner mapping of a nested retrieval is performed first, then the outer mapping uses the results of the inner mapping as a set of constants.

For example:

Find part number of all parts supplied by more than one supplier:

```
SELECT P#

FROM    SP, SPX

WHERE   P# IN (IN is equivalent to = )

        SELECT P#

        FROM    SP

        WHERE   SP.S#>  = SPX.S#;
```

### 3.1.6 Additional Aspects of Qualification

None found.

## 3.2  Retrieval and Representation

### 3.2.1 Database Queries

A query block is represented by a SELECT list, a FROM list and a WHERE tree containing the list of items to be retrieved, the table referenced and the Boolean combination of simple predicates specified by the user. A single SQL statement may have many query blocks because a predicate may have one operand which is itself a query.

### 3.2.2 Retrieval of Information about Database Constituents

System R automatically maintains catalogs that describe all tables, views, images, links, assertions, and triggers that are known to the system. These catalogs are kept in the form of tables which may be queried in the same way as any other table. Each catalog entry has space for a comment which may be filled in by the creator of the relevant object.

### 3.2.3 Retrieval of System Performance Data

The operating system schedules periodic checkpoints and maintenance usage and performance statistics for reorganization and accounting purposes.

### 3.2.4 Report Generation

The SQL select clause can be used to generate output in report form. Uniqueness of tuples can be specified by the keyword UNIQUE. The GROUPED BY clause can be used to select tuples satisfying a unique property of a group. A predicate in a HAVING clause may compare an aggregate property of the group to a constant or to another aggregate property of the same group. The ORDER BY clause will sort on a specific attribute.

### 3.2.5 Constraints and Limitations

When a user queries a relation, a security check is made as to whether he has access to the relation involved before any operation is done.

Views can be used to accomodate queries into certain sections of a relation in which other information is privileged.

### 3.2.6 Additional Aspects of Retrieval and Presentation

Data can be retrieved for the purpose of insertion into other relations and updates in other relations.

## 3.3 Alteration

### 3.3.1 Insert Facilities

Relations and views can be altered by insertion.  A relation or view can be added by inserting one tuple or a set of tuples. Attributes not given values in the insertion assume null values. For example:

```
    INSERT INTO P: ' <P7', 'WASHER', 'GREY', 2, 'ATHENS'>;
```

A query result can be used as a table for insertion in another relation.

For example:

```
    INSERT INTO    P:
    SELECT         *
    FROM           W
    WHERE          COLOR = 'RED';
```

### 3.3.2 Delete Facilities

Deletion alters relations and views by removing a row or rows satisfying some condition.  Rows are specified by a WHERE clause syntactically identical to a query WHERE clause.

For example:

```
    DELETE S
    WHERE  S#=
           SELECT *
           FROM   W
           WHERE  STATUS=20;
```

### 3.3.3 Modify Facilities

Updates can be used to alter rows in a relation by changing specific data values. As in the DELETE and INSERT facilities, the parameter in the WHERE clause is considered a table in itself. An update is similar to delete except the SET clause is used to specify the updates to be made.

For example:

> Change the color of P2 to yellow
>
> UPDATE P
>
> SET COLOR = 'YELLOW'
>
> WHERE P# = 'P2';

For example:

> Increase QHO by 10% if they are in the W table.
>
> UPDATE P
>
> SET    QHO = QHO*1.1
>
> WHERE  P1 IN
>
> > SELECT *
> >
> > FROM W ;

### 3.3.4 Commit and Undo Facilities

A transaction recovery scheme is provided which allows a transaction to be backed out to the beginning of the transaction. Transaction recovery occurs when the RESTORE_TRANSACTION is issued. The effect is to undo all changes made by that transaction. See Section 3.4.5.

### 3.3.5 Additional Alteration Facilities

No additional features found.

3.4   Additional Functional Capabilities

3.4.1 Arithmetic and String Operations

Simple addition, subtraction, multiplication and division are supported in qualifications and update functions.  A user may construct arithmetic operations in the SELECT clause.

3.4.2 Sorting

A user may specify a query to be presented in ascending or descending order using the keywords ORDER BY

For example:

```
SELECT      S#,SNAME          (GIVES NAME AND NUMBER
FROM        S                 OF SUPPLIERS IN LONDON
WHERE       CITY = 'LONDON'   ALPHABETIZED BY SUPPLIERS'
ORDER BY    SNAME;            NAMES)
```

3.4.3 Library Functions

The functions AVG, MAX, MIN, SUM and COUNT are supported and can be used in queries.

For example:

```
SELECT AVG (QTY)          (GIVES AVERAGE QUANTITY
FROM   SP                 OF S1'S PARTS)
WHERE  S# = "S1";
```

3.4.4 User Defined Functions

System R allows a user to add additional functions to the system by placing routines written in SQL and, say PL/I, in a special function library.

### 3.4.5 Transactions

The system permits a series of alterations to be placed in a
transaction block, with the statements inside to be executed
as an atomic operation without interference by other users.
A three leveled locking technique can be used to handle
various concurrency problems.

For example:

        BEGIN TRANSACTION

              .

              .

              .

        END TRANSACTION ;

### 3.4.6 Multi-Tuple Alterations

See Sections 3.3.1, 3.3.2 and 3.3.3.

### 3.4.7 Grouping

A relation can be partitioned into groups according to values
of some attribute.  Then a built-in function may be applied to
each group.  Each item in the SELECT clause must be a unique
property of a group instead of a tuple.

For example:

        SELECT    P#,(COUNT(S#)

        FROM      SP

        GROUP BY P#;

All set functions AVG, MAX, MIN, SUM and COUNT can be used in
this manner.

3.4.8 Exception Handling Mechanisms

Error Messages and codes are returned for invalid SQL commands
and access violations.

3.4.9 Additional Functional Capabilities

None.

# 4.0 DEFINITION, GENERATION AND ADMINISTRATION FACILITIES

## 4.1 Definition Facilities

### 4.1.1 Constituents of a Database Definition

A database is defined through the definition of relations or table, view, tuple (row), column, (attribute). Views are thought of as derived relations, and rows and columns are used for base and derived relations. Access paths are maintained by the system.

### 4.1.2 Database Definition

A database is defined through the definition of relations (base and derived). There is no known limit to the number of relations allowed.

### 4.1.3 Relation Definition

A relation is defined through the keywords CREATE TABLE:

For example:

```
CREATE TABLE   X
STATUS DECIMAL (4)
SNAME  CHARACTER (20)
CITY   CHARACTER (40);
```

There is no known restriction on the number of rows or columns. A static derived relation can be defined by:

For example:

```
ASSIGN TO X       (SNAME, STATUS, CITY)
           SELECT  SNAME, STATUS, CITY
           FROM    S;
```

The command KEEP TABLE (table-name) causes a temporary
table (such as one made through the ASSIGN clause) to
become permanent.  A relation can be deleted by the DROP
TABLE command.

4.1.4  View Definition

Views can be created and dropped dynamically.  Dynamic
derived relations are defined by the example:

```
DEFINE VIEW V60 AS
        SELECT      S#,SNAME
        FROM        S
        WHERE       S#>'S1';
```

A view is not stored physically.  It is a dynamic windown on
a data base.

4.1.5  Tuple Definition

Tuples are implicitly defined when tables are defined.

4.1.6  Attribute Definition

Attributes are defined when tables are defined.

4.1.7  Domain Definition

Domains are defined within attributes.

4.1.8  Definition of Additional Database Constituents

A user may define a TRIGGER to be executed upon the occurrence
of a specified action (READ, INSERTION, DELETION or UPDATE).
An example of a TRIGGER definition is:

```
            DEFINE TRIGGER  T1
          ON UPDATE OF S(S#)
            (UPDATE SP
              SET S# = NEW.S#);


            UPDATE S
            SET S# = 'S6'
            WHERE S# = 'S1';
```

When a supplier's number is changed in relation S, make the
same change in its derived relation SP.

Trigger can be deleted via the DROP TRIGGER command.

Assertions can be defined by:  (See Section 2.8)


```
          ASSERT N ON SP:<QTY 10,000 >;
```

## 4.2 Generation Facilities

### 4.2.1   Constituents of Database Generation

The database is generated by populating the relations of the
database. Insertion commands both through SQL or a high-level
language may be used for the population.

### 4.2.2   Generation of Database Constituents

Base relations may be populated by the insert command.  Static
derived relations are populated automatically.  Dynamic derived
relations use access paths to indicate what tuples are to be
included in the generation.

## 4.3 Data Base Redefinition

### 4.3.1   Renaming Database Constituents

Aliases are allowed using the keyword SYNONYM.  Nothing found
on renaming.

4.3.2  Redefining Database Constituents

Relations and tuples can be redefined by the addition of
attributes via the EXPAND command.  There is no known limit
on the addition of attributes.  Indexes on tables can be added
and destroyed.

## 4.4  Database Regeneration and Reorganization

### 4.4.1  System - Controlled

The RSS permits new stored tables or new indexes to be
created at any time, or existing ones destroyed without
dumping and reloading the data.  New fields can be added.
Add or delete pointer chains across existing tables can
be defined at any time.

### 4.4.2  DBA - Controlled

A table or other object may be dropped or authorized for use
only by the user who created it.  User-ids have, therefore,
been used to represent the role of the DBA and not specific
persons.  The DBA can created, control and destroy those
portions of the database which he has created.  Private users
can create relations for their own private use.  All the query
facilities are available to the DBA.  Private users have certain
authorization restrictions as determined by the DBA.

## 4.5  Database Dictionary

SQL is an integrated data definition and data manipulation language.
In System R the description of the database is stored in user visible
'system' tables which may be read using the SQL language.  The creation

of a table or an access path results in new entries in these
system tables. Users defining tables and other objects are
encouraged to include English text which describes the 'meanings'
of the objects. Later, others may retrieve all tables with
certain attributes or may browse among the descriptions of
defined tables (if they are so authorized).

5.0  INTERFACES AND DBMS ARCHITECTURE

    5.1  System Architecture

        System R architecture is  divided into two subsystems, Relational

        Data System (RDS) and Research Storage System (RSS).

        The Relation Data Interface (RDI) is the external interface of

        System R which can be called directly from a programming language.

        SQL is embedded within the RDI.

        RSI (Relation Storage System) is an internal interface which

        handles access to single tuples of base relations.

    5.2  Interface Descriptions

        5.2.1  SQL Description

            SQL is a non-procedural, mapping oriented relational language.

            SQL is English-like free-format narrative.  SQL can either

            stand alone or can be embedded in COBOL or PL/I.  SQL statements

            are prefixed by $-signs when embedded.  SQL has been implemented

            as a stand alone interactive language or as an embedded batch-

            oriented language.

        5.2.2  Research Storage System (RSS)

            The interfaces to these two subsystems are called:

                    Relational Data Interface (RDI)

                    Relational Storage Interface (RSI)

            The architecture of System R is shown on the following page.

            Some of the subsystems are shown.

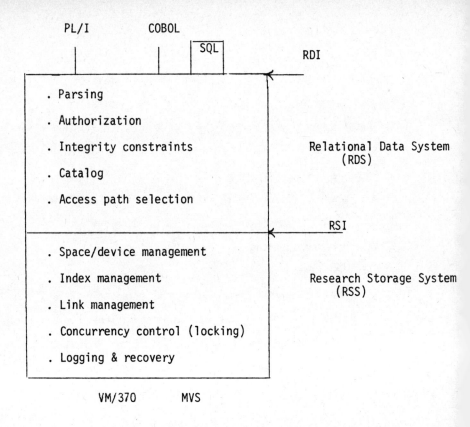

## 5.2.2.1  RDI Operators

The RDI (Relational Data Interface) is the external interface of
System R which can be called directly from a programming language.
SQL is embedded within the RDI.  System R uses the following RDI
operators:  SEQUEL, FETCH, FETCH_HOLD, OPEN, CLOSE, KEEP, DESCRIBE,
BIND, BEGIN_TRANS, END_TRANS, SAVE, RESTORE and RELEASE.

SQL statements embedded in PL/I programs and host-language
variables appearing in those statements are prefixed with
$-signs as shown below:

```
$UPDATE PARTS

SET    PNAME=$X

WHERE  STATUS=$Y;
```

An INTO clause delivers the query result to the host program.
For example:

```
$SELECT PNAME, STATUS

INTO    $X, $Y

FROM    P

WHERE   P#=$Z;
```

This returns only the first tuple in the query result.  To
process more than one tuple, a cursor is required.  A cursor
is a symbolic name associated with a query for the purpose
of retrieving a query result, tuple by tuple.  In the following
example, PARTS is the symbolic or cursor name:

```
$LET PARTS BE

SELECT PNAME, STATUS

INTO    $X, $Y

FROM    P

WHERE   P#=$Z;
```

The OPEN statement binds the value of the input variable and
prepares to deliver tuples in accordance to the query.  The
FETCH clause causes a new tuple to be delivered into the

program value specified by the query.  The CLOSE statement
informs the system that no further fetches will be issued
by the query:

        $OPEN PARTS;

        $FETCH PARTS;

        $CLOSE PARTS;

After the execution of each SQL statement, a status code is
returned to the host program in a variable called SYR_CODE.
The FETCH statement can be used in conjunction with the status
code to process all tuples of a given relation.

        DO WHILE(SYR_CODE=OK);

         $FETCH PARTS;

         PUT SKIP LIST $X, $Y;

        END;

The DESCRIBE statement returns a description of the number of
fields and data types of the result into an array indicated in
the query.  SQL statements may be dynamically defined by the
PREPARE statement.  The PREPARE statement indicates to System R
that, at run time, the character type variable specified will
contain a SQL statement which should be optimized and associated
with the appropriate name.  Unknown parameters are indicated by
question marks.  To execute the prepared command, the EXECUTE
command is issued.  All statements not beginning with SELECT
are handled by means of the EXECUTE command.

## 5.2.2.2  RSI OPERATORS

RSI (Relational Storage Interface) is an internal interface
which handles access to single tuples of base relations.  All
data is stored in a collection of logical address spaces called
segments.  The OPEN_SEGMENT operator makes a segment available
for processing.  When the SAVE_SEGMENT command is issued, disk
pages bound to segments are brought up-to-date.  The RESTORE_
SEGMENT command restores the original segment value.  CLOSE_
SEGMENT commands make the segment unavailable for further
processing.  Records can be fetched across a particular access
path through the OPEN_SCAN command.  The records can then be
accessed by a sequence of NEXT commands.

A user may determine which records will be children of a given
parent.  The relative order of the children under a given parent
can be determined by the CONNECT and DISCONNECT operations.

Lock operations provide concurrency protection of relations and
segments within relations.

## 6.0  OPERATING ASPECTS

### 6.1  Security

#### 6.1.1  Access Control

When a SQL statement is translated and the access path chosen
for the operation in question, a check is made to see if the
user involved is authorized to operate on the relation.  Logon authorization  is performed by the virtual memory monitor.
a user can control access to the data objects the user creates
by use of the GRANT and REVOKE operations.

GRANT [auth] table-name to user-list

[WITH GRANT OPTION] ;

REVOKE [operation-list ON]  table-name

FROM user-list;

#### 6.1.2  Capability

A user has the capability of granting to or revoking from other
uses the following privileges regarding relations he has created:
READ, INSERT, DELETE, UPDATE (by column), EXPAND, IMAGE (to define
images on the relation), LINK (to create links on the relation),
CONTROL (to make assertions or define triggers pertaining to the
relation ) and GRANT (grant the right to grant).  [8]

### 6.2  Physical Integrity

#### 6.2.1  Concurrency Control

System R permits multiple users to be active simultaneously,
performing a variety of activities.  These simultaneous activities
are supported by the automatic locking subsystem built into the
RSS.

The transaction mechanism allows a user to keep his view of the database constant throughout his operations, ignoring other user requests.

System R provides the user with a choice of three levels of locking. Level 3, to which the system defaults, provides the most complete protection by allowing one user to complete a transaction without intervention from another user. For example, data read by a user cannot be updated by another user until the first user has terminated. Level 2 and Level 1 provide locking at a lower degree. Level 1 allows other users to read data that is currently being updated. Level 2 also allows other user to read data that is currently being updated, however, Level 2 locks each record before reading it to make sure it is committed at the time of the read. The lock is released immediately after the read has been completed.

### 6.2.2  Crash Recovery

System R has complete facilities for transaction backout and system recovery. Recovery compensates for system failures of the magnetic media (Disk Head Crash). Almost all recovery information is kept on disk and a non-catastrophic restart is transparent to operations.

## 6.3 Operating Environment

### 6.3.1  Software (Operating System)

System R requires the VM/370 operating system for best operation. IBM reference manuals describe the system in detail.

## 6.3.2  Hardware

System R has been implemented on Virtual Machine/370, an IBM System/370.  The system requires at least one direct access storage device.

The system requires storage on any 370 Direct Access Device (e.g., IBM's 3330 Disk Drive).  Magnetic tape is required for backup to support audits and database reconstruction after system failure.

System R can handle multiple users concurrently accessing the database.  Any System/370 compatible  terminal may be utilized.  System R can operate on any IBM 370 with dynamic address translation capability.

# 7.0 ESSENTIALLY RELATIONAL SOLUTIONS FOR GENERALIZED DBMS PROBLEMS

System R incorporates the following claimed advantages of the
Relational Approach:

Simplicity - System R has only one major structure, the
table, and operations for manipulation of the
table.

Uniformity - System R queries exhibit closure.

Data Independence -  Ordering and indices are strictly
optional, while access paths are
transparent to users.  SQL is a
non-procedural language.

Permits optimization - Each data access path is found
after an optimization routine
is used.

Interfaces are high level.

Multiple views are supported.

## 8.0 DATABASE APPLICATIONS USING THE SYSTEM

System R was evaluated by IBM for approximately two and one-half years.
The results of this evaluation can be found in "A History and Evaluation
of System R", RJ2843 (36129), IBM Research Laboratory, San Jose,
California  95193.  The evaluation consisted of two parts:  (1) experiments
performed on the system at the San Jose Research Laboratory and (2) actual
use of the system at a number of internal IBM sites and three selected
customers.  The typical experimental databases were smaller than 200
Megabytes with less than ten concurrent users.  A summary of their results
follows:

1) Several user sites were able to install System R, design and load
   a database, and run application programs in a matter of days.

2) Indexes could be created and dropped without impacting users or
   application programs.

3) Joins on several tables degraded performance.

4) The users felt that the SQL language was easy to learn.  Users
   with no experience were able to learn a subset of the language
   in one sitting.  SQL was judged generally successful in
   meeting its design goals.

5) All SQL statements were reduced to machine code by selecting
   code fragments from a library of approximately one-hundred
   fragments.  In a typical short transaction of less than 50,000
   instructions, 80% of the instructions were executed by the RSS
   access module.  The remaining 20% were executed using the

access module and the application program.  Code generation adds a small amount of CPU time and no I/O time.  If this results in a routine which runs more efficiently, the cost of code generation is paid back after a few record fetches.

6)  A B-tree index was used to represent access paths.  This proved to be appropriate for programs with many record accesses, but was not cost-efficient when only a few resources were accessed.

7)  View definition and controlling authorization was found to be powerful, flexible and convenient.  User suggestions included developing the concept of group users, implementing a command which changed ownership and optionally saving views and authorization when base relations are dropped.

8)  Experimentation has shown that a "Write-Ahead Log" protocol is superior to the "Shadow-Box" protocol for the System R recovery system.

9)  It was found that most users ran under the Level 3 option of the security system.  In fact, the Level 2 option proved to be more expensive than Level 3.

10)  It was found that, in a small number of cases, a query could hold a lock when its time slice ended, thus holding up other queries until it received another time slice.  The lock release protocol was changed to correct this.

ADDENDUM TO 1.2.1 SYSTEM


The documents in the public domain concerning System R are not consistent with

the implementation of System R, release 4.0.  The following is a list of the

inconsistencies with the Section in which they appear.


| Item | Explanation | Section |
|------|-------------|---------|
| 1. Links | not implemented | 2.3.2, 2.3.4, 2.5.2, 3.2.2, 4.4.1, 6.2.2 |
| 2. Set operators | not implemented | 2.3.2, 3.1.3, 3.3.3 |
| 3. Assertions | not implemented | 2.3.3, 2.4.3, 2.5.3, 2.8, 3.2.2, 4.1.8, 6.2.2 |
| 4. Triggers | not implemented | 2.3.3, 2.8, 3.2.2, 4.1.8, 6.2.2 |
| 5. Natural join | System R will not perform an equi-join on common attribute names without those names being specified in the WHERE clause | 3.1.4 |
| 6. Nonequi-joins | System R will perform nonequi-joins, but it will not optimize them | 3.1.4 |
| 7. User defined functions | not implemented | 3.4.4 |
| 8. DECIMAL | not on implemented data type | 4.1.2 |
| 9. ASSIGN TO | not implemented | 4.1.2 |
| 10. KEEP TABLE | not implemented | 4.1.2 |

| 11. | RDI operators | the System R host language interface uses a precompiler which translates SQL statements into the appropriate RDI calls. Therefore, the applications programmer codes SQL instead of the listed RDI operators | 5.2.2.1 |
| 12. | IMAGE | the syntax to create an index is CREATE INDEX | 6.2.2 |
| 13. | Operating system | System R was also implemented on MVS | 6.3.1 |
| 14. | Domains | System R does not support the domain constituent | 2.1, 2.6.1, 2.7.2 4.1.7 |
| 15. | View definition | A more correct definition is: A view may be defined to be the result of any SQL statement. | 2.4.1 |
| 16. | Key definition | A more correct definition is: unique index and specifying the "NO NULL" option for each column of the index in the CREATE TABLE statement | 2.5.1 |

# 4. Feature Summaries and Comparisons

The objective of this chapter and of the RTG's work is to identify the features that constitute an RDBMS. Specifically, this chapter analyses the significance and frequency of the features given in the feature catalogue. This is done by summarizing and comparing, in a tabular form, the results obtained in the 14 RDBMS feature analyses.

Some feature analysis authors differed in their interpretation of some feature catalogue entries. This led to several errors some of which were corrected on consultation with the feature analysis authors. Corrections were made in the summary and comparison tables but were not necessarily made in the original feature analysis. Another result of misinterpretation was an overlap between sections of the feature analyses and consequently between sections of this chapter.

## 4.1  Database Constituents

### 4.1.1  Definitions -

Analysis of the feature catalogue indicated that the following seven constituents appeared in a majority of the systems evaluated:

1.  Database. The relational database is a collection of relations. Depending on the system, relations can be base relations, views, and/or snapshots.

2.  Relation. A relation is a set of relation elements of the same type. A relation may be presented to the user as a table of rows and columns.

3.  Tuple. A relation element is called a tuple. A tuple is a row in the tabular presentation of a relation.

4.  Attribute. The attributes of a tuple are defined by a tuple type. The legal values of an attribute are chosen from a specific set of values called domains.

5.  User defined domain. The set of values over which an attribute value can range is called a domain. A user defined domain allows the user to describe specific domains, such as the domain COLOR where COLOR can be red, yellow, blue, or green.

6. View. A view is a relation derived from existing relations. After its declaration, modification to its defining relations is reflected in the view, according to its definition.

7. Snapshot. A snapshot is a relation derived from existing relations. After its declaration, it is independent of its defining relations and does not reflect updates made to its defining relations.

The following concepts were listed as constituents for systems that were analyzed.

8. Transaction/Lock. A transaction/lock is a set of queries to be executed without interference from any other query. A lock is normally an interactive command, while a transaction is usually batch. In some systems, however, a transaction can be issued in either batch or interactive mode.

9. Trigger. A trigger is a set of user specified commands that is executed automatically after a specific situation has occurred in the database. For example, modification of a specific relation may cause a trigger to be activated.

10. Authority/Assertion. Authority and assertion allow control privileges over a relation.

11. Relational Dictionary. This means that the data dictionary is presented to the user in relational form and can be queried using relational operators.

12. Relation Logging. A user can request that a log be maintained of all atomic changes to a specified relation.

13. Workspace. A workspace is an area where a relation can be manipulated and changed without affecting the database.

14. Image. An image defines the output picture for the data.

15. Index. An index is an access mechanism that can be defined for faster access.

16. Macro. A macro is a set of queries defined by a name. When the name is issued, the macro is automatically executed.

4.1.2   Results -

TABLE 4.1   DATABASE CONSTITUENTS

|                          | ASTRAL | IDAMS |
|--------------------------|--------|-------|
| 1.  Database             | Yes    | Yes   |
| 2.  Relation             | Yes    | Yes   |
| 3.  View                 | Yes    | Yes   |
| 4.  Snapshot             | Yes    | No    |
| 5.  Tuple                | Yes    | Yes   |
| 6.  Attribute            | Yes    | Yes   |
| 7.  Domain (user defined)| Yes    | Yes   |
| 8.  Other                | Module, Transaction, Trigger, Index, Procedures, Dictionary | Transaction, Index, Macro, Dictionary, Relation Logging |

TABLE 4.1   DATABASE CONSTITUENTS (continued)

|                        | IDM    | INGRES | MRDS  |
|------------------------|--------|--------|-------|
| 1. Database            | Yes    | Yes    | Yes   |
| 2. Relation            | Yes    | Yes    | Yes   |
| 3. View                | Yes    | Yes    | Yes   |
| 4. Snapshot            | Yes    | Yes    | Yes   |
| 5. Tuple               | Yes    | Yes    | Yes   |
| 6. Attribute           | Yes    | Yes    | Yes   |
| 7. Domain (user def.)  | No     | No     | Yes   |
| 8. Other               | Transaction, Macro, Index, Relation Logging | Index, Macro, Authority | Transaction, Macro |

TABLE 4.1   DATABASE CONSTITUENTS (continued)

| | MRS | NOMAD | ORACLE |
|---|---|---|---|
| 1. Database | Yes | Yes | Yes |
| 2. Relation | Yes | Yes | Yes |
| 3. View | No | Yes | Yes |
| 4. Snapshot | No | Yes | Yes |
| 5. Tuple | Yes | Yes | Yes |
| 6. Attribute | Yes | Yes | Yes |
| 7. Domain (user defined) | No | No | No |
| 8. Other | Index, Transaction | | Macro, Transaction |

TABLE 4.1   DATABASE CONSTITUENTS (continued)

| | PASCAL/R | PRTV | RAPPORT |
|---|---|---|---|
| 1. Database | Yes | Yes | Yes |
| 2. Relation | Yes | Yes | Yes |
| 3. View | No | Yes | No |
| 4. Snapshot | Yes | Yes | No |
| 5. Tuple | Yes | Yes | Yes |
| 6. Attribute | Yes | Yes | Yes |
| 7. Domain (user defined) | Yes | Yes | No |
| 8. Other | Relational Dictionary | Workspace Macro | Index, Transaction |

TABLE 4.1   DATABASE CONSTITUENTS (continued)

|  | SYSTEM R | QBE | RAPID |
|---|---|---|---|
| 1. Database | Yes | Yes | Yes |
| 2. Relation | Yes | Yes | Yes |
| 3. View | Yes | No | Yes |
| 4. Snapshot | Yes | Yes | No |
| 5. Tuple | Yes | Yes | Yes |
| 6. Attribute | Yes | Yes | Yes |
| 7. Domain (user defined) | No | Yes | Yes |
| 8. Other | Index Transaction, Dictionary | Macro, Authority, Image, Index Transaction, Dictionary | Index |

### 4.1.3   Observations On Database Constituents -

The 14 feature analyses indicate uniformity in the following database constituents: database, relation, tuple, and attribute. Snapshots and views, while not supported by all of the systems, are well represented with ten systems supporting snapshots and ten systems supporting views. PASCAL/R supports snapshots as a temporary relation only. User defined domainis are supported by only half of the systems. Under the heading of other database constituents it was found that the transaction, relational dictionary, and macro are the most prevalent.

TABLE 4.1   DATABASE CONSTITUENTS SUMMARY

| | |
|---|---|
| 1. Database | Supported by 14 Systems |
| 2. Relation | Supported by 13 Systems |
| 3. View | Supported by 10 Systems |
| 4. Snapshot | Supported by 10 Systems |
| 5. Tuple | Supported by 14 Systems |
| 6. Attribute | Supported by 14 Systems |
| 7. User Defined Domain | Supported by  6 Systems |

## 4.2 Functional Capabilities

32 features of the functional capabilities of an RDBMS were considered. They involved qualification, retrieval and presentation, alternation, and additional operations. Table 4.2 characterizes these features for the 14 DBMSs and presents a summary.

| TABLE 4.2 OPERATIONS | | |
|---|---|---|
| | ASTRAL | IDAMS |
| 1. Retrieval tuple handling | Duplicates always removed | Duplicates always removed |
| 2. Nesting | Fully | Fully |
| 3. Closure | Fully closed | Fully closed |
| 4. Set membership operator | Yes | Yes |
| 5. Set operators (union, intersection, difference, equality) | Yes | No |
| 6. Group by operator | No | Yes |
| 7. Arithmetic operators | Yes | Yes |
| 8. String operators | Yes | Yes |
| 9. Transaction operators | Yes | No |
| 10. Existential quantifier | Implied | Implied |
| 11. Universal quantifier | Explicit | Implied |
| 12. Boolean operators | Yes | Yes |
| 13. Query language environment | Stand alone | Stand alone and host |
| 14. Self-join capability | Full | Full |
| 15. Equi-join capability | Full | Full |
| 16. Natural join capability | Full | Implicit |

| TABLE 4.2 OPERATIONS (continued) | | |
|---|---|---|
| | ASTRAL | IDAMS |
| 17. Projection capability | Explicit/ implicit | Implicit |
| 18. Sort capability | Explicit | Explicit |
| 19. Insert | Explicit | Explicit |
| 20. Delete | Explicit | Explicit |
| 21. Modify | Explicit/ implicit | Explicit |
| 22. Update over more than one relation | No | No |
| 23. Commit / undo | Implicit | Implicit |
| 24. Triggers | Yes | No |
| 25. Aggregate functions | Yes | Yes |
| 26. User defined functions | Yes | Yes |
| 27. Library functions | Yes | Yes |
| 28. User defined error conditions (exit capabilities) | Yes | No |
| 29. Format of schema information | Relational | Relational |
| 30. System performance data available | No | Yes |
| 31. Report generator | No | Yes |
| 32. Relationally complete | Yes | Yes |

TABLE 4.2  OPERATIONS (continued)

| | IDM | INGRES | MRDS |
|---|---|---|---|
| 1. Retrieval tuple handling | Duplicates removed under user request | Duplicates removed under user request | Duplicates removed under user request |
| 2. Nesting | Fully | Fully | Fully |
| 3. Closure | Fully closed | Fully closed | Restricted |
| 4. Set membership operator | No | No | No |
| 5. Set operators (union, intersection, difference, equality) | No | No | No |
| 6. Group by operator | Yes | Yes | No |
| 7. Arithmetic operators | Yes | Yes | Yes |
| 8. String operators | Yes | No | Yes |
| 9. Transaction operators | Yes | No | No |
| 10. Existential quantifier | Explicit operation | Implied | Implied |
| 11. Universal quantifier | Implied | Implied | Implied |
| 12. Boolean operators | Yes | Yes | Yes |
| 13. Query language environment | Stand alone | Stand alone and host | |
| 14. Self-join capability | Full | Full | Full |
| 15. Equi-join capability | Full | Full | Full |
| 16. Natural join capability | Full | Full | Full |

TABLE 4.2   OPERATIONS (continued)

| | IDM | INGRES | MRDS |
|---|---|---|---|
| 17. Projection capability | Implicit | Implicit | Implicit |
| 18. Sort capability | Explicit | No | No |
| 19. Insert | Explicit | Explicit | Explicit |
| 20. Delete | Explicit | Explicit | Restricted |
| 21. Modify | Explicit | Explicit | Explicit and restricted |
| 22. Update over more than one relation | No | Yes | |
| 23. Commit / undo | Explicit | No | No |
| 24. Triggers | No | No | No |
| 25. Aggregate functions | Yes | Yes | Yes |
| 26. User defined functions | No | No | Yes |
| 27. Library functions | No | Yes | |
| 28. User defined error conditions (exit capabilities) | Yes | Yes | No |
| 29. Format of schema information | Relational | Relational | Other |
| 30. System performance data available | Yes | No | No |
| 31. Report generator | No | Yes | No |
| 32. Relationally complete | Yes (self-contained) | Yes (self-contained) | |

TABLE 4.2  OPERATIONS (continued)

| | MRS | NOMAD | ORACLE |
|---|---|---|---|
| 1. Retrieval tuple handling | Duplicates removed under user request | Duplicates removed under user request | Duplicates removed under user request |
| 2. Nesting | Restricted | Restricted | Fully |
| 3. Closure | | Fully closed | Fully closed |
| 4. Set membership operator | | Yes | Yes |
| 5. Set operators (union, intersection, difference, equality) | No | No | No |
| 6. Group by operator | Restricted | Yes | No |
| 7. Arithmetic operators | No | Yes | Yes |
| 8. String operators | No | Yes | No |
| 9. Transaction operators | No | No | Yes |
| 10. Existential quantifier | Implied operation | Implied | Implied |
| 11. Universal quantifier | Implied | Implied | Implied |
| 12. Boolean operators | Yes | Yes | Yes |
| 13. Query language environment | Stand alone | Stand alone | Stand alone |
| 14. Self-join capability | None | Full | Full |
| 15. Equi-join capability | Full | Full | Restricted |
| 16. Natural join capability | Full | Full | Restricted |

| TABLE 4.2 OPERATIONS (continued) | MRS | NOMAD | ORACLE |
|---|---|---|---|
| 17. Projection capability | Implicit | Implicit | Implicit |
| 18. Sort capability | No | Explicit | Explicit |
| 19. Insert | Explicit | Explicit | Explicit |
| 20. Delete | Explicit | Explicit | Explicit |
| 21. Modify | Explicit | Explicit | Explicit |
| 22. Update over more than one relation | No | No | No |
| 23. Commit / undo | No | Implicit | No |
| 24. Triggers | No | Yes | No |
| 25. Aggregate functions | Yes | Yes | Yes |
| 26. User defined functions | No | Yes | No |
| 27. Library functions | | Yes | Yes |
| 28. User defined error conditions (exit capabilities) | No | Yes | No |
| 29. Format of schema information | Other | Other | Relational |
| 30. System performance data available | No | Yes | No |
| 31. Report generator | No | Yes | Yes |
| 32. Relationally complete | | Yes (self-contained) | No |

| | PASCAL/R | PRTV | RAPPORT |
|---|---|---|---|
| TABLE 4.2 OPERATIONS (continued) | | | |
| 1. Retrieval tuple handling | Duplicates always removed | Duplicates always removed | Duplicates never removed |
| 2. Nesting | Fully | Fully | None |
| 3. Closure | Fully closed | Fully closed | No |
| 4. Set membership operator | Yes | No | |
| 5. Set operators (union, intersection, difference, equality) | Yes | Yes | No |
| 6. Group by operator | No | Yes | No |
| 7. Arithmetic operators | Yes | Yes | Yes |
| 8. String operators | Yes | Yes | No |
| 9. Transaction operators | No | No | Yes |
| 10. Existential quantifier | Explicit | Implied | Implied |
| 11. Universal quantifier | Explicit | Implied | No |
| 12. Boolean operators | Yes | Yes | Limited |
| 13. Query language environment | Stand alone and host | Stand alone | Stand alone and host |
| 14. Self-join capability | Full | Full | Restricted |
| 15. Equi-join capability | Full | Full | Restricted |
| 16. Natural join capability | Full | Full | Restricted |

| | PASCAL/R | PRTV | RAPPORT |
|---|---|---|---|
| TABLE 4.2   OPERATIONS (continued) | | | |
| 17. Projection capability | Explicit | Explicit | Restricted (only on output) |
| 18. Sort capability | Restricted | No | Explicit |
| 19. Insert | Explicit | Implicit | Explicit |
| 20. Delete | Explicit | Implicit | Explicit |
| 21. Modify | Explicit | Implicit | Explicit |
| 22. Update over more than one relation | No | No | No |
| 23. Commit / undo | No | No | Explicit |
| 24. Triggers | No | No | No |
| 25. Aggregate functions | No | Yes | Yes |
| 26. User defined functions | Yes | Yes | Yes |
| 27. Library functions | No | Yes | No |
| 28. User defined error conditions (exit capabilities) | No | No | Yes |
| 29. Format of schema information | Relational | Other | Other |
| 30. System performance data available | Yes | No | Yes |
| 31. Report generator | Yes | No | No |
| 32. Relationally complete | Yes (self-contained) | Yes (self-contained) | No |

| | SYSTEM R | QBE | RAPID |
|---|---|---|---|
| **TABLE 4.2   OPERATIONS (continued)** | | | |
| 1. Retrieval tuple handling | Duplicates removed under user request | Duplicates always removed | Duplicates removed under user request |
| 2. Nesting | Fully | Fully | Restricted |
| 3. Closure | Fully closed | Fully closed | Restricted |
| 4. Set membership operator | Yes | Yes | No |
| 5. Set operators (union, intersection, difference, equality) | Union, inter-section | Yes | No |
| 6. Group by operator | Yes | Yes | No |
| 7. Arithmetic operators | Yes | Yes | No |
| 8. String operators | No | No | No |
| 9. Transaction operators | Yes | No | Yes |
| 10. Existential quantifier | Implied | Implied | Implied |
| 11. Universal quantifier | Implied | Implied | Implied |
| 12. Boolean operators | Yes | Yes | Yes |
| 13. Query language environment | Stand alone and host | Stand alone and host | Stand alone |
| 14. Self-join capability | Full | Full | Full |
| 15. Equi-join capability | Full | Full | Full |
| 16. Natural join capability | Full | Full | Full |

TABLE 4.2  OPERATIONS (continued)

| | SYSTEM R | QBE | RAPID |
|---|---|---|---|
| 17. Projection capability | Implicit | Explicit | Restricted (only on output) |
| 18. Sort capability | Explicit | Explicit | No |
| 19. Insert | Explicit | Explicit | Explicit |
| 20. Delete | Explicit | Explicit | Explicit |
| 21. Modify | Explicit | Explicit | Explicit |
| 22. Update over more than one relation | Yes | Yes | No |
| 23. Commit / undo | Explicit | Explicit | No |
| 24. Triggers | No | No | No |
| 25. Aggregate functions | Yes | Yes | No |
| 26. User defined functions | No | No | No |
| 27. Library functions | Yes | Yes | No |
| 28. User defined error conditions (exit capabilities) | Yes | No | Yes |
| 29. Format of schema information | Relational | Relational | Other |
| 30. System performance data available | No | No | Yes |
| 31. Report generator | No | No | No |
| 32. Relationally complete | Yes (self-contained) | Yes (self-contained) | No |

```
-----------------------------------------------------------------
|                                                               |
|              TABLE 4.2   OPERATIONS SUMMARY                   |
|---------------------------------------------------------------|
|                            | Duplicates removed               |
|  1.  Retrieval tuple handling | under user request:       8   |
|                            | Dupl. always removed:     5      |
|---------------------------------------------------------------|
|                            | Full nesting:            10      |
|  2.  Nesting               | Restricted nesting:       3      |
|                            | Nesting not allowed:      1      |
|---------------------------------------------------------------|
|                            | Full closure:             9      |
|  3.  Closure               | Restricted closure:       2      |
|                            | Not closed:               1      |
|---------------------------------------------------------------|
|  4.  Set membership operator | Supported by 7 systems         |
|                            | Not supported by 5 systems       |
|---------------------------------------------------------------|
|  5.  Set operators         | Supported by 6 systems           |
|---------------------------------------------------------------|
|                            | Full:                     7      |
|  6.  Group by operator     | Restricted:               1      |
|                            | Not supported:            6      |
|---------------------------------------------------------------|
|  7.  Arithmetic operators  | Supported by 11 systems          |
|---------------------------------------------------------------|
|  8.  String operators      | Supported by 7 systems           |
|---------------------------------------------------------------|
|  9.  Transaction operators | Supported by 6 systems           |
|---------------------------------------------------------------|
|                            | Explicit:                 2      |
| 10.  Existential quantifier | Function provided by other      |
|                            | operator combinations:   12      |
|---------------------------------------------------------------|
|                            | Explicit:                 2      |
| 11.  Universal quantifier  | Function provided by other       |
|                            | operator combinations:   11      |
|                            | Function not supported:   1      |
|---------------------------------------------------------------|
| 12.  Boolean operators     | Full:                    13      |
|                            | Limited:                  1      |
|---------------------------------------------------------------|
| 13.  Query language environment| Stand alone:          5      |
|                            | Stand alone and host:     6      |
|---------------------------------------------------------------|
| 14.  Self-join capability  | Supported by 12 systems          |
|---------------------------------------------------------------|
|                            | Full:                    12      |
| 15.  Equi-join capability  | Restricted:               1      |
|                            | Not supported:            1      |
|---------------------------------------------------------------|
| 16.  Natural join capability | Supported by 11 systems        |
-----------------------------------------------------------------
```

```
!-----------------------------------------------------------!
¦                                                           ¦
¦        TABLE 4.2   OPERATIONS SUMMARY (continued)         ¦
¦-----------------------------------------------------------¦
¦                          ¦ Explicit:              4       ¦
¦ 17. Projection capability ¦ Implicit:              8       ¦
¦                          ¦ Restricted to output:  2       ¦
¦-----------------------------------------------------------¦
¦                          ¦ Explicit:              8       ¦
¦ 18. Sort capability       ¦ Restricted:            1       ¦
¦                          ¦ Not supported:         5       ¦
¦-----------------------------------------------------------¦
¦ 19. Insert                ¦ Explicit:             13       ¦
¦                          ¦ Implicit:              1       ¦
¦-----------------------------------------------------------¦
¦                          ¦ Explicit:             12       ¦
¦ 20. Delete                ¦ Implicit:              1       ¦
¦                          ¦ Restricted:            2       ¦
¦-----------------------------------------------------------¦
¦                          ¦ Explicit:             12       ¦
¦ 21. Modify                ¦ Restricted:            1       ¦
¦                          ¦ Implicit:              1       ¦
¦-----------------------------------------------------------¦
¦ 22. Update over more      ¦ Supported by 3 systems        ¦
¦     than one relation     ¦                                ¦
¦-----------------------------------------------------------¦
¦                          ¦ Explicit:              4       ¦
¦ 23. Commit / undo         ¦ Implicit:              4       ¦
¦                          ¦ Not supported:         6       ¦
¦-----------------------------------------------------------¦
¦ 24. Triggers              ¦ Supported by 2 systems        ¦
¦-----------------------------------------------------------¦
¦ 25. Aggregate functions   ¦ Supported by 12 systems       ¦
¦-----------------------------------------------------------¦
¦ 26. User defined functions ¦ Supported by 8 systems        ¦
¦-----------------------------------------------------------¦
¦ 27. Library functions     ¦ Supported by 7 systems        ¦
¦-----------------------------------------------------------¦
¦ 28. User defined error    ¦ Supported by 7 systems        ¦
¦     conditions            ¦                                ¦
¦-----------------------------------------------------------¦
¦ 29. Format of schema      ¦ Relational:            8       ¦
¦     information           ¦ Other:                 5       ¦
¦-----------------------------------------------------------¦
¦ 30. System performance    ¦ Yes:                   7       ¦
¦     data available        ¦ No:                    7       ¦
¦-----------------------------------------------------------¦
¦ 31. Report generator      ¦ Yes:                   5       ¦
¦                          ¦ No:                    9       ¦
¦-----------------------------------------------------------¦
¦ 32. Relationally complete ¦ Yes:                   9       ¦
¦                          ¦ No:                    2       ¦
!-----------------------------------------------------------!
```

4.3  Schema Definition


4.3.1  Descriptions –


    Schema definition features of a system can  be  put  into eleven categories.  A description of each follows:

1.    Define Database.  An explicit command allows  a  user  to define  an  entire  database.  Defining one  or  more relations is not considered to be an explicit command for defining an entire database.

2.    Generate Database.   An  explicit  command  exists  for populating  a  database.  In  addition  to  this,  the generation facility can dump data from the  database  and into the database (i.e., a fast load/unload facility).

3.    Destroy database.  An explicit command exists  that  will destroy an entire database.  Destroying one relation at a time is not considered  to  be  an  explicit  command  to destroy a database.

4.    Define Relation.  An explicit command defines a relation.

5.    Destroy Relation.   An  explicit  command  destroys  a relation.

6.    Reorganize Relation.  An explicit command  reorganizes  a relation.

7.    Define Snapshot.  An explicit command defines a snapshot.

8.    Define View.  An explicit command defines a view.

9.    Drop Attribute.  An explicit command causes an  attribute to  be  deleted  from a relation if the original relation still exists.  A projection command that chooses all  but the  unwanted  attribute (and forms this into a relation) is not considered to be an explicit command to delete  an attribute.

10.    Add Attribute.  An explicit command will add an attribute to  a  relation.  A  join  command  that  forms  another relation (which includes all attributes of  the  original relation  and  an additional attribute) is not considered to be an explicit command to add an attribute.

11.    Rename Attribute.  An explicit  command  will  rename  an attribute.  A  command  which  allows  a  synonym for an attribute name is not considered to be  a  command  which renames an attribute.  The original name of the attribute must not exist after this command is issued.

12.   Define Tuple.  An explicit command defines a tuple.

Other schema definitions listed for the  systems  include
displaying  and  modifying  a  directory,  specifying  backup,
defining a secondary index, checking a domain, grouping a  set
of  relations,  encoding  and  decoding  data, and opening and
closing a relation.


4.3.2   Results –


|  TABLE 4.3   SCHEMA DEFINITIONS | ASTRAL | IDAMS |
|---|:---:|:---:|
| Define database | Yes | Yes |
| Generate database | No | Yes |
| Fast load / unload | No | Yes |
| Destroy database | Yes | Yes |
| Define relation | No | Yes |
| Destroy relation | Yes | Yes |
| Reorganize relation | Yes | No |
| Define snapshot | Yes | No |
| Define view | Yes | Yes |
| Drop attribute | No | No |
| Add attribute | No | No |
| Rename attribute | Yes | No |
| Define tuple | Yes | No |
| Other | | Index |

TABLE 4.3  SCHEMA DEFINITIONS (continued)

| | IDM | INGRES | MRDS | MRS |
|---|---|---|---|---|
| Define database | Yes | Yes | Yes | No |
| Generate database | Yes | Yes | No | |
| Fast load / unload | Yes | Yes | No | |
| Destroy database | Yes | Yes | No | Yes |
| Define relation | Yes | Yes | Yes | Yes |
| Destroy relation | Yes | Yes | No | Yes |
| Reorganize relation | Yes | No | No | Yes |
| Define snapshot | Yes | Yes | Yes | |
| Define view | Yes | Yes | Yes | |
| Drop attribute | No | No | No | Yes |
| Add attribute | No | No | No | Yes |
| Rename attribute | Yes | No | Yes | Yes |
| Define tuple | No | No | No | |
| Other | Open, close | | Index, check domain | Display database, backup |

TABLE 4.3  SCHEMA DEFINITIONS (continued)

| | NOMAD | ORACLE | PASCAL/R | PRTV |
|---|---|---|---|---|
| Define database | Yes | No | Yes | Yes |
| Generate database | Yes | No | Yes | No |
| Fast load / unload | Yes | No | Yes | No |
| Destroy database | Yes | No | Yes | Yes |
| Define relation | Yes | Yes | Yes | Yes |
| Destroy relation | Yes | Yes | No | Yes |
| Reorganize relation | Yes | No | Yes | Yes |
| Define snapshot | Yes | Yes | Yes | Yes |
| Define view | Yes | Yes | No | Yes |
| Drop attribute | Yes | No | No | Yes |
| Add attribute | Yes | Yes | No | Yes |
| Rename attribute | Yes | No | Yes | Yes |
| Define tuple | No | No | Yes | No |
| Other | Group a set of relations, encode/ decode | | | |

TABLE 4.3  SCHEMA DEFINITIONS (continued)

| | RAPPORT | SYSTEM R | QBE | RAPID |
|---|---|---|---|---|
| Define database | Yes | Yes | Yes | Yes |
| Generate database | Yes | Yes | Yes | |
| Fast load / unload | Yes | Yes | Yes | |
| Destroy database | No | Yes | Yes | |
| Define relation | Yes | No | | No |
| Destroy relation | No | Yes | Yes | Yes |
| Reorganize relation | Yes | No | Yes | No |
| Define snapshot | No | No | Yes | No |
| Define view | No | Yes | No | Yes |
| Drop attribute | No | Yes | Yes | Yes |
| Add attribute | No | Yes | Yes | Yes |
| Rename attribute | Yes | No | Yes | Yes |
| Define tuple | No | No | No | Yes |
| Other | | | | Open, close, status |

```
---------------------------------------------------------------
|              TABLE 4.3   SCHEMA DEFINITIONS SUMMARY           |
---------------------------------------------------------------
| Define database     | Supported by 12 systems |
---------------------------------------------------------------
| Generate database   | Supported by  8 systems |
---------------------------------------------------------------
| Fast load / unload  | Supported by  8 systems |
---------------------------------------------------------------
| Destroy database    | Supported by 10 systems |
---------------------------------------------------------------
| Define relation     | Supported by 13 systems |
---------------------------------------------------------------
| Destroy relation    | Supported by 11 systems |
---------------------------------------------------------------
| Reorganize relation | Supported by  8 systems |
---------------------------------------------------------------
| Define snapshot     | Supported by  9 systems |
---------------------------------------------------------------
| Define view         | Supported by 10 systems |
---------------------------------------------------------------
| Drop attribute      | Supported by  6 systems |
---------------------------------------------------------------
| Add attribute       | Supported by  7 systems |
---------------------------------------------------------------
| Rename attribute    | Supported by 10 systems |
---------------------------------------------------------------
| Define tuple        | Supported by  3 systems |
---------------------------------------------------------------
```

4.3.3   Observations -


     In general, the  systems  reviewed  deal  with  relations
rather   than   with   the  database itself.  All systems have the
ability to define a relation, and a great majority allows  the
user  to destroy and reorganize relations and define snapshots
and views.  In several systems, the database  is  defined  and
populated  implicitly  when  the  relations  are  defined  and
generated.  Most systems have explicit commands to drop,  add,
and   rename   attributes.  Only three systems explicitly define
tuples.  In the other systems, a tuple is  defined  implicitly
when the relation of which it is an element is defined.

## 4.4 Additional Definition, Generation, And Administration Facilities

### 4.4.1 Background –

Additional definition, generation, and administration facilities are shown in Table 4.4. These facilities were chosen based on their importance for the relational model as determined by the RTG. Facilities are considered to be not applicable (N/A) if the constituent about which the facility is defined is not supported by the system.

1. Attribute Synonyms. An explicit command exists to define a synonym for an attribute name of a relation.

2. Relation Synonym. An explicit command exists to define a synonym for a relation name.

3. Duplicate Tuples. The system supports storage of duplicate tuples. This may be due to the way the system has been implemented or it may be a user option.

4. Can a view be defined over more than one relation, for example, in the case of join, union, intersection, and relative complement operations?

5. Can a view be defined from other views, for example, can a dynamically derived relation be used in the definition of another dynamic derived relation?

6. User/DBA can define a mapping to update a view, for example, a view can be explicitly updated, causing updates to be mapped down to its defining relations?

7. Selection Criterion. Tuples of a relation can be selected based on meeting a user specified criterion.

8. Aggregate Function. The system supports aggregate functions such as MIN, MAX, and COUNT.

9. Primary Keys. The system requires primary keys as part of the logical data definition.

10. Keys can be modified. A user can modify a key value.

11. Keys can be declared unique. Once a key is declared, its value must be unique for each tuple. Note that this feature allows, at the user option, definitions of "primary" and "candidate" keys for certain relations.

12. Concatenated Key. A key can consist of more than one attribute of a relation.

13. Views inherit keys. When a view is declared, the key is inherited from its underlying relations.

14. Null valued keys are supported. A primary key may have a null value.


4.4.2  Results -

```
------------------------------------------------------------
|                                                          |
|          TABLE 4.4   ADDITIONAL FACILITIES               |
|                               --------------------       |
|                               |  ASTRAL  |  IDAMS  |      |
|------------------------------------------------------    |
|  Attribute synonyms           |   Yes    |   No    |      |
|------------------------------------------------------    |
|  Relation synonyms            |   Yes    |   No    |      |
|------------------------------------------------------    |
|  Duplicate tuples             |   No     |   Yes   |      |
|------------------------------------------------------    |
|  Can view be defined over     |   Yes    |   Yes   |      |
|  more than one relation       |          |         |      |
|------------------------------------------------------    |
|  Can view be defined          |   Yes    |   No    |      |
|  from other views             |          |         |      |
|------------------------------------------------------    |
|  User/DBA can define mapping  |   No     |   Yes   |      |
|  to update view explicitly    |          |         |      |
|------------------------------------------------------    |
|  Selection criterion          |   Yes    |   Yes   |      |
|------------------------------------------------------    |
|  Aggregate function           |   Yes    |   Yes   |      |
|------------------------------------------------------    |
|  Primary keys required        |   Yes    |   No    |      |
|------------------------------------------------------    |
|  Key can be modified          |   Yes    |   Yes   |      |
|------------------------------------------------------    |
|  Key can be declared unique   |   Yes    |   Yes   |      |
|------------------------------------------------------    |
|  Concatenated primary key     |   Yes    |   Yes   |      |
|------------------------------------------------------    |
|  Views inherit keys           |   Yes    |   No    |      |
|------------------------------------------------------    |
|  Null valued keys allowed     |   No     |   No    |      |
------------------------------------------------------------
```

TABLE 4.4   ADDITIONAL FACILITIES (continued)

| | IDM | INGRES | MRDS | MRS |
|---|---|---|---|---|
| Attribute synonyms | Yes | No | Yes | No |
| Relation synonyms | Yes | No | Yes | No |
| Duplicate tuples | Yes | No | Yes(view)<br>No (snap-<br>shot) | Yes |
| Can view be defined over more than one relation | Yes | Yes | Yes | N/A (*) |
| Can view be defined from other views | Yes | No | Yes | N/A |
| User/DBA can define mapping to update view explicitly | No | No | No | N/A |
| Selection criterion | Yes | Yes | Yes | Yes |
| Aggregate function | Yes | Yes | Yes | Yes |
| Primary keys required | No | No | Yes | No |
| Key can be modified | Yes | Yes | No | N/A |
| Key can be declared unique | Yes | No | Yes | N/A |
| Concatenated primary key | Yes | No | Yes | N/A |
| Views inherit keys | No | Yes | Yes | No |
| Null valued keys allowed | No | No | Yes | No |

(*)  N/A = not applicable

TABLE 4.4  ADDITIONAL FACILITIES (continued)

|  | NOMAD | ORACLE | PASCAL/R | PRTV |
|---|---|---|---|---|
| Attribute synonyms | Yes | Yes | Yes | No |
| Relation synonyms | No | Yes | Yes | Yes |
| Duplicate tuples | Yes | Yes | No | No |
| Can view be defined over more than one relation | Yes | Yes | N/A | Yes |
| Can view be defined from other views | No | Yes | N/A | Yes |
| User/DBA can define mapping to update view explicitly | No | No | N/A | No |
| Selection criterion | Yes | Yes | Yes | Yes |
| Aggregate function | Yes | Yes | No | Yes |
| Primary keys required | No | No | Yes | No |
| Key can be modified | Yes | Yes | No | N/A |
| Key can be declared unique | Yes | Yes | Yes | N/A |
| Concatenated primary key | Yes | No | Yes | N/A |
| Views inherit keys | No | N/A | N/A | N/A |
| Null valued keys allowed | Yes | No | No | N/A |

```
+------------------------------------------------------------------+
|                                                                  |
|     TABLE 4.4   ADDITIONAL FACILITIES (continued)                |
|             +-----------+-----------+---------+-----------+       |
|             | RAPPORT   | SYSTEM R  |  QBE    |  RAPID    |       |
+-----------------------------------------------------------+------+
```

| | RAPPORT | SYSTEM R | QBE | RAPID |
|---|---|---|---|---|
| Attribute synonyms | Yes | No | | No |
| Relation synonyms | No | Yes | | No |
| Duplicate tuples | No | Yes | No | Yes |
| Can view be defined over more than one relation | N/A | Yes | N/A | No |
| Can view be defined from other views | N/A | Yes | N/A | |
| User/DBA can define mapping to update view explicitly | N/A | Yes | N/A | |
| Selection criterion | Yes | Yes | Yes | Yes |
| Aggregate function | Yes | Yes | Yes | No |
| Primary keys required | Yes | No | No | Yes |
| Key can be modified | No | Yes | | Yes |
| Key can be declared unique | Yes | Yes | Yes | No |
| Concatenated primary key | Yes | Yes | Yes | Yes |
| Views inherit keys | N/A | Yes | N/A | No |
| Null valued keys allowed | No | Yes | No | Yes |

```
-----------------------------------------------------------------
|                                                               |
|            TABLE 4.4   ADDITIONAL DEFINITION,                 |
|        GENERATION, AND ADMINISTRATION FACILITIES             |
|                     SUMMARY                                   |
|---------------------------------------------------------------|
| Attribute synonyms          |  Supported by  7 systems        |
|-----------------------------------------------------------------|
| Relation synonyms           |  Supported by  7 systems        |
|-----------------------------------------------------------------|
| Duplicate tuples            |  Supported by  9 systems        |
|-----------------------------------------------------------------|
| Can view be defined over    |  Supported by  9 systems        |
| more than one relation      |                                 |
|-----------------------------------------------------------------|
| Can view be defined         |  Supported by  6 systems        |
| from other views            |                                 |
|-----------------------------------------------------------------|
| User/DBA can define         |                                 |
| mapping to update           |  Supported by  2 systems        |
| view explicitly             |                                 |
|-----------------------------------------------------------------|
| Selection criterion         |  Supported by 14 systems        |
|-----------------------------------------------------------------|
| Aggregate function          |  Supported by 12 systems        |
|-----------------------------------------------------------------|
| Primary keys required       |  Supported by  5 systems        |
|-----------------------------------------------------------------|
| Key can be modified         |  Supported by  8 systems        |
|-----------------------------------------------------------------|
| Key can be declared unique  |  Supported by 11 systems        |
|-----------------------------------------------------------------|
| Concatenated primary key    |  Supported by 10 systems        |
|-----------------------------------------------------------------|
| Views inherit keys          |  Supported by  4 systems        |
|-----------------------------------------------------------------|
| Null valued keys allowed    |  Supported by  4 systems        |
-----------------------------------------------------------------
```

4.4.3  Observations -


     The selection criterion facility is supported by  all  of
the  systems.   Often  used  with  selection  is the aggregate
function which is found in ten of the systems.  Eight  of  the
systems  support  duplicate tuples;  however, in most of these
systems, the user can specify  if  he  wishes  to  see  unique
tuples  only.   Synonyms  are  allowed for both attributes and
relations in seven of the systems.  The domain of an attribute
can be operated on in only five of the systems.  An example of
such an operation might be limiting the domain of an attribute

SALARY such that the fixed decimal value is greater than zero and less than 100,000. In most systems the domain is an implicit entity used in the definition of attributes.

Primary keys are supported in eleven of the systems. A majority of the systems that support keys allow modification of key values and allow a key to be a concatenation of attribute values.

Views can be defined in terms of more than one relation in seven of the nine systems which support views. Less than half of the systems allow views to be defined in terms of other views, to inherit keys of their defining relations, and to be defined prior to run time. Only two systems allow the explicit update of views.

## 4.5 Functional Classes

### 4.5.1 Definitions -

In analyzing the feature catalogue, twelve different functional classes were defined. These classes were used to group logically relational functions and are described below.

1. Database Schema Definition. These functions are included in interfaces 1, 4 of ANSI/SPARC DBMS framework and include the conceptual and external schema source definitions.

2. Database Retrieval. These functions include the set oriented and record-at-a-time oriented retrievals from the database. They include functions found in interfaces 7, 8, 9, 10, 11 of the ANSI/SPARC DBMS framework.

3. Database Altering. These functions include the set oriented and record-at-a-time oriented inserts, modifications, and deletes in the database. They include functions found in interfaces 7, 8, 9, 10, 11 of the ANSI/SPARC DBMS framework.

4. Integrity Constraints. These functions include the definitions of constraints on data values and their relationships. They include functions that would be in interfaces 1, 4 of the ANSI/SPARC DBMS framework.

5. Database Generation and Regeneration. These functions include facilities, separate from the database altering functions, for logical bulk loading, unloading, and reloading of relations. These functions can be found in

interface 39 of the ANSI/SPARC DBMS framework.

6. Database Schema Redefinition and Renaming. These functions include facilities for renaming attributes and relations, adding or deleting attributes to already existing relations, and adding or deleting entire relations. These functions would be supported through functions 1 and 4 of the ANSI/SPARC framework.

7. Report Generation. These functions include facilities that would be found in interface 8 of the ANSI/SPARC framework and are used for formatting and producing printed reports.

8. Special Data Entry. These functions would include screen entry or form entry processors and correspond possibly to function 11 of the ANSI/SPARC framework.

9. Security Definition and Monitoring. These functions are used to define protection and access rights, and to indicate whether and how security violations are to be housed. They would be included in functions 1 and 4 of the ANSI/SPARC framework.

10. Database Utilities. These functions would support physical dumping and loading of databases, and rollback and rollforward from database logs. They could correspond to function 24 of the ANSI/SPARC framework.

11. Definition of Storage Structure and Access Paths. These functions are used to define the static internal schema of the database and as such are similar to function 13 of the ANSI/SPARC framework.

12. Database Dictionary. These functions are used for retrieval of schema data and auxiliary user supplied textual descriptions, and can include functions found in functions 34, 35, 36, 37, 38, 2, 3, 5, 6, 14 and 15 of the ANSI/SPARC architecture.

4.5.2  Results -

| TABLE 4.5  FUNCTIONAL CLASSES | | |
|---|---|---|
| | ASTRAL | IDAMS |
| 1.  Database schema definition | DD commands static | DD commands dynamic |
| 2.  Database retrieval<br>    Set-oriented | Yes | Yes |
|     Record-at-a-time | Yes | |
| 3a) Database insert<br>    Set-oriented | Yes | Yes |
|     Record-at-a-time | Yes | |
| 3b) Database modify<br>    Set-oriented | Yes | Yes |
|     Record-at-a-time | Yes | |
| 3c) Database delete<br>    Set-oriented | Yes | Yes |
|     Record-at-a-time | Yes | |
| 4.  Integrity constraints | DD commands | DD commands |
| 5.  Database generation, regeneration | Bulk load | Utility |
| 6.  Database schema redefinition and renaming | Indirect | DD command |
| 7.  Report generation | | QL operator |
| 8.  Special data entry | | Utility |
| 9.  Security, monitoring | | Utility |
| 10. Load/dump/recovery | Yes | Yes |
| 11. Definition of access paths | DD utility | Implicit by optimizer |
| 12. Database dictionary | QL access | Special commands |

| TABLE 4.5 FUNCTIONAL CLASSES (continued) | | | |
|---|---|---|---|
| | IDM | INGRES | MRDS |
| 1. Database schema definition | QL commands dynamic | QL commands dynamic | Utility static |
| 2. Database retrieval Set-oriented | Yes | Yes | Yes |
| Record-at-a-time | | Yes | Yes |
| 3a) Database insert Set-oriented | Yes | Yes | |
| Record-at-a-time | | Yes | Yes |
| 3b) Database modify Set-oriented | Yes | Yes | Yes |
| Record-at-a-time | | | Yes |
| 3c) Database delete Set-oriented | Yes | Yes | Yes |
| Record-at-a-time | | | Yes |
| 4. Integrity constraints | QL commands | QL commands | DD utility |
| 5. Database generation, regeneration | Logical bulk load | Logical bulk load | Logical bulk load |
| 6. Database schema redefinition and renaming | Indirect | Indirect | Indirect |
| 7. Report generation | | Print command | Print command |
| 8. Special data entry | | | Prompting |
| 9. Security, monitoring | QL commands | QL commands | DD utility |
| 10. Load/dump/recovery | Yes | Yes | Yes |
| 11. Definition of access paths | QL commands | QL commands | DD utility |
| 12. Database dictionary | QL access | QL access | Special commands |

| | MRS | NOMAD | ORACLE |
|---|---|---|---|
| TABLE 4.5 FUNCTIONAL CLASSES (continued) | | | |
| 1. Database schema definition | QL commands dynamic | QL commands dynamic | QL dynamic |
| 2. Database retrieval Set-oriented | Yes | Yes | Yes |
|     Record-at-a-time | | Yes | Yes |
| 3a)Database insert Set-oriented | | | Yes |
|     Record-at-a-time | Yes | Yes | Yes |
| 3b)Database modify Set-oriented | Yes | Yes | Yes |
|     Record-at-a-time | Yes | Yes | Yes |
| 3c)Database delete Set-oriented | Yes | Yes | Yes |
|     Record-at-a-time | Yes | Yes | Yes |
| 4. Integrity constraints | | DD command | |
| 5. Database generation, regeneration | Logical bulk load | Logical bulk load | Logical bulk load |
| 6. Database schema redefinition and renaming | Indirect | Indirect | Indirect |
| 7. Report generation | | Print command | Utility |
| 8. Special data entry | | | Prompting |
| 9. Security, monitoring | QL commands | QL commands | DD utility |
| 10.Load/dump/recovery | Yes | Yes | |
| 11.Definition of access paths | QL commands | QL commands | QL commands |
| 12.Database dictionary | QL access | Special commands | QL access |

| TABLE 4.5 FUNCTIONAL CLASSES (continued) | PASCAL/R | PRTV | RAPPORT |
|---|---|---|---|
| 1. Database schema definition | Utility static | QL command dynamic | Utility static |
| 2. Database retrieval     Set-oriented | Yes | Yes | Yes |
|     Record-at-a-time | Yes | Yes | Yes |
| 3a) Database insert     Set-oriented | Yes | Yes | No |
|     Record-at-a-time | Yes | Yes | Yes |
| 3b) Database modify     Set-oriented | Yes | | No |
|     Record-at-a-time | Yes | Yes | Yes |
| 3c) Database delete     Set-oriented | Yes | Yes | Yes |
|     Record-at-a-time | Yes | Yes | Yes |
| 4. Integrity constraints | DD utility | None | DD utility |
| 5. Database generation, regeneration | Logical bulk load | Logical bulk load | Utility |
| 6. Database schema redefinition and renaming | Indirect | QL commands | Indirect |
| 7. Report generation | Print command | Utility | Print command |
| 8. Special data entry | | Utility | No |
| 9. Security, monitoring | | | |
| 10. Load/dump/recovery | Yes | Yes | Yes |
| 11. Definition of access paths | DD utility | | DD utility |
| 12. Database dictionary | QL access | QL access | Special commands |

| TABLE 4.5 FUNCTIONAL CLASSES (continued) | | | |
|---|---|---|---|
| | SYSTEM R | QBE | RAPID |
| 1. Database schema definition | QL command dynamic | QL command dynamic | User program, dynamic |
| 2. Database retrieval    Set-oriented | Yes | Yes | Yes |
|    Record-at-a-time | | Yes | Yes |
| 3a) Database insert    Set-oriented | Yes | Yes | |
|    Record-at-a-time | Yes | Yes | Yes |
| 3b) Database modify    Set-oriented | Yes | Yes | |
|    Record-at-a-time | Yes | Yes | Yes |
| 3c) Database delete    Set-oriented | Yes | Yes | Yes |
|    Record-at-a-time | Yes | Yes | Yes |
| 4. Integrity constraints | QL command | QL command | DD utility |
| 5. Database generation, regeneration | Utility | Logical bulk load/ unload | Logical bulk load/ unload |
| 6. Database schema redefinition and renaming | QL command | QL command | Utility |
| 7. Report generation | Print command | Print command | Utility |
| 8. Special data entry | Utility | | Forms |
| 9. Security, monitoring | Utility | QL command | |
| 10. Load/dump/recovery | Yes | Yes | Yes |
| 11. Definition of access paths | QL command | QL command | DD utility |
| 12. Database dictionary | QL access | QL access | Utility |

```
|-----------------------------------------------------------|
|            TABLE 4.5   FUNCTIONAL CLASSES SUMMARY          |
|-----------------------------------------------------------|
|1.  Database schema     |Separate utility:   3 systems      |
|    definition          |Q.L. commands   :   8 systems      |
|                        |User program    :   2 systems      |
|                        |DD commands     :   1 system       |
|-----------------------------------------------------------|
|2.  Database retrieval  |                                   |
|        Set-oriented    |Supported by 13 systems            |
|        Record-at-a-time|Supported by 11 systems            |
|-----------------------------------------------------------|
|3a) Database insert     |                                   |
|        Set-oriented    |Supported by  9 systems            |
|        Record-at-a-time|Supported by 12 systems            |
|-----------------------------------------------------------|
|3b) Database modify     |                                   |
|        Set-oriented    |Supported by 11 systems            |
|        Record-at-a-time|Supported by 11 systems            |
|-----------------------------------------------------------|
|3c) Database delete     |                                   |
|        Set-oriented    |Supported by 13 systems            |
|        Record-at-a-time|Supported by 10 systems            |
|-----------------------------------------------------------|
|                        |Q.L. commands:      6 systems      |
|4.  Integrity constraints|D.D. utility :     5 systems      |
|                        |None         :      2 systems      |
|-----------------------------------------------------------|
|5.  Database generation,|Bulk load                          |
|    regeneration        |Supported by 13 systems            |
|-----------------------------------------------------------|
|6.  Database schema rede-| Insert         :   9 systems      |
|    finition and renaming| Utility        :   1 system       |
|                        | Separate command:  4 systems      |
|-----------------------------------------------------------|
|7.  Report generation   |Print command:  7 systems          |
|                        |Utility      :  4 systems          |
|-----------------------------------------------------------|
|8.  Special data entry  |Prompting of att. names: 4 systems |
|                        |Forms approach        : 3 systems  |
|-----------------------------------------------------------|
|9.  Security, monitoring|Q.L. commands    :   6 systems     |
|                        |Part of data def.:   2 systems     |
|-----------------------------------------------------------|
|10. Load/dump/recovery  |Supported by 13 systems,           |
|                        |others depend on O.S.              |
|-----------------------------------------------------------|
|11. Definition of       |Q.L. commands    :   7 systems     |
|    access paths        |Part of data def.:   5 systems     |
|                        |Implicit         :   1 system      |
|-----------------------------------------------------------|
|12. Database dictionary |Q.L. access      :   9 systems     |
|                        |Special commands:    4 systems     |
|-----------------------------------------------------------|
```

### 4.5.3   Observations –

The features of 14 relational systems were analyzed in order to locate the existence of these functional classes. Note that this analysis is concerned with the existence of these classes and the functional similarity rather than with their power or completeness.

There appears to be uniformity in many of the systems in some of the classes. These classes, in decreasing order of uniformity, include set oriented retrieval operations (ignoring duplicate removal), set oriented tuple deletion and modification operations, record-at-a-time insertion operations, query language style commands to define the database, and query language style commands to retrieve those definitions. These classes of functions appear somewhat similar in about 50% of the systems.

Other function classes are either not present in more than 50% of the systems or exhibit considerable variability in their style.

### 4.6   Interface Flavors

### 4.6.1   Definitions –

The functions of the various systems can be characterized by expected uses of the function.  Three such categories include:

1. Interactive End User Interface.  In this function the user issues 'query' language commands through a keyboard (CRT or hard copy) terminal to access the database.

2. Host Programming Language Interface.  In this function a programming language such as COBOL, PL/1, or FORTRAN is used to access the database.  These functions can be implemented with the use of a preprocessor which maps database commands to host language subroutine calls, with direct (user controlled) subroutine calls, or with actual extensions to an existing (or new) language and compiler.

3. Special Interfaces. These functions generally require special hardware, such as graphics terminals, for accessing the database.

## TABLE 4.6   INTERFACE FLAVORS

| | Host Programming Language | | | |
|---|---|---|---|---|
| Interactive end user | Pre-processor | Calls | New language | Special interface |
| 1. ASTRAL | | | | Yes | |
| 2. IDAMS | Yes | | Yes | | Skeleton forms |
| 3. IDM | | | | | Back end machine |
| 4. INGRES | Yes | Yes | | | CUPID |
| 5. MRDS | Yes | | Yes | | |
| 6. MRS | Yes | | | | Interactive subsystem (tuple editor) |
| 7. NOMAD | Yes | | Yes | Yes | Screen editor for data |
| 8. ORACLE | Yes | | Yes | | Forms for data, editor for commands |
| 9. PASCAL/R | Yes | | | Yes | Various utilities |
| 10. PRTV | Yes | | Yes | | |
| 11. RAPPORT | Yes | Yes | | | |
| 12. SYSTEM R | Yes | Yes | | | |
| 13. QBE | Yes | | Yes | | QBE tabular form |
| 14. RAPID | | | Yes | | Various utilities |
| | 11 systems | 3 systems | 7 systems | 3 systems | 9 special interfaces have been defined |
| | 12 systems | | | | |

4.6.2  Observations -

The availability of these interfaces in the systems analyzed are shown in Table 4.6. Most systems support an interactive end user interface and a host programming language interface.   The realization of the programming language functions vary considerably, as did the special functions.


4.7  System Architectures

4.7.1  Results -

The systems analyzed can be loosely grouped into two types of architectures.   Those architectures are shown in Figure 4.1.  Systems of the Type A architecture have separate utilities for defining the database and for manipulating the data items.  In those systems the data definitions are stored in an internal form where they are accessed (retrieval only) in order to process data manipulation commands.  Some systems in this architecture also store the data definitions in relations for convenient and powerful access by database users.   Systems of the Type A architecture include MRDS, NOMAD, PASCAL/R and RAPPORT.

Systems of the Type B architecture, on the other hand, generally have one query level type interface (for both retrieval and update) through which schema commands and data manipulation commands can be freely intermixed.  Systems with this type of architecture include IDM, INGRES, MRS, ORACLE, PRTV, SYSTEM R and QBE.


4.7.2  Observations -

A few observations can be made about the architecture and functions of the systems.  First, many of the systems store system data in relations.  Those relations, protection permitting, can be accessed by the same retrieval commands that access user relations.  However, special create or define commands are required to populate the system data.  In a few systems it may be possible to apply 'user relation' update commands to the system's relations.

Secondly, in most of the systems, the record-at-a-time operators appear to go through the same level of function as do the set-at-a-time operators.  In no system it is made explicit to the user that the 'user set oriented operators' are mapped to the 'user individual record oriented operators'.

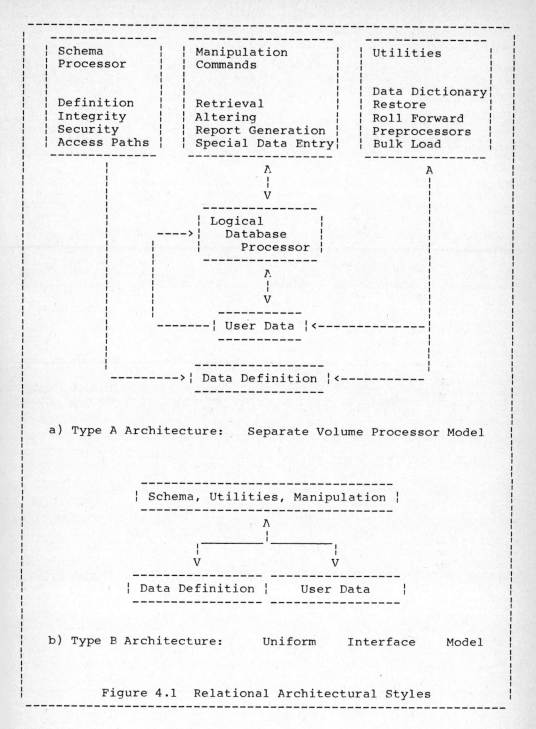

a) Type A Architecture:   Separate Volume Processor Model

b) Type B Architecture:   Uniform   Interface   Model

Figure 4.1   Relational Architectural Styles

## 4.8 Operational Aspects

### 4.8.1 Definitions –

In section 6 of the feature analysis, the security, concurrency control, and crash recovery mechanisms of the 14 relational database systems were reviewed. Information was provided in the following areas:

1. Security - User Related. This section, labelled access control, was concerned with how (and if) users were identified to the DBMS. Three types of identification were identified:

   a. User Id from Operating System. The DBMS, through a system call, identifies the current user in order to determine the users capabilities.

   b. Passwords. The DBMS requires a user to supply a password in order to determine the user's capabilities.

   c. File Access Control. The Operating System controls access to the database files. For some DBMSs, this method is the only form of access control. For others, the O.S. control is used in conjunction with user identification of type a. or b. For the latter type of system, the DBMS itself is the owner of the database files.

2. Security -- Data Related. This section, labelled capabilities, was concerned with the granularity and/or level of protection.

   a. Item protected for most systems was a relation, view, or both, but had to be explicitly named. Some systems allowed protection on specific attributes of relations.

   b. Value based protection indicated that the data value can be used to define the items to be protected. Note this feature is distinct from the value dependent view mechanism in that the value based granules need not be 'named'.

3. Concurrency Control. This section was concerned with the consistency of the database during multiple user update. The particular items noted were:

a.  Multiple User Updates.  Could users simultaneously (at least from their perspective) update the database?

b.  Multiple Update Commands.  If so, could the user group multiple update commands into a transaction?

c.  Degree of Consistency.  If multiple users could simultaneously update the database, what degree of consistency was permitted?  Degree 3 consistency implies that no user sees the update of another user until the other user has completed a transaction (possibly a one command transaction).  Some DBMSs achieve Degree 3 consistency by locking everything that a transaction reads or writes and holding those locks until the end of the transaction.  With Degree 1 consistency, one user can see updates of other user transactions that have not been completed.  Some of the DBMSs achieve Degree 1 consistency by locking records (or pages) while they are in main memory but not when the records are returned to the disk.

d.  Explicit Locks.  If multiple users could simultaneously update the database, can they explicitly preclaim resources by requesting locks for those resources?

4.  Crash Recovery.  Does the system make any provisions for protecting the consistency of the database in the presence of system and disk crashes?

a.  Database Back-up and Restore.  Does the Database System have special functions for backing up the disk copy of the database and restoring the database from that back-up?  If the database system does not have those functions, some feature analyses suggested that operating system file dump and restore utilities could be used on the database files.

b.  Logging.  Is logging of record changes or page changes supported? By supported we mean that the log can be 'rolled forward' together with the DB dump/restore to return the database to a consistent state in the case of a disk crash.

c.  Recovery from System Crash.  Does the system have any provisions for protecting the database from inconsistency due to ,for example, soft (non-disk damaging) crashes?

4.8.2   Results -

TABLE 4.8   OPERATIONAL ASPECTS

|  | ASTRAL | IDAMS |
|---|---|---|
| 1. Security (user related) | | |
| a. User id from O.S. | | Yes |
| b. Passwords | | Yes |
| c. File access by O.S. | | Yes |
| 2. Security (data related) | | |
| a. Item of protection | | Relations/views |
| b. Based on data value | | |
| 3. Concurrency control | | |
| a. Multiple user update | Yes | Yes |
| b. Multiple commands per transaction | Yes | Yes |
| c. Degrees of consistency | 3 | 3 |
| d. Explicit locks | Yes | No |
| 4. Crash recovery | | |
| a. DB back-up/restore | Yes | Yes |
| b. Logging | Yes | Page |
| c. Recovery from system crashes | Yes | Yes |

TABLE 4.8   OPERATIONAL ASPECTS (continued)

|  | IDM | INGRES | MRDS |
|---|---|---|---|
| 1. Security (user related) | | | |
| a. User id from O.S. | Yes | Yes | |
| b. Passwords | | | |
| c. File access by O.S. | | Yes | Yes |
| 2. Security (data related) | | | |
| a. Item of protection | Views/ relations/ attributes | Relations/ attributes | View/ relations |
| b. Based on data value | | Yes | |
| 3. Concurrency control | | | |
| a. Multiple user update | Yes | Yes | Yes |
| b. Multiple commands per transaction | Yes | No | Yes |
| c. Degrees of consistency | 3 | 3 | 3 |
| d. Explicit locks | No | No | Yes |
| 4. Crash recovery | | | |
| a. DB back-up/restore | Yes | O.S. | O.S. |
| b. Logging | Record | | |
| c. Recovery from system crashes | Yes | Yes | Yes |

TABLE 4.8  OPERATIONAL ASPECTS (continued)

| | MRS | NOMAD | ORACLE |
|---|---|---|---|
| 1. Security (user related) | | | |
| a. User id from O.S. | | Yes | Yes |
| b. Passwords | | | Yes |
| c. File access by O.S. | Yes | Yes | |
| 2. Security (data related) | | | |
| a. Item of protection | Relation | Relation/ attributes | View/ relations |
| b. Based on data value | | Yes | |
| 3. Concurrency control | | | |
| a. Multiple user update | | Yes | Yes |
| b. Multiple commands per transaction | | Yes | Yes |
| c. Degrees of consistency | | 1 | 3 if explic. preclaim 1 otherwise |
| d. Explicit locks | | | Yes |
| 4. Crash recovery | | | |
| a. DB back-up/restore | Yes | O.S. | O.S. |
| b. Logging | | | |
| c. Recovery from system crashes | | Yes | |

TABLE 4.8  OPERATIONAL ASPECTS (continued)

| | PASCAL/R | PRTV | RAPPORT |
|---|---|---|---|
| 1. Security (user related) | | | |
| a. User id from O.S. | | | Yes |
| b. Passwords | Yes | | Yes |
| c. File access by O.S. | Yes | Yes | Yes |
| 2. Security (data related) | | | |
| a. Item of protection | | | Attributes |
| b. Based on data value | | | Yes |
| 3. Concurrency control | | | |
| a. Multiple user update | No | No | Yes |
| b. Multiple commands per transaction | | | Yes |
| c. Degrees of consistency | | | 1, 3 |
| d. Explicit locks | | | Yes |
| 4. Crash recovery | | | |
| a. DB back-up/restore | O.S. | O.S. | Yes |
| b. Logging | | | Record |
| c. Recovery from system crashes | | | Yes |

TABLE 4.8   OPERATIONAL ASPECTS (continued)

| | SYSTEM R | QBE | RAPID |
|---|---|---|---|
| 1. Security (user related) | | | |
|    a. User id from O.S. | Yes | Yes | |
|    b. Passwords | | | |
|    c. File access by O.S. | Yes | Yes | Yes |
| 2. Security (data related) | | | |
|    a. Item of protection | Views/ relations attributes | Relation/ attribute | View |
|    b. Based on data value | | Yes | |
| 3. Concurrency control | | | |
|    a. Multiple user update | Yes | No | Yes |
|    b. Multiple commands per transaction | Yes | | Yes |
|    c. Degrees of consistency | 3, 2 or 1 User selects | | |
|    d. Explicit locks | Yes | | Yes |
| 4. Crash recovery | | | |
|    a. DB back-up/restore | Yes | Yes | Yes |
|    b. Logging | Page, tuple | Page | Page |
|    c. Recovery from system crashes | Yes | Yes | |

TABLE 4.8   OPERATIONAL ASPECTS SUMMARY

| | | |
|---|---|---|
| 1. Security (user related) | | |
|    a. User id from O.S. | | 8 systems |
|    b. Passwords | | 4 systems |
|    c. File access by O.S. | | 11 systems |
| 2. Security (data related) | | |
|    a. Item of protection | Views : | 6 systems |
| | Relations : | 9 systems |
| | Attributes (R,W): | 6 systems |
|    b. Based on data value | | 4 systems |
| 3. Concurrency control | | |
|    a. Multiple user update | | 10 systems |
|    b. Multiple commands per transaction | | 9 systems |
|    c. Degrees of consistency | Level 3: | 8 systems |
| | Level 1: | 4 systems |
|    d. Explicit locks | | 7 systems |
| 4. Crash recovery | | |
|    a. DB back-up/restore | 7 systems (O.S. for others ) | |
|    b. Logging | Record: | 4 systems |
| | Page  : | 3 systems |
|    c. Recovery from system crashes | | 8 systems |

### 4.8.3   Observations -

The results shown in Table 4.8 indicate that there   is   a
variety   of   approaches   to these operational aspects of DBMSs
and that many aspects of the approaches do not seem related to
the relational model.

The results are important, however, establishing the fact
that   some   of   the   relational   systems   are   in   some   sense
'complete' DBMSs;   they are suitable for shared databases used
by   multiple   users   simultaneously updating the database, and
they allow   for   environmental   realities   such   as   integrity
violations and soft and hard crashes.

# 5. References

We distinguish between two kinds of references:

1. <u>Relational Bibliography</u>, i.e., partial list of publications of importance to the relational approach.

2. <u>Reference Papers</u>, i.e., additional documents used in preparing the RTG's work.

## 5.1 Relational Bibliography

[AMBLE79] Amble, T., K. Bratbergsengen and O. Risnes. "ASTRAL: A Structured and Unified Approach to Data Base Design and Manipulation". Proc. IFIP TC-2 Working Conf. on Data Base Architecture, Venice, June 1979, North Holland 1979.

[ASTR80a] Astrahan, M.M., W. Kim and M. Schkolnick. "Evaluation of System R Access Path Selection Mechanism". Research Report RJ 2797, IBM Research Laboratory, San Jose, California, April 1980.

[ASTR80b] Astrahan, M.M. et al. "A History and Evaluation of System R". Research Report RJ2843, June, 1980.

[ASTR76] Astrahan, M.M. et al. "System R: Relational Approach to Database Management". ACM TODS, Vol. 1, No. 20, June 1976.

[BEER78] Beeri, C., P. Bernstein, and N. Goodman. "A Sophisticate's Introduction to Database Normalization Theory". Proc. 4th VLDB, Berlin, 1978.

[BJOR80] Bjorner, D. "Formalization of Database Models". in "Abstract Software Specifications", Springer Lecture Notes in Computer Science No. 86, Springer Verlag Heidelberg, New York, 1980.

[BJOR73] Bjorner, D. et al. "The Gamma-0 n-ary Relational Data Base Interface Specifications of Objects and Operations". Research Report RJ1300, IBM Research Laboratory, San Jose, California, April 1973.

[BLAS79] Blasgen, M.W. et al. "System R: An Architectural Update". Research Report RJ2581, July 1979.

[BLAS77] Blasgen, M.W. and K.P. Eswaran. "Storage and Access in Relational Data Bases". IBM Systems Journal, Vol. 16, No. 4, 1977.

[BOYCE73] Boyce, R.F. and D.D. Chamberlin. "Using a Structured English Query Language as a Data Definition Facility". Research Report RJ1318, December 1973.

[BROD82] Brodie, M.L. and J.W. Schmidt (Eds.). "Report of the ANSI Relational Task Group". ACM SIGMOD Record, July 1982.

[BROD81] Brodie, M.L. and S.N. Zilles (Eds.). Proc. Workshop on Data Abstraction, Databases and Conceptual Modelling, Pingee Park, June 1980, ACM SIGART, SIGMOD, SIGPLAN, January/February 1981.

[BROD80b] Brodie, M.L. "Data Abstraction, Database, and Conceptual Modelling: An Annotated Bibliography." NBS Special Pub. 500-59, May 1980.

[BROD80e] Brodie, M.L. "Standardization and the Relational Approach to Databases". Proc. 6th VLDB, Montreal, October 1980.

[BUNE79] Bunemann, P. and R.E. Frankel. "FQL - A Functional Query Language". Proc. 1979 SIGMOD, Boston, May 1979.

[CHAM81] Chamberlin, D.D. et al. "Support for Repetitive Transactions and Ad Hoc Queries in System R". ACM TODS, Vol. 6., No. 1, March 1981.

[CHAM77] Chamberlin, D.D. et al. "Data Base System Authorization". Research Report RJ2041, July 1977.

[CHAM76a] Chamberlin, D.D. "Relational Data Base Management Systems". Computing Surveys, Vol. 8, No. 1, March 1976.

[CHAM76b] Chamberlin, D.D. et al. "SEQUEL 2: A Unified Approach to Data Definition, Manipulation and Control". IBM Journal of Research and Development, November 1976.

[CHAM75] Chamberlin, D.D., J.N. Gray and I.L. Traiger. "Views, Authorization and Locking in a Relational Data Base System". Proc. 1975 AFIPS National Computer Conf., 1975.

[CHANG79] Chang, C.L. "On Evaluation of Queries Containing Derived Relations in a Relational Database". Research Report RJ2667, IBM Research Laboratory, San Jose, California, October 1979.

[CODD82] Codd, E.F. "Relational Database: A Practical Foundation for Productivity", CACM 25, 2, February 1982.

[CODD80] Codd, E.F. "Data Modells in Database Management" in [BROD81].

[CODD79a] Codd, E.F. "Derivability, Redundancy and Consistency of Relations Stored in Large Data Banks". Research Report RJ2599, IBM Research Laboratory, San Jose, California, August 1979.

[CODD79b] Codd, E.F. "Extending the Relational Data Base Model to Capture More Meaning". ACM TODS, Vol. 4, No. 4, 1979.

[CODD74] Codd, E.F. "Recent Investigations in Relational Data Base Systems". IFIP Congress, Amsterdam, North Holland, 1974.

[CODD72] Codd, E.F. "Relational Completeness of Database Sublanguages". in Data Base Systems, Courant Computer Science Symposium 6, Prentice Hall, 1972.

[CODD71] Codd, E.F. "A Database Sublanguage founded on the Relational Calculus". Proc. ACM SIGFIDET Workshop, San Diego, Calif., November 1971.

[CODD70] Codd, E.F. "A Relational Model of Data for Large Shared Data Banks". CACM, Vol. 13, No. 6, June 6, 1970.

[DATE81] Date, C.J. "An Introduction to Database Systems", Third Edition, Addison Wesley, 1981.

[DATE80] Date, C.J. "An Introduction to the Unified Database Language (UDL)". Proc. 6th VLDB, October 1980, Montreal, Canada.

[DATE79] Date, C.J. "An Architecture for High Level Database Extensions" (UDL: COBOL and PL/I Version). IBM Santa Teresa Laboratory, San Jose, California, April 1979.

[DAYAL78] Dayal, U. and P.A. Bernstein. "On the Updatability of Relational Views". Proc. 4th VLDB, Berlin, September 1978.

[DELO80] Delobel, C. "An Overview on the Relational Data Theory". IFIP Congress, Tokyo, North Holland, 1980.

[DRIS78] Driscoll, J.R., B.A. Dutton and K.C. Kinsley. "A Relational Storage Scheme Suitable for Derived Views". Proc. of the 1978 ACM Annual Conf., 1978.

[FAGIN79] Fagin, R. "Normal Forms and Relational Database Operators". Research Report RJ2471, IBM Research Laboratory, San Jose, California, February 1979.

[FURT78] Furtado, A.L. "Formal Aspects of the Relational Model". Information Systems 3, 2, 1978.

[FRY76] Fry, J.P. and E.H. Sibley. "Evolution of Database Management Systems". Computing Surveys, Vol. 8, No. 1, March 1976.

[GALL78] Gallaire, H. and J. Minker (Eds.) "Logic and Databases". Plenum Press, New York, 1978.

[HALL75a] Hall, P.A.V. "Optimization of a Single Relational Expression in a Relational Data Base System". Research Report UKSC 76, June 1975.

[HALL75b] Hall, P.A.V., P. Hitchcock and S.P.J. Todd. "An Algebra of Relations for Machine Computation". Conf. Record of 2nd ACM Symposium on Principles of Programming Languages, Palo Alto, California, January 1975.

[HANS76] Hansel, A. "A Formal Definition of a Relational Database System". Research Report UKSC 80, 1979.

[HEATH71] Heath, I.J. "Unacceptable File Operations in a Relational Data Base". ACM SIGFIDET Workshop, 1971.

[HELD75] Held, C.D., M. Stonebraker and E. Wong. "INGRES: A Relational Database System". Proc. ACM Pacific 75 Regional Conference, 1975.

[HITC76] Hitchcock, P. "User Extensions to the Peterlee Test Vehicle". Systems for Large Data Bases. Amsterdam, 1976.

[HOUS79] Housel, B.C. "QUEST: A High Level Data Manipulation Language for Network, Hierarchical, and Relational Databases". Research Report RJ2588, July 1979.

[JARD79] Jardine, C. and J. Owlett. "Applying a Relational Database System to Historical Data". IBM UK Technical Note 74, 1979.

[JONES78] Jones, S.E. and D.R. Ries. "A Relational Data Base Management System for Scientific Data". Lawrence Livermore Laboratory, February 1978.

[KIM79] Kim, W. "Relational Database Systems". ACM Computing Survey, Vol. 11, No. 3, September 1979.

[LACR76] Lacroix, M. and A. Pirotte. "Generalized Joins". ACM SIGMOD Record, Vol. 8, No. 3, 1976.

[LACR77a] Lacroix, M. and A. Pirotte. "ILL: An English Structured Query Language for Relational Databases". Proc. IFIP TC-2 Working Conference on Modelling in Database Management Systems, Nice, France, January 1977, Nijssen, Ed.), North Holland, 1977.

[LACR77b] Lacroix, M. and A. Pirotte. "Domain Oriented Relational Languages". Proc. 3rd VLDB, October 1977.

[LACR78] Lacroix, M. and A. Pirotte. "Example Queries in Relational Languages". Tech. Note 107, MBLE Research Laboratory, Brussels, Belgium, revised April 1978 (see also Research Reports 351 and 367).

[LACR80] Lacroix, M. and A. Pirotte. "User Interfaces for Database Application Programming". Proc. 74th Infotech State of the Art Conference on Databases, London, October 1980.

[LACR81] Lacroix, M. and A. Pirotte. "Associating Types with Domains of Relational Databases" in [BROD81].

[LAME80] Lamersdorf, W. and J.W. Schmidt. "Semantic Definition of PASCAL/R". Berichte Nr. 73 and 74, University of Hamburg, Federal Republic of Germany, July 1980.

[LORIE79] Lorie, R.A., R. Casajuana and J.L. Becerril. "GSYSR: A Relational Database Interface for Graphics". Research Report RJ2511, April 1979.

[McDO75] McDonald, N. and M. Stonebraker. "CUPID: The Friendly Query Language". Proc. ACM Pacific 75 Regional Conference, April 1975.

[MYLO75] Mylopoulos, J., S. Schuster and D. Tsichritzis. "A Multi-Level Relational System". Proc. 1975 AFIPS National Computer Conf., 1975.

[OWENS71] Owens, R.C. "Evaluation of Access Authorization Characteristics of Derived Data Sets". Proc. ACM SIGFIDET Workshop on Data Description, Access and Control, 1971.

[OWLE77] Owlett, J. "Deferring and Defining in Databases" in "Architecture and Models in Data Base Management Systems". Proc. of the IFIP Working Conf. on Modelling in Data Base Management Systems, November 1977.

614

[PIRO79] Pirotte, A. "Fundamental and Secondary Issues in the Design of Non-Procedural Languages". Proc. 5th VLDB, Rio de Janeiro, October 1979.

[PIRO78] Pirotte, A. "Linguistic Aspects of High Level Relational Languages". Infotech State of the Art Report on Data Base Technology, Vol. 2, 1978.

[PIRO77a] Pirotte, A. "The Entity-Property-Association Model: An Information-Oriented Data Base Model". Proc. ACM International Computing Symposium, ICS77), North Holland, 1977.

[PIRO80] Pirotte, A. "High Level Database Query Languages" in "Logic and Databases" in [GALL78].

[SAND81] Sandberg, G. "A Primer on Relational Data Base Concepts". IBM Systems Journal, Vol. 21, No. 1, 1981.

[SCHM82] Schmidt, J.W. and W. Lamersdorf. "Relational Data Model: A Definition and its Formalization". Bericht Nr. 88, University of Hamburg, Federal Republic of Germany, March 1982.

[SCHM80a] Schmidt, J.W. and M. Mall. "PASCAL/R Report". Bericht Nr. 66, University of Hamburg, Federal Republic of Germany, January 1980.

[SCHM79] Schmidt, J.W. "Parallel Processing of Relations: A Single-Assignment Approach". VLDB5, Rio de Janeiro, 1975.

[SCHM77] Schmidt, J.W. "Some High Level Language Constructs for Data of Type Relation". ACM TODS, Vol. 2, No. 3, September 1977.

[SELI79] Selinger, P.J. et al. "Access Path Selection in a Relational Database System". Research Report RJ2429, January 1979.

[SHIP81] Shipman, D. "The Functional Data Model and the Data Language DAPLEX". ACM TODS, Vol. 6, No. 1, March 1981.

[SMITH77] Smith, J.M. and D.C.P. Smith. "Database Abstraction: Aggregation and Generalization". ACM TODS Vol. 2, No. 2 June 1977.

[STON80b] Stonebraker, M. "Retrospection on a Database System". ACM TODS, Vol. 5, No. 2, June 1980.

[STON78] Stonebraker, M. "Concurrency Control and Consistency of Multiple Copies of Data in Distributed INGRES". ERL Technical Memorandum Reprint 1702, University of California, August 1978.

STON76] Stonebraker, M. et al. "The Design and Implementation of INGRES". ERL Technical Memorandum Reprint 1468, University of California, September 1976.

[STON75] Stonebraker, M. "Implementation of Integrity Constraints and Views by Query Modification". Proc. ACM SIGMOD, San Jose, May 1975.

[STRN71] Strnad, A.J. "The Relational Approach to the Management of Data Bases". IFIP Congress 1971, Ljubljana, 1971.

[TODD77a] Todd, S.P.J. "Automatic Constraint Maintenance and Updating Defined Relations". IFIP Congress 1977, Toronto, North Holland, 1977.

[TODD76] Todd, S.P.J. "The Peterlee Relational Test Vehicle - A System Overview". IBM Systems Journal, No. 4, 1976.

[TODD74] Todd, S.P.J. "Implementation of the Join Operator in Relational Data Bases". IEEE/IERE Colloquium on Information Structure and Storage Organisation, London, April 1974.

[TSIC78] Tsichritzis, D. and A. Klug. "The ANSI/X3/SPARC DBMS Framework." Report of the Study Group on a Database Management System. Information Systems, Vol. 3, No. 4, 1978.

[ULLM80] Ullman, J.D. "Principles of Database Systems". Computer Science Press, 1980.

[VERH76] Verhofstad, J.S.M. "The PRTV Optimiser: The Current State". Research Report UKSC 83, May 1976.

[WONG77] Wong, H.K.T. and J. Mylopoulos. "Two Views of Data Semantics: A Survey of Data Models in Artificial Intelligence and Database Management". INFOR, Vol. 15, No. 3, October 1977.

[ZLOOF77] Zloof, M.M. "Query-By-Example: A Data Base Language". IBM Systems Journal, No. 4, 1977.

[ZLOOF75a] Zloof, M.M. "Query-By-Example". AFIPS Conf. Proc., Vol. 44, AFIPS Press, Montvale, N.J., 1975.

[ZLOOF75b] Zloof, M.M. "Query-By-Example: The Invocation and Definition of Tables and Forms". Proc. 1st VLDB, Framingham, Massachusetts, September, 1975.

## 5.2  Reference Papers

[BEKIC79] Bekic, H., D. Bjorner, W. Henhapl and C.B. Jones. "A Formal Definition of PL/1 Subset, Parts I and II". Tech. Report TR25.139, IBM Laboratory, Vienna, December 1979.

[BJOR78] Bjorner, D., and C.B. Jones. "The Vienna Development Method: The Meta Language." Springer Verlag, New York, 1978.

[BRAT80] Bratbergsengen, K. et al. "A Neighbor Connected Processor Network for Performing Relational Algebra Operations". ACM 5th Workshop on Computer Architecture for Non-Numeric Processing, ACM SIGMOD Vol. 10, No. 4, March 1980.

[BROD80a] Brodie, M.L. "A Functional Framework for Database Management Systems". TR-78, Dept. of Computer Science, University of Maryland, February 1980.

[BROD80c] Brodie, M.L. and J.W. Schmidt. "Feature Catalogue of Relational Concepts, Languages and Systems". RTG Working Doc. 80-81, May 1980.

[BROD80d] Brodie, M.L. and J.W. Schmidt. "Issues in Investigating a Standard for the Relational Approach to Databases". Proc. NBS Conf. of DBMS Standards, Gaithersburg, MD, September 1980.

[CCA80] Computer Corporation of America. "Overview of NBS Strawman Architecture for Family of DBMS Standards". Presented at NBS Conference, September 1980.

[CHILDS77] Childs, D.L. "Extended Set Theory". Proc. 3rd VLDB, Tokyo, October 1977.

[CODA73,78] CODASYL Data Description Language Committee, Journal of Development, 1973 and 1978.

[CODA69,71] CODASYL Database Task Group Reports 1969 and 1971.

[CODD81a] Codd, E.F. "The Significance of the SQL/Data System Announcement". Computerworld, February, 1981.

[CODD81b] Codd, E.F. "The Capabilities of Relational Database Management Systems". IBM Research Laboratory Report, RJ3132, May 11, 1981.

[DONA76] Donahue. "Complementary Definitions of Programming Language Semantics". Lecture Notes in Computer Science No. 42, Springer Verlag, Heidelberg, New York, 1976.

[EARL71] Earley, J. "Towards an Understanding of Data Structures". CACM, Vol. 14, No. 10, October 1971.

[EGLI74] Egli, H. "Programming Language Semantics Using Extensional Lambda-Calculus Models". TR-206, Cornell University, April 1974.

[EPST80a] Epstein, R. and P. Hawthorn. "Aids in the 80's". DATAMATION, February 1980.

[EPST80b] Epstein, R. and P. Hawthorn. "Design Decisions for the Intelligent Database Machine". Proc. of the 1980 NCC.

[ERBE80] Erbe, R. et al. "Integrated Data Analysis and Management for the Problem Solving Environment". Information Systems, Vol. 5, 1980.

[GOGU77] Goguen, J.A., J.W. Thatcher and E.G. Wagner. "An Initial Algebra Approach to the Specification, Correctness, and Implementation of Abstract Data Types". RC6487, IBM Yorktown Heights, New York, April 1977.

[GORD79] Gordon, M.J.C. "The Denotational Description of Programming Languages". Springer Verlag, Heidelberg, New York, 1979.

[GUTT78] Guttag, J.V. and J.J. Horning. "The Algebraic Specification of Abstract Data Types". Acta Informatica 10, 1978.

[HARD80] Hardgrave, W.T. "Positional Set Notation". National Bureau of Standards, February 1980.

[HARD78] Hardgrave, W.T. "The Relational Model: A Reformulation of some Mathematical Aspects Using Positional Set Notation". IFSM T.R. No. 25, Dept. of Information Systems Management, University of Maryland, March 1978.

[HARD76] Hardgrave, W.T. "Set Processing: A Tool for Data Management". IFSM T.R. No. 6, Dept. of Information Systems Management, University of Maryland, April 1976.

[HOARE74] Hoare, C.A.P. and P.E. Lauer. "Consistent and Complementary Formal Theories of the Semantics of Programming Languages". Acta Informatica 3, 1974.

[HOARE73] Hoare, C.A.P. and N. Wirth. "An Axiomatic Definition of the Programming Language PASCAL". Acta Informatica 2, 1973.

[JOHN79a]  Johnson, H.R., J.A.  Larson  and  J.D.  Lawrence.
    "Data  Description  Language  for  Network and Relational
    Modelling".  Sperry Univac, Roseville, Minnesota, 1979.

[JOHN79b]  Johnson, H.R., J.A.  Larson  and  J.D.  Lawrence.
    "Network  and  Relational Modelling in a Common Data Base
    Architecture  Environment".  Research  Report  TMA00720,
    Sperry Univac, Roseville, Minnesota, March 1979.

[LEHM79]  Lehmann, H.  et al.  "Integrated Data  Analysis  and
    Management  System,  Command  Language  User's  Guide".
    Scientific Center, Heidelberg, TN 79.04., July 1979.

[LUCAS71]  Lucas, P.  "Formal  Definition  of  Programming
    Languages and Systems".  IFIP Congress 71, August 1971.

[MILLS79]  Mills,  H.D., R.C.  Linger  and  B.I.  Witt
    "Structured  Programming  Theory  and Practice".  Addison
    Wesley, 1979.

[OSBO79]  Osborn, Sylvia L.  "Towards a  Universal  Relational
    Interface".  IEEE, August 1979.

[SCHA81]  Schauer, U.  et al.  "Integrated Data  Analysis  and
    Management  System,  Publication  of  the Gesellschaft f.
    Informatik (GI) Special Interest Group  on  Methods  Data
    Bases, February 1981.

[SCOTT72]  Scott, D.  "Lattice Theory, Data Types, and  Formal
    Semantics".  NYU Symposium on Formal Semantics, Prentice
    Hall, 1972.

[STON80a]  Stonebraker, M.  "A Tale of Three Standards".  Proc
    1980  NBS  Workshop  on  a  Family of DBMS Standards, NBS
    Publication, October 1980.

[TODD77b]  Todd, S.P.J.  "Database  Research  at  the  IBM  UK
    Scientific Centre, Peterlee:  A Survey".  Research Report
    UKSC 93,1977.

[VERH79]  Verhofstad, J.S.M.  "An  Evaluation  of  the  PRTV
    Optimiser".  Research Report UKSC 91, 1979.

[ZLOOF78a]  Zloof, M.M.  "Query-by-Example:  Operations on the
    Transitive  Closure".  IBM  Research  Report RC5526, IBM
    Thomas J.  Watson Research Center,  Yorktown  Heights,New
    York, February 1978.

[ZLOOF78b]  Zloof, M.M.  "Security and  Integrity  within  the
    Query-By-Example  Data  Base  Management  Language".  IBM
    Research Report RC6982, February, 1978.

[ZLOOF76]  Zloof, M.M.  "Query-By-Example:  Operation  on
    Hierarchical Data Bases". AFIPS Conf. Proc., NCC45, 1976.

# Operating Systems

An Advanced Course

By **M. J. Flynn, J. N. Gray, A. K. Jones, K. Lagally, H. Opderbeck, G. J. Popek, B. Randell, J. H. Saltzer, H. R. Wiehle**

Editors: **R. Bayer, R. M. Graham, G. Seegmüller**

Springer Study Edition
Reprint. 1979. 100 figures, 14 tables. X, 593 pages
ISBN 3-540-09812-7
(Originally published in the series *Lecture Notes in Computer Science,* Volume 60)

*From the reviews:* "Despite its description as 'An Advanced Course' this book is much more akin to a set of conference proceedings; the 'course', given in July 1977 and again in April 1978, takes the form of a series of presentations bordering on, or even consisting of, research topics in a number of areas connected with the entire spectrum of operating systems...
The course organisers, the editors of this book and its several contributors are to be congratulated. There is a minimum of the repetition which so often mars such a product, and yet the internal linkages between the various facets are present. I found much that was new, and appealing, in terms of new techniques, new results and especially valuable, new ways of looking at familiar situations. The main emphasis is on the abstract modelling of three aspects of current advances in operating systems; the invocation, allocation and control of resources; improvements in reliability by co-operation between software and specific functions of the hardware; and the provision of efficient and secure interprocess communications, especially where the communicating processes are under distinct local managements."

*The Computer Journal*

**Contents:** Introduction. – Models: The Object Model: A Conceptual Tool for Structuring Software. Computer Organization and Architecture. – Issues and Results in the Design of Operating Systems: Naming and Binding of Objects. Issues in Kernel Design. Protection Mechanisms and the Enforcement of Security Policies. Synchronization in a Layered System. Reliable Computing Systems. Notes on Data Base Operating Systems. Common Carrier Provided Network Interfaces. Design Issues for Secure Computer Networks. – Future Outlook and Research Problems: On System Specification. Research Problems of Decentralized Systems with Largely Autonomous Nodes.

Springer-Verlag
Berlin
Heidelberg
New York

# Data Base Design Techniques I:

Requirements and Logical Structures

NYU Symposium, New York, May 1978

Editor: **S. B. Yao, S. B. Navathe, J. L. Weldon, T. L. Kunii**

1982. V, 227 pages.
(Lecture Notes in Computer Science, Volume 132)
ISBN 3-540-11214-6

# Data Base Design Techniques II:

Physical Structures and Applications

Proceedings, Tokyo, November 1979

Editor: **S. B. Yao, T. L. Kunii**

1982. V, 170 pages.
(Lecture Notes in Computer Science, Volume 133)
ISBN 3-540-11215-4

The design of data base organizations is one of the most important steps in the development of a computerized information system. In the past, data base design activities consisted of trial and error approaches using ad hoc techniques: systematic method was lacking. Practitioners have in the meantime working on design methodologies, with independent researchers developing theories and models.

This two-volume work (Lecture Notes in Computer Science, Volumes 132, 133) brings together these different approaches to facilitate the exchange of ideas.

Two symposia were held to compare and summarize various new developments in data base design: *The NYU Symposium on Data Design* and *The Symposium on Data Base Engineering*.

The organizers of both symposia have edited many excellent papers covering a wide range of data base design models and methods for inclusion herein. Both practioners and researchers in the field of data base design will find these two books useful. Although not conceived as textbooks, they can also be used as the basis for advanced seminars on data base systems.

Springer-Verlag
Berlin
Heidelberg
New York